# YOUR CAREER

## How To Make It Happen

Julie Griffin Levitt
Boise State University
Boise, Idaho

Fourth Edition

VISIT US ON THE INTERNET
www.swep.com
www.thomson.com

South-Western
EDUCATIONAL PUBLISHING
Thomson Learning™

Cincinnati • Albany, NY • Belmont, CA • Bonn • Boston • Detroit • Johannesburg • London • Madrid
Melbourne • Mexico City • New York • Paris • Singapore • Tokyo • Toronto • Washington

**Vice President/Director of Publishing:** Peter D. McBride
**Team Leader:** Eve Lewis
**Acquisitions/New Business Development Manager:** Susan Carson
**Project Manager:** Penny Shank
**Editor:** Timothy Bailey
**Production, Art & Design Coordinator:** Patricia Matthews Boies
**Manufacturing Coordinator:** Kathy Hampton
**National Career Development, English, Communication Consultant:** Carolyn Love, Ph.D.
**Marketing Manager:** Mark Linton
**Cover & Internal Design:** Doug Klocke/Photonics Graphics
**Compositor:** A. W. Kingston Publishing Services

**Photo Credits:** All photos copyright PhotoDisc Inc. 1997-'99

**Contributing Authors:** Richard Rapp
Lynne Whaley



ISBN: 0-538-72191-X
2 3 4 5 6 7 8 9 BM 07 06 05 04 03 02 01 00
**PRINTED IN THE UNITED STATES OF AMERICA**

# Table of Contents

## PART 1 • PLANNING YOUR CAREER



## PART 2 • YOUR JOB SEARCH

# Career Action Assignments

## PART 1 • PLANNING YOUR CAREER

## PART 2 • YOUR JOB SEARCH



## PART 3 • CAREER SEARCH DOCUMENTS

## PART 4 • YOUR INTERVIEW

## PART 5 • AFTER YOUR INTERVIEW

Dear Reader:

Welcome to *Your Career: How to Make It Happen*—The Career Power Kit!

Typically, 97% of the students in my classes have secured their jobs using the techniques in this text—before they finish the course! This text is your career power kit. It contains all the tools you need to assess, plan, and succeed in achieving your job search and career goals.

**Get the Competitive Advantage**

Did you know that people who develop sound job search and career planning skills are **80 percent more successful** in landing top jobs than those who don't develop these skills? *Your Career: How to Make It Happen* provides the career management/job search tools to give you this huge competitive edge!

**Learn How to Make Your Career Happen**

This text provides the most thorough, practical career management and job search advice and guidelines available on the topic today. These offer big career dividends for you—top jobs, promotions, and career success! *Your Career: How to Make It Happen* shows you exactly how to:

- Develop proactive, success attitudes
- Verify promising job and career goals
- Tap into prospective employers
- Develop the best career network
- Use the Internet to your advantage
- Master the electronic resume
- Launch an efficient, successful job search
- Develop winning resumes and cover letters
- Develop a top notch career portfolio
- Interview like a pro
- Negotiate a top salary and benefits package
- Succeed in the changing workplace

The success of these tools and guidelines keeps *Your Career: How to Make It Happen* in high demand; this fourth edition is completely updated and clearly reflects the needs of the 21st Century workplace.

Take charge of your career with these practical tools—use them to gain competitive advantage and achieve your full career potential.

Sincerely,

Julie Levitt

Julie Levitt

# Preface

*"A technological revolution is changing the way we engineer careers and look for employment. Your Career: How to Make It Happen doesn't just look ahead to the 21st Century—it is the 21st Century! Cyberspace job search techniques, preparation of winning career search documents, Internet exercises, and career success strategies create new windows of opportunity for students to reach full career potential."*

*Linda Welther*
*Education Supervisor*
*ITT Technical Institute*

## THE PURPOSE OF THIS BOOK

This text provides the job and career management tools to reach your full career potential. You will develop essential career success skills through class activities and direct practice in the business community.

## KEY FEATURES

The key features of *Your Career: How to Make It Happen* include the following:

- **Employer Quotes:** Quotes from leading employers introduce each chapter and highlight important concepts from the employer's perspective.
- **Success Tips:** Over 100 easy Success Tips highlight the key steps you can take to achieve full job satisfaction and career potential.
- **Career Bulletins:** Each chapter also highlights special bulletins on the primary topics.
- **Career Actions—Your Competitive Edge:** Hands-on assignments in each chapter take you to the business community to research employers, learn about application requirements, practice meeting business people in your career field, and practice interviewing. These assignments polish your career management skills so you can achieve your immediate and future goals. Some of these assignments include:
  - Effective job search organization
  - Development of essential Internet skills
  - Preparation of winning resumes, cover letters, and career portfolios
  - Actual career networking
  - Interview practice
- **Internet-Linking Software:** Available as a supplement is the all-new Internet-Linking program, ***WebGuide: Your Online Career Search.*** *WebGuide* provides a convenient, direct link to top Web resources providing the very latest in career information, resume writing and interviewing strategies, and job opportunities. This program automatically maintains links and site updates.

*Your Career: How to Make It Happen* emphasizes the important role the Internet plays in successful job search/career planning and integrates Internet assignments throughout. *WebGuide* activities are also included for additional Internet skill development, a priority for 21st Century career success.

This *WebGuide* Icon signals a *WebGuide* activity. *WebGuide: Your Online Career Search* (ISBN 0-538-72204-5) is available from South-Western Educational Publishing; call 800-354-9706.

## ACKNOWLEDGMENTS

This book reflects the influence of many people skilled in career management education. Foremost in this category is the thorough and professional writing and subject matter guidance provided by:

**Karen Schneiter**
Rochester Community and Technical Colleges
Rochester, MN

I am also grateful to the following reviewers and instructors who gave suggestions and support:

**Karen Keasler**, Southeastern Illinois College, Harrisburg, IL

**Jackie Marshall**, Ohio Business College, Loraine, OH

**Laurie Shapero**, Miami-Dade Community College, Miami, FL

**David Tipps**, Miller-Motte Business College, Wilmington, NC

**Mortina Williams**, Three Rivers Community College, Poplar Bluff, MO

Grateful acknowledgment is made to Mr. Richard Rapp, Associate Vice-President for Student Affairs and Director of the Career Center, Boise State University. Mr. Rapp contributed significantly by writing Chapter 20 and by editing and advising on the text.

Mr. Rapp has personally assisted over 15,000 people in finding appropriate career employment. He also serves in leadership roles in local and national career planning and placement organizations.

Lynne Whaley researched and wrote Chapter 4, as well as the resumes, cover letters, and thank-you letters. She has expertise in resume writing, corporate administration, complex equipment sales, business education, and business ownership.

Special acknowledgement is also made to Dona Orr, business instructor, College of Technology, Boise State University. She developed the all-new bank of tests that greatly enhance evaluation.

In addition, the following people deserve recognition for their technical contributions to this edition. Mary Seroski, who produced the PowerPoint slide supplement; Linda Welther, ITT Technical Institute, who contributed research and chapter content; and Janis Petersen, Joan Lecther, Becky Beus, and Troy Van Houten of Micron Technology, Incorporated, who provided technical support.

Grateful acknowledgement is made to Dr. and Mrs. Richard Griffin, the sources of inspiration and experience upon which Chapter 1 of this text is based.

Finally, and importantly, I wish to recognize Dr. Monte Levitt who provided artwork and the personal support so essential to developing this comprehensive writing project.

## ABOUT THE AUTHOR

Julie Griffin Levitt is a business educator, corporate trainer and consultant, lecturer, and author of numerous educational publications. She teaches and consults in the areas of career planning and job search skills, office occupations, communications, supervision, and motivation in Boise, Idaho.

She has taught job-seeking and career planning skills at the secondary and postsecondary levels. The job placement ratio of her students is 97 percent or better.

# Orientation: What's In It For You?

*"As a former Personnel Recruiter for a Fortune 500 company, I strongly recommend this book to anyone who is looking for a challenging, well-compensated career. I only wish this book was on the market when I was looking for a career!"*

*Darryl Wright*
*Leadership & Employee Development*
*Corporate Training & Education*
*Micron Technology, Inc.*

## WHAT BENEFITS WILL YOU GAIN FROM THIS BOOK?

You will develop all the tools you need to manage your career successfully and gain the following benefits:

- **The right job and the right career moves:** This text will prepare you to get the right job or promotions and succeed in your career through practice and development of proven career management techniques.
- **Competitive advantage:** You will learn and apply strategies that give you the winning advantage when competing for good jobs.
- **Convenient career management tools:** You will develop three personalized career management tools that help you achieve lifetime career goals. These are described briefly below, in greater detail throughout the text, and in a summary in "Appendix C: Career Management and Marketing Tools."

1. **Lifetime Career Database.** You will create an easily updated base of information you can use immediately and throughout your life as you complete the activities in this text. At the same time, you will be compiling a timesaving base of information you can use for every future career activity. Your Lifetime Career Database will consist of personal data; content for resumes, cover letters, and applications; reference lists; summaries of your qualifications, education, training, and more. You can easily update this base of information any time you seek a promotion, consider a new job, or even pursue a new career.
2. **Career Portfolio.** You will prepare a master set of documents and other items that provide evidence of your skills, abilities, achievements, experience, and other job qualifications. This "Career Portfolio," is a complete documentation of your employability.
3. **Interview Marketing Kit.** This is a professional looking binder or case containing selected items from your "Career Portfolio" for each job interview. You will tailor the contents of your Interview Marketing Kit for each interview by choosing items that match the specific needs of individual employers. This tailored evidence of your qualifications will greatly enhance your interview effectiveness.

The authoring team conducts active, ongoing job seeking and career development research. They refine and enhance the instructional materials as required to meet the changing needs of the job market. This text reflects over 20 years of professional expertise in career development.

## SKILLS YOU WILL DEVELOP

The importance of developing career development skills is obvious. Through the information and practical exercises you apply directly to your job search and career development, you will gain skills you can use throughout your working career. You will learn:

- How to assess your occupational qualifications.
- How to identify and confirm the best job and career choices.
- How to use the Internet to increase your job search and career management success.
- How to prepare an electronic resume, cover letter, and online employment application.
- How to organize your job search to find the best possible job in the shortest possible time.
- How to research prospective employers and your career field.
- How to succeed in the application process (application, resume, and cover letter).
- How and where to look for a job.
- How to get interviews and succeed in them.
- How to follow up an interview successfully.
- How to adjust quickly and achieve peak success in a new position
- How to apply techniques on the job that result in maximum career advancement.
- How to evaluate the pros and cons of changing jobs or careers or relocating, and how to plan for such changes.
- How to deal effectively with being laid off, downsized, or terminated.

## DEVELOP LIFETIME CAREER SKILLS AND INFORMATION

Each chapter of this book contains Career Actions—special assignments to help you develop skills and compile information necessary for getting the job you want, succeeding in it, and advancing your career. Many of these assignments have corresponding perforated worksheets at the end of the chapters, while others are to be prepared using separate paper.

### Develop Lifetime Career Information

The information you assemble in the Career Action assignments is essential for developing your resumes, cover letters, employment applications, networking lists, etc., throughout your life. Completed Career Actions will form a convenient database of information you can quickly access and update any time you pursue a job or career goal. You will be making a smart investment in your lifetime career success as you create this important Lifetime Career Database.

### Use a Computer to Enter and Store Key Career Action Information

Most people will make at least eight job or career moves in their lifetimes. You can use the information you compile about yourself in the Career Actions as the foundation for every one of these career moves. This is why we recommend you enter and store electronically (on diskette or other computer storage media) much of your Career Action information using word processing or database software. The Career Actions that are most appropriately entered and stored electronically contain the following notation:

Career Database Appropriate

## WHO CAN USE THIS BOOK?

This text is written for anyone seeking employment, a promotion, or a career change. This includes students (vocational, college, and university level) as well those currently working in or reentering the workforce. This book is appropriate for students of traditional age as well as for adults reentering postsecondary systems for additional training or those who are simply planning for a new job, promotion, or career.

## THIS TEXT IS WIDELY APPLICABLE

The information and techniques in this text apply to the vast majority of career fields today. These include, but are not limited to administration, management, computer technology, information systems, electronics, engineering, accounting, marketing, merchandising, health care services, retail sales, customer service, government, education, and nonprofit organizations.

## YOU ARE PART OF THE SCRIPT

Consider this book to be a partial script. You, the principal player in the development of your own career, will fill in the blank lines. You will be carefully coached and directed through exercises that will help you identify, confirm, and realize your job and career goals. Good communication skills are vital to achieving career success. For this reason, you will be given ample guidance, practice, and real applications in developing winning resumes and cover letters and in developing verbal and nonverbal skills required to get and succeed in job interviews.

## YOU WILL LEARN BY DOING

You can gain an 80 to 100 percent advantage over your competition using this text. Through the practice assignments, you will develop the essential job search and career planning skills that give you this competitive advantage. The goal of this text is to help you get the most suitable job possible and to develop your career successfully. You won't just read about how to succeed in a job search, you will practice the skills in your business community through class and outside Career Action assignments.

Some of these assignments include researching your career field and target job; submitting resumes and cover letters for evaluation; taking practice interviews in actual offices, and more.

## THE INTERNET WILL BE YOUR CAREER PARTNER

Using the Internet is a must for successful job search and career management in the 21$^{st}$ Century. This is why *Your Career: How to Make It Happen* incorporates important exercises throughout to build your Internet skills. Job applicants who use the Internet for employer and industry research and for professional electronic communications with employers always outdistance those applicants who don't use this important tool. You will be counted among the Internet-savvy applicants when you complete this text.

## HOW TO GET THE MOST FROM THIS BOOK

Review the learning objectives listed at the beginning of each chapter before you read the chapters to see exactly what you will learn. An overall summary is presented in the first paragraphs of each chapter to clarify the content.

The assignments are designed to focus on your personal job and career goals, not on generalized theories. Reading alone will not give you the practice to develop these skills adequately. You will be an active doer, taking charge of your own career success by taking the guided steps necessary to ensure it. To get the best results read each chapter, study and complete all the assignments. The path is clearly laid out for you to reach your job and career goals.

## EVALUATION

To assess your understanding of the principles of each chapter and identify any areas you may need to review, three levels of evaluation are provided with the curriculum for *Your Career: How to Make It Happen*:

**Critical Thinking Questions** are included at the end of each chapter. The purpose of these questions is to prompt your consideration of how the key concepts of the chapter apply directly to you and your career goals.

**Chapter Tests** are provided in the Instructor's Manual and on the Instructor's Resource CD. Your instructor may use these to evaluate your mastery of the key concepts of each chapter.

**Career Competency Assignments** are also provided in the Instructor's Manual, which give you essential practice to outdistance your competition. They verify that you can perform the skills for successful career management. Your instructor will determine procedures for the use of this evaluation material.

## APPENDIX ITEMS

Four important appendix items are included at the end of this book:

- **Appendix A:** Sample Business Letter and E-Mail Formats
- **Appendix B:** Internet Resources
- **Appendix C:** Career Management and Marketing Tools
- **Appendix D:** Reference Reading for Career Planning and Job Search.

## A FINAL WORD OF ADVICE AND ENCOURAGEMENT

National studies verify that job seekers who are persistent, informed of current job market trends, and organized in their approach are at least 80 percent more successful in attaining their career goals than those without this training. The tools to succeed in your career are conveniently organized in this book. Apply these to maximize your career potential and the quality of your working life. It's your career—make it happen with these winning success tools.

CHAPTER 1

# Reach Your Full Career Potential

> **A positive attitude, flexibility, and a varied skill set have become the keys to success. When setting goals, be assertive for your own goals, but also for the company's goals – that is the ultimate in career development.**
>
> *Nancy Porte*
> *Director of Professional Services*
> *The Career Builder Network*
> *www.careerbuilder.com*

## *In this chapter, you will*

- Use affirmation statements and positive self-talk to help achieve your goals.
- Identify techniques for successfully setting and achieving your goals.
- Improve assertive behavior and apply it in your job search.

Access the Internet and locate additional success strategies.

Access the Internet and complete a success action plan.

Chapter 1 outlines guidelines to help you strengthen career-boosting skills, attitudes, and strategies that persuade employers to hire and promote. You will learn and apply eight strategies to give you the competitive edge in achieving career success and reaching your full potential.

# GET THE COMPETITIVE EDGE WITH EIGHT SUCCESS STRATEGIES

Successful leaders in all fields from business to entertainment consistently use the eight success strategies discussed in this chapter to help them achieve their career goals. These strategies focus on positive attitudes and actions. Worldwide, Olympic sports psychologists coach competitors to achieve maximum performance by learning and applying these strategies. Renowned motivational experts, such as Anthony Robbins, Dennis Waitley, Stephen Covey, and Brian Tracy, teach these strategies to help business leaders, politicians, and performers reach their peak potential.

Review and use the eight strategies that follow to help achieve your full career potential; they profoundly affect career success at every step.

1. Positive Thinking and Behavior
2. Visualization
3. Positive Self-Talk
4. Affirmation Statements
5. Dynamic Goal Setting
6. Positive Action
7. Assertive Behavior
8. Self-Esteem Builders

Figure • 1-1 Project positive energy in person and on the phone. People can hear enthusiasm.

These eight mental success strategies and behaviors are major career enhancers that help transform goals into realities. Pay close attention to any that are new ideas for you. They provide wide-ranging benefits; you can use them to:

- Create and sustain your inner drive
- Increase your confidence
- Provide mental and physical energy
- Guide you toward goals
- Help you project competence, enthusiasm, and presence
- Improve performance

## SHOCKING BUT TRUE

The most qualified person is not always the one who gets the job or promotion. The person hired is the one the employer perceives as the most qualified. Chapter 1 explains exactly how you can use success strategies that project competence and persuade employers to hire and promote.

## Positive Thinking and Behavior

*Positive thinking* is making a conscious effort to think with an optimistic attitude and to anticipate positive outcomes. *Positive behavior* means purposely acting with energy and enthusiasm. When you think and behave positively, you guide your mind toward your goals and generate matching mental and physical energy.

Positive thinking and behavior are often deciding factors in landing top jobs—your first job, a promotion, a change of jobs—whatever career step you are targeting. That's because the subconscious is literal; it accepts what you think as fact. The function of the subconscious is to support thoughts and behavior by triggering matching physiological responses. This subconscious function is called *autosuggestion*, and research has proved it has a powerful impact on the mind and body.

**SUCCESS TIP**

**Think and act positively: these strategies actually improve outcomes because they direct your subconscious to support your efforts.**

Positive thinking causes the brain to generate matching positive chemical and physical responses. Thinking positively actually boosts your ability to perform and your ability to project enthusiasm, energy, competence, and confidence—the qualities interviewers look for when they hire and promote candidates. Negative thinking causes the brain to stimulate matching negative chemicals and physical responses that decrease energy, creativity, and mental and physical performance and that diminish performance and self-confidence.

Follow these steps to form the positive habit and boost your success.

1. **Deliberately motivate yourself each day.** Think of yourself as successful, and have positive expectations for everything you attempt.

2. **Project energy and enthusiasm.** Employers hire people who project positive energy and enthusiasm. Develop the habit of speaking, moving, and acting with these qualities.

Figure • 1-2: You project your positive self-image.

## INTERVIEWERS SAY THIS IS A BIG HIRING ADVANTAGE

Applicants who project enthusiasm and positive behavior generate a positive chemistry that rubs off. Hiring decisions are influenced largely by this positive energy.

3. **Practice this positive expectation mind-set** until it becomes a habit, and your subconscious will stimulate the physiological responses that increase your self-esteem and your performance. This habit will help you reach your peak potential.

> **"Our minds can't tell the difference between real experience and one that is vividly and repeatedly imagined."**
>
> —Denis Waitley, The Seeds of Success

4. **Dwell on past successes.** Focusing on past successes to remind yourself of your abilities helps in attaining goals. For example, no one is ever born knowing how to ride a bicycle or how to use a computer keyboard. Through training, practice, and trial and error, we master new abilities. During the trial-and-error phases of development, remind yourself of past successes; look at mistakes as part of the natural learning curve. Continue until you achieve the result you want. You fail only when you quit trying!

## Visualization

***Positive visualization*** is purposely forming a mental picture of your successful performance and recalling the image frequently. Visualization improves performance because the positive picture triggers your subconscious to generate matching positive physiological responses that increase performance.

Athletic champions and successful people throughout the world use positive visualization to boost their performance and to achieve goals. Positive visualization actually improves learning and skill development while strengthening confidence and performance. Have you used it personally or in a group to help improve performance? This is definitely a technique you want to apply in the job search process.

Apply the visualization techniques below to boost your success in job searches, interviews, and attaining goals:

1. **Relax.** Sit in a chair, close your eyes, breathe deeply, and clear your mind.

2. **Mentally draw a picture or create a mental video** that shows you succeeding in your goal. To project a positive and competent image, visualize yourself doing just that—walking and speaking with confidence, maintaining excellent posture, and projecting dignity.

3. **Make the picture detailed and visualize success.** Do not permit any negative visions or thoughts (fear, failure, anxiety, error). See yourself as already having achieved your goal.

**SUCCESS TIP**

**Visualize your positive performance. Your brain then triggers positive responses that enhance performance.**

4. **Incorporate pictures, words, actions, senses.** Mentally "practice" exactly what you plan to say or do. This "mental rehearsal" strengthens your actual performance.

5. **Dwell on the image; be able to recall it instantly.** Repeat the visual picture as often as possible before the actual event.

## Positive Self-Talk

***Positive self-talk*** means purposely giving yourself positive reinforcement, motivation, and recognition—just as you would do for a friend. Congratulate yourself when you do well, and remind yourself of your accomplishments, abilities, strengths, and skills. Keep a to-do list, check off accomplishments, and review your progress periodically.

**"Always bear in mind that your own resolution to succeed is more important than any other one thing."**

—Abraham Lincoln

Figure • 1-3: Winning athletes use visualization, affirmation, and positive self-talk to improve performance and reach their goals. You can too!

**Make Self-Talk Work for You.** What we habitually say to ourselves has a profound impact on our self-image, our self-esteem, and therefore our performance and success. Remember, your subconscious triggers physiological responses that match the pictures and thoughts you have of yourself to make them happen. Make this work for you by purposely keeping your self-talk positive. Following are some good examples of positive self-talk:

- I did a good job on that report; a lot of effort went into it.
- Well done! I passed another class, and I'm one step closer to my degree.
- Terrific! I am maintaining my exercise schedule.
- I can do this.

**Stop Negative Self-Talk.** Often, we are quick to nag ourselves (we all want to be perfect). Negative self-talk is damaging, however, because the subconscious literally believes what we say about ourselves. Any time you catch yourself using negative self-talk, stop. Focus instead on the best course of action you can take, and ***do it***. Keep your thoughts, mental pictures, and self-talk positive.

Can you rephrase the negative self-talk examples below to make them positive?

- I don't think I can learn to operate that new software.
- This goal is too difficult; I'll probably never make it anyway.

Make positive communication a habit. Focus on the positive in goal statements, self-talk, and all communications. Compare the following phrases, and notice how the positive words convey confidence, commitment, and enthusiasm.

| NEGATIVE . . . | POSITIVE |
|---|---|
| I'll try | I will |
| I should do | I will do |
| I have to | I want to/I choose to |

## Affirmation Statements

*Affirmation statements* are positive self-statements or reminders to help achieve goals. They are positive messages with a punch—mental bumper stickers—to motivate your subconscious to work for you. The guidelines below explain how to use this powerful mental reminder technique:

1. **Make the statements personal.** Use *I*, your name, or *you*.
2. **Keep affirmations short!** If you can't remember them, how can you use them?
3. **Phrase them positively.** The mind accepts as truth the words you give it. Use positive words only. Leave out negative words:

   **Negative:** I will not be nervous during my interview.

   **Positive:** I will be calm and self-assured during my interviews.
4. **Include a positive emotion.** A phrase that triggers a positive emotion strengthens the affirmation. Example: "My goal is *valuable*, and it *excites* me."
5. **Phrase affirmations as fact.** Phrase a goal as if it has happened—is happening (even if you haven't achieved it yet). Your subconscious believes mental messages and works to make them reality.
   - I am making good progress on my goal.
   - I am strengthening my speaking abilities.
6. **Say your affirmations at least once a day.** Repetition enhances self-confidence, acts as a reminder, and stimulates your subconscious to help you achieve your goal.

**Complete Career Action 1-1**

**SUCCESS TIP**

**Use positive self-talk and affirmation statements to trigger matching positive physical responses that enhance performance.**

## Dynamic Goal Setting

*Career goal setting* involves recording clear objectives and required actions to achieve them. The most common reason people don't achieve their goals is that they never set them in the first place. Follow the steps below to focus your efforts and to maximize your goal achievement.

# CAREER ACTION 1–1

## Practice Positive Self-Talk and Affirmation Statements

**DIRECTIONS:** On a separate sheet of paper, write your responses following the directives below:

1. Take a moment to recall a goal you have been striving to achieve and are making progress on. Then write a positive statement about your progress.
2. Describe one or more of your work skills or abilities that fit the requirements of the job you are or will be seeking. Write complete sentences.
3. Write an affirmation statement to use as a reminder and to help you achieve an important career goal.

1. **Define your goals clearly in writing.** Writing down your goals increases the likelihood of achieving them by 80 percent! Writing goals increases your sense of commitment, clarifies the achievement process, and helps you remember important details.
2. **Identify and focus on the benefits** (to you and others) of achieving goals. This is a strong motivator.
3. **Define the purpose of your goals.** Link your goals to a practical, specific purpose, but also base them on inspiration, not just logic; this also increases motivation.
4. **Identify supportive forces for you.** For example, supportive forces for improving writing skill include instructors, books, workshops, and a good writer to coach you and edit your writing.
5. **Develop an action plan, set deadlines, and act.** Establish subgoals; divide each main goal into logical, progressive steps. Set deadlines for completing each step, and complete steps on time.
6. **Establish priorities.** Take action in order of priority.
7. **Make a public commitment.** If appropriate, share your goals with someone who encourages you to go the extra mile—to increase your sense of responsibility and provide motivation.
8. **Be realistic about limitations.** Don't set a short-term goal to get a job requiring a lot more education. Set separate goals to get the education, take an interim job, and then reach the ultimate goal.
9. **Use positive self-talk and affirmation statements.** Do this every day! Write your statements down and post them prominently.
10. **Use positive visualization.** This boosts goal achievement.
11. **Practice.** Practice new skills regularly. Get additional information, coaching, and feedback on your progress.

12. **Evaluate and revise goals as necessary.** Evaluate your progress; experiment with new methods if you're not getting the results you want, and, if necessary, revise your goals.

13. **Persevere.** Stay the course until you succeed!

14. **Reward yourself.** Rewards are motivators. As you make progress toward your goals, do something nice for yourself.

15. **Record progress on your goals.** As simplistic as it seems, a long series of check marks on your calendar motivates by providing a sense of accomplishment—do it. But don't let missing an occasional daily goal deter you; keep focusing on the ultimate goal.

> **"When we set goals, the magic begins: The switch turns on, the current starts to flow, and the power to accomplish becomes a reality."**
>
> —Wynn Davis, The Best of Success

## Positive Action

Taking regular positive action (no matter how small) and making progress toward goals both provide real evidence of achievement and increase confidence and creativity. This boosts your momentum; action fuels more action! Deliberately plan and take regular actions toward your goals to maximize your success.

For example, if you have a long-term goal of specializing in one area of your career field, you can take momentum-building, intermediate actions. Examples are listed below:

- Research to learn exactly what skills you need to qualify in the specialty. Contact specialists in your area to learn what skills they require. These actions will give you concrete information for outlining appropriate goal steps.
- Take courses to help you develop these skills. As you complete each one, you will be a step closer to your final goal.
- Consider working in an entry-level position for a firm noted in your targeted specialty area. Then get additional training or education to work up to the specialty.

Get help in arranging to complete an internship or work study program with a firm noted in your target specialty area.

**Complete Career Action 1-2**

**Set goals that support your needs and you'll find it's much easier to stay focused on achieving your goals.**

## Assertive Behavior

*Assertive behavior* is standing up for your own rights; expressing yourself honestly, courteously, and comfortably; and observing the rights of others. Assertive behavior promotes equality and a healthy balance in human relationships. Assertion is based on human rights—especially the right to be treated with respect in all situations. Other human rights include the right to (a) be listened to and taken seriously, (b) say

## CAREER ACTION 1–2

### Practice Dynamic Goal Setting and Positive Actions

**DIRECTIONS:** On a separate piece of paper, answer each of the following questions.

1. Identify a goal that is important to you. Review and follow the guidelines for dynamic goal setting on pages 6–8.
2. Write down your goal, describing it by addressing goal-setting guidelines 1-5.
3. Identify 3 to 5 positive actions you can take in the next ten days to achieve this goal.
4. Follow up by actually completing all fifteen guidelines.

"yes" or "no" with conviction, (c) express your opinion, and (d) ask for what you want.

**Assertive Behavior Is Critical in Your Job Search.** Why is assertiveness critical to a successful job search and career potential? Assertiveness conveys self-esteem and capability.

Employers hire people who behave confidently and are able to convey their job qualifications comfortably and clearly. They want employees who strengthen human relations and project competence in the workplace through assertive behavior. They hire applicants who demonstrate assertiveness in interviews, resumes, and all communications. To reach your fullest career potential, be assertive and tactful in expressing yourself and respect the rights of others.

**Assertive Behavior Is Critical to Workplace Success.** Personality types fall into three general categories: nonassertive, aggressive, and assertive. Nonassertive and aggressive employees are often detrimental in organizations; employers avoid hiring them.

Nonassertive people become unhappy because they permit others to abuse their rights; they project their feelings of unhappiness to others in the workplace. They have difficulty expressing thoughts or feelings because of a lack of confidence; this projects a weakness in personal and company effectiveness. No one wants to hire a person who projects these qualities to clients or customers.

Aggressive people violate the rights of others with domineering, pushy behavior. Their goal is to dominate because they fear loss of control. Overly aggressive employees drive business away by being annoying or brash; therefore, employers avoid hiring them.

Assertive behavior is essential to achieving career success. Assertive people are confident, express their needs and opinions comfortably, and are sensitive to the feelings and needs of others. Employers want assertive employees because assertive behavior projects capability and confidence and promotes a healthy, productive working environment.

Figure • 1-4: Everyday encounters give you an opportunity to build your assertiveness skills.

**Building Your Assertiveness Skills.** Being assertive requires having healthy self-esteem; therefore, a key to improving assertiveness is to strengthen self-esteem. Because all the success strategies and behaviors discussed in this chapter build self-esteem, they also enhance assertiveness. If you need to improve your assertiveness skills, focus on the suggestions in the next section of this chapter.

Practice assertiveness; strive to deal with others in a confident, positive way without appearing boastful or overbearing. Force yourself to be more open, to express your ideas and needs, and to perform with greater confidence (you may have to pretend at first). At the same time, dare to show your respect for others more openly. The winning combination is *assertiveness + respect.*

The benefits of increasing your assertiveness are great, and they include increased confidence and a professional image. The more often you act assertively, the easier it will be for you; you will find that people respect assertiveness.

**Exercises for Developing Assertiveness.** Review the following techniques for improving your assertiveness. Practice expressing your feelings and needs calmly and clearly. Also, demonstrate acceptance and respect for others by praising them when they perform or behave well.

1. **Initiate a friendship.** Invite the person to have coffee or lunch; take time to get to know him or her.

2. **Express your opinion** in a meeting or conversation, particularly when you believe strongly in it—even if everyone else doesn't appear to agree.

3. **Join a professional or service organization or club,** and volunteer to serve on a committee. What a way to network *and* build your assertive skills!

4. **Compliment someone** on a skill, talent, or positive quality.

5. **Tell someone when she or he has offended you unfairly.** Evaluate first to be certain the person was actually unfair; being unjustifiably sensitive can impair your assertiveness.

6. **Return faulty merchandise,** and get an immediate replacement or free repair.

7. **Initiate a conversation** with a stranger before or after a class, meeting, or social event. (Just try it, you'll like it!)

8. **Design your own assertive exercises.** Develop exercises to meet your specific areas of need for improvement.

9. **Read more about assertiveness.** Several good books are available on developing assertiveness. Many are listed in the Reference Reading section at the end of this book. Ask your librarian if you want more information.

**Complete Career Action 1-3**

# CAREER ACTION 1–3

## Improve Assertiveness

**DIRECTIONS:** Review the previous information on assertiveness and the sample assertiveness exercises. Select at least two activities for practicing assertiveness—exercises provided in the chapter or others more pertinent to your needs. Write out your plans for improving assertiveness skills through the exercises you choose.

SUCCESS TIP

**Behave assertively to enhance interview and career success.**

## Self-Esteem

Projecting the confidence and competence that is so important in your job search and throughout your successful career requires a healthy self-esteem (belief in your abilities and your worth).

Think how easy it is to project a confident and competent image when you feel good about yourself; you automatically project confidence. By developing the success habits outlined in this chapter, you can strengthen your self-esteem.

**Enhancing Your Self-Esteem.** Begin by describing yourself in writing; you might want to ask a friend or family member to help. Make two lists: one of your positive traits and one of your negative traits. Which list is longer? If it's your positive list, you have a good base for self-esteem. If it's your negative list, you will have to work harder to develop a good sense of self-confidence. By doing so, you will also strengthen your assertive abilities because good self-esteem makes assertive behavior easier.

Next, identify negative images you want to change. Begin with the trait you think you should improve first. For example, a negative trait may be a lack of initiative, expressiveness, or organization.

Improving self-image often requires developing a positive habit, such as reading more to improve vocabulary or exercising to improve fitness. Your efforts to increase your positive characteristics and decrease negative ones will improve your self-confidence, making it easier to increase your assertiveness.

After you identify the traits you want to improve, develop a plan for doing so. Write your goal in positive terms as shown in Figure 1-5 on page 12.

Write your Action Plan so you can evaluate it daily, as in the example in Figure 1-5 on improving punctuality. This makes progress easy to evaluate and provides reinforcement. Put a red check mark on your calendar each day you make progress in your goal; this is surprisingly motivational. Be creative. Gold stars and a "Congratulations" sign on the refrigerator can work wonders!

Action Plan

Goal: To be punctual for all activities

Personal Action Plan for Achieving Goal: I will set my alarm to sound thirty minutes earlier each morning. I will get ready for work with no interruptions. I will leave for work promptly at 7:30 every morning so I have fifteen minutes leeway for travel delays.

Time Frame for Action Plan: I will stick to this plan for thirty days, marking my calendar with a large X through every day I succeed in being punctual for all activities; arrival at work; return from breaks or lunch; arrival at social activities, classes, meetings, or other activities.

Figure • 1-5: Action Plan

**Effects of Negative Self-Esteem and Fear.** Negative self-image holds us back by promoting fear of failure. It prevents us from taking risks that lead to growth and development. The result is stagnation, even regression, not successful development.

Sometimes we base our behavior on imagined fears, not on facts. We allow fear to limit our full potential. Following are tips for dealing constructively with fears and enhancing your success.

1. When working on a challenging goal, such as public speaking, avoid negative images. Concentrate on developing your relevant skills and knowledge; then plan and act positively and visualize your success.
2. Assess the situation. Get training or additional information if necessary.
3. Seek support from those who motivate you.
4. Act with courage and conviction, and be persistent.

Figure • 1-6: Enhance your career achievements by writing down your strengths, weaknesses, and goals.

**Maintaining a Healthy Self-Esteem.** We all feel changing levels of self-esteem resulting from life experiences. Because of this, we need to work deliberately at strengthening and maintaining self-esteem, just as we do at maintaining good physical health. Techniques you can use to strengthen your self-esteem are outlined below:

1. **Believe it can be done, and make a commitment.** Remember how positive suggestion influences your subconscious positively!
2. **Identify your strengths** in writing, and dwell on past successes.
3. **Set written goals** for improvement, and take action.
4. **Practice positive self-talk.**
5. **Visualize your success.**
6. **Make positive action a habit.**
7. **Surround yourself with a positive environment.** (Positive people, reading, viewing, and listening material.)
8. **Look good to feel good.** Looking your best boosts your confidence, and others respond positively to a good appearance.
9. **Keep fit.** Take care of your body, mind, and spirit. Exercise, eat properly, rest, take time for yourself, and balance work with other life activities.

**Complete Career Action 1-4 on page 15.**

## APPLY THE EIGHT SUCCESS STRATEGIES

Use the eight success strategies emphasized in this chapter to reach your full career potential. Apply these mental success strategies regularly throughout your job search and lifetime career. Pursue your career goals with an assertive belief in yourself and your rights, and practice thinking and acting positively. Success is not a one-time destination; it's a lifelong journey.

**Complete Career Action 1-5 on page 16.**

### CHECKLIST FOR APPLYING EIGHT SUCCESS STRATEGIES

Check each of the following actions that you are currently taking to increase your career success:

- ☐ Think and act positively.
- ☐ Visualize your positive performance.
- ☐ Use positive self-talk.
- ☐ Use affirmation statements.
- ☐ Write clear short-term and long-term goals, and revise them when necessary.
- ☐ Take regular action to achieve defined goals.
- ☐ Practice assertive behavior.
- ☐ Maintain self-esteem through positive thinking and actions.

## CRITICAL THINKING QUESTIONS

1. Which of the eight success strategies do you think will be most useful for strengthening your career planning and job search success?
2. How can projecting enthusiasm and positive expectations help you in an interview?
3. Explain the effects that positive and negative thoughts, images, and self-talk have on performance.
4. Would you rate your own assertiveness skills as excellent, good, or needing improvement? If you need improvement, what specific actions can you take to strengthen them?

# CAREER ACTION 1–4

## Access the Internet, and Locate Additional Success Strategies

**PURPOSE:** To achieve peak success in competing for top jobs, you need to use the success strategies emphasized in this chapter. You also need good Internet research skills. In this assignment, you will practice using your Internet skills in the following search.

**NOTES:** (a) Because the content of Web sites is subject to change without notice, be aware that the link listed below may not match the current content of the Web site referenced in this assignment. (b) Also be aware that some Web sites are beginning to omit the introductory "http://" from their Web site addresses. If you find that a Web site address listed in this text doesn't take you to the site indicated, try taking off the http://, and you may then find it will work successfully.

**DIRECTIONS:** Launch your Web browser, and follow the steps below.

1. Go to the Cyber Nation Web site: ***http://www.cybernation.com/***
2. Scroll down, and click on the ***Enter Your Cyber Nation Here*** button.
3. Scroll down to locate the "Victory" button; then, under this heading, click on the photo or the text below it.
4. Click on ***The You Can Do It Center*** button.
5. Click the ***Get Inspired by These Success Tips*** button. Locate one or two success tips or articles that interest you most. Then prepare a written summary of the information and how you can use it.

**NOTE TO NEW INTERNET USERS:** For online directives or tutorials for using the Internet, check out the following Internet search engines and the *WebGuide* program activity before you complete **Career Action 1–4**.

**INTERNET SEARCH ENGINES**

| | |
|---|---|
| AltaVista | ***http://www.altavista.com/*** |
| Excite | ***http://www.excite.com/*** |
| Infoseek | ***http://www.infoseek.com/*** |

CONTINUED ON NEXT PAGE

# CAREER ACTION 1–4

CONTINUED

| | |
|---|---|
| Lycos | ***http://www.lycos.com/*** |
| Yahoo (See "How to Search the Web") | ***http://www.yahoo.com/business/employment/*** |

*WEBGUIDE* ACTIVITY
The supplemental software, *WebGuide: Your Online Career Search,* is described in the Preface of this textbook. If you are using this software, access the Main Menu of the program, and click on "Searching the Web," then click on the items displayed and review the content.

# CAREER ACTION 1–5

## Access the Internet, and Develop a Success Action Plan

**DIRECTIONS**: Launch your Web browser, and follow the steps below.

1. Access the South-Western Educational Publishing Web site:

   ***http://www.swep.com/***

2. Select ***Career Development*** (postsecondary level).
3. Select *Your Career: How to Make It Happen.*
4. Locate the **Success Action Plan** form.
5. Read the instructions, and enter your answers on the **Success Action Plan** form.
6. Print your completed form, and save it. In Chapter 2, you will be instructed to file this form with other career data for future use.

CHAPTER 2

# Take a Look at Yourself

> "Be courageous! Dare to explore what you love and what is most important to you. Don't waste time assessing yourself as you are now. Dream and plan for who you want to be in the future."
>
> *Betty Jo Matzinger Lash*
> *Associate Director*
> *Georgetown University Career Center*

## *In this chapter, you will:*

- Document your education, work experience, and other activities related to a potential career that you will use in your job search and career development.
- Identify the career-related skills you developed through your education and work experience.
- Identify your personal, school-related, and work-related accomplishments.
- Begin to build your Lifetime Career Database.

Use the Internet to complete personal assessments for planning and confirming your career choices.

In Chapter 2, you will take a complete inventory of your education, training, experience, accomplishments, values, work preferences, and performance traits. This personal inventory is an essential tool for developing or confirming your career target and for conveying your qualifications to potential employers.

## KNOWING YOURSELF IS A MUST FOR YOUR CAREER SUCCESS

In promoting yourself throughout your career, you are the person who must sell the product—you. Successful salespeople know their products. And you must know your qualifications and communicate them effectively to employers in your resume, cover letter, and interviews. You must also understand what is important to you in life and in work situations. The Career Actions in this chapter will help you thoroughly inventory your training, education, and experience and identify the values and work preferences that will play an important role in choosing a career or accepting a job offer. In the next chapter, you will assess this information about yourself from an employer's perspective and consider it carefully in making a good job match.

> "Nothing is particularly hard if you divide it up into small jobs."
>
> —Henry Ford

### Your Personal Career Inventory

Your Personal Career Inventory consists of basic information about you that an employer may find helpful when considering you for a job. This includes basic personal data and information about (a) your education and professional training; (b) work experience, skills, and accomplishments; and (c) people you can use as references.

### Record Personal Information

The first step in recording your Personal Career Inventory is to record basic personal data you will be asked to provide on most job applications, such as information about how you can be reached, hobbies, and professional memberships. Keep this information handy, updated, and accurate so you always have a ready reference.

### Review Education and Training

The next step in completing your Personal Career Inventory is to document your education and training, including dates, places, career-relevant courses and activities, skills, and accomplishments obtained through your education and training. This information will help you identify or confirm an appropriate career choice, develop resumes and cover letters, and prepare for job interviews.

#### DEVELOP A CAREER DATABASE

In this textbook, you are collecting important data you can use to help achieve lifetime job and career goals. This includes data you will record in many Career Actions as well as drafts of job search documents that will form your Lifetime Career Database (also see Appendix C of this text). Much of this information is appropriately entered and stored using a computer to provide easy editing capabilities for updating your data throughout your lifetime career.

**IMPORTANT:** Look for this notation at the bottom of selected Career Actions:

**Career Database Appropriate**

This indicates the information you record for this Career Action is appropriately prepared and stored using word processing or database software and that you should store electronic and hard copies in your Lifetime Career Database.

Take your time when completing this section of your Inventory; be sure the information is complete and accurate. Put yourself under a microscope, and look at every detail carefully. You may want to ask people who know you well to help you document your accomplishments. Consider scholarships, honors, and awards you have received and competitions in which you have participated. When reporting accomplishments, be as specific as possible. For example:

- **Won first place in schoolwide business math competition**

When identifying the skills and accomplishments you developed through your education and training, consider two kinds of skills (or competencies) that employers are seeking: job-specific skills and transferable competencies. You will identify both kinds of skills and competencies in **Career Action 2-1**.

**Job-Specific Skills.** Job-specific skills are the technical abilities that relate *specifically* to a particular job. For example, in accounting, preparing a balance sheet by using accounting software customized for a client is a job-specific skill. Relining brakes on a vehicle is a job-specific skill for an auto mechanic; and processing a dental X ray and operating medical diagnostic equipment are also job-specific skills.

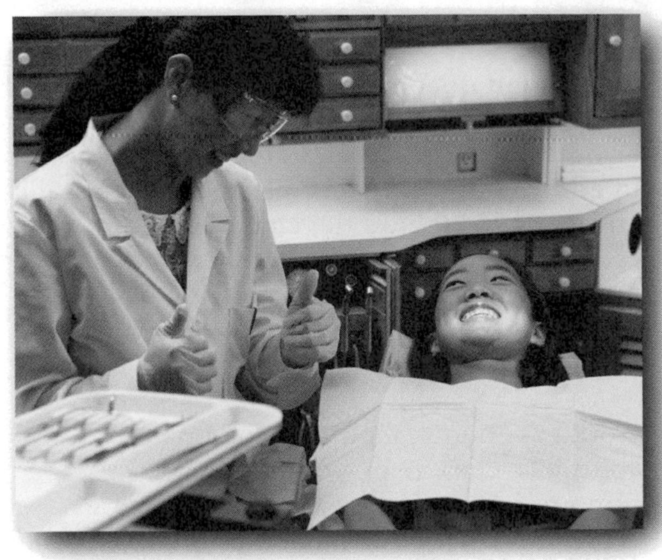

Figure • 2-1: Dental technicians must have job-specific skills as well as transferable skills, such as the ability to work with people in difficult situations.

**Transferable Competencies.** Transferable competencies are abilities you have that can be applied in more than one work environment. For example, both accountants and auto mechanics are required to have such transferable competencies as the ability to read, write, use mathematics; and use computers. Transferable competencies may also include such things as ability to work well with others, lead, organize work and materials, solve problems, make decisions, and manage resources.

**Complete Career Action 2-1**

# CAREER ACTION 2-1

## Education and Training Inventory

**DIRECTIONS:** Turn to page 25, and complete each section of the form that applies to you. Be thorough in providing details.

**Career Database Appropriate**

## List Experience and Skills

Just as you documented your education and training, you will identify all of your work or other experiences in **Career Action 2-2**. In addition to dates and places, list the skills and knowledge you developed and any accomplishments, achievements, or recognition you received during your work activities. Be sure to include both job-specific skills and transferable competencies.

Work experience should include paid or volunteer work (e.g., volunteering on community service projects, fund-raising programs, environmental cleanup programs), internships, or cooperative education experience. Be specific about the contributions you made. For example:

- Raised 20 percent more in contributions over previous year.
- Reduced time required to process a reprint by 10 percent.
- Suggested new file management procedures that reduced filing error rate by 25 percent.

**Complete Career Action 2-2**

"All our dreams can come true, if we have the courage to pursue them."

—Walt Disney

## Identify Job References

The final step in completing your Personal Career Inventory is to identify your job references. A job reference is someone who can vouch for your capabilities, skills, and suitability for a job. References are most often people who have been your teachers and coaches in school or your coworkers or supervisors in volunteer and paid work environments. Therefore, you should review your inventory of education and work experience for potential job references.

Identify people who can *and are willing* to confirm (from firsthand observation) your good performance on the job, in school, or in other activities. Employers usually want at least three job references listed on application forms; ideally, these are supervisors or employers or others who know your work well. Relatives or classmates are not appropriate references. The more references you have available, the better for your current and future job campaign.

If you are qualified to work in two different fields, such as retail sales and accounting, you will get the best results by having one

# CAREER ACTION 2-2

## Experience and Skills Inventory

**DIRECTIONS:** Turn to page 29, and complete each section of the form that applies to you. Be as specific and thorough as possible.

**Career Database Appropriate**

set of references targeted for each of the two fields, or a total of six references (three in sales-related fields and three from accounting fields). Some organizations ask for different types of references. For example, an employer may ask for personal, as well as professional references.

Use **Career Action 2-3** to identify people you can list as your references. Make note of how they know you and in what areas they can speak about your performance.

**Complete Career Action 2-3**

# CAREER ACTION 2-3

## Develop a Database of Potential Job References

**DIRECTIONS:** Identify at least three (but as many as you can) potential job references from your education/training and experience/skills inventories. Also consider contacts at professional associations. Using either the form provided in **Career Action 2-3** (on page 31) or a database, record their names, addresses and other contact information. Plan to contact each reference and ask him or her to write you a letter of reference.

**Career Database Appropriate**

## SELF-ASSESSMENT

Another important part of knowing yourself is having an accurate assessment of your personal values, work preferences, and job-related performance traits. Understanding the personal factors that influence your performance and job satisfaction will help you make good choices when setting job and career targets and when considering specific job offers.

### Values

*Webster's New World Dictionary* defines "value" as "that which is desirable or worthy of esteem for its own sake; the social principles, goals, or standards held or accepted by an individual." By working in a job that matches your values, you greatly increase the chances of enjoying and succeeding in your job. **Career Action 2-4** will help you identify and prioritize your values.

### Work Environment

Most people spend a lot of time in their work environment; to maximize your success, identify the work environments you prefer and perform best in. For example, if you are an extrovert, you probably won't enjoy working in an isolated environment. **Career Action 2-4** will help you clarify what is important to you in a work environment.

SUCCESS TIP

**Identify your skills, abilities, work experience, values, and work preferences to achieve a good job match.**

**Complete Career Action 2-4**

# CAREER ACTION 2-4

## Values and Work Environment Preferences Inventory

**DIRECTIONS: Career Action 2-4** will help you identify and prioritize the values that are important to you and the kinds of work environments you find acceptable. Remember, there are no wrong answers in defining what's important to you. Turn to page 33, and complete **Career Action 2-4** now.

### Personal Qualities and Work Performance Traits

To get the job you want, you must be able to sell your personal qualities, positive job performance traits, and enthusiasm. In **Career Action 2-5**, you will identify these qualities and traits to help find a suitable job target match.

Knowing your personal qualities and work performance traits will also help you decide what type of work you are best suited for.

**Complete Career Action 2-5**

# CAREER ACTION 2-5

## Personal Qualities and Work Performance Traits

**DIRECTIONS:** Now turn to page 35, and follow the directions to complete **Career Action 2-5**.

## SELF-ASSESSMENT RESOURCES

Many self-assessment resources speed the process of making and confirming a successful career choice. Which of the resources listed below could you use to improve your career planning?

**Note:** Some services may have a fee attached to them.

- **Your school career services staff and counselors.** These specialists can provide a wide variety of aptitude and interest tests.
- **The Internet.** You can find excellent information on careers and jobs on the World Wide Web. Many sites offer online tools to assess your career interests and values and to help match the results with appropriate careers and jobs.
- **Commercial software packages.** Some commercial software packages are available over the Internet and through school career services offices.

**Complete Career Action 2-6**

# CAREER ACTION 2-6

## Self-Assessment Test

**NOTE:** Because the content of Web sites is subject to change without notice, be aware that the links listed below may not match the current content of the Web sites referenced in this assignment.

1. The supplemental software program, *WebGuide: Your Online Career Search,* is described in the preface of this textbook. If you are using this software, access the Main Menu of the program, and click on ***Self-Assessment***. Then click on ***Keirsey Personality Test*** and complete the test. Then use the ***Keirsey Personality Matrix*** to determine your personality type.

2. Or go to the Internet address: ***http://www.keirsey.com/***, click on ***The Keirsey Temperament Sorter II***, and complete the test. Then return to the home page, click on ***The Four Temperaments***, and review the data.

3. Complete the test, and score the results; then list four jobs you think might suit your personality type.

4. Complete the following on-line personal asssessment to help confirm your career directions: ***Birkman Quiz (http://www.review.com/birkman)***

## Your Lifetime Career Database

The Personal Career Inventory you have just completed clearly documents your education, working experience, and qualifications—information you will refer to repeatedly in the future whenever you are looking for a job or considering new career options. In **Career Action 2-7**, you will use this personal inventory material to begin compiling your Lifetime Career Database, a collection of job and career reference information. Any time you make a job or career change, you will find the information in this database valuable (e.g., updating your resume, completing employment applications, interview preparation). Look for the "Career Database Appropriate" notation at the bottom of selected Career Actions in this book. This notation is a reminder for you to use a word processing or a database program to enter and store the information. File electronic and hard copies in your Lifetime Career Database. You'll be glad you did!

**Complete Career Action 2-7**

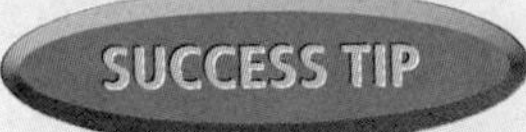


**Begin compiling your Lifetime Career Database; place a copy of your Personal Career Inventory in it now.**

# CAREER ACTION 2-7

## Begin Lifetime Career Database

**DIRECTIONS:** In Appendix C, Career Management Tool 1, Lifetime Career Database, follow all the instructions to set up your own Lifetime Career Database File, and begin organizing your job search and career development data. Then, in this file, store all your completed Career Actions, including the **Success Action Plan** from **Career Action 1-5**. As you progress through this book, continue to store all completed Career Actions in this file.

Figure • 2-2: The right career is one that complements your skills, interests, values, and environmental preferences.

### CHECKLIST FOR SELF-ASSESSMENT

Check each of the following actions that you are currently taking to increase your career success:

- ☐ Identify your skills, abilities, work experience, values, and work preferences to achieve a good job match.
- ☐ Begin compiling your Lifetime Career Database; place a copy of your personal inventory information in it now. (Save disk and hard copies of completed Career Actions if you use a computer.)

## CRITICAL THINKING QUESTIONS

1. Why is it important in career planning and a job search to assess and document thoroughly your education, training, work experience, and accomplishments?
2. Explain why it is useful to identify your work performance traits and career-related personal qualities.
3. What should be compiled in your Lifetime Career Database; how will it be useful to you throughout your career?

# CAREER ACTION 2-1

## Education and Training Inventory

**DIRECTIONS:** This inventory of your education and training contains four sections: (1) High School Inventory, (2) Business, Vocational, or Technical Education Inventory, (3) College or University Inventory, and (4) Seminars and Workshops Inventory. Complete each section that applies to you; list information related to your career target. Be thorough in documenting your accomplishments and achievements.

### HIGH SCHOOL INVENTORY

Name of School: ______________________________

Address: ______________________________

______________________________

Dates of Attendance: __________ to __________ Date of Diploma: __________

Grade Point Average: __________ G.E.D. (Date): __________

1. **Career-Related Courses.** List the career-related courses you completed.

______________________________

2. **Career-Related Activities.** Describe your involvement in school, extracurricular, community, and other activities. (Examples: clubs, sports, organizations, volunteer)

______________________________

3. **Career-Related Skills.** List the skills you developed in high school and other activities. Include both job-specific skills and transferable competencies. (Examples: operating a computer, calculating numbers, persuading others, using specific tools/equipment, organizing and leading others, working in a team)

______________________________

4. **Accomplishments, Achievements, and Recognition.** List all special accomplishments, achievements, or recognition you received in high school and through other activities. (Examples: selected to play lead in musical production, selected to serve on state debate team, awarded first place in competition.) List any scholarships or honors you earned. Also summarize praise received from teachers, peers, others.

______________________________





CONTINUED ON NEXT PAGE

# CAREER ACTION 2-1

(CONTINUED)

**BUSINESS, VOCATIONAL, OR TECHNICAL EDUCATION INVENTORY**

**DIRECTIONS:** Complete one of these sets of questions for each school attended. Before writing on this form, duplicate it if you have attended more than one business, vocational, or technical school.

Name of School: ______________________________

Address: ______________________________

______________________________

Dates of Attendance: __________ to __________ Grade Point Average: __________

Type of Degree, Diploma, or Certificate: __________ Date Received: __________

1. **Career-Related Courses.** List the career-related courses you completed.

______________________________

2. **Career-Related Activities.** Describe your involvement in school, extracurricular, community, and other activities. (Examples: sports, clubs, volunteer work, student organizations—Business Professionals of America)

______________________________

3. **Career-Related Skills.** List the skills you developed through your classes and other activities. Include both job-specific skills and transferable competencies. (Examples: operating a computer, using specific software, presenting and creating oral and written communication, calculating numbers, persuading others, operating specific equipment/machinery, using specific tools, organizing and leading others, working as a team member, studying, analyzing, and researching data)

______________________________

4. **Accomplishments, Achievements, and Recognition.** List all special accomplishments, achievements, or recognition you received for your school and other activities. List any scholarships or honors you earned. (Examples: awarded first place in state business education skills competition, earned service award, earned perfect attendance award, served as class officer, inducted into National Vocational-Technical Honor Society, restored two-bedroom apartment)

______________________________



CONTINUED ON NEXT PAGE

# CAREER ACTION 2-1

(CONTINUED)

## COLLEGE OR UNIVERSITY INVENTORY

**NOTE:** Before writing on this form, duplicate it if you have attended more than one college or university.

Name of School: ______________________

Address: ______________________

______________________

Dates of Attendance: __________ to __________ Grade Point Average: __________

Type of Degree, Diploma, or Certificate: __________ Date Received: __________

1. **Career-Related Courses.** List the career-related courses you completed that may be of value in your career.

______________________

2. **Other Activities.** Describe your involvement in school, extracurricular, community, volunteer, and other activities. (Examples: clubs, offices held, volunteer work, community projects or programs)

______________________

3. **Career-Related Skills.** List the skills you developed through your classes and other activities. Include both job-specific and transferable competencies. (Examples: supervising, marketing, finance, sales, teaching, accounting, computer operation or programming, nursing, caretaking, physical fitness/therapy, specific software use, electronic applications, oral and written communication, calculating numbers, persuading and leading others, working as a team member, researching)

______________________

4. **Accomplishments, Achievements, and Recognition.** List all special accomplishments, achievements, or recognition you received for your school activities. List any scholarships or honors you earned. (Examples: served as class officer, won scholarship, prepared lesson plans in student teaching that were used as model for campus, selected for only paid internship in business department, won regional award)

______________________

CONTINUED ON NEXT PAGE

# CAREER ACTION 2-1

(CONTINUED)

## SEMINARS AND WORKSHOPS INVENTORY

**DIRECTIONS:** List below the seminars or workshops you have attended. If necessary, add to the list of seminars and workshops (a) by keying in the additional information if you are using a computer for this activity or (b) by using additional paper if you are handwriting this activity.

Name of Seminar/Workshop: ______________________________

Offered by: ____________________ Date(s): ____________________

Career-related concepts or skills I learned: ______________________________

Name of Seminar/Workshop: ______________________________

Offered by: ____________________ Date(s): ____________________

Career-related concepts or skills I learned: ______________________________

Name of Seminar/Workshop: ______________________________

Offered by: ____________________ Date(s): ____________________

Career-related concepts or skills I learned: ______________________________

Name of Seminar/Workshop: ______________________________

Offered by: ____________________ Date(s): ____________________

Career-related concepts or skills I learned: ______________________________

Name of Seminar/Workshop: ______________________________

Offered by: ____________________ Date(s): ____________________

Career-related concepts or skills I learned: ______________________________

# CAREER ACTION 2-2

## Experience and Skills Inventory

**DIRECTIONS:** Complete one set of questions for each position or project (cooperative work experience, internship, volunteer/paid work experience, military experience). Begin with the most recent experience, and continue in reverse chronological order. Two copies of the form are provided; duplicate the form for additional job experiences.

POSITION TITLE: ______________________________

Name of organization: ______________________________

Address: ______________________________

Telephone Number: ______________ Salary (if paid experience): ______________

Circle Type of Experience: (1) Cooperative, (2) Volunteer, (3) Internship, (4) Paid Work

Dates of Employment or Involvement: ______________________________

Supervisor Name/Title: ______________________________

1. **Career-Related Skills.** List the job-specific skills, transferable competencies, and responsibilities you developed in this position.

   ______________________________

2. **Accomplishments and Achievements.** List all of your accomplishments in this position, preferably in measurable terms. (Examples: increased sales by 20 percent, reduced order processing time by 15 percent by developing more efficient processing methods, named employee/volunteer of the month, supervised evening shift of eight employees)

   ______________________________

3. **Praise Received.** Summarize praise received from employers, coworkers, customers.

   ______________________________

   ______________________________

Why did you leave? ______________________________

Performance rating (circle one): High Very Good Good Needs Improvement Poor

CONTINUED ON NEXT PAGE

# CAREER ACTION 2-2

(CONTINUED)

POSITION TITLE: ______________________________

Name of organization: ______________________________

Address: ______________________________

Telephone Number: ______________ Salary (if paid experience): ______________

Circle Type of Experience: (1) Cooperative, (2) Volunteer, (3) Internship, (4) Paid Work

Dates of Employment or Involvement: ______________________________

Supervisor Name/Title: ______________________________

1. **Career-Related Skills.** List the job-specific skills, transferable competencies, and responsibilities you developed in this position.

   ______________________________

2. **Accomplishments and Achievements.** List all of your accomplishments in this position, preferably in measurable terms. (Examples: increased sales by 20 percent, reduced order processing time by 15 percent by developing more efficient processing methods, named employee/volunteer of the month, supervised evening shift of eight employees)

   ______________________________

3. **Praise Received.** Summarize praise received from employers, coworkers, customers.

   ______________________________

   ______________________________

Why did you leave? ______________________________

Performance rating (circle one): High Very Good Good Needs Improvement Poor

# CAREER ACTION 2-3

## Develop a Database of Potential Job References

**DIRECTIONS:** Use this form to list at least three people who would recommend you to prospective employers. List more references if possible. Select people who can attest to your work-related abilities, attitudes, and skills. Always get permission to use their names as references during your job search.

Name: ______________________________

Title and Organization: ______________________________

Address: ______________________________
Street City State ZIP Code

Telephone: ______________________________
Home Work Fax

E-Mail Address: ______________________________

How I know this reference: ______________________________

Date permission to use as a reference received: ______________________________

Date of reference letter on file: ______________________________

Date of last personal contact: ______________________________

Name: ______________________________

Title and Organization: ______________________________

Address: ______________________________
Street City State ZIP Code

Telephone: ______________________________
Home Work Fax

E-Mail Address: ______________________________

How I know this reference: ______________________________

Date permission to use as a reference received: ______________________________

Date of reference letter on file: ______________________________

Date of last personal contact: ______________________________

CONTINUED ON NEXT PAGE

# CAREER ACTION 2-3

(CONTINUED)

Name: ____________________

Title and Organization: ____________________

Address: ____________________

Street City State ZIP Code

Telephone: ____________________

Home Work Fax

E-Mail Address: ____________________

How I know this reference: ____________________

Date permission to use as a reference received: ____________________

Date of reference letter on file: ____________________

Date of last personal contact: ____________________

Name: ____________________

Title and Organization: ____________________

Address: ____________________

Street City State ZIP Code

Telephone: ____________________

Home Work Fax

E-Mail Address: ____________________

How I know this reference: ____________________

Date permission to use as a reference received: ____________________

Date of reference letter on file: ____________________

Date of last personal contact: ____________________

# CAREER ACTION 2-4

## Values and Work Environment Preferences Inventory

### PART 1: VALUES

**DIRECTIONS:** Review the values listed below, and rank the importance of each as it relates to your career and job goals (H = high, M = medium, and L = low).

| Value | Ranking (H, M, L) |
|---|---|
| 1. Adventure (risk taking, new challenges) | |
| 2. Education/Learning/Wisdom | |
| 3. Social needs (need for relationships with people) | |
| 4. Self-Respect/Integrity/Self-Discipline | |
| 5. Helping/Serving | |
| 6. Recognition/Respect from others | |
| 7. Freedom/Independence (working independently with minimal supervision) | |
| 8. Security (job, family, national, financial) | |
| 9. Spiritual needs | |
| 10. Expression (e.g., creative, artistic) | |
| 11. Responsibility (reliability, dependability) | |
| 12. Others (List other values below, and rank each one) | |
| | |
| | |
| | |
| | |
| | |





CONTINUED ON NEXT PAGE

# CAREER ACTION 2-4

(CONTINUED)

## PART 2: WORK ENVIRONMENT PREFERENCES

**DIRECTIONS:** In the boxes to the right, place a check mark next to each work environment condition you prefer.

| Work Environment | Check Those Preferred |
|---|---|
| 1. Indoor work | ☐ |
| 2. Outdoor work | ☐ |
| 3. Factory setting | ☐ |
| 4. Office setting | ☐ |
| 5. Working alone | ☐ |
| 6. Working with people | ☐ |
| 7. Working with things | ☐ |
| 8. Working with data | ☐ |
| 9. Working with ideas | ☐ |
| 10. Challenge | ☐ |
| 11. Predictable, orderly, structured work | ☐ |
| 12. Pressure work | ☐ |
| 13. Problem solving | ☐ |
| 14. Standing while working | ☐ |
| 15. Sitting while working | ☐ |
| 16. Busy surroundings | ☐ |
| 17. Quiet surroundings | ☐ |
| 18. Exciting, adventurous conditions | ☐ |
| 19. Safe working conditions/environment | ☐ |
| 20. Creative | ☐ |
| 21. Nonsmoking environment | ☐ |

Others (List other conditions you are seeking in your job target)

______________________________

______________________________

______________________________

# CAREER ACTION 2-5

## Personal Qualities and Work Performance Traits

**DIRECTIONS:** (a) Rate yourself on each of the personal qualities and work performance traits listed below by using a scale of high, average, or low (H, A, L). For example, if you think you have a high degree of dependability, write *H* in the space to the right of Dependability. Be sure to list other qualities or traits that are important for success in your targeted career. (b) In preparing your resume and preparing to interview well, you should be able to prove that you have these traits by giving examples of how you actually used them successfully. At the bottom of the form, write at least five brief, positive examples of how you have used these qualities or traits.

| Personal Quality or Work Performance Trait | Rating (H, A, L) |
|---|---|
| 1. Initiative/Resourcefulness/Motivation | |
| 2. Dependability | |
| 3. Punctuality | |
| 4. Flexibility | |
| 5. Creativity | |
| 6. Patience | |
| 7. Perseverance | |
| 8. Humor | |
| 9. Diplomacy | |
| 10. Intelligence | |
| 11. High energy level | |
| 12. Ability to work well with a team | |
| 13. Ability to set and achieve goals | |
| 14. Ability to plan, organize, prioritize work | |
| 15. Outgoing personality | |
| 16. Ability to handle conflict | |
| 17. Optimistic attitude | |
| 18. Realistic attitude | |
| 19. Enthusiastic attitude | |
| 20. Willingness to work | |
| 21. Orderliness of work | |
| 22. Attention to detail | |

CONTINUED ON NEXT PAGE

## CAREER ACTION 2-5

(CONTINUED)

**Others** (List and rank other positive personal qualities or work performance traits)

| Personal Quality or Work Performance Trait | Rating (H, A, L) |
|---|---|
| | |
| | |
| | |
| | |
| | |
| | |
| | |
| | |
| | |
| | |
| | |

**Examples:** List at least five positive examples of how you have used some of these qualities and traits in the past.

Example: ____________________________________________

Example: ____________________________________________

Example: ____________________________________________

Example: ____________________________________________

Example: ____________________________________________

Example: ____________________________________________

Example: ____________________________________________

CHAPTER 3

# What Do Employers Want?

"When hiring for any position, I look for people who have a grasp of computers and good communication skills. I also look for people who can work well with others, adapt easily to change, and be creative when looking for new ways to do things."

*Debbie Bornholdt*
*Human Resource Project Manager*
*QVC, Electronic Retailer*
*West Chester, PA*

## *In this chapter you will:*

- Assess your skills and work attitudes from an employer's perspective.
- Use the Internet to enhance your self-assessment and career planning activities.

- Use the Internet to research current trends in developing a career portfolio; begin listing appropriate items for your own.
- Set a career target.

Chapter 3 identifies the skills, work attitudes, and other qualifications that employers focus on in making hiring decisions. The chapter guides you through a self-assessment from the employer's perspective. The assessment will help you identify your most important qualifications that you will need to present to an employer during your job search. This chapter also identifies excellent career and job-planning resources to help confirm appropriate goals. Finally, Chapter 3 explains the importance of developing a career portfolio and provides Internet resources for additional information on this topic.

## WHAT EMPLOYERS WANT

Employers want to hire employees who have the specific and transferable work skills required for a job, who have work values compatible with their organizations, and who have the personal qualities necessary to be successful in the organizations. The more clearly you convey your skills that relate to your job target, the greater your chance of landing your ideal job.

### Job-Specific Skills

Employers seek job-specific skills (skills and technical abilities that relate *specifically* to a particular job). Two examples of job-specific skills are (a) using specialized tools and equipment and (b) using a custom-designed software program for a specific field of work.

**SUCCESS TIP**

**Identify your job-specific skills and transferable competencies to convince employers you fit the job.**

### Transferable Skills and Attitudes

In addition to job-specific skills, employers need workers who have transferable competencies: basic skills and attitudes that are required for all types of work. These skills and attitudes required for workplace success can be transferred or applied from one job or work environment to another, making employees responsive to change. Examples include using a computer, communicating effectively, and performing basic math. Other examples include traits such as responsibility, self-control, and honesty.

Both a construction supervisor and an accountant must work well with others, manage time, solve problems, read, and communicate effectively—all transferable competencies. They both must be competent in these areas even though framing a house and balancing a set of books (the job-specific skills for each field) are not related. In every occupation, transferable competencies are as important as technical expertise and job-specific skills.

The way specific jobs are performed changes frequently as continual improvements are made in tools, technology, and quality procedures. As a result, some job-specific skills and even entire jobs become obsolete. Electronics, for example, has revolutionized the field of vehicle engine mechanics. Transferable work competencies are not tied to a specific job but can be transferred from one job to another and even from one career field to another.

**Complete Career Action 3-1**

## CAREER ACTION 3-1

### Skills and Competencies Profile

**DIRECTIONS:** Turn to page 47, and complete **Career Action 3-1** now.

**Career Database Appropriate**

## Skills for the Future—SCANS

Many educational, business and government organizations are identifying the workplace competencies they think are essential to keep the United States competitive in the 21st Century. One of the most important reports on this topic is known as SCANS (the Secretary's Commission on Achieving Necessary Skills). SCANS was published by the U.S. Department of Labor and identified the transferable competencies essential for career and business success in the 21st Century.

> **"Choose a job you love, and you will never have to work a day in your life."**
> —Confucius

Because technology and other factors rapidly change the way work is processed, employers need adaptable employees with foundational work competencies who are creative thinkers and problem solvers. This is the only way employers can continue to operate and compete successfully. They also want employees who are responsible, comfortable with technology and complex systems, able to learn and work in teams, and who have a passion for continuous learning.

Figure 3-2 on page 40 is a summary of the SCANS study results identifying the skills and competencies that employers nationwide are seeking when hiring and promoting employees at all levels. Notice that the SCANS study addresses transferable competencies rather than job-specific skills.

## THE ROLE OF TRANSFERABLE COMPETENCIES

Employees with strong transferable competencies and basic skills are most successful in managing change because they have the basic skills and attitudes necessary to adapt. Two of the most influential transferable competencies are demonstrating enthusiasm and working well with others. During your job search, you will need to provide clear examples of both the job-specific skills and the transferable competencies most relevant to your job target.

Figure • 3-1: Employers want employees who are responsible, comfortable with technology, and able to work in teams.

## The Five Workplace Competencies Employers Want Most

1. **RESOURCES:** Identifies, organizes, plans, allocates, and manages resources.

2. **INTERPERSONAL:** Works well with others.

3. **INFORMATION:** Acquires, organizes, interprets, and uses information.

4. **SYSTEMS:** Understands complex social, organizational, and technological systems and interrelationships.

5. **TECHNOLOGY:** Works with a variety of technologies (tools, equipment, computers).

## The Foundation Skills and Personal Qualities Employers Want Most

1. **BASIC SKILLS:** Reads, writes, performs arithmetic and mathematical operations, listens, and speaks.

2. **THINKING SKILLS:** Thinks creatively, makes decisions, solves problems, visualizes, knows how to learn, reasons.

3. **PERSONAL QUALITIES:** Displays responsibility, self-esteem, sociability, self-management, integrity, and honesty.

**NOTES:** The ability to work well with others (interpersonal competence) is considered the most important of these components. It is essential so that work teams can solve problems and make the most effective decisions.

Most tasks require employees to use several of these eight components simultaneously.

Figure • 3-2: Summary of SCANS Skills and Competencies

# ASSESSING YOURSELF FROM AN EMPLOYER'S PERSPECTIVE

In Chapter 2, you identified specific skills that you had developed in school and work environments. This chapter has provided you with insights on how employers view skills and competencies. Now it is time to review your inventory and self-assessment from an employer's perspective. How would an employer categorize your skills and personal qualities?

**Complete Career Action 3-2**

# CAREER ACTION 3-2

**SCANS Inventory**

**DIRECTIONS:** Turn to page 51, and complete **Career Action 3-2** now. As you read the summary of competencies, foundation skills, and personal qualities listed, think about and check each one you've developed.

**Career Database Appropriate**

## CAREER PLANNING RESOURCES

By using several career planning resources, you can speed the process of making and confirming your career choice and greatly improve your chance of making a successful decision. Review the following resources, and place a check mark next to those you could use to improve your career planning.

**NOTE:** Comprehensive sources of job information are provided in Chapter 6, and you may want to review those briefly now because some of them can also be career planning resources.

Figure • 3-3: Use resources at your school or public library to access information about careers and jobs.

Use a variety of career planning resources to help choose and validate appropriate career and job goals.

☐ **Your school career services staff and counselors.** These counselors specialize in assisting students and alumni with career planning. They provide aptitude and interest tests, as well as current information about the job market and occupational fields.

☐ **The Internet.** A wealth of career planning and job information is available through the Internet. Many sites offer online tools to assess your career interests and values and to help match the results with appropriate careers and jobs.

See your school career services staff and counselors for recommendations for productive Web sites. Also check out the career center or career services Web sites of your local colleges or universities; many of these are excellent.

## SUCCESSFUL CAREER PLANNING REQUIRES FLEXIBILITY

Changing technologies and a global economy cause some careers to become obsolete or vastly changed. Broaden your options in today's rapidly changing technological environment by preparing to qualify for two closely related career goals requiring similar education, training, and general capabilities. Ask a knowledgeable career counselor to help you identify multicareer goals appropriate for your interests and abilities. Continually work at developing your career flexibility.

- ☐ **Computerized career information systems.** To use this service, users complete a computerized questionnaire regarding their personal interests and abilities. The program then provides a list of occupations consistent with the user's answers. Other information provided may include job descriptions, hiring requirements, employment prospects, and education and training requirements. Check with your school career counselor or state department of education to locate the nearest computerized system.
- ☐ **City, county, state, and federal employment or human resources departments.** For information about government occupations, contact the employment or human resources department that manages employment in your target field.
- ☐ **Career planning publications.** Ask your school career services counselor and librarian for help in locating books, magazines, and articles about your field and current job target.
- ☐ **People you know.** Contact people whom you have observed or known, admire, and have jobs just like the one you dream of. Ask them to help you explore your readiness for a similar job or career.
- ☐ **Volunteer work.** Volunteering can be a big asset when you apply for the job you want; it demonstrates exceptional initiative; it also helps you get a feel for a job and career. You can volunteer on a part-time or temporary basis or arrange an internship through your school.

**Complete Career Action 3-3**

**"Formulate and stamp indelibly on your mind a mental picture of yourself succeeding. Hold this picture tenaciously. Never permit it to fade. Your mind will seek to develop this picture!"**

—Norman Vincent Peale

# CAREER ACTION 3-3

## Internet Career Planning Resources

**NOTE:** Because the content of Web sites is subject to change without notice, be aware that the links listed below may not match the current content of the Web sites referenced in this assignment.

1. Select "Your Career Search" from the main menu of *WebGuide: Your Online Career Search.* Then complete item 1, Jobs of tomorrow; and item 8, Link your education and your career.

2. Surf the following Web sites for information on career selection. Then prepare a summary of your findings or print useful information.

   **Bureau of Labor Statistics** *http://stats.bls.gov/*

   **America's Career InfoNet** *http://www.acinet.org/*

   **The Catapult** *http://www.jobweb.org/catapult/*
   Under "Help Guides and Career Library Resources," click on *Career Choices*.

   **JobSmart** *http://www.jobsmart.org/*
   Click on *Career Guides*.

# SET YOUR CAREER TARGET

The work you have completed in this chapter has prepared you for this next step in your career. You now have all the information you need to set your career target. You may want to use the visualization skills from Chapter 1 to help you in defining your personal career objectives. Together with friends and associates, brainstorm careers that are appropriate. Think about work, hobbies, and volunteer experiences you have enjoyed in the past. What kind of work do you want to do? Where would you like to do this work? How much do you want to get paid for your work? What is the best career match for your unique skills, experiences, values, and interests? The form for **Career Action 3-4** will help you organize your thoughts.

**Complete Career Action 3-4**

# CAREER ACTION 3-4

## My Career Target

**DIRECTIONS:** Turn to page 54, and complete **Career Action 3-4** now.

## YOUR CAREER PORTFOLIO

The *portfolio* is a collection of documents and other items that demonstrate your skills, abilities, achievements, experience, and training. The purpose of the career portfolio is to organize examples of your skills and achievements that you can present during interviews as proof of your qualifications. Developing and using a career portfolio provides tangible proof of your qualifications. It also demonstrates important skills that employers are seeking: critical thinking, analyzing, planning, and preparation.

Examples of appropriate portfolio items include an official copy of your transcript(s); your resume; exemplary samples of your work, such as business writing, graphic artwork, and printed samples from software presentations. Other appropriate items include evidence of specialized computer usage, such as desktop publishing and Web site creation; awards; work performance evaluations; and letters of reference.

Portfolio samples can be from paid or volunteer work, internships, cooperative education, clubs, community activities, and more. A more comprehensive list of appropriate items and ideas for building your portfolio is contained in the "Career Portfolio" section of Appendix C, "Career Management Tools." Additional activities are presented later in this text to help you in developing an effective portfolio.

Begin considering what you have done or accomplished that best demonstrates your qualifications for the job you want. For example, to demonstrate your computer skills, you could include your transcript listing related coursework or a diskette containing examples of documents you developed using specific computer skills. To demonstrate a strong background in foreign languages, you could include in your portfolio your transcripts listing appropriate coursework and a letter of

Figure • 3-4: Assemble a portfolio of items that demonstrate your abilities and accomplishments.

recommendation from a teacher or employer who is familiar with your language skills.

For now, you can use a folder to store items that you identify for use later in your career portfolio. Begin listing appropriate items in **Career Action 3-5**.

**Complete Career Action 3-5**

**Begin listing items that will be appropriate for your career portfolio that demonstrate your job qualifications, such as school transcripts, hard copy or electronic samples of exemplary work, and letters of recommendation.**

# CAREER ACTION 3-5

## List Appropriate Portfolio Items

**DIRECTIONS:** Take a moment now to list items that seem appropriate to include in your Career Portfolio. As you progress through the upcoming chapters, add other items to your list. Later, you will be instructed to begin assembling your actual portfolio.

1. ______________________________

2. ______________________________

3. ______________________________

4. ______________________________

5. ______________________________

6. ______________________________

7. ______________________________

8. ______________________________

9. ______________________________

10. ______________________________

Figure • 3-5: Collect portfolio items that will demonstrate your qualifications for prospective employers.

## CHECKLIST FOR ASSESSING YOURSELF FROM AN EMPLOYER'S PERSPECTIVE

Check each of the following actions that you are currently taking to increase your career success:

- ☐ Identify your job-specific skills and transferable competencies to convince employers you fit the job.
- ☐ Use a variety of career planning resources to help in choosing and validating appropriate career and job goals.
- ☐ Develop a career portfolio of items to demonstrate your job qualifications for prospective employers.
- ☐ Start collecting items that will demonstrate your job qualifications for prospective employers.

## CRITICAL THINKING QUESTIONS

1. Why is it important to develop a broad career base that is flexible enough to encompass at least two fields?
2. Which career planning resources will be most helpful in your job search and career planning activities, and why?
3. Why do employers value employees who have the workplace competencies and foundation skills identified in the SCANS report?

# CAREER ACTION 3-1

## Skills and Competencies Profile

### Part 1: Job-Specific Skills

**DIRECTIONS:** Review **Career Actions 2-1 and 2-2** to refresh your memory regarding the job-specific skills and transferable competencies you developed through your education, training, and experiences. Then identify and list below the ten most important job-specific skills related to your current career target (examples: using job-specific computer software; operating specific equipment or tools; performing specific tasks such as developing X-rays).

**My Most Important Job-Specific Skills Related to My Career Target**

1. ______________________________
2. ______________________________
3. ______________________________
4. ______________________________
5. ______________________________
6. ______________________________
7. ______________________________
8. ______________________________
9. ______________________________
10. ______________________________

**NOTE:** In Chapter 9 (resume development) and Chapter 11 (the interview), you are asked to prove that you have these skills by documenting examples of times you used them—providing "proof by example." Employers ask for these examples, and you need to be prepared to give them.

CONTINUED ON NEXT PAGE

# CAREER ACTION 3-1

(CONTINUED)

**Part 2: Basic Skills and Attitudes**

**DIRECTIONS:** (a) Review the following skill categories and related transferable competencies. (b) Check the boxes to the left of every skill category that applies to you in any way. (c) Circle each transferable competency you have developed (those listed after each skill category). For example, under the first category, "Art," circle any transferable competency you have developed: "Drawing, designing, painting," and so on. List under "other" any additional transferable competencies you have that relate to each category.

| SKILL CATEGORY | RELATED TRANSFERABLE COMPETENCIES |
|---|---|
| ☐ **Art:** | Drawing, designing, painting, sculpting, computer graphics design<br>Other: ______ |
| ☐ **Athletics:** | Physical strength, physical ability, physical coordination, coaching, physical development, agility, team sports, individual sports<br>Other: ______ |
| ☐ **Communication:** | Explaining/persuading, strong grammar/vocabulary, organizing thoughts clearly, communicating logically, listening, speaking, good telephone/reception skills, writing, knowledge of foreign languages<br>Other: ______ |
| ☐ **Computer Technology:** | Computer operation, researching, training, testing, workflow analysis, evaluating, writing instructions, programming<br>Other: ______ |
| ☐ **Creativity:** | Innovative, imaginative, idea person, bold<br>Other: ______ |



CONTINUED ON NEXT PAGE

# CAREER ACTION 3-1

(CONTINUED)

| SKILL CATEGORY | RELATED TRANSFERABLE COMPETENCIES |
|---|---|
| ☐ **Engineering:** | Researching, testing, designing, constructing, analyzing, evaluating, controlling, electronic technology<br>Other: ________________ |
| ☐ **Human Relations:** | Counseling, diplomacy, negotiating, patience, outgoing, teamwork ability, understanding, resolving conflict, handling complaints<br>Other: ________________ |
| ☐ **Management:** | Analyzing data, directing, delegating, evaluating performance, organizing people/data/things, leading, making decisions, managing time, motivating self/others, planning, budgeting money/resources, solving problems, supervising, interviewing/hiring people, owning/operating a business<br>Other: ________________ |
| ☐ **Manual/ Mechanical:** | Good manual dexterity, building, operating, maintaining/repairing, assembling, installing, carrying, loading, lifting, cooking, driving/operating vehicles, performing precision work, assessing spacial relationships, operating heavy equipment<br>Other: ________________ |
| ☐ **Mathematical:** | Mathematical computations, accuracy, analyzing data, mathematical reasoning, statistical problem solving, analyzing cost effectiveness, budgeting, applying formulas, collecting money, calculating<br>Other: ________________ |
| ☐ **Office:** | Keyboarding, data entry, computer operation, text processing, data processing, office equipment operation, filing/retrieving records, recording data, computing data, record keeping, telephone skills, business writing<br>Other: ________________ |

CONTINUED ON NEXT PAGE

# CAREER ACTION 3-1

(CONTINUED)

| SKILL CATEGORY | RELATED TRANSFERABLE COMPETENCIES |
|---|---|
| ☐ **Outdoor Activities:** | Animal care, farming, landscaping, grounds care, boating, navigating, oceanographic studies, forestry, logging, mining, fishing, horticulture<br>Other: ______ |
| ☐ **Performing:** | Speaking, acting, dancing, singing, musical ability, comedy, conducting<br>Other: ______ |
| ☐ **Sales/ Promotion:** | Persuading, negotiating, promoting, influencing, selling, projecting enthusiasm, organizing, handling rejection, following up<br>Other: ______ |
| ☐ **Scientific Activities:** | Investigating, researching, analyzing, systematizing, observing, diagnosing<br>Other: ______ |
| ☐ **Service/General:** | Serving, referring, receiving, billing, handling complaints, good customer relations, good listening skills, patience, managing difficult people, helping others, relating to others<br>Other: ______ |
| ☐ **Service/Medical:** | Nursing, diagnosing, treating, rehabilitating, counseling, consoling, sympathizing, managing stress/emergencies, good interpersonal skills<br>Other: ______ |
| ☐ **Training/ Teaching:** | Teaching skills/knowledge, tutoring, researching instructional content, organizing/developing content, explaining logically/clearly, demonstrating clearly, coaching others, evaluating learning, addressing all learning styles<br>Other: ______ |

# CAREER ACTION 3-2

## SCANS Inventory

**DIRECTIONS:** Check the boxes to the left of each competency, skill, or quality that you've developed, and circle the portions of the detailed descriptions of each item that apply to you.

### PART 1: WORKPLACE COMPETENCIES

**RESOURCES:** Identifies, organizes, plans, and allocates resources

- ☐ **Manages Time:** Selects relevant, goal-related activities; ranks them in order of importance; allocates time to activities; understands, prepares, follows schedules
- ☐ **Manages Money:** Uses budgets, keeps records, makes adjustments to meet objectives
- ☐ **Manages Material and Facilities:** Acquires, stores, allocates, and uses materials or space efficiently
- ☐ **Manages Human Resources:** Assesses skills and distributes work accordingly, evaluates performance, and provides feedback

**INTERPERSONAL:** Works well with others

- ☐ **Participates as Team Member:** Contributes to group effort
- ☐ **Teaches Others New Skills**
- ☐ **Serves Clients/Customers:** Works to satisfy customers' expectations
- ☐ **Exercises Leadership:** Communicates ideas to justify position, persuades/convinces
- ☐ **Negotiates Decisions:** Works toward agreements involving exchange of resources, resolves divergent interests
- ☐ **Works with Cultural Diversity:** Works well with people from diverse backgrounds

**INFORMATION:** Acquires and uses information

- ☐ **Acquires/Evaluates Information**
- ☐ **Organizes/Maintains Information**
- ☐ **Interprets/Communicates Information**
- ☐ **Uses Computers to Process Information**

CONTINUED ON NEXT PAGE

# CAREER ACTION 3-2

(CONTINUED)

**SYSTEMS:** Understands complex social, organizational, technological systems and interrelationships

- ☐ **Understands Systems:** Knows how social, organizational, and technological systems work and operates effectively with them
- ☐ **Monitors/Corrects Performance:** Distinguishes trends, predicts impacts on system operations, diagnoses deviations in systems' performance and corrects malfunctions
- ☐ **Improves/Designs Systems:** Suggests modifications to existing systems and develops new or alternative systems to improve performance

**TECHNOLOGY:** Works with a variety of technologies

- ☐ **Selects Technology:** Chooses procedures, tools, or equipment including computers and related technologies
- ☐ **Applies Technology to Task:** Understands overall intent and proper procedures for setup and operation of equipment
- ☐ **Maintains/Troubleshoots Technology:** Prevents, identifies, or solves problems with equipment, including computers and other technologies

## PART 2: FOUNDATION SKILLS AND PERSONAL QUALITIES

**BASIC SKILLS:** Reads, writes, performs arithmetic/mathematical operations, listens, speaks

- ☐ **Reading:** Locates, understands, and interprets written information including material in documents such as manuals, graphs, and schedules
- ☐ **Writing:** Communicates thoughts, ideas, information, and messages in writing; and creates documents such as letters, directions, manuals, reports, graphs, and flowcharts
- ☐ **Arithmetic/Mathematics:** Performs basic computations and approaches practical problems by choosing appropriately from a variety of mathematical techniques
- ☐ **Listening:** Receives, attends to, interprets, responds to verbal messages and other cues
- ☐ **Speaking:** Organizes ideas and communicates orally



CONTINUED ON NEXT PAGE

# CAREER ACTION 3-2

(CONTINUED)

**THINKING SKILLS:** Thinks creatively, makes decisions, solves problems, visualizes, knows how to learn, and reasons

- ☐ **Creative Thinking:** Generates new ideas
- ☐ **Decision Making:** Specifies goals and constraints, generates alternatives, considers risks, and evaluates and chooses best alternative
- ☐ **Problem Solving:** Recognizes problems and devises and implements plan of action
- ☐ **Knowing How to Learn:** Uses efficient learning techniques to acquire and apply new knowledge and skills
- ☐ **Reasoning:** Discovers a rule or principle underlying the relationship between two or more objects and applies it when solving a problem

**PERSONAL QUALITIES:** Displays responsibility, self-esteem, sociability, self-management, integrity, and honesty

- ☐ **Responsibility:** Exerts a high level of effort, perseveres towards goal attainment
- ☐ **Self-Esteem:** Believes in own self-worth, maintains a positive view of self
- ☐ **Sociability:** Demonstrates understanding, friendliness, adaptability, empathy, politeness
- ☐ **Self-Management:** Assesses self accurately, sets personal goals, monitors progress, and exhibits self-control
- ☐ **Integrity/Honesty:** Chooses ethical courses

### Fine-Tune Your Competencies List

**DIRECTIONS:** Review the items you identified in **Career Action 3-2**. Then select the ten strongest of these competencies and basic skills related to your current job target, and list them below.

| | |
|---|---|
| 1. ____________________ | 6. ____________________ |
| 2. ____________________ | 7. ____________________ |
| 3. ____________________ | 8. ____________________ |
| 4. ____________________ | 9. ____________________ |
| 5. ____________________ | 10. ____________________ |

**NOTE:** You expand on this information in Chapters 9 and 11.

# CAREER ACTION 3-4

## My Career Target

**DIRECTIONS:** Answer the following questions about your current career target.

1. In what career field are you planning to seek employment? (Examples: accounting, office management, health care, teaching, administration, construction, computer technology)

2. List the specific job or jobs that you are targeting in your employment search. (List every job you are qualified for and interested in pursuing; maximize your job options.)

3. What specific activities are you most interested in performing in your ideal job? What energizes and excites you most?

4. Are you willing to travel or relocate? Explain.

CHAPTER 4

# Explore Contemporary Workplace Issues

> **"Today, without question, information is the most valuable commodity on the planet. The ability of my team to articulate, educate, and navigate through the changing communication channels of the future is a harbinger of the company's success."**
>
> *Lee Duffey, president and founder*
> *Duffey Communications, Inc.*
> *Altanta, GA*

## *In this chapter you will:*

- Integrate personal financial management into your career strategies.
- Identify what globalization means to your career.

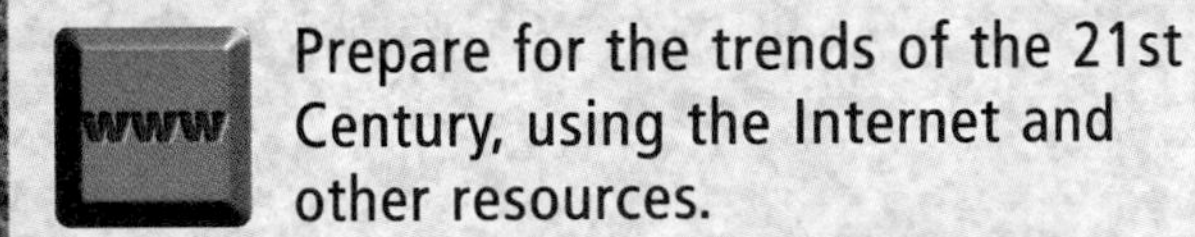

- Prepare for the trends of the 21st Century, using the Internet and other resources.
- Learn how employers expect you to work responsibly with others.

Chapter 4 provides an overview of some prominent issues you will face in the workplace of the 21st Century: an increasingly global economy, continuously changing technology, evolving workplace equity, and complex challenges to high ethical standards. This chapter also discusses the importance of, and provides guidelines for, managing personal finances responsibly. Use this chapter to help plan for the future and to develop the competencies, skills, and resources that will best support your career success.

## TAKE CHARGE OF YOUR SUCCESS

Take charge of your career success: Follow the example of the most successful companies by spending adequate time on strategic planning and action. Study local, national, and international business issues; anticipate the impact they will have on your industry; and develop the skills and marketing approach that will best support your career objectives.

### Cultivate Success

Be entrepreneurial: Advance your career with the same five competencies SCANS identifies for business success. Develop your foundation skills, personal qualities, and workplace competencies to manage your career.

1. **Resources.** Use your educational, social, and economic resources to support your professional development.

2. **Interpersonal.** Cultivate your ability to work well with others by taking applicable classes and by volunteering.

3. **Information.** Acquire and use information about business, political, and social trends and issues.

4. **Systems.** Seek knowledgeable mentors, take classes, and network to enhance your understanding of social, organizational, and technological systems in your industry.

5. **Technology.** Adapt to the ever-increasing rate of technological change by continuously updating your knowledge of tools, equipment, and software.

Figure • 4-1: Learn to manage your personal finances, and keep your living below your income.

Finally, remember that of all the variables that influence career success—job skills, people skills, opportunities—the most important one is attitude: YOUR attitude. Employers hire people with positive attitudes.

### Manage Your Personal Finances

Many goals require both personal effort and money: a home, a car, and an education. Managing money well is also essential for achieving career success. Often, employers will not hire people with a history of poor money management such as defaulting on educational loans or other lines of credit. Keeping expense payments current provides many benefits: (a) protecting credit status, (b) avoiding disqualification for employment, and (c) being accepted for future loans at favorable interest rates.

**Balance Wants and Resources.** Plan and control your money with a well-designed monthly budget. (See the Monthly Budget Planner on pages 58 and 67.) Required income varies with individual circumstances, and a budget will reveal the amount of money you need to survive. Knowing this figure will be crucial for you to negotiate salary offers realistically.

## MANAGING YOUR FINANCES PROVIDES MAJOR BENEFITS

The rewards for budgeting your income and expenses, saving money, and investing wisely include (a) earning a good credit rating, (b) maintaining your employment competitiveness, (c) negotiating realistic wages, (d) keeping financial peace of mind, and (e) providing money to achieve financial goals such as a car, a home, an education, retirement security, and travel.

**Track Income.** Tracking your sources of year-round income will help you anticipate and plan for income changes or variances. For example, you may earn quite a bit of money over the summer months but find that during the school year income is down and expenses are up.

**Track Expenses.** Where does your money go? To manage your finances successfully, you need to allocate money for all your needs, including living, schooling, and personal expenses. Categorize and budget your expenses. If your actual expenses exceed budgeted amounts, determine where expenses can be cut.

**Set Up a Regular Savings Plan.** Regular contributions to a savings plan will allow you to save money to pay back college or other loans. Keep in mind you must pay a minimum amount per month on your student loan regardless of the balance. Savings will also help you accumulate the extra cash you may need if you choose a job that involves relocation expenses. Start-up expenses such as deposits for rent, utilities, and telephone can be costly.

**Use Credit Wisely.** Establishing and maintaining good credit is a must for successful career development. Opening a credit account and using it wisely helps people build the all-important positive credit rating. In contrast, using credit beyond what you can afford creates a destructive cycle of charging, paying only the minimum payment, carrying an increasing balance over to the next month, and charging more because you don't have the cash to make needed purchases. Below are eight credit-smart tips:

1. Avoid using credit beyond what you can afford.

2. Develop good budgeting and checking account management skills before getting a major credit card.

3. Practice with a debit card. Debit cards are used like credit cards but work like checking accounts.

4. Shop around for a credit card with good terms such as no annual fee, grace periods, and the lowest interest rates. **Warning:** Most cards offer low initial interest rates that eventually increase, sometimes significantly.

5. Use only one credit card and use it sparingly.

6. Pay more than the monthly minimum payment. Credit seems affordable because the minimum payment is small, but the amount paid in finance charges can really add up. Remember: Credit card companies are in business to make credit profitable for *them*.

7. Make sure the credit card company receives your payment before the due date.

8. Never use credit to extend your paycheck.

The Consumer Credit Counseling Service (CCCS) offers a "College Student Budget Packet" and excellent credit counseling to anyone, free of charge. The CCCS can be found in most cities nationwide. It is a program funded by the United Way and accredited by the Council on Accreditation of Services to Children and Families.

Some major credit card companies are accessible via the Internet. MasterCard's Web site offers students a variety of budget and credit card information at **http://www.mastercard.com/students/**.

Credit experts offer the following additional tips for getting ahead financially: (a) Protect the income you need for rent, utilities, and food by *not* promising it to the credit card companies. (b) Purchase a vehicle you can afford. Your standard of living always falls when you owe too much.

Use good budgeting skills, make informed choices, and exercise common sense to avoid a financial fiasco that can tarnish your credit rating for a lifetime.

## CCCS-RECOMMENDED QUESTIONS TO ASK BEFORE YOU USE CREDIT:

- Do I really need it?
- Do I have to have it today?
- What will happen if I don't buy it now?
- Why have I gotten along without it until now?
- Are there credit-free ways I can pay for it?

**Complete Career Action 4-1**

# CAREER ACTION 4-1

## Master Your Money with a Common Cent$ Budget

**DIRECTIONS:** Copy the Monthly Budget Planner on page 67, and follow the steps below to prepare your monthly budget.

1. Add your additional item names to column B.
2. Put appropriate amounts in columns C and D.
3. For each numbered item, subtract column D from column C; place answer in column E. Mark differences over budget with a negative (–) sign and those under budget with a positive (+) sign.
4. Subtotal each category in each column.
5. In columns C and D, put the total for line 3 on line 32 and the total for line 31 on line 33.
6. Subtract line 33 from line 32, and put answer on line 34.

### Manage Your Career Development

Since the 1980s, downsizing has become a common practice. People who relied entirely on one employer to help them develop a successful career were suddenly unemployed. The demands of the marketplace have made it more cost-effective for employers to hire workers for the duration of specific projects and then to reassign or lay people off.

**SUCCESS TIP**

**Think of yourself as an entrepreneur and of employers as clients who contract for your skills and abilities. Build a successful career by negotiating well and delivering top value.**

Today, you must be entrepreneurial: Think of yourself as a contractor and of your employers as clients. Accept complete responsibility for managing your career. Concentrate on developing skills applicable to several closely related fields, and take jobs that further your career goals.

## UNDERSTAND WHAT GLOBALIZATION MEANS TO YOUR CAREER

For the first part of the 21st Century, experts predict global trade among nations will increase three to four times faster than individual national economies. Success in this larger, more competitive market requires innovative, quality, timely, and efficiently produced products. To meet the upcoming challenges, many companies are restructuring as follows:

1. Distributing design, marketing, and customer service operations across the globe
2. Moving manufacturing plants to locations that offer the appropriate combination of education and low labor costs
3. Purchasing product components from outside suppliers
4. Reducing the number of permanent employees
5. Relying on specialized teams, often made up of short-term workers, to meet critical deadlines
6. Recruiting highly skilled workers worldwide

In short, globalization is increasing competitive pressures, blurring economic boundaries, and relocating well-educated workers.

### Appreciate the Major Role of Quality Assurance Programs

In the early 1980s, the European economies lagged behind those of the United States and Japan. After realizing that their many different production standards made them less competitive, Europeans began requiring suppliers of regulated products to meet the quality assurance standards (ISO 9000 series) adopted by the International Organization of Standards (known as ISO). Companies worldwide are establishing Total Quality Management (TQM) programs to achieve ISO 9000 series certification.

Reassure employers you understand the importance of quality by submitting well-prepared job search documents. Study the TQM literature, and know how the quality process applies to your industry. During job interviews, ask employers about quality programs. If you consider out-of-country positions, research the applicable quality issues. Let employers know you appreciate the significance of quality.

## Provide Service for Two Kinds of Customers

TQM has taught companies that success in today's marketplace requires satisfying two kinds of customers: internal and external. Internal customers are employees who build on the work of coworkers and are dependent on receiving quality work to complete their own jobs successfully. External customers contribute to successful companies by purchasing the final products and services. In the worldwide market, customer service means delivering satisfactory results to both types of customers.

Identify the internal and external customers for any job you consider. Research your industry so you can speak knowledgeably about current customer service issues and can give examples of how you handle typical customer concerns in a positive way.

## Develop a Worldwide Perspective

Meet the challenges of globalization by developing a worldwide perspective. Demonstrate an understanding of the global competitive factors of your industry, and show a willingness to learn about international cultures. Advise employers if you are willing to travel or if you speak more than one language. As trading opportunities expand, career possibilities will also broaden and require more skills and more world awareness.

**SUCCESS TIP**

**Use a two-pronged approach when preparing for a successful career in a global economy: (a) Learn about the economic, political, social, and technological trends in the world; and (b) provide quality products and excellent service to all your customers.**

# PREPARE FOR THE TRENDS OF THE 21ST CENTURY

From everyday transactions with stores and banks to sophisticated international operations, technology removes time zone and geographic barriers, revolutionizes tools, and changes the processes we use in working and making decisions. Technology will continue to evolve and affect our lives and careers at an ever-increasing pace. Incorporate technology into your career by keeping current on technological trends, by frequently updating your skills, and by keeping a flexible, positive attitude.

## The Virtual Office

One of the fastest growing trends worldwide is the virtual office, or *teleworking*: working in nontraditional locations through the use of advanced communications and computer technology. Some companies are reducing permanently

Figure • 4-2: Laptop computers allow people to work in nontraditional locations.

assigned desks and introducing work stations equipped with computers or computer hookups, telephones, and basic office supplies. Employees who travel among company locations can plug their laptops into the company computer network and start working. In addition, some companies are expanding the use of teleworking by letting their employees *telecommute*: work at home and use technology to communicate with coworkers and clients. Develop your technical and organizational skills, and remain flexible so you can work comfortably and productively in the virtual office environment.

**"It's kind of fun to do the impossible."**
—Walt Disney

## Telephone and Computer Networks

Networks, which use computer and communications technology to link resources, make it easy for people to find, send, or receive information. Voice and data networks can provide nearly instantaneous access to items as diverse as company records, public chat rooms, and unwanted viruses.

**Businesses That Use Networks Must Be Security Conscious.** Anyone with a computer, a telephone line, and a modem can access the worldwide Internet. Like any other society, the Internet has its share of vandals. Small companies that use the Internet to send inter- and intra-company e-mail, to sponsor company Web sites, or to conduct monetary transactions usually protect their computers with *host-based* security programs. These special programs are installed on each computer to protect it from unauthorized access and from viruses.

Although any business may use the public Internet, many companies are setting up private, closed computer networks—called *intranets*. These intranets are used for internal communications and to protect business information from competitive spying or sabotage. Companies typically restrict intranet access to company-owned, employee-operated computers. Some companies even prohibit remote access, but most issue passwords to allow employees who travel or telework to use the intranet via telephone lines and modems.

Companies often use firewall security systems to protect their intranets but allow their employees to access the Internet. *Firewalls* use special combinations of hardware and software to restrict the types of information that can enter or leave intranets. Firewalls can also be configured to provide network managers with usage patterns, the number of attempts to breach the system, or other information.

**Privacy Is Nonexistent on Networks—Internet or Intranet.** Network managers have full access to network information, including in-house e-mail. Even if both the sender and the receiver delete a message from their computers' memories, the message still exists in the backup files of the sending and receiving servers. Protect your privacy: Do not send private information over the Internet, and transmit only legal, ethical company business over intranets. Also, use passwords to protect the confidentiality of company information or sensitive personnel records.

## Increased Work Pace

Technology has increased the work pace by reducing distance and time as barriers to communication. In the past, the pressures of decision making and the demands of work processes were buffered by the time it took for information to travel from one point to another. No one expected business information to be quickly available to all workers or to be routinely delivered to people who were traveling, on vacation, or at home.

**Expectations Have Changed.** People expect quicker results and faster decisions because information is now available swiftly from almost any location to workers at any level. The current direction is toward larger, more complex workloads, which has led to an increased sense of urgency for employees and to a growing infringement of work on leisure time.

## Lean Organizations Require Team Emphasis

The availability of management information to all employees, the rapid rate of technological advances, and the competitive pressures of globalization have combined to result in unpredictable staffing needs and fundamental shifts in the working structures of companies. The shifts are away from management-directed systems toward "flat," team-directed systems that increase each individual's responsibilities.

Companies are using a skilled core group of leaders to develop strategies and goals and to manage work teams that perform the design, production, marketing, and servicing tasks. Technology, instead of middle managers, now transfers information between core groups and work teams. Flatter, leaner organizations respond more efficiently to competitive pressures and create a need for flexible, problem-solving team leaders.

## Growth in Service and High-Tech Jobs

Globalization, advancing technology, and the aging of baby boomers (the 76 million people born between 1946 and 1964) are stimulating a long-term shift from a manufacturing-based economy to a service-based economy. Expect to see the greatest number of job openings in the service sector: information technology, business services, health care, personal services, tourism, and entertainment.

SUCCESS TIP

**Sharpen your technological and team skills so you can work productively with the flatter, leaner organizations that use the latest in computer and communications technology. Show employers you adapt well to change by demonstrating flexibility and by focusing on problem solving.**

## Impact of Baby Boomer Retirements

Only 12 percent of the pre-baby boomer generation chose to remain in the workforce after the traditional retirement age of sixty-five. If global markets continue to expand and if boomers (who make up 52 percent of today's working population) retire at the same rate as their parents, employers could face a serious labor shortage and a rapid rise in recruitment, training, and benefit costs. Current projections, however, show that several factors will keep 75 to 80 percent of baby boomers working in some capacity after traditional retirement ages:

- **Lack of money.** Most baby boomers over age sixty-five will need to work (a) to supplement Social Security, (b) to combat the effects of inflation, (c) to offset reduced or nonexistent pensions, (d) to pay rising Medicare and medical rates, and (e) to maintain their pre-age-sixty-five standards of living.

- **Healthier elderly and longer life spans.** In the 1930s, the average life expectancy was sixty-two years; today it is eighty years.

- **Personal satisfaction.** The National Institute on Aging published a survey that showed 75 percent of older workers would prefer to phase down from full-time to part-time work instead of retiring abruptly.

## PROTECT YOUR INDEPENDENCE

Take charge of your retirement planning *now*. Start saving for retirement at the beginning of your career. Your reward? More lifestyle options later in life.

SUCCESS TIP

Research the compensation and benefits plans offered by various-sized firms in your industry. Recognize that employers may offer attractive, unusual benefits packages to enhance wages.

### Tailored Benefits Packages

Employers are using additional benefits to attract new workers and to slow the transition of baby boomers to retirement. The trend for all employers is to beef up compensation plans by using strategies similar to those listed below.

- **Offer personalized benefits.** Approve fixed-amount employer contributions that employees use to pay for their choices from a smorgasbord of benefits such as (a) child care; (b) long-term care insurance; (c) elder-care services; (d) family-care leave of absence; (e) work/life programs; (f) domestic partner benefits; (g) prepaid legal, auto, home, and funeral insurance; and (h) convenience or "concierge" services.

- **Allow workers to pay for additional benefits at group rates.**

- **Offer flexible working schedules.**

- **Restructure jobs** into part-time (including shared jobs), temporary, telecommuting, or contractual assignments.

- **Reorganize the compensation system** to reward people quickly for performance.

- **Expand compensation packages** to include extra training, exposure to key decision makers, and increased recognition.

## WORK RESPONSIBLY WITH OTHERS

Working responsibly with others will be the hallmark of a successful career in the 21st Century. Economic, legal, and social forces worldwide will make it increasingly important to respect and value cultural, gender, and physical diversity in coworkers. Successful companies will view employee differences as assets to the teamwork that ensures successful customer service in diverse markets.

### Promote Workplace Equity

To meet competitive pressures today, employers are working to integrate diversity into their businesses. Companies that meet and exceed legal requirements for workplace equity have increased productivity because all employees feel valued and respected for their contributions. Most businesses with more than 15 employees have an official diversity policy to ensure compliance with the four federal laws that set the tone for workplace equity in the United States:

1. **The (Revised) Fair Labor Standards Act (incorporates the Equal Pay Act),** which applies to almost all businesses and defines the forty-hour workweek, covers the federal minimum wage, sets requirements for overtime, places restrictions on child labor, and prohibits compensating men and women differently for doing the same job.

2. **Title VII of the Civil Rights Act** makes workplace discrimination with respect to race, color, sex, national origin, and religion illegal for companies that employ 15 or more people.

3. **The Age Discrimination in Employment Act** prohibits companies that employ 20 or more from discriminating against employees who are age forty or older.

4. **The Americans with Disabilities Act** prohibits employers with 15 or more employees from discriminating against people with physical or mental disabilities and requires employers to make "a reasonable accommodation" for the needs of disabled employees as long as the accommodation does not represent an undue hardship to the employer.

Promote workplace equity by demonstrating respect for others and openness to different perspectives. Further your career by relating positively to others in regard to physical abilities, gender, race, culture, age, religion, or sexual orientation.

## Respect Privacy and Confidentiality of Your Company, Coworkers, Customers, and Suppliers

Working responsibly with others includes respecting individual, company, and customer privacy. Coworkers do not like having their privacy violated, and employers dismiss and often sue employees who "leak" proprietary information, abuse the company's computer system, or violate a nondisclosure agreement. Customers and suppliers also are assertive in protecting their confidential business information. They may take legal action or refuse to do business with people who violate their trust.

**Treat Coworkers As You Would Want to Be Treated.** The openness of most working environments makes true privacy impossible, but the expectation of privacy remains. If you develop a reputation for being discreet and courteous, you will learn more, progress further, and become a respected member of the team.

**Guard Your Company's Business Information.** By accepting employment, you agree to join your employer's team and to help your company succeed. Because giving away company-confidential material would undermine the ability of your employer to compete in the marketplace, you have a moral and legal obligation to protect product, marketing, or management information. Before discussing work-related information with your coworkers, make sure you are in an appropriate location. Take reasonable precautions to protect important business information.

**Honor Confidentiality Agreements with Customers and Suppliers.** Ask your supervisor about your company's policies regarding confidentiality or nondisclosure agreements. These agreements state that your company's representatives will not disclose or use clients' or suppliers' business information except for the legitimate purposes detailed in the agreement. Make sure you know what customers or suppliers expect you to do with sensitive information before you accept it. If you have any doubts, check with appropriate management personnel.

**SUCCESS TIP**

**Follow the lead of the most successful companies: Respect diversity, honor confidentiality, and maintain a high ethical standard.**

## Practice Ethics in the Workplace

According to one dictionary, *ethics* means "the moral principles which determine the rightness or wrongness of particular acts or activities." Nothing will damage your career as drastically as losing your reputation for ethical behavior! In general, members of the business community will expect you to be honest, open, accurate, law-abiding, and trustworthy. Fraud, dishonesty, manipulation, and conspiracy not only are unethical but also lead to career-devastating legal consequences.

**Make Ethical Decisions.** Most of us believe we know the difference between right and wrong, but applying our principles and maintaining our integrity in the business world can be challenging.

**Refuse to Take Unethical Actions.** If you know an action is wrong, refuse to do it. If you aren't sure what to do, ask. Most companies make personnel, management, and legal resources available to employees. You also have the right to consult with your own spiritual or legal advisers.

If you have any reservations about an action, don't let yourself be "talked into" it by someone in authority, by someone who says "it's done all the time," or by someone who says you "must" make an immediate decision. If you take an unethical action, you are the one who will have to live with the resulting loss of reputation and with the personal and legal consequences. Protect your long-term career: Uphold your personal principles and values.

**Complete Career Action 4-2**

### CAMP ON YOUR PRINCIPLES

When you are confronted with a situation, however small, that leaves you uncertain about the right course of action, think CAMP.

**Conscience:** Does the action go against your conscience?

**Allowable:** Is the action allowed by law?

**Media:** Would you want the action publicized in the media?

**Policy:** Does the action follow company policy?

## CAREER ACTION 4-2

### Use the Internet to Research Contemporary Workplace Issues

**Directions:** Turn to page 68, and complete **Career Action 4-2**.

## CHECKLIST FOR EXPLORING CONTEMPORARY WORKPLACE ISSUES

Check each of the following actions that you are currently taking to increase your career success:

- ☐ Master your money with common cent$ by using a monthly budget.
- ☐ Think of yourself as an entrepreneur and of employers as clients who contract for your skills and abilities.
- ☐ Use a two-pronged approach when preparing for a successful career in the global economy of the 21st Century: (a) learn about the economic, political, social, and technological trends; and (b) provide quality products and excellent service to your customers.
- ☐ Show employers you adapt to change by demonstrating flexibility, focusing on problem solving, and working well with teams.
- ☐ Research the compensation and benefits plans offered by the various-sized firms in your industry.
- ☐ Respect diversity, honor confidentiality, and maintain high ethical standards.

## CRITICAL THINKING QUESTIONS

1. Why is it important to manage your personal finances well?
2. List five ways you can use credit wisely.
3. How is technology changing the way people work?
4. Why should you practice high ethical standards in the workplace?

# CAREER ACTION 4-1

## Prepare Your Monthly Budget

**MONTHLY BUDGET PLANNER FOR MONTH OF**

| A<br>Category | B<br>Item | C<br>Budgeted | D<br>Actual | E<br>Over (–) or Under (+) |
|---|---|---|---|---|
| 1. Income | Wages | | | |
| 2. | Other | | | |
| 3. | Total Income | | | |
| 4. Expenses | Rent/Mortgage | | | |
| 5. | Car Payment | | | |
| 6. | Child Care | | | |
| 7. | Insurance | | | |
| 8. | | | | |
| 9. | Loans | | | |
| 10. | | | | |
| 11. | Savings | | | |
| 12. | Allowance | | | |
| 13. | Food/Living Items | | | |
| 14. | Home Utilities | | | |
| 15. | | | | |
| 16. | Telephone(s) | | | |
| 17. | Cable TV | | | |
| 18. | Transportation | | | |
| 19. | | | | |
| 20. | School Expenses | | | |
| 21. | Credit Cards | | | |
| 22. | | | | |
| 23. | Medical Care | | | |
| 24. | Clothes/Shoes | | | |
| 25. | Hobbies/Sports | | | |
| 26. | Entertainment | | | |
| 27. | Charity | | | |
| 28. | Gifts | | | |
| 29. | Vacations | | | |
| 30. | Other | | | |
| 31. | Total Expenses | | | |
| 32. Totals | Total Income | | | |
| 33. (less) | Total Expenses | | | |
| 34. | Difference* | | | |

* If your expenses exceed your income, reassess your budget.

# CAREER ACTION 4-2

## Use the Internet to Research Contemporary Workplace Issues

**DIRECTIONS:** Use the Internet to research one or more of the contemporary issues listed, or select a workplace issue that especially interests you. Write a brief summary of your findings below, or use separate paper for your report.

**NOTE:** Since the content of Web sites is subject to change without notice, be aware that the links listed below may not match the current content of the Web sites referenced in this assignment.

1. **Global Perspective:** Try the search string "international and business."

   Also check these Web sites:
   a. Michigan State University: *http://ciber.bus.msu.edu/*
      (Click on *International Business Resources on the WWW*)

   b. The Association for International Business: *http://www.earthone.com/*

2. **The Workplace:** Try the following three search strings: (a) "the workplace," (b) "business and intranets," and (c) "telecommuting and virtual and office." Also check the Excite Netscape Web Directory site *http://excite.netscape.com/directory/* (Click on *Business*, then *Careers*, and then *Workplace*)

3. **Tailored Benefits Packages:** Try the following two search strings: (a) "workplace and benefits" and (b) "work and life and benefits." Also check the Excite Netscape Web Directory site *http://excite.netscape.com/directory/*
   (Click on *Business*, then *Careers*, then *Workplace*, and then *Benefits*)

**Summary of Internet Research Findings**

________________________________________

________________________________________

________________________________________

________________________________________

________________________________________

________________________________________

CHAPTER 5

# Organize Your Winning Network

> Students should pursue nothing less then their dreams when they search for a job. My advice is to choose something you really want to do and then establish a network of support people who can help you find the right avenues to pursue your dreams.
>
> *Charles Widger*
> *Managing Partner*
> *Brinker Capital*

***In this chapter you will:***

- Develop a personal support system list of people who can motivate you in your job search and provide moral support.
- Prepare a job search network list of people who can help you find solid job leads and provide professional suggestions for enhancing your job search preparation.

Use the Internet to search for current job search networking tips.

Chapter 5 explains the need and methods for developing two important support groups to help you achieve your career goals: (a) a personal support system to motivate and encourage you and (b) a network of people who can help identify solid job leads.

# YOUR PERSONAL SUPPORT SYSTEM IS YOUR COACHING TEAM

What is a personal job search support system? Your *support system* is the group of people who can motivate, advise, and encourage you (like a personal coaching team) during your job search and throughout your developing career. This is the group of people who can help you strengthen your winning attitude and successful job search and career development strategies. Good choices for your personal support system include your family; friends; school, work, or social acquaintances; former or current employers; career services staff and counselors from your school; and instructors—people who are willing to provide motivational and instructional support during your job search.

## Members of Your Support System Play Many Important Roles

One support member could provide the extra energy to boost your motivation and commitment; another could help soothe your ego after a job rejection. Still another support member who is skilled in writing can help you polish your resumes and cover letters. These people sustain you and bolster your ego; they motivate you when you need a "push." They are valuable people who can help you stretch to reach your full potential.

SUCCESS TIP

**Develop a personal support system of people who can (a) motivate and encourage you, (b) help with resumes and job search letters, and (c) act as sounding boards for job search planning.**

## Identify Your Support System Members Now!

Select your support system members for the following qualities:

1. Ability to motivate you.
2. Ability to help you develop or edit effective job search communications (people who have good English and writing skills).
3. Ability to help with solid job leads in your field, ability to share similar experiences and job search progress information (for example, another job seeker who is either in the same or another occupational field).

**Complete Career Action 5-1**

**"There is no such thing as a self-made man. You will reach your goals only with the help of others."**

—George Shinn

# DEVELOP A LARGE NETWORK—THE NO. 1 SOURCE OF JOB LEADS

Did you know that 65 percent of jobs in the United States are identified through job search networking? Getting the job you want is a numbers game; the more people you make aware of your search, the more solid leads you will obtain. *Networking* is actively making as many people as possible aware of your job search. It is also seeking

# CAREER ACTION 5-1

## List Your Personal Support System Members

**DIRECTIONS:** Who always boosts your morale and encourages you to keep striving toward your goals? These people should be tops on your list! Review the list of three areas you should consider in selecting support members. Write below as many names of support members as possible.

______________________________________________

______________________________________________

______________________________________________

______________________________________________

**NOTE:** This assignment is designed to get you started in developing your personal support system. Use separate paper or a computer to finalize the names, addresses, and telephone numbers of all the people you want on your team. They will become part of your larger "job search network" (explained in the next section of this chapter).

job leads and referrals from them to prospective employers. Networking is the number one source of successful job leads because employers hire more people referred to them personally (through networking) than through any other source. Therefore, the larger your network, the greater your odds are of linking to someone who knows a viable prospective employer. So, tap into this number one source, build your successful network, and get the word out now.

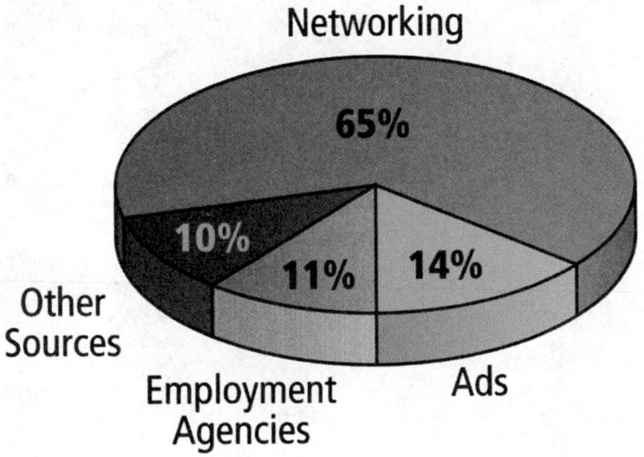


Figure • 5-1: Networking is #1 source of job leads.

## Networking Pays Off: A Case History

Consider this actual experience: After Kwame completed a computer electronics training program, he sent out resumes to all his prospects. Because he had overlooked a good source in his network, landing a job took him several more months than necessary. Six months into his job search, he was describing his job target to Juan, the owner of the printshop where he had been duplicating his resumes. From past experience, Juan knew that Kwame's computer and technology abilities were good. A few days later, the printshop owner mentioned this to one of his regular customers (head of a communications satellite company). This woman had been looking for someone with Kwame's skills for five months, so she called Kwame for an interview; as a result, Kwame landed an ideal job. Kwame could definitely have speeded the process by including the printshop owner in his network from the start.

Don't let this happen to you; include on your network list absolutely everyone you know.

## Networking Sources

The network of people who can help you mushrooms with each new contact you make. People who know you personally are the most likely to help you. Your network begins with people you know who link to others, increasing your chances of discovering good job prospects.

Review the list of networking sources below to help identify prospects for your support network:

1. Friends
2. Relatives
3. Current and former employers
4. Colleagues or coworkers
5. Teachers
6. Career fairs
7. Counselors
8. Classmates
9. People from your place of worship
10. Neighbors
11. Members of your clubs, professional associations, volunteer groups
12. Web sites, bulletin boards, news and chat groups
13. Professionals (physicians, dentists, accountants)
14. People you do business with (salespeople, clerks, other)
15. People you spend leisure time with (sports, hobbies, other)
16. Service people (letter carrier, hairdresser or barber, librarian, clerks, gas attendant, other)
17. People your children or siblings associate with (parents, teachers, club leaders, etc.)
18. Who else do you know? (*Don't overlook anyone*!) Whom do they know? They might have connections exactly where you need them.

## Networking Expands Your Potential

You could easily have 100 to 500 acquaintances. Multiply that number by two (two referrals from each person), and the potential is astounding! This is why networking is the top source of job leads.

Figure • 5-2: Your personal network is larger than you think. Consider contacts where you work and play.

## HOW TO CREATE A STRONG NETWORK

1. Contact people who can help with your career preparation and job search.
2. Discuss your job target with them; leave a copy of your resume and a brief outline of your job target and your qualifications.
3. Respect their time.
4. *Ask them for the names of at least two other people* to contact to find job leads and information.
5. Contact these two people; repeat the process.
6. Follow up on every lead; be persistent.
7. Within one day, send a thank-you note on quality stationery.
8. Stay in touch throughout your search.
9. Let them know when you get your job.

**NOTE:** To get the most from networking, follow *all* the steps above.

The following guidelines will help you get the most from your networking efforts.

- **Ask Everyone for Referrals.** As you meet with network members, ask them to refer you to at least two other people who may be able to provide useful information or job leads. You don't have to be vague about it, be direct. "Do you know anyone in my field who might have a job opening?" If the answer is *no,* ask, "Do you know anyone else who might know a prospective employer in my field?" Be persistent (and courteous); it pays!
- **Put Career Fairs High on Your List.** Career fairs are expanding rapidly and are an excellent networking source because you can connect with so many potential employers in a short time period. Check with your school career services center to find out what is offered in your area.
- **Broaden Your Network.** Join and be active in professional associations and other relevant groups in your field. They are a great resource for keeping informed of new industry developments, which employers consider important.
- **REMEMBER: It's a Numbers Game.** The more people who know about your job search goals and qualifications, the greater your chance of finding the ideal job! Maximize your networking efforts to maximize your potential

**Complete Career Action 5-2**

# CAREER ACTION 5-2

## Job Search Network List

Sharpen your memory and your pencil. On separate paper or using a computer, write the name of everyone you can think of for your job search network. Then, develop a master job search network list. Include the name of each person you contact, the person's mailing address, e-mail address, and telephone number. Also include space to record the dates you contact the person and to make notes of needed follow up.

**Career Database Appropriate**

## Meet with Members of Your Network

Schedule a meeting with each person on your network list to inform him or her of your job search goals. Explain the type of job you are looking for and the skills, education, work experience, and other abilities you have to qualify for this job. With this information, your network can more effectively help you.

Always leave a copy of your resume with each networking contact. Unless you already have a top-notch resume, don't begin your networking yet. Guidelines for researching employers and for preparing a winning resume are outlined in Chapters 6 through 9. After you have completed the assignments in Chapter 9, you will be ready to begin networking.

If you already have a well-prepared resume, you can begin your networking as soon as you are ready to start your formal job search. If you're ready, you can start today! But first review Chapter 9, "Creating a Winning Resume," to verify that your existing resume is as strong as it can be.

**Conduct organized networking meetings: Review your job target and qualifications, leave a resume, ask for referrals, get references, send thank-you letters, and follow up.**

**Update Your Network List.** Update your job search network list periodically. Eliminate people who, over time, are reluctant or have too many other commitments to permit their involvement.

**Establish References.** During your networking, seek influential references who are willing to vouch for your qualifications. *Always ask permission* to use their names as references you can give to prospective employers. These references should be people who can attest to your good job, school, or other performance and to your desirable character traits and values and who are willing to write letters recommending you to employers. Add their names to the list of references you recorded in **Career Action 2-3**.

## Maintain Active Communication

Communicate with your network members regularly to update them on your job search progress. Ask them to recommend additional job search strategies or job leads. It is best to contact the members of your network in person. Otherwise, use the telephone or e-mail to update these people regarding your job search status and to get additional assistance and encouragement from them. Every job hunter can use regular encouragement. Someday you can return the favor or extend it to another person who needs and deserves it.

Figure • 5-3: Form a career network with class members. Help each other find leads and provide encouragement when needed.

**Complete Career Action 5-3**

# CAREER ACTION 5-3

## Use the Internet to Search for Current Job Search Networking Tips

**DIRECTIONS:** Search for articles on networking tips that relate to areas presented in Chapter 5 (job search networking and motivation). You can use any of the sites listed below or others you identify. **Select at least two articles that interest you most, and write a summary of each one.**

**NOTE:** Since the content of Web sites is subject to change without notice, be aware that the links listed below may not match the current content of the Web sites referenced in this assignment.

1. **JobSmart** *http://www.jobsmart.org/*
   Click on *Hidden Job Market*; then click on *Get Networked*; browse through the article, link to others listed.

2. **Career Magazine** *http://www.careermag.com/*
   Check out the current columns on the home page; also click on *Articles*, and browse through current articles and archives.

3. **National Business Employment Weekly** *http://www.nbew.com/*
   Click on *Resumes, Networking and Interviewing*, and review the articles on networking.

Also use search engines to help identify job search networking and motivation tips.

## TIPS FOR BEST USE OF REFERENCES

- Always ask permission to use someone as a reference in your job search. Never give a prospective employer the name of a reference who hasn't given you this permission. Always thank references for allowing you to use their names.
- Never identify someone as a reference who would not recommend you highly.
- Don't use relatives as references.
- Ask each reference to write a letter of reference for you that you can provide to employers.
- Keep in touch with your references. Know how to reach them, and let them know when you will be using their names.

## CHECKLIST FOR ORGANIZING A WINNING NETWORK

Check each of the following actions that you are currently taking to increase your career success:

- ☐ Develop a support system: people who motivate and help you with resumes and letters.
- ☐ Develop a large job search network to help find job leads.
- ☐ Conduct organized networking meetings: Review your job target and qualifications, leave a resume, ask for referrals, get references, send thank-you letters, and follow up.

## CRITICAL THINKING QUESTIONS

1. What is networking?
2. List the steps for effective networking.
3. Are neighbors and fellow club members as useful for networking as teachers or coworkers? Why?

CHAPTER 6

# Engineer an Efficient Job Search

> **"Look for all possible opportunities when planning your job search and internship. Take advantage of on-campus college recruiting and other services such as mock interviews, career counseling, and skills assessment. Employers now look for applicants who are well-rounded and involved in activities and who gain work experience through internships."**

*Fred Burke*
*Assistant Director of Career Planning*
*Miami University*
*Oxford, Ohio*

## *In this chapter you will:*

Use the Internet to research job listings and job trends information.

- Identify and use printed, human, Internet, and organizational sources of job information.
- Use tools for organizing and conducting your job search efficiently.

This chapter identifies many good resources to help you find jobs fast, including networking, direct employer contact, school career services centers, Internet sites, professional associations, and newspapers and other publications. The resources presented are based on extensive research with employment and placement counselors, with recent job seekers, and through the Internet. The more types of resources you use to find your ideal job, the greater your choices will be and the more quickly you will get optimum results. Chapter 6 also provides practical, efficient tools for organizing your job search to achieve your goals quickly.

# SOURCES OF JOB LEADS

The following comprehensive summary of sources of job leads and information will help you find prospective employers. However, don't limit yourself to the sources listed here. Use your imagination and initiative; some of the most rewarding jobs are uncovered in personally creative ways. Your own career objectives determine which sources are most useful to you.

## Networking

Friends, relatives, and acquaintances such as current and former employers, coworkers, and teachers are statistically the best source of job leads for two reasons:

1. People who know you are the most likely to have interest in your well-being and success. Therefore, they are the most likely to help you in your job search.

2. A personal referral from a friend, relative, or acquaintance is highly influential with prospective employers if the employers know and respect the person referring you. Employers trust recommendations from people they know more than they do from others.

Since it's the most productive source, focus your efforts on networking (getting help from people you know) to identify prospective employers.

**Focus your job search energy on networking; it's the #1 source of job leads.**

## Direct Employer Contact: Direct Bids and Information Surveys

Applicants who have training in job search techniques often find jobs through direct employer contact because they are organized and act professionally in making contacts by telephone, in writing, and in person. One effective method of obtaining solid job leads is through information interviews or surveys (meetings arranged to get general career information and advice from prospective employers or from employees holding jobs similar to the applicant's target). During these meetings, many job seekers obtain job leads as well as good career advice. We refer to these as *career information surveys* and discuss the topic further in Chapter 7.

SUCCESS TIP

**Concentrate on direct telephone or face-to-face contacts with employers; the most successful strategies involve direct contact with the hiring authority.**

## School Career Services Centers

School career services centers are good sources for obtaining job search information. Typically, these offices (a) maintain listings of local, regional, and national employers and lists of job openings; (b) assist with job search skills, interviewing, and resume and letter writing; (c) arrange and schedule on-campus interviews for students with prospective employers; (d) help research employer and salary information; and (e) provide career planning and job search counseling.

## Hot Internet and Job Information Web Sites

Many Web sites serve as job bank connections for employers and applicants. Once you get the hang of Internet research, you'll be amazed at the vast amount of usable and current information you can link to from just one search. If you're already skilled at Internet research, this is not news to you. Hone your cyberspace research to get the edge on your competition.

All types of employers have Web sites on the Net, including privately owned companies, government agencies, nonprofit organizations, and educational institutions. The Internet is also a great resource for worldwide job searches. Many excellent Internet job search sources are listed in **Career Action 6-1**. Don't limit yourself to these. Ask school career services staff and others for help in obtaining specific employer Web site addresses.

Employer Web sites typically provide: (a) general information about the organization, (b) general information about jobs available in the organization, and (c) instructions for submitting applications and resumes. Chapters 9 and 10 of this text provide more information about the electronic application and resume.

**SUCCESS TIP**

**Include the Internet as a job search tool. If jobs in your field are heavily advertised through the Net, it could be a top job lead source for you.**

## Leaders in Your Occupational Field

Recognized leaders in your occupational field can be excellent sources of job leads. Successful people are usually knowledgeable about the employment needs of their peers and competitors. One of these people may even consider hiring you after learning of your job target and qualifications. Be sure to include this valuable source in your job search.

## Professional, Vocational, and Trade Associations

Virtually every profession, vocation, and trade in the United States has one or more associations to keep members informed of changing technology, methods, and trends. Such groups typically provide educational publications, workshops, and continuing education courses. They often announce job openings during meetings and in their publications.

The Internet and many libraries have information on professional, vocational, and trade associations. For example, you will find associations for information technology, accounting, sales and marketing, writing, health care, teaching, and business management. Your career services staff and the reference librarian can help you identify organizations related to your interests and locate issues of their publications. Check current and back issues for help-wanted advertisements, and look for information about employment and job market trends.

## Employment Directories

Directories listing employers in local areas and defined geographic regions are available throughout the United States. Some employer specialty directories are also available in specific areas, such as manufacturing. To find such directories, check public, state, college, or university libraries; your school career counseling center; the Internet; and area chambers of commerce.

Figure • 6-1: Your local newspaper is a valuable source for job openings and hiring trends in your community.

## DON'T MISS A GOOD OPPORTUNITY: READ EVERY AD

Be thorough; read every listing. Advertisements don't always appear under a logical job heading, and you may miss an important lead by looking only under the obvious heads.

## Want Ads (Newspapers, Other Print Media, and Internet)

Check for job openings posted in a variety of ways:

- **Newspapers.** Look in the help-wanted and other sections of newspapers from all areas that may interest you. Also read the business sections, front pages, living sections, regional or city news, and sports pages of these newspapers. You can learn much relating to the hiring, expansion, downsizing, or startup of organizations in the area. Many newspapers also post their classified ads on the Internet.



- **Internet.** Check the job listings and want ads on the Internet by using the same cross-checking procedures. The Internet permits quick, convenient access and linking to an enormous number of sources. You can also subscribe to online employment publications such as the *National Business Employment Weekly* (**http://www.nbew.com/**) through the Internet.

- **Journals and other publications.** Check the classified sections of professional journals in your field, your school newspaper and bulletin boards, and publications that target job seekers (such as the *National Employment Weekly*, published by *The Wall Street Journal*).

**Want Ads: Good Sources of Job Market Trends.** Get the most out of want ads listed in print media and on the Internet. Use them to learn which kinds of employers are hiring and which appear to be expanding (indicated by several ads from the same organization). You can learn what experience, additional courses, and training you need for employment or advancement in your field.

Be alert for companies, agencies, industries, and regions that advertise actively—even for jobs that require more experience and education than you have now. Active advertising indicates that other positions may be open and indicates growth and job opportunities.

**SUCCESS TIP**

**Don't limit your search to published job announcements; they represent only 15% of available jobs.**

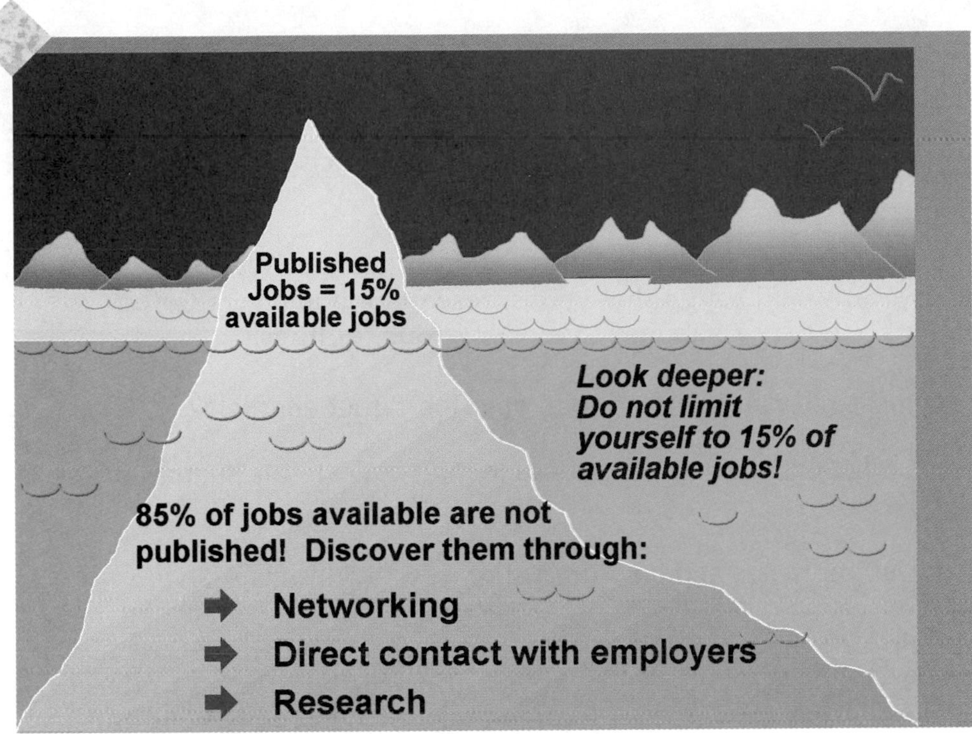


Figure • 6-2: Published job openings: just the tip of the iceberg!

**Review Old Ads.** Search the Internet and back issues of newspapers for ads that are 12 to 18 months old (check microfilm in your library). If a company was hiring three months ago, it's a job lead for you. The company may not have found the right person, may have let the last person go, or may now be expanding. Contact the firm, and ask to schedule a career information survey; it could provide a good lead or even a job offer (see Chapter 7 for survey details).

If an advertised job differs slightly but is still related to your target, pursue the lead anyway. You could find yourself interviewing for an unadvertised job that fits your goals. Don't overlook the "blind" ads requesting that resumes be sent to an anonymous box number. Some companies run blind ads to limit the number of individual contacts required to review applications. A well-prepared resume and cover letter can help you land a job this way.

SUCCESS TIP

**Don't limit your search to published announcements; they represent only 15% of available jobs.**

Help-wanted advertisements are a limited resource for finding just the right job, but don't let a choice opportunity slip through your fingers for lack of attention. **Perhaps family members or friends will help you with this daily task.**

## Small Businesses

A fast-growing trend is the availability of more job openings in small businesses than in large firms. This is a clear reason to research small businesses seriously as an employment source. Information about small business openings is available through chambers of commerce, your school career services center, employer directories, and help-wanted advertisements.

**Complete Career Action 6-1**

# CAREER ACTION 6-1

## Use the Internet to Find Job Listings and Information

**DIRECTIONS:** Use the Internet to access the sites listed under the *WebGuide* and Internet activities below. Browse through these sites, researching answers to the following three questions. Prepare a summary report of your findings.

1. Which sites had the most relevant information to your job target and field?
2. Summarize or print job listings you find for your field, and indicate the sources of the listings.
3. Summarize other useful job trends and job information you find in this search.

***WebGuide* Activity:** At the *WebGuide* Main Menu, select "Your Job Search." Complete Activity #6, "Search for a job," by visiting the sites listed in the activity, and summarize answers to the three questions listed above in the "Directions" of this assignment.

**Internet Activity:** Access the following Web sites, and summarize answers to the three questions listed in the "Directions" of this assignment, listed above.

**NOTE:** Since the content of Web sites is subject to change without notice, be aware that the links listed below may not match the current content of the Web sites referenced in this assignment.

**WEB SITES**

| | |
|---|---|
| America's Job Bank | http://www.ajb.dni.us/ |
| CareerMosaic | http://www.careermosaic.com/ |
| CareerPath | http://www.careerpath.com/ |
| Catapult | http://www.jobweb.org/catapult/ |
| JobBank USA | http://www.jobbankusa.com/ |
| JobWeb | http://www.jobweb.org/ |
| Monster.com | http://www.monster.com/ |
| The Online Career Center | http://www.occ.com/ |

**SEARCH ENGINES TO LOCATE SPECIFIC EMPLOYER WEB SITES**

| | |
|---|---|
| Alta Vista | http://www.altavista.com/ |
| Excite | http://www.excite.com/ |
| Lycos | http://www.lycos.com/ |
| Yahoo | http://www.yahoo.com/ |

## Private Employment Agencies

Private employment agencies can be useful sources for finding prospective employers, particularly if the one you select specializes in your field. Generally, the job applicant pays the agency a fee for securing a permanent job. Before considering such an agency, research the following:

1. Does the firm have a good reputation? Check for references with the staff at your school career services center, employers who work with the agency to obtain employees, other job seekers, and the Better Business Bureau. Don't take just one person's word. Also visit the agency you are considering.

2. How long has the agency been in business? What has happened to past clients?

3. Does the agency have expertise in placing people in your field?

4. If you would accept employment out of your local area, does the agency belong to a nationwide or regional system? Is it familiar with job opportunities, hiring trends, and salaries throughout the areas you would consider?

5. What services will the agency provide for you, and what would it expect you to do?

6. What are the costs to you? Get a written agreement spelling out every service you will receive, including how long counseling will take and how long you are entitled to the agency services.

7. Read every word of the contract, and make certain you are willing to accept all the conditions. Have the agency clarify how it handles client dissatisfaction with job placement. Firms that provide a full refund guarantee are usually the most reputable.

Figure • 6-3: When you visit an agency, be prepared to fill out forms and take employment tests.

## State Employment Services

Through the U.S. Department of Labor, each state has an employment agency that includes an employment services office. Names for the state employment offices vary throughout the nation; many incorporate the term *career center*. You can call the main state information number and ask for the number of the employment services office.

Such offices provide career counseling, job search techniques, and information on area job openings. Many offices maintain computerized data with up-to-the-minute information on job openings in the service regions. The job hunter is not charged a fee for this assistance.

## Employment Contractors

Employment contractors serve clients (employers, not job applicants) who need permanent employees or temporary help to handle extra work projects or to cover for regular employees on vacation or sick leave. Clients (the employers) often don't want to spend the time interviewing for jobs or handling the record keeping required to manage employees, so they deal with the employment contractors to handle these responsibilities.

Contract work is one of the most accessible means of reentering the job market and is a stepping stone between unemployment and employment. This arrangement offers two major benefits: (a) It gives both the employer and the employee an opportunity to check for a "good fit" without making a permanent commitment up front, and (b) the employment contractor takes care of the administrative details. Many people find full-time jobs through this source by gaining experience in the temporary jobs. To locate these companies, look in the Yellow Pages of your telephone directory under "Employment Contractors." The contract job may not fit your career target perfectly, but it can provide some outstanding benefits, including those listed below:

- Reentry to the job market
- Experience you may lack
- References for work done well
- Additions to your list of solid job leads
- Possibly a full-time job
- On-the-job training and hands-on practical skill development
- Income now

**NOTE:** As with private employment agencies, always review the employment contract thoroughly, and check carefully to verify the reputation of the employment contractor.

## Public Agencies: City, County, State, and Federal

City, county, and state agencies employ people in a variety of professional, technical, clerical, and other positions. Most agencies have a civil service system, which requires application and some preemployment testing through a central human resources department. Consult your local telephone directory to locate the numbers of these agencies.

Federal agencies also employ people in a variety of positions. Your local state employment office can refer you to the regional federal offices in areas that interest you. The Internet has good links to the federal jobs Web site, and Federal Job Information Centers are listed under "U.S. Government" in the blue pages of major area telephone directories. Request information regarding federal employment application procedures from your school career services center or your local state employment office.

Figure • 6-4: Federal and other government agencies offer many and varied career opportunities.

## Human Resources Departments in Private Industry

Contact human resources departments of private companies to learn about current job openings and testing, application, and hiring procedures. If no job openings are available, ask whether you can leave your application and resume on file for future openings. If these are accepted, ask whether any action is required on your part to keep your file open (for example, confirming your status every six months). Also ask these contacts whether they have suggestions for other job lead sources in your field. Some organizations have telephone recordings of information about current job openings.

## Career Fairs

The primary reason employers go to community- or school-sponsored career fairs is to find new talent, so go; you have to be there to be discovered! Career fairs are good sources of job leads and employer information; they are beneficial to both employers and job seekers because they provide opportunities to explore employment matches in a relaxed, face-to-face format. These fairs are efficient ways to contact many employers in one day. Career fairs are also offered on the Internet (search the Web sites listed in **Career Action 6-1** for career fairs; many also advertise on-line career fairs).

The following guidelines explain how to get the most out of on-site career fairs:

1. Take copies of your perfected resume and your business portfolio.

2. Arrive early and stay late to take advantage of this great networking opportunity.

3. Wear business-smart clothes. Make a positive, professional first impression by wearing standard business attire.

4. Plan your remarks. Be professional: Shake hands, introduce yourself, promote yourself by summarizing your qualifications briefly, and ask pertinent questions.

5. Visit the less attractive firms first to perfect your marketing pitch before visiting your main employer targets.

## Educational Institutions

For a teaching job, contact the human resources departments of school districts that interest you to find out about their application and hiring procedures. Also ask your school career services staff for help in locating jobs in education. Look in telephone directories for areas you would consider.

If no openings are currently available, request permission to leave your application and resume on file for future openings. Ask how you should follow up to keep your file updated and active. Also, check out the possibility of being certified to do substitute teaching—this can be a great way to prove your abilities and possibly work into a regular teaching position.

## Self-Employment

Self-employment is a mushrooming trend worth considering. This form of employment continues to skyrocket because organizations are downsizing and outsourcing tasks to control costs.

**Start by Learning under Another Employer.** To succeed in owning your own business, adequate education, training, and knowledge are essential. In addition to getting adequate formal schooling or training, you can increase your chance of successful self-employment by first working for someone who has succeeded in the field. Learn what works and what the pitfalls are as an employee, not as a new business owner.

If you lack extensive experience, it is more difficult to succeed in self-employment or contract work because prior work experience and accomplishments provide the credibility to land work contracts.

Self-employment is definitely worth considering, however, if you have good experience and can get endorsements from people who are satisfied with your performance.

Figure • 6-5: If you want to start your own business, learn all you can by working for someone already successful in that field.

**Research to Succeed.** If you are seriously interested, interview people in your field who are successfully self-employed to learn what methods they have used. Also obtain and study information from the Internet, your library, or bookstores on the subject of self-employment.

**Networking Is Essential.** To run your own business successfully, you must network with people in your field and with potential clients or customers. Market yourself by being active and visible. Take an active role in the most viable professional, trade, or other associations and clubs related to your career field.

**Start Small and Build.** A good way to begin self-employment is to do it part-time to develop a client base and references. Volunteer to give workshops or demonstrations to groups to prove your skills. Begin small, keeping your expenses at an absolute minimum, and expand only with demand.

**Consider self-employment if you have adequate experience; this is projected to be one of the largest sources of employment in the near future.**

## Nonprofit Organizations

Nonprofit organizations are good sources for jobs in public relations, solicitation, writing, management, health care, and other fields. They can offer growth opportunities, valuable work experience, and opportunities to demonstrate community service.

Examples of nonprofit organizations are the United Way, representing several organizations; the Red Cross; the March of Dimes; professional and vocational associations; federal grant support projects; Head Start programs; and health clinics for migrant workers. Look under "Associations" or "Social Services Organizations" in the Yellow Pages.

## Classified Telephone Directories

Collect classified sections or Yellow Pages of telephone directories from all areas you would consider for employment. Most of these directories are available on CD and the Internet (see http://www.bigyellow.com/). Look for employers in your field under all related headings (check the easy-reference indexes). This source provides comprehensive, readily available listings of current employers.

## Library

Ask your local reference librarian for help in finding directories (business, product, company, etc.) related to your field of interest. These directories list names, addresses, telephone numbers, and general information about employers in your field. Also ask knowledgeable people in your field to suggest additional library job search resources.

## Chambers of Commerce

Contact the local chamber of commerce in each of your geographic target areas. Chambers have complete, current lists of employers and often have names and telephone numbers of company executives. Most chambers also have information on new organizations that plan to locate in the area.

## The Military

The military is a good source of employment and provides important training and experience. Talk with your career services staff and local recruiting officers to obtain information and compare the offerings available.

Figure • 6-6: Internships can develop into full-time employment.

## Internships, Cooperative Education, and Volunteering

You can gain much in training internships, cooperative education programs, or volunteer work. You gain important experience and references who will verify your qualifications; and you demonstrate personal initiative—a highly favorable attribute—which enhances your employability.

## Reference Reading

Excellent publications are available to strengthen your career planning and job search in specific areas—particularly publications that specialize in your field. Ask your librarian and school career services staff for suggestions.

## The Hidden Job Market

Because 85% of job openings are never published, personal search is required to uncover them. Many job openings are actually created by the applicants. Such jobs are part of the hidden job market. To uncover the hidden job market, research the target organization thoroughly to discover where you can provide a useful service or offer money-making or money-saving ideas. Then, present your qualifications for this useful job or service so convincingly that the employer is motivated to create a job for you. This hidden job market is created through your own ingenuity. This source of employment is discussed further in Chapter 12.

SUCCESS TIP

**Allocate job search time in relation to the proven success rate of each:**
**Networking (65% success rate)**
**Advertisements (14% success rate)**
**Employment Agencies (11% success rate)**
**All other Sources (10% success rate)**

## PERSONAL AWARENESS OF MARKET TRENDS

Throughout your job search (and even before), look actively for all job leads—from people, television, radio, newspapers, the Internet, books, magazines, and general personal awareness. Be aware of what is happening in your city and state, the nation, and the world. Notice how changing technology shapes new jobs and revises or eliminates traditional jobs. Through this awareness, you can learn what trends are emerging.

Major job market trends favor health care and fitness, information processing, electronics, computerization, robotics, energy development, and services to the elderly, to name a few. Can you market your abilities in any of these areas? What other job market trends do you see emerging?

## ORGANIZING AN EFFECTIVE JOB SEARCH

The energy you put into organizing your job search directly affects the speed and success of your search. The following techniques will help you maximize your efforts.

### Compile Your List of Prospects

This chapter provides many excellent resources for identifying prospective employers. Use any of the suggestions that apply to your occupational field. Also use the following **Career Action** to prepare records of prospective employers you identify through your job search activities.

**Complete Career Action 6-2**

## CAREER ACTION 6-2

### Job Leads Source List

**Directions:** To organize your traditional sources of job leads, turn now to page 92 and review the directions for preparing your Job Leads Source List.

**Career Database Appropriate**

### Develop Prospective Employer Records

To identify prospective employers, research each source you list on the Job Leads Source List (**Career Action 6-2**). Fill out a Prospective Employer Record for each job lead.

Duplicate the blank form on page 93 so you will have plenty of copies.

If you prefer, you can create your own form on a computer and store the information for future reference. When it comes time to send your cover letters and resumes, you can search for the "Hot Prospects" first to maximize both your potential and time in the job search. If you don't have access to a computer, you can use index cards to make your prospective employer records and file them in a box alphabetically. Use colored file tags to mark hot prospects.

"Everyone who's ever taken a shower has an idea. It's the person who gets out of the shower, dries off, and does something about it that makes a difference."

—Nolan Bushnell

Prospective employer records provide vital information on the employers and help ensure you don't forget any of them during your job search.

### Narrow Your List

After you have completed your Prospective Employer Records, concentrate on the employers who could best use your abilities. For now, eliminate those who offer a slim chance for employment.

If you plan to do a direct mailing in your job search, narrowing your list of prospects is especially important. (A direct-mail job search consists of mailing cover letters with requests for interviews along with your resume to prospective employers.) Don't start this type of campaign until you have completed all the reading, assignments, and activities for Chapters 1 through 10 of this book. A direct mailing of unsolicited resumes is statistically not a productive job search method unless you have high-demand skills.

### The Job Market Is Not Always Organized—You Must Be!

Employers use a variety of hiring techniques. Their processes may be simple or complex, well or poorly organized, short or long. You, the job applicant, must be well organized—even if the job market is not. As you progress through this book, your pool of job-seeking tools will increase. Use these tools to develop your own efficient, speedy, and *successful* job-seeking campaign.

## PLANNING TIME FOR YOUR JOB SEARCH

If you are just finishing school, you will be competing with other new graduates for employment. The sooner you start your job search, the greater your advantage will be. Employers sometimes view a long delay between school or your last job and application for employment as a lack of either initiative or employability.

### Your Job Search: A Full-Time Job

The best job search campaign includes daily activities and a minimum of 25 to 30 hours per week. If you're employed now and seeking another position, you will have to look at your job search as a second job and won't be able to devote as much time to it.

### SUCH JOB SEARCH ZEAL!

My neighbor couldn't figure out why her son wasn't making progress in his job search. I got a good clue when I heard the message he left for her on their answering machine: "Mom, I'm going to look for a job. I'll be back in 30 minutes."

## Tips for Job Search Management

The following tips will help you manage your job search time effectively:

1. Set up an organized job search headquarters so you can easily lay your hands on anything you need and can follow up on leads effectively. Use labeled file folders for your job search schedules, job lead lists, prospective employer records, and so on. Organize your stationery, copies of your resumes, and other documents or materials you'll need in your job search process.

2. Prepare a weekly job search schedule. Use a monthly calendar to schedule your activities one or more weeks in advance. Record the number of hours to be spent each day and which hours of the day they will be.

3. Prepare a daily job search plan. Plan your daily job search activities at least one day in advance. This gives you an immediate plan of action and helps you ward off procrastination. Use the Daily Job Search Organizer form on page 94 to help you in planning your daily goals. Duplicate the form so you'll have enough for each day of your job search.

4. If at all possible, begin your job search while you're still employed, either part-time or full-time. (Employers consider applicants who are currently employed to be more employable than those who are unemployed. Why? Being employed is proof that the applicant can do a job adequately enough to keep it.)

SUCCESS TIP

**Write out your job search schedule to increase your sense of commitment and improve your organizational effectiveness.**

5. If you aren't employed, begin your search the moment you know you need to get a job. If you will graduate in June and will need a job, start your search preparations in January or before!

6. Procrastination is the job seeker's biggest enemy. Never make excuses for not working on your job search, even for one day. Persistence, in contrast, can be one of your greatest allies. Report for work on your search as you would for a full-time job.

7. Employers expect you to be punctual for all scheduled meetings; never be late. A prospective employer will not consider you further if you are late for a meeting or appointment.

8. Follow up every job lead immediately. Delays can cost you the job you are seeking.

## Develop a Job Search Routine

Establish a routine to help you stay focused and efficient. The following are appropriate daily activities:

- **Look the part every day.** Dress and groom yourself for success.

- **Organize your job search work area daily,** including your files, references, and related forms and materials. If possible, have a telephone and a computer in your work area.

- **Make telephone contacts** to arrange meetings, to communicate with your network, and so on.
- **Work on new leads.** Research, make telephone and written contacts, and arrange meetings.
- **Follow up.** Write thank-you letters, review leads, and take appropriate actions.
- **Arrange meetings** to (a) network, (b) gather information, and (c) interview.

**SUCCESS TIP**

**Organize your job search to gain an advantage over those who don't plan an efficient search.**

- **Develop prospective employer records.**
- **Develop and follow a daily job search schedule.**
- **Be persistent.**
- **Follow up.**

## CHECKLIST FOR ORGANIZING A WINNING JOB SEARCH

Check each of the following actions that you are currently taking to increase your career success:

- ☐ Focus job search energy on networking (the #1 job lead source).
- ☐ Concentrate on direct telephone or face-to-face contacts with employers.
- ☐ Include the Internet as a job search tool.
- ☐ Dont limit your search to published job announcements; they represent only 15% of available jobs.
- ☐ Consider self-employment if you have adequate experience.
- ☐ Allocate your time in relation to the proven success rate of the top job search strategies: networking, advertisements, and employment agencies.
- ☐ Plan and organize your job search to gain an advantage over those who don't.

## CRITICAL THINKING QUESTIONS

1. Why should you make a conscious effort to tell everyone about your job search?
2. How can professional or trade associations help the job seeker?
3. How can you obtain employment information from organizations in private industry?
4. What sources do you think will be most useful for you to use in your own job search?

# CAREER ACTION 6-2

## Job Leads Source List

**DIRECTIONS:** Review each of the sources of job information presented in this chapter, including the Internet sites you used in **Career Action 6-1**. Then, list those sources you think would be effective in your job search. (Do not limit yourself to the sources suggested in this chapter. Make additional copies of this form if necessary.)

Name of source: ______________________________

Address of source: ______________________________

Internet address: ______________________________

Telephone number: ______________________________

Action plans for using this source: ______________________________

Name of source: ______________________________

Address of source: ______________________________

Internet address: ______________________________

Telephone number: ______________________________

Action plans for using this source: ______________________________

Name of source: ______________________________

Address of source: ______________________________

Internet address: ______________________________

Telephone number: ______________________________

Action plans for using this source: ______________________________

Name of source: ______________________________

Address of source: ______________________________

Internet address: ______________________________

Telephone number: ______________________________

Action plans for using this source: ______________________________

# PROSPECTIVE EMPLOYER RECORD

**Name of Organization:** ______________________________

**Address of Organization:** ______________________________

**Internet Address:** ______________________________

**Telephone Number:** ______________ **Fax Number:** ______________

**Job Target Title:** ______________________________

**Job Target Description:** ______________________________

______________________________

**Person to Contact** (name and title): ______________________________

______________________________

**Source of Information:** ______________________________

**Referred by** (person who will refer me): ______________________________

**Hiring Status:** Position Open ________ No Position Open Now ________

**Other:** ______________________________

**Potential:** Hot Prospect ________ Possible ________ Long Shot ________

**Date Resume and Cover Letter Sent:** ______________________________

**Interview Follow Up:** ______________________________

______________________________

**Comments:** ______________________________

______________________________

______________________________

# DAILY JOB SEARCH ORGANIZER

**Directions:** Record the name of the employer, the person you plan to contact and whether it will be a personal visit, Internet contact, phone call, or letter. Record the purpose of the contact and any necessary follow-up (send a thank-you note, resume, other). Summarize other job search goals you plan for the day. Complete the last two sections of the form at the end of the day, including a summary of progress made and a list of new job leads. Also note whether or not you achieved the purpose of the contact.

**Date:** ________ **Number of hours to be spent on job search:** ________ **From:** ________ **To:** ________

| | Employer, Name of Contact, and Job Target | Form of Contact (personal visit, phone call, letter, Internet contact) | Purpose of Contact | Purpose Achieved (Yes/No) |
|---|---|---|---|---|
| 1. | | | | |
| | | | | |
| 2. | | | | |
| | | | | |
| 3. | | | | |
| | | | | |

**Other Goals for Today** (research, support system/network contact, schedule appointments, etc.):

______________________________________________

Summary of Progress Made: ______________________________

New Job Leads: ______________________________

Miscellaneous Notes/Reminders: ______________________________

CHAPTER 7

# Investigate Job, Application, and Hiring Procedures

"We select the applicants for our branch of Microsoft from a corporate resume database. This database is made up of all of the resumes that are submitted online through our Microsoft Web site. I can run a query on the type of experience and job skills I am looking for, and the computer will do a search for me."

*Carrie Fellhoelter*
*Senior Human Resource Administrator*
*Microsoft Corporation*
*Dallas, Texas*

## *In this chapter you will:*

- Survey people holding jobs similar to the one you will be seeking to learn about the scope of their jobs and the hiring procedures used by their employers.

Use the Internet to search for current information about application and hiring procedures.

- Prepare a Job Qualifications Profile to help in marketing your skills by identifying your current job target and by relating your qualifications directly to the target.

In this chapter, you will learn more about existing jobs similar to the one you want and about the application and hiring procedures typical in your field. You will complete surveys to obtain this information directly from people working in your career field. You will also use the Internet to locate additional tips regarding current hiring and job application procedures. The answers will help you get just the job you're looking for. Finally, Chapter 7 guides you through the preparation of your Job Qualifications Profile, which will help you develop content for your successful self-marketing.

### OUTSIDE ASSIGNMENTS GIVE YOU THE COMPETITIVE EDGE!

The outside assignments in this book will give you decided advantages over your competition. These assignments provide:

- **Practice:** These assignments take you into the business community for research and practice. You will schedule and participate in meetings and practice communicating about your career and job targets.
- **Information:** You obtain current information about the scope of jobs in your field and the hiring procedures.
- **Competitive Edge:** You get the edge over applicants who don't do these activities.

Carry out these assignments professionally. Often, they provide good job leads, and sometimes they even result in job offers!

## THE CAREER INFORMATION SURVEY

In this survey, you will contact two people holding jobs similar to your job target. Your objective is to meet them at their job sites to learn about the scope of their jobs and the hiring procedures used by their employers. This information will help prepare you for a successful job search.

SUCCESS TIP

**Contact employees in your field to get current information about the scope of their jobs and hiring procedures.**

### Sample Questions for Career Information Survey

In preparation for your survey meetings, make a list of questions you will ask your contacts. Following are some sample questions:

A. Questions Regarding the Job Scope and Career Development

1. Is the firm privately owned, a government agency, or a nonprofit organization? (Ask only if you don't already know.)
2. What are the main goals of the organization? Is it a product- or service-oriented firm? (Ask only if you don't know.)
3. What skills, education, experience, and knowledge are required to qualify for a position such as yours?
4. What personal qualities or traits are important in your work?
5. What are your specific duties?
6. What do you like most/least about your job?
7. What is the average starting salary range for a position such as yours?
8. What employee benefits are offered in this position (health insurance, retirement savings programs, other)?

9. What changes do you anticipate in this field in the future?

10. What additional or ongoing education or training do you need to achieve your future career goals?

11. Does the employer offer on-the-job training for this position? If so, what does it involve?

12. Is continuing education for the position encouraged by the employer? If so, what kinds of programs are available or promoted, and are fees paid by the employer?

13. Would it be possible to get a written description of your job if one is available?

14. What professional association would you recommend for staying informed in this career field?

15. What publications would you recommend (books, journals, etc.)?

16. Could you suggest other people to help me with my research?

17. Do you have any advice for planning my career and job search?

B. Sample Questions Regarding the Application, Interview, and Hiring Procedures

1. What are your general procedures for applying for positions such as the one I will be seeking?

2. Do you have an employment application form I could see, or could I a get a copy of one to review as a reference?

3. What are the interview procedures (one person interviewing the applicant, team interviewing, multiple interviews, typical length of interviews, testing)?

4. Could you tell me what types of questions are typically asked during interviews? Are applicants asked to give specific examples of how they have used the skills required for the job they are seeking or how they have handled specific work situations?

5. What do you think is important to show in a resume for a position such as the one I will be seeking?

6. Do you have any advice for preparing and interviewing successfully?

## Study the Work Environment of Your Contacts

Through careful observation at the job site, you can learn about the working conditions for the type of job you want. So, prior to the survey, also make a list of questions to ask yourself about this environment. Following are some examples:

1. What type of work area does my contact have? Does my contact work at a desk, share office space, other?

2. What equipment (if any) does my contact use?

3. Is the work environment appropriate for the type of work?

4. Is the environment quiet, noisy, slow- or fast-paced?

5. Does my contact interact with others—with whom and how often?

6. What type of dress is appropriate?

7. Is the atmosphere formal or informal?

8. Are work areas spotless or relaxed looking?

## How to Spot a Top Place to Work

Be alert to the work atmosphere, and listen for comments from your contacts. Employees of desirable workplaces often mention freedom, trust, pride, teamwork, fair pay and benefits, opportunities for growth, recognition, and fairness in management. Ask about and watch for these characteristics during your meetings. Keep these qualities in mind as you select your actual job prospects.

Now prepare your own questions about the job and work environment.

**Complete Career Action 7-1**

Figure • 7-1: You can learn a lot about the workplace by watching how people interact. Be observant. Does the place you're visiting seem like a place you'd like to work?

## CAREER ACTION 7-1

### Career Information Survey Worksheet

**DIRECTIONS:** Prepare a Career Information Survey Worksheet by preparing two sets of questions:

1. Prepare the career information questions you will ask your contact during your survey meeting (those regarding the job, career development, and hiring procedures).

2. Prepare the work environment questions you want to answer for yourself through observation.

Some of the sample questions listed earlier may apply to your field, but develop your own additional questions for each list. The goal is to clarify your understanding of the particular job, the occupational field, the typical work environment, and the hiring procedures. Allow space after each question to record the information you obtain. Place these questions in a professional binder to use during your surveys; projecting a professional image is important in all outside assignments!

## Making Your Appointment for a Survey Meeting

To make your appointment, contact at least two organizations employing people in your occupational field. Making the initial contact in person is preferable. If you can't do that, use the telephone, but first review the telephone techniques outlined in Chapter 12.

**SUCCESS TIP**

**Dress and act professionally in all outside assignments to project competence and to encourage job leads.**

Ask to speak with a person whose job is similar to your job target. Emphasize that you are carrying out an assignment from your instructor or doing research in your field. Explain that you want to learn directly about your occupational field as part of your career-planning research. **Never say you're looking for a job.**

Figure • 7-2: If you can't make the initial contact in person, schedule your survey meeting over the telephone.

Strangers are more likely to help you with career-planning research than with getting a job. Follow the guidelines below in making your appointment:

1. **Be clean, neat, and properly dressed if you make your appointment in person.**
2. **Introduce yourself.**
3. **State your purpose**—completing an assignment from your instructor at (name your school). If you are using this book independently, state that you are conducting career research.
4. **Request an appointment** to ask a few questions about the person's job and the occupational field.
5. **Confirm the date and time.** If you're making your initial contact in person, the individual may offer to meet with you immediately. **Be prepared by having your binder and questions with you!**
6. **Always thank the person for his or her time and assistance.**

## Survey Tips for Hard-to-Reach Employers

Some high-tech and large companies are less easily accessed for career survey meetings. If yours is such an organization, follow the guidelines below to identify people you can meet with for the survey.

1. **Turn to your network.** Ask *everyone* in your job search network (friends, family, school counselors, etc.) to help you identify people working in your targeted employment field—someone you could meet with to gather career information. Your network can provide opportunities that would not otherwise be available for you.

2. **Search the Internet.** Some firms that have computerized hiring processes provide application and hiring information through their company Web sites or through third-party job bank/job-posting Web sites. If your target employer uses this process, obtain its company or third-party Internet addresses, search for the application and hiring information, and print your findings or prepare a written summary to submit as your report for **Career Action 7-2**.

3. **Choose a closely related employer target.** If you are unable to meet with your preferred target employer, schedule a meeting with a closely related organization. This valuable face-to-face meeting will give you the important practice necessary to outdistance your competition.

SUCCESS TIP

**Use the Internet to research job descriptions and hiring information of hard-to-reach employers.**

Complete Career Action 7-2

## BE COURTEOUS, FRIENDLY, AND PROFESSIONAL

Learn your contact's name, and use it when you first meet the person, when you leave, and in follow-up. People like to be remembered, and this enhances your professional image.

## Your Career Information Survey Meeting

**REMEMBER:** Dress and act professionally for all outside assignments. If you make a good impression, this assignment could develop into firm job leads for you. (See Chapter 11 for appropriate grooming guidelines.)

In every communication with prospective employers, emphasize your interest in *developing a career,* not in "just getting a job." This emphasis implies you are serious about finding the best match between you and the employer so that both gain maximum results.

Figure • 7-3: Your information survey interview is as important as a job interview. Dress well. Be professional and positive; you'll gain contacts, career information, and job leads.

# CAREER ACTION 7-2

## Internet Research of Hiring Procedures

**DIRECTIONS:** Identify at least two major company or organizational Web sites that offer information regarding employer application and/or hiring processes. Prepare a short report of your findings.

**NOTE:** Since the content of Web sites is subject to change without notice, be aware that the links listed below may not match the current content of the Web sites referenced in this assignment.

1. **Tips for finding Web sites for companies or organizations:** Using your Web browser, try entering the company name or initials followed by *.com*. For example, if you are trying to find the Web address for "Windings," try entering *windings.com* in the URL address field.

2. **Web site resources for finding major employers:**

   a. Companies Online — *http://www.companiesonline.com/*

   b. Monster.com — *http://www.monster.com/*

   c. Hoover's Online — *http://www.hoovers.com/*

   d. Job Options — *http://www.joboptions.com/*

   e. Virtual Job Fair — *http://www.virtualjobfair.com/*

   f. Wall Street Research Net — *http://www.wsrn.com/*

Also try using search engines to locate employer Web sites.

**NOTE:** Move quickly through your prepared questions, and avoid wasting time. It's OK to make a very few brief notes of your contact's answers, but don't write out every answer completely. Do this as soon as possible after the meeting.

**Be Aware During the Survey.** Make careful **mental notes** throughout these meetings. After the meeting, record your findings fully on the survey worksheets you prepared for **Career Action 7-1**.

**Job Leads from the Survey.** If your contacts offer to help you with job leads, accept the help enthusiastically, making complete notes of any information offered. Do not make a direct bid for their help; don't be pushy.

## Apply the Eight Success Strategies

Always practice the eight success strategies during your survey meetings. Review the principles presented in Chapter 1, and apply them in your meetings. People consider the way you conduct your job search to be a direct indication of the way you would carry out work assignments on the job or interact with others as an employee. Therefore, conduct your career information survey meetings professionally and with energy, enthusiasm, and attention to detail.

**Complete Career Action 7-3**

# CAREER ACTION 7-3

## Participate in Career Information Survey Meeting

**DIRECTIONS:** Schedule and participate in your career information survey meeting(s); write the answers to your survey questions, and be prepared to discuss your findings in class.

**IMPORTANT NOTES:**

- Schedule as many of these meetings as possible; the benefits of gaining current information and possible job leads are great.
- Also consider contacting people in your field who screen, interview, or hire job applicants to discuss the job hiring processes in particular. This could put you closer to a future job interview if you perform impressively during your information-gathering meeting.
- Small companies often have only a few employees; the company owner may also be the hiring authority.

## Following Up the Meeting

Within one day of your meeting, write follow-up letters of thanks to the people who helped you with the assignment. Use fine-quality stationery, and handwrite or type it neatly. If a contact offers to help you with a job lead, take or mail a copy of your resume to your contact within the next week. (This person could become a key part of your job search network!) If you don't already have a resume, review Chapter 9 carefully, and prepare one, following the guidelines in that chapter. If you have a resume prepared, compare it to the guidelines provided in Chapter 9. Sample resumes and summaries are provided on pages 137-154.

> "Sooner or later, those who win are those who think they can."
>
> —Richard Bach

## DISCUSSION OF THE SURVEY RESULTS

Classroom sharing of survey results helps prepare you to handle the widest possible variety of application and hiring procedures.

**NOTE:** If you are using this book independently, focus on how you can use the survey information in your actual job search.

Figure • 7-4: Classroom sharing of survey experiences will help you handle a wider variety of application and hiring procedures. Focus on how you can use survey information in your job search.

**Develop a Job Qualifications Profile to market yourself successfully to employers.**

## JOB QUALIFICATIONS PROFILE: A SNAPSHOT TO PERSUADE EMPLOYERS

The Job Qualifications Profile organizes the qualifications information you summarized about yourself in Chapters 2 and 3. This profile will give you a solid description of your abilities that relate to your job target. This is exactly the information employers need from you to show evidence of a good match between the job and the applicant—you! Follow the steps below to start developing this summary:

> "Act as if what you do makes a difference. It does."
>
> —William James

1. **Clearly identify your job target.** If you have not yet done this, a career counselor could help you. Refer also to the information in Chapter 3 to identify other sources of career-planning information and assistance.
2. **Write a clear description of your targeted job.** Obtain job descriptions from prospective employers. If this isn't feasible, ask your school career counselor or librarian to help you locate a general written description of your job target in the *Dictionary of Occupational Titles,* published by the U.S. Department of Labor. For more complete descriptions of major occupations, refer to the printed version of the *Occupational Outlook Handbook* or the online version (http://stats.bls.gov/ocohome.htm), also a publication of the U.S. Department of Labor.
3. **Refer to the information compiled in Chapters 2 and 3.** This information will help you complete the rest of the Job Qualifications Profile form outlining your abilities as they relate to your job target.

4. **Copy the profile form** (Career Action 7-4) **for multiple job targets.** If you are prepared for employment in more than one field or area, prepare one Job Qualifications Profile for each target. Develop the broadest possible career-planning base by including as many options as possible.

Your Job Qualifications Profile will serve as the solid core of information for your lifetime job search and career planning. As you develop new skills and gain more experience, training, and education, your goals will change or expand. You can repeat the self-analysis exercises in this book at any time during your career. Your Job Qualifications Profile will always present a well-organized summary of your qualifications related directly to your current job target. This profile provides the snapshot of your qualifications necessary to persuade an employer to hire you for the job you want.

**Complete Career Action 7-4**

## CHECKLIST FOR INVESTIGATING THE JOB, APPLICATION, AND HIRING PROCEDURES

Check each of the following actions you are currently taking to increase your career success:

- ☐ Contact employees in your field to get current information about the scope of their jobs and hiring procedures.
- ☐ Dress and act professionally in all outside assignments to project competence and to encourage job leads.
- ☐ Use the Internet to research job descriptions and hiring information of hard-to-reach employers.
- ☐ Develop a Job Qualifications Profile to market yourself successfully to employers.

## CRITICAL THINKING QUESTIONS

1. What benefits can you gain by scheduling career information survey meetings?
2. What is the most significant information you obtained from the outside assignment for this chapter?
3. How can you use your Job Qualifications Profile information in your job search and interviews?

# CAREER ACTION 7-4

## Job Qualifications Profile

**DIRECTIONS:** Supply the information called for below on this Job Qualifications Profile. Refer to your completed **Career Actions** from Chapters 2 and 3.

**Career Database Appropriate**

**NOTE:** Copy this form, and use it to develop a summary for each of your job targets.

1. Title of job target:

______________________________________________

______________________________________________

______________________________________________

2. Description of job:

______________________________________________

______________________________________________

______________________________________________

3. My education and training related to the job target:

______________________________________________

______________________________________________

______________________________________________

4. My work experience related to the job target:

______________________________________________

______________________________________________

______________________________________________

5. My accomplishments related to the job target:

______________________________________________

______________________________________________

______________________________________________

CONTINUED ON NEXT PAGE

# CAREER ACTION 7-4

(CONTINUED)

6. Praise or recognition I have received related to the job target:

7. How my skills relate to the job target:

8. How my values relate to the job target:

9. How my work environment preferences relate to the job target:

10. How my personality traits relate to the job target:

11. What appeals to me about this job:

CHAPTER 8

# Research Prospective Employers

> **It is very likely I will ask applicants, 'Why do you want to work here?' If they are knowledgeable about our organization, applicants can answer this question effectively.**
>
> *Caroline Carlson*
> *Associate Staffing Manager*
> *Kraft Foods*

## *In this chapter you will:*

Use Internet, printed, and people resources for research on prospective employers, your job target, and your career field.

- Expand your job search and career-planning vocabulary through review of job descriptions, employment applications, job advertisements, and selected newspaper and journal articles.

Chapter 8 explains how to gather current information about your field and about prospective employers so you can custom-fit your job search communications and emphasize your related strengths and suitability for the job. Many excellent resources for researching employers are presented, including research with recognized leaders in your field, career fairs, several Internet sites, libraries, and professional or trade associations. Doing this research gives you a major advantage over candidates who don't research.

## COMPLETE INDUSTRY, EMPLOYER, AND JOB RESEARCH FOR BIG PAYOFFS!

Research gives applicants a big competitive edge. Employers nationwide say applicants who research employers well increase their employability as much as 25 percent! Figure 8.1 illustrates the competitive advantage that you can gain over other applicants through employer research.

The advantages of researching your career field and employers affect the success of your job search in many ways:

- **Competitive Edge:** Employers view candidates who don't have solid knowledge of the employer's business and industry as weak choices. Many applicants don't bother to research employers. If you do, you get the competitive edge.

- **Better Career Decisions:** Having current knowledge of the employer, industry, and job target equip you to make informed career decisions about employers and to assess your interest in, and qualifications for, specific jobs.

- **Improved Ability to Market Your Skills and Get Hired:** Researching employers improves your ability to discuss specifically how your qualifications match the employer's purpose, goals, and needs. Employers are most willing to invest training time and money in applicants who demonstrate initiative and commitment through their employer and industry knowledge.

- **Compensating for Lack of Experience:** Industry knowledge helps you compensate for lack of actual or extensive job experience.

> **"Knowledge itself, therefore, turns out to be not only the source of the highest-quality power...It is, in fact, the ultimate amplifier."**
>
> —Alvin Toffler, *Powershift*

- **Increased Confidence:** Being well informed helps you communicate more clearly, feel more confident, and project greater competence.

## WHAT YOU SHOULD KNOW

Strengthen your employability by improving your knowledge in the following three areas:

1. **General Information about the Occupational Field.** Learn about the products; services; current and predicted industry trends; general educational requirements, job descriptions, growth outlook, and salary ranges in the industry.

2. **Information about Prospective Employers.** Learn whether the organization is publicly or privately owned. Verify company names, addresses, products or services (current, predicted, and trends); reputation; performance; divisions and

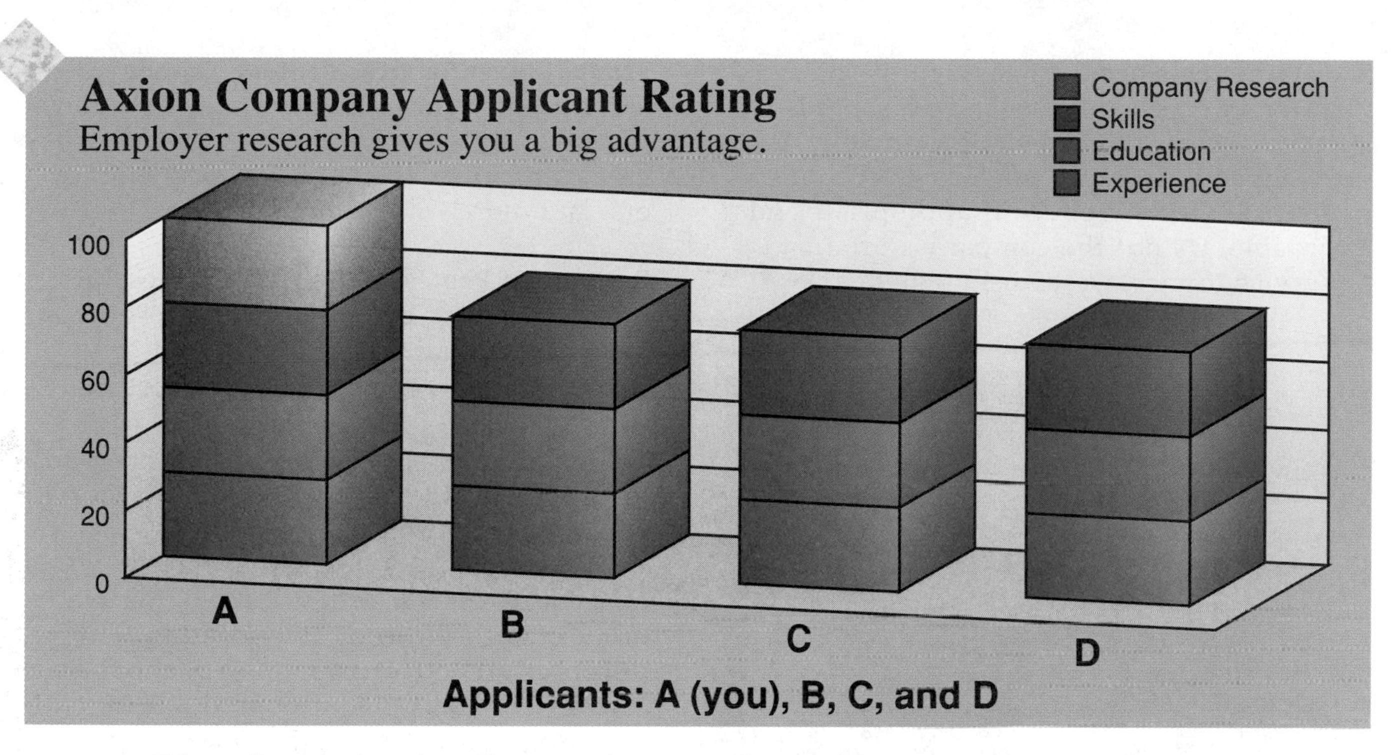


Figure • 8-1: This applicant-rating graph illustrates the power of research.

subsidiaries; locations (U.S. and global); predicted growth indicators; number of employees; company philosophies and procedures; predicted job openings; salary ranges; and listings of managers of your targeted department within the organization. Also learn about the competitors.

3. **Information about Specific Jobs.** Obtain job descriptions; identify the required education and experience; and determine prevalent working conditions, salary, and fringe benefits.

**Gain the competitive advantage by researching to learn about employers; they expect you to be knowledgeable about the job, the company, and the industry.**

# USE MANY SOURCES OF INFORMATION

This section identifies resources for industry, company, and job information.

## People Resources

People are strong resources for learning about the character and function of an organization and for gathering general information about the industry. If your target employer is a small organization, people are typically the best research sources.

**Employees of Your Target Employer.** Current or previous employees know about hiring procedures; employee satisfaction levels; job descriptions and responsibilities; skills, education, and experience required for jobs; company objectives; salary information; and opportunities for advancement. Don't rely only on opinion, however, particularly if it's extremely negative or overly positive.

**Your Target Employer.** Whenever possible, visit target employers to get a personal perspective. Be sure to dress appropriately. Ask for company literature, such as a brochure or a stockholder's report. If appropriate and affordable, try out the company's product or service to increase your knowledge.

Figure • 8-2: You can often get annual reports and other literature by calling the company.

**Customers, Clients, or Patients.** Ask customers, clients, or patients their opinions of the employer's service, reliability, products, and general reputation.

**Competitors.** Research competitors of your target employer to learn about the industry. Compare positions available, pay rates, benefits, and the education, skills, and experience required.

**Teachers, Professors, and Counselors.** These people often have good knowledge about local employers and the industry. Since they may serve as job references for you, always demonstrate excellent performance, punctuality, and reliability in dealing with them. One of them may open the door to your career!

**School Career Services Centers.** School career services staff generally have comprehensive resources for learning about industries, specific companies, specific jobs, local employers, and more.

**Recognized People in the Field.** Successful people in your field are excellent resources for learning about the industry and prospective employers. Complete **Career Action 8-1** to learn more about your career field through discussions with experienced leaders. It could lead you directly to the job you are hoping for!

**IMPORTANT NOTE:** Do not ask for a job or an interview during this meeting. The purposes are to learn all you can about your career field and to identify methods of updating your industry information and skills.

**Complete Career Action 8-1**

## Career Fairs

As noted earlier, career fairs offered by communities and schools and on the Internet are remarkable sources of employer information. It would take hundreds of hours to reach the number of companies individually that you can access in one career fair day.

Use fairs to gather company literature and to find out directly what job skills and knowledge are required, to learn keywords you can emphasize in your resume, and even to schedule interviews.

## Libraries

Check out the reference sections of college, university, or public libraries for extensive employer and industry information available in printed, microfilm, and electronic CD-ROM format. Reference librarians can help you locate appropriate resources.

# CAREER ACTION 8-1

## Contact Recognized People in Your Field

**OBJECTIVE:** To gather industry information so you can communicate well during your job search, making you a more persuasive candidate.

**DIRECTIONS:** Follow these steps for researching trends and information sources in your industry.

1. **Contact at least two people recognized for their ability and accomplishments.** Ask school career services staff, teachers, family, and friends for recommendations.
2. **Schedule a time, date, and place to meet.** Call and ask whether your contact can meet with you to discuss career development questions.
3. **Be well dressed and on time.** Such meetings can lead to referrals or job offers.
4. **Project professionalism.** Place your neatly prepared survey questions in a professional binder (sample questions are listed below; add others of your own).
5. **Be prepared to discuss your findings in class, or submit a summary report.**

### SAMPLE QUESTIONS FOR CAREER ACTION 8-1

1. In your opinion, what are the most important current trends in the industry? Where can I learn more about these trends?
2. To remain well informed about the industry:
   a. What publications (books, periodicals, etc.) do you recommend?
   b. What Internet Web sites do you recommend?
   c. What professional or trade associations do you recommend?
3. What skills, education, and experience are necessary for my job target?
4. What new terminology or industry buzzwords do you suggest I know to increase my preparation? (**NOTE:** This information can be applied to **Career Action 8-3**.)
5. How did you succeed in the field? Would you recommend the same or a similar approach for me?
6. Do you have other suggestions to improve my employability in the field (further education, training, research, reading, etc.)?

**Career Database Appropriate**

The following list of resources will help in completing your research and preparation.

- *Dun and Bradstreet's Million Dollar Directories*
- *Thomas' Register of American Manufacturers*
- *Standard and Poor's Stock Reports*
- *Value Line Investment Survey*
- *Moody's Manuals*
- *Business Periodicals Index*
- *Readers' Guide to Periodical Literature* and *Business Periodicals Index*
- *Job Choices*—excellent National Association of Colleges and Employers magazine. Check school career services centers.
- *Occupational Outlook Handbook*—published by the U.S. Department of Labor, Bureau of Labor Statistics, and usually available in school career services centers.
- Area telephone directories
- *Fortune* and *Forbes* magazines and *The Wall Street Journal*
- *Standard and Poor's Register of Corporations, Directors, and Executives*

**NOTE:** Also ask reference librarians for assistance in locating international business information if your target employer has international holdings or is based outside the United States.

## The Internet: Another Galaxy of Information

The Internet is exploding with public and private Web sites to research industries and employers. Use the Web to gather information about products and services, corporate history, recent trends, and more.

**Web Sources.** The following search engines and Web sites will help you maximize your Internet research effectiveness:

- **Search engines:** Use search engines to conduct a general search for specific employers or specific career topics. Look here for recent news about your industry and target companies. Examples are listed below:

  AltaVista
  ***http://www.altavista.com/***

  Excite
  ***http://www.excite.com/***

  Infoseek
  ***http://www.infoseek.com/careers/***

  Lycos
  ***http://www.lycos.com/***

  Yahoo
  ***http://www.yahoo.com/***

- **Financial sites:** Use these sites to access sales and earnings information and recent news about public companies. Examples are listed below:

  American Stock Exchange
  ***http://www.amex.com/***

  New York Stock Exchange
  ***http://www.nyse.com/***

  NASDAQ
  ***http://www.nasdaq.com/***

- **Employer sites:** Visit sites of employers that interest you. Always check out the **What's New** or **News** items to get current, updated information. Review company mission statements, product information, services, and overview information. Review the **jobs, human resources**, and **career opportunities** sections to gather job and hiring information.

  Mine the entire employer site, searching for special nuggets of information you can use during your job search to demonstrate your Internet skills. Print out pages you want for special reference.

**Don't Limit Yourself to the Internet.** Although electronic information is valuable and sometimes the most up-to-date information source, many important facts vital to evaluating an employer can only be found in print sources.

Figure • 8-3: Use your library's historical and electronic resources to find articles and information on companies that interest you.

Often the Internet just provides summaries of topical information; the full text is available only through library research. In addition, employer Web sites emphasize their positive aspects only, so don't rely only on this source.

## RESEARCHING LOCAL AND SMALL FIRMS

If you want a job with a local or small firm, the following are good resources for research: people in the field, the area chamber of commerce, the area Better Business Bureau, local newspapers, telephone directories, and local libraries. Also learn about the occupational field in general (local, national, and global trends; professional associations; etc.).

### Professional or Trade Associations

Nearly every industry has professional or trade associations that provide journals, newsletters, and reports of current industry information, related trends, and technological changes. Many have membership lists (good prospective employer resources). Employers are impressed with applicants who know about their industry associations and publications.

Enhance your employability by joining a well-known professional or trade association in your field and reading their publications. Many have student chapters or memberships. Such extra effort can give you the power to outdistance your competition. Check *The Encyclopedia of Associations* to locate major associations.

**Complete Career Action 8-2**

# CAREER ACTION 8-2

## Printed, People, and Internet Research of Employers

**DIRECTIONS:** Use printed, people, and Internet resources to research at least two companies that interest you. Learn about (a) company products or services, (b) company objectives, (c) company locations, (d) earnings information, (e) trends, and (f) other information that interests you. Prepare a written summary of your findings.

**NOTE:** Since Web site content is subject to change, the links listed below may not match the current content of the Web sites.

1. ***WebGuide* RESOURCES:** From the *WebGuide* main menu, select "Advanced Research." Under "Job Search Sites," click on *Career Mosaic* and then *Job Hunt: Online Meta-List*. Under "Resumes, Cover Letters, and Interviews," click on *What Color Is Your Parachute Netguide* (see "Research").

2. **INTERNET LINKS:** Check these.

   **Companies Online** *http://www.companiesonline.com/*

   **JobSmart** *http://jobsmart.org/*
   (Click on *Hidden Job Market*; then click on *Researching Companies*)

   **Hoovers Online** *http://www.hoovers.com/*

   **Wall Street Research Net** *http://www.wsrn.com/*

3. Refer to the Printed, People, and Internet Resources for Employer Research form beginning on page 118 for additional research and resource ideas.

# DEVELOP AND INCREASE YOUR CAREER-RELATED VOCABULARY

A strong career-related vocabulary projects competence; employers view this as a good indicator of job- and industry-related knowledge. For this reason, continually increasing your job- and career-related vocabulary is important. **Career Action 8-3** is designed to help you do this.

**Develop and regularly increase your job/career-related vocabulary to demonstrate competence and knowledge.**

All the sources listed in this chapter will also be useful for building your job search and career-planning vocabulary. Your vocabulary can help or hurt you in your lifetime career; start now to build a vocabulary that strengthens your career.

**Complete Career Action 8-3**

# CAREER ACTION 8-3

## Job Search and Career Development Vocabulary

1. Obtain two general job descriptions for the type of job you are seeking. Get these directly from employers, from people currently working in similar jobs, from job postings, or from the Internet. If you can't find at least two written descriptions, obtain verbal descriptions from people working in your field and write them out. Also, get one or more general job descriptions for your job target from the *Occupational Outlook Handbook.*

2. Obtain at least two application blanks for the type of job you are seeking. Note that some employers only provide applications online; access these through their Web sites, and download them.

3. Obtain at least two advertisements for positions similar to your job target. Check newspapers, professional journals, the Internet, your career services center, and so on.

   a. Read carefully through all the job target material you obtain. Underline all action verbs (for example: *compile, analyze, operate, supervise*) and all key nouns used to describe required or related skills, education, and experience, including the specific names of software programs or computer-related knowledge (for example: *operator, operation, accounts receivable, instructor/instruction, writing, analyzing, designing, evaluation, management, computing, computations, Word, Excel, UNIX*). Underline vocabulary, abbreviations, special terminology, and buzzwords unique to your field.

   b. Make a list of these terms, with the correct spelling and definitions. If you don't know the definition of a term, find it. Categorize the terms as follows: (a) action verbs, (b) key nouns, (c) specialized terminology, (d) abbreviations, and (e) industry buzzwords.

4. Keep this vocabulary list, add to it whenever possible, and use the terms to shine in your resumes, cover letters, interviews, and follow-up communications.

**Career Database Appropriate**

**"The next best thing to knowing something is knowing where to find it."**

—Samuel Johnson

## YOU ARE WHAT YOU SAY!

Competing applicants with equal education, training, and experience are judged on their verbal and written command of industry vocabulary. Develop a strong vocabulary to help land your ideal job.

## APPLY YOUR INDUSTRY, EMPLOYER, AND JOB RESEARCH

Apply the information you obtain from your research as you write your resumes and cover letters and as you interview. Complete all the Career Actions in Chapter 8 to gather this essential information.

Figure • 8-4: Refer to Chapter 9 to see how you can use the information you find in your research to prepare powerful, targeted resumes.

**IMPORTANT NOTES:** Review the Printed, People, and Internet Resources for Research of Employers beginning on page 118 to identify resources for answering specific research questions.



Don't limit yourself to the resources listed in this textbook. Ask school career services staff and reference librarians to help identify resources most valuable for your career objectives. Ask members of your network for their help in obtaining the most current and useful employer information.

## RESEARCH INTERVIEWERS

Round out your research by trying to learn about the interviewer. This can strengthen your competitive position by giving you information that helps you communicate comfortably and connect positively during your interview.

### Learn about the Interviewer *Before* You Are Interviewed

Get the interviewer's name from the company when you schedule an interview. If you know anyone who works or worked with the interviewer or who knows the interviewer personally, contact that person to learn as much as you can.

### What to Research

In researching the interviewer, learn as much as you can about the following:

- The interviewer's special interests or activities.
- The interviewer's work philosophy, goals and objectives, and achievements.
- The general development of the interviewer's career.

If possible, find out how the interviewer prefers to be contacted for a job: by letter, in person, by telephone, by e-mail? This information can help you approach the interviewer in his or her preferred style and can help you phrase your remarks to meet the interviewer's interests and needs.

People who know the interviewer are the best resources for obtaining information about interviewers for small organizations. Don't press a secretary, receptionist, or other employee too hard for information about the interviewer, however. Often, word will get back to the interviewer! If you are courteous, you may get some useful information, but tread lightly; avoid coming across as "pushy."

**SUCCESS TIP**

**Research to learn all you can about the interviewer to help you communicate comfortably and connect positively during your interview.**

## CHECKLIST FOR RESEARCHING PROSPECTIVE EMPLOYERS

Check each of the following actions that you are currently taking to increase your career success:

- ☐ Gain competitive advantage by researching to learn about prospective employers; they expect you to be knowledgeable about the job, the company, and the industry.
- ☐ Develop and regularly increase your job/career-related vocabulary to demonstrate competence and knowledge.
- ☐ Research to learn all you can about the interviewer to help you connect positively during your interviews

## CRITICAL THINKING QUESTIONS

1. What are the advantages of researching your occupational field and your targeted job?
2. What should you try to learn about the interviewer?
3. Name at least two Internet Web sites you have visited that provide useful information about employers. Give at least two examples of the types of information you have found at each site.

# CAREER ACTION 8-2

## Printed, People, and Internet Resources for Research of Employers

### QUESTIONS ABOUT THE INDUSTRY

1. What is the general job description for your occupational career choice?

   **References:** (a) school career services staff, (b) *Occupational Outlook Handbook*, (c) reference library.

   **Internet:** (a) school career services Web sites; (b) U.S. Department of Labor's *Occupational Outlook Handbook* ***http://stats.bls.gov/ocohome.htm/***, (c) employer Web site addresses.

2. What is the occupational outlook projection for your field? (Will occupational opportunities grow, diminish, stay the same? By what percentage? Over what period of time?)

   **References:** (same as #1).

   **Internet:** (same as #1) and America's Career InfoNet ***http://www.acinet.org/***.

3. What is the current general salary range for your occupational field and for your job target?

   **References:** (a) people in the field, (b) *Occupational Outlook Handbook*, (c) school career services staff.

   **Internet:** (same as #1; under the Department of Labor's *Occupational Outlook Handbook*, select ***Occupational Cluster*** and then choose the title of your field and a subtitle if necessary; then click on ***Earnings***.

4. What occupations are closely related to your first occupational choice?

   **References:** (a) *Occupational Outlook Handbook*, (b) school career services staff.

   **Internet:** (same as #1).





CONTINUED ON NEXT PAGE

# CAREER ACTION 8-2

(CONTINUED)

## QUESTIONS ABOUT PROSPECTIVE EMPLOYERS

1. What are the products or services of prospective employers you have identified?

   **References:** (a) people in the field, (b) *Dun & Bradstreet's Million Dollar Directories*, (c) annual reports of the employer, (d) *Moody's Manuals*.

   **Internet:** (a) employer Web sites—look for products/services and annual reports of the employer, (b) Companies Online (http://www.companiesonline.com/), (c) Monster.com (http://www.monster.com/), (d) Hoovers Online (http://www.hoovers.com/), (e) Internet search engines.

2. What is the size of the employer organization, its number of employees, the sales assets, and stock market standing?

   **References:** (a) people, (b) *Dun & Bradstreet's Million Dollar Directories*, (c) *Standard and Poor's Buyers' Compendium of American Industry*, (d) annual reports of the company.

   **Internet:** (a) all sources listed in #1, (b) Wall Street Research Net (http://www.wsrn.com/), financial information Web sites.

3. Has the company shown consistent and substantial growth? What is the financial and competitive position of the company in the industry?

   **References:** (a) people in the field, (b) company annual reports, (c) *Fortune* magazine, (d) *Forbes* magazine, (e) *The Wall Street Journal*, (f) *Value Line Investment Survey*, (g) *Dun & Bradstreet's Million Dollar Directories*.

   **Internet:** (a) all sources listed in #1, (b) annual reports of the employer, (c) financial information Web sites.

4. Who are the competitors?

   **References:** (a) people in the field, (b) *Dun & Bradstreet's Million Dollar Directories*, (c) telephone directory Yellow Pages, (d) chamber of commerce, (e) *Fortune* magazine, (f) *Forbes* magazine, (g) *The Wall Street Journal*.

   **Internet:** (a) BigYellow (http://www1.bigyellow.com/), (b) the Wall Street Research Net (http://www.wsrn.com/).

CONTINUED ON NEXT PAGE

# CAREER ACTION 8-2
(CONTINUED)

5. What are the current trends in the industry, and are technological changes occurring or anticipated in the field?

   **References:** (a) people in the field, (b) professional and trade associations, (c) publications in the field, (d) *The Wall Street Journal.*

   **Internet:** (a) employer Web sites (b) America's Career InfoNet (http://www.acinet.org/), (c) Wall Street Research Net (http://www.wsrn.com/), (d) Internet search engines.

## QUESTIONS ABOUT THE JOB ITSELF

1. What is the title of the position you will be seeking?

   **References:** (a) the company or organization—check with the human resources department or the department or employer you are targeting, (b) people currently in the field and knowledgeable about your job target.

   **Internet:** (a) employer Web sites (check under **human resources, employment opportunities**, etc.), (b) other sites you found useful in the previous questions.

2. What are the job description, duties, and responsibilities of the job and the required skills, education, and training?

   **References:** (a) the employer organization—many provide written job descriptions on request, (b) employees of the company or people working in similar jobs.

   **Internet:** (a) employer Web sites (check under **human resources, employment opportunities**, etc.), (b) other sites you found useful in the previous questions.

**NOTE:** This question will help you identify the requirements of the position so you can relate your qualifications for it in your search communications. Do your research carefully, and be complete in your answer. The one who benefits is *you*!

CHAPTER 9

# Prepare a Winning Resume

> I do an initial read through of all resumes to make sure they are clear and concise. If a resume is poorly written or has obvious typos, I will not read it a second time. A sloppy resume is not considered because it shows lack of effort and attention to detail. The second time I read a well-written resume, I look for specific skills and related experience that is pertinent to the position I am hiring for.
>
> *Tracy Bradshaw*
> *Project Director*
> *KRA Corporation*

*In this chapter you will:*

- Identify the elements of a winning resume.
- Identify critical differences among traditional, scannable, and electronic resumes.
- Write a clear, appropriate job objective.
- Outline the content for your paper resume.
- Prepare and evaluate your paper resume draft; make corrections; and produce a final resume.
- List appropriate keywords to use in a cyber-resume.

Create a cyber-resume. Use *WebGuide* or the Internet to access and research a resume-posting Web site.

Most employers select candidates to interview largely on the basis of their resumes. The selection is based on a quick visual screening or a quick computerized search of resumes submitted by applicants. Employers look for a match between their needs and applicants' qualifications. Because this initial resume screening takes only a few seconds, you must learn how to write resumes that will be chosen by both types of screening processes (visual or computerized). This chapter explains how to do that.

## WHAT IS A RESUME?

A resume is a short document detailing your qualifications for a particular job or job target.

The traditional resume has been an attractively and sometimes elaborately formatted hard copy document. Because a growing number of employers are electronically scanning resumes into resume-tracking and search software, the trend is moving toward a simple but attractively formatted document. Heavily formatted resumes do not scan well.

### Scannable Paper Resume

A scannable paper resume is a dual-purpose, hard copy resume designed to be visually appealing; to be delivered by regular mail, by hand, or by fax; and to be scannable by computer software.

Most paper resumes must now be specially formatted so they can be scanned correctly into computers and processed by resume-tracking programs. A scannable resume contains less complex formatting than was used previously in traditional resumes.

Figure • 9-1: Your resume may be circulated to managers within a company by e-mail or fax.

### Cyber-Resume

A cyber-resume (also called an electronic resume) is designed to be delivered via e-mail or via an Internet resume service. We use the term *cyber-resume* in referring to an electronic resume. This resume must be completely stripped of word processing codes and is, therefore, a plain-looking document. Cyber-resumes must be specially formatted (explained later in this chapter) so they can be transmitted electronically to employers, be easily read on screen through an e-mail program, and be transmitted directly to a resume-tracking program for processing.

Find out from employers what term they use for cyber-resumes (e.g., electronic resumes); use that term in all your correspondence with them. Because cyber-resumes save employers the scanning step, many employers highly prefer this format.

## WHAT MAKES A WINNING RESUME?

A winning resume is a resume that gets you a job interview. Before you can write a winning resume, you need to understand what happens to a resume after it is received. Following is a typical scenario.

ABC Company receives your resume (along with many others) in response to an advertisement in the newspaper or on the Internet. ABC Company is one of a growing number of companies that electronically scan all resumes so the contents may be stored in an electronic database for easy distribution and retrieval.

Since hiring managers don't have time to interview everyone who submits a resume, all the resumes are reviewed to select the candidates who appear most qualified. This review and selection may be done by a person or by software that searches resumes for *keywords*—words the company has instructed the software to search for. Resumes with the largest number of keywords are selected for the next review step.

The selected resumes are reviewed again, and the resumes of potential candidates may be circulated (in hard copy format or online) to the hiring authorities. These people choose candidates who appear to meet job needs and who may work well with existing employees.

From that scenario, you can infer that a winning resume is one that achieves four objectives:

1. Quickly shows that the candidate has the qualifications necessary for the job.
2. Demonstrates that the candidate can meet the employer's needs.
3. Suggests that the candidate is someone who is likeable and works well with others.
4. Appeals to both human and electronic reviewers.

The table on the next page gives you some quick guidelines for achieving these four key objectives in your resume. The balance of this chapter walks you through all stages of writing winning traditional, scannable, or electronic resumes. Following the instructions for development of resume content are guidelines for formatting resumes for electronic processing.

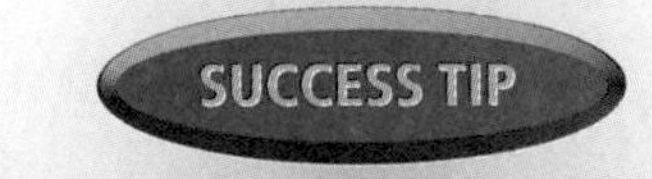


**Begin by taking inventory of your qualifications.**

## PREPARE TO WRITE YOUR RESUME

Before you begin writing your resume, you should have done the following:

- Completed a thorough inventory of your education and skills (see Chapters 2 and 3).
- Considered the kind of work environment you will thrive in.
- Set a career target (see Chapter 3).
- Completed research to identify specific companies or job titles that interest you.

If you have not already done so, complete Chapters 2 and 3 of this book before beginning to write your resume.

## FIVE STEPS TO PREPARING YOUR RESUME

Writing a resume that gets you an interview does not happen on the first try. It requires completing these five carefully planned steps:

1. Decide on Your Job Objective
2. Choose the Most Appropriate Resume Format
3. Organize Carefully and Write Forcefully
4. Fine-Tune Each Section of Your Resume
5. Finalize and Produce Your Resume

Don't rush the process. If you skip or skimp on any of these steps, you will greatly diminish your chance of achieving the purpose of your resume: getting the interview and, ultimately, the job.

## FOUR KEYS TO WRITING A WINNING RESUME

| KEY | WHY | HOW |
|---|---|---|
| **Quickly show you have the qualifications for the job.** | The first cut on a resume takes only seconds.<br><br>Your qualifications for a job must be quickly apparent to a reviewer. | Include a clear job objective.<br><br>Include a keyword section and/or a capabilities section at the top of your resume.<br><br>List most pertinent data first. |
| **Demonstrate you can meet the employer's needs.** | Once past the initial qualifications review, employers want to know whether you can apply your skills to solving their problems. | Reflect your knowledge of the job and the employer in your resume content.<br><br>Include examples of work-relevant accomplishments—for example, reduced errors, saved money, increased sales and productivity. |
| **Suggest that you are likeable.** | Employers want to work with people who have positive personal and performance traits. | Emphasize your enthusiasm, cooperation, and dependability.<br><br>Stress activities, teamwork, and leadership.<br><br>Effective words include accurate, cooperative, creative, flexible, organized, and self-directed. |
| **Pass both human and electronic reviews.** | More and more employers are scanning resumes for electronic processing reviews. | Include a keyword section, and use keywords throughout your resume to pass electronic reviews.<br><br>Use action words to demonstrate accomplishments and to appeal to human readers.<br><br>Format your resume for clear scannability. |

## Step One: Decide on Your Job Objective

The first step in writing a successful resume is to specify a concise, written objective. Your entire resume will be organized around this objective. Therefore, if you have more than one job objective, write separate resumes for each job objective.

**Write a clear, appropriate job objective to focus your entire resume.**

Complete Career Action 9-1

# CAREER ACTION 9-1

## Write Your Job Objective

**DIRECTIONS:** Write a job objective for the job you have targeted. You may want to use one of the job descriptions you collected earlier as a reference for this assignment. Write an objective to mirror the needs stated in the job description you are referencing.

## Step Two: Choose the Most Appropriate Resume Format

The most common resume formats are chronological, functional, and combination. Review the following descriptions of these resume formats, and consider which one best meets your needs:

- **Chronological:** Use this format to show skill development, work experience, and a logical career progression that relates directly to the job target. Choose this format to emphasize steady, related work experience that does not contain major employment gaps or numerous job changes. Place at the top of the resume the information category that best supports your job objective. List employment history with the most recent experience first, and stress the major accomplishments and responsibilities of each position. Avoid repeating details common to several positions. (See Figure 9-5 on page 137.)

- **Functional:** Use the functional format if you lack work experience directly related to your job target. This format is also appropriate if you have gaps in employment; it emphasizes your capabilities related to the job target. Clearly identify your skills that relate to the job objective, and substantiate these with measurable accomplishments. Use separate paragraphs to emphasize each skill category. Arrange the paragraphs in order of importance to the objective, listing the most important skill first. (See Figure 9-6 on page 138.)

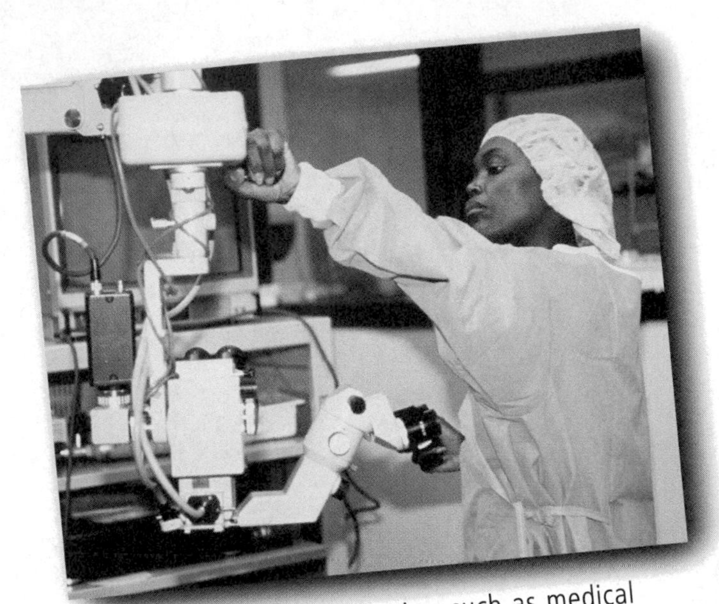

Figure • 9-2: A clear job objective, such as medical technician, will help you determine the best way to organize your resume, select appropriate keywords, and present your experience.

- **Combination:** Capture employers' attention by immediately emphasizing the match between your skills and the position requirements. Consider this format if you want to emphasize your skills or if you have limited experience. List your skills just below the position objective. Then incorporate accomplishments in a chronological list of job experiences. Add credibility by linking your achievements with specific employers and time periods. Place your education summary where it best supports your objective. (See Figure 9-7 on page 139.)

Figures 9-5 through 9-16 provide excellent models to help you prepare your own winning resume. Examine carefully the content and format of each one, and read each of the explanatory summaries provided. Use a colored pen to mark the examples and explanations that are most relevant to you.

**SUCCESS TIP**

**Choose the resume format that best supports your job objective.**

## Step Three: Organize Carefully and Write Forcefully

Use the following general guidelines as you write and edit your resume.

**Write Concisely and Clearly.** Convey your qualifications as clearly and concisely as possible, but don't omit pertinent information that could cost you the interview.

You can write more concisely if you avoid using dated expressions and overly complex terms. Some common examples and alternatives are shown below:

| DATED/EXPRESSIONS | CONCISE |
|---|---|
| at this point in time | now |
| left no stone unturned | used every possible method |

| COMPLEX/WORDY | CONCISE |
|---|---|
| utilized | used |
| manifested | showed |

**Use Numbers and Specific Examples.** Your resume will be clearer and more powerful if you use specific terms and examples to indicate accomplishments. Notice the impact these specific examples have:

| GENERAL/VAGUE | SPECIFIC |
|---|---|
| reduced costs significantly | reduced costs by 20 percent |
| the leading producer | top producer of 60 employees |

The most persuasive resumes highlight applicants' accomplishments with numbers to emphasize how the accomplishments could meet the employer's needs. Use numbers whenever possible to show the magnitude and credibility of your achievements.

Notice how the numbers in the second example below strengthen the accomplishment:

> Processed more orders than any other member of the work team.

> Processed **40 percent** more orders than any other member of the work team.

**TIP**: Try adding the word *that* to an accomplishment statement: "Developed a new filing system that reduced filing time by 25 percent." If necessary, use an estimated measurement (approximately or averaged).

**Use numbers and action verbs to describe your accomplishments.**

**Use Action Verbs and Omit *I* and *My*.** To satisfy resume search software, you need to include keywords, which are usually nouns that reflect employer needs. Ultimately, however, you want a person to view your resume, so you also need to include action terms, which are persuasive to human readers.

When writing action statements, complete sentences are unnecessary. Employers want to find the important information quickly. Omit *I*, *me*, and *my* to increase conciseness and to avoid sounding like a braggart (employers assume that the resume is about you). Use action verbs and phrases to show that you take initiative and actively participate in problem-solving and decision-making processes (*wrote proposal, improved process, increased sales*).

Notice how the specific action verbs in the second example convey a stronger image.

> My duties included reviewing marketing trends, analyzing statistical data, and preparing annual sales reports.

> **Conducted** extensive market research; **analyzed**, **diagramed**, and **reported** results of sales data; and **wrote** annual sales reports.

Use a thesaurus to find just the right words to convey your qualifications accurately and clearly. Notice how the use of more specific action verbs in the second example (*designed* and *implemented*) increases the clarity of the description and the scope of the responsibility. Specific verbs also convey a greater sense of accomplishment.

> **Started up** the inventory-tracking system.

> **Designed** and **implemented** the inventory-tracking system.

Review the following accomplishment statements to get a feel for writing them:

> **Organized** and **trained** volunteers who solicited contributions and **raised $55,000** for citywide "elder-help" campaign.

> **Coordinated** school student-body elections and **reduced** final ballot processing time by **25 percent**.

# IDENTIFY MARKETABLE ASSETS

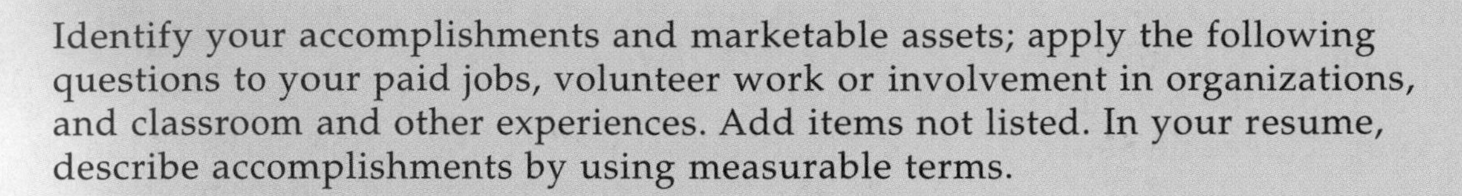

Identify your accomplishments and marketable assets; apply the following questions to your paid jobs, volunteer work or involvement in organizations, and classroom and other experiences. Add items not listed. In your resume, describe accomplishments by using measurable terms.

1. How have I increased my skills and/or knowledge?
2. How have I solved problems or made decisions or recommendations? Were the results effective? Explain in measurable terms (use numbers, percentages, etc.).
3. Have I organized or planned tasks, activities, and projects? Explain.
4. Did I work well under pressure and meet critical deadlines? Explain.
5. Have I cut costs (by reducing processing time, reducing errors or waste, etc.)? Explain.
6. What equipment have I operated, and what software can I use?
7. Did I work with a team? What did I contribute? Did I lead others? Explain.
8. What reports and documents have I written?
9. Have I helped train or develop others? Explain.
10. Did I manage money for any group? Explain.
11. How can I measure the results of my work (numbers of customers served, percentage increase in production, percentage decrease in costs or errors, etc.)?
12. What personal qualities or traits increase my ability to perform and achieve results?

**Use Keywords Strategically.** Keywords name attributes that qualified candidates must have. Specific words or short phrases that describe employer-valued qualifications are good keywords. Examples are capabilities (skills, knowledge, specialties), licenses or certifications, experiences, awards, education, and degrees.

Using keywords is essential for resumes that are likely to be processed by resume-tracking software. Include keywords throughout your resume. Repeat critical keywords; the more keywords the search software identifies, the more likely it is that your resume will be selected and you will be called for interviews.

Also use synonyms for keywords; employers may use different terms as search criteria. For example, *budget* may be a synonym for *forecast*, *BA* for *Bachelor of Arts*, and *supervisor* for *manager*.

Figure • 9-3: Study job ads and descriptions carefully to identify the keywords, targeted vocabulary, and industry terminology you should use in your resume.

**Tailor Your Basic Resume to Specific Openings.** Employers expect resumes to be tailored for specific positions. With word processing software, you can easily tailor your resumes to specific job titles, job advertisements, and employers. The targeted approach is 100 percent more effective than the one-fits-all resume. Here are some ways you can tailor your resume:

- Use capabilities and keywords in your job objective and within your resume that match those in the job ad.
- Identify the name of the company or industry.
- Use appropriate industry terminology.

SUCCESS TIP

**Tailor your resume to meet the needs of the employer. Match your resume to the job description: Use specific terms and industry terminology.**

**Include Keywords, Targeted Vocabulary, and Industry Terminology from an Employer's Job Descriptions.** What better words for you to use in describing how you are qualified for the job than the words employers use in job descriptions and advertisements! For example, if you are applying for a computer programming position and the job description calls for the ability to "debug software," include this term when describing your qualifications.

**Limit Your Resume to One or Two Pages.** Keep your traditional and scannable hard copy resume to one page unless you have extensive working experience; then two pages are acceptable. Employers prefer paper resumes to be brief. Make every word count, and put the emphasis on how you meet employers' needs. Electronic resumes will probably be longer for reasons discussed later in this chapter. The content, however, should be as concise as possible.

## Step Four: Fine-Tune Each Section of Your Resume

As you write your resume, apply the writing guidelines to your work. Remember: You may not want to include all the sections described in this segment, or you may present them in a different order.

**Contact Information.** Be sure to provide your name, mailing address, telephone number (including message phone), fax number, and e-mail address, if appropriate. Place all the contact details at the top of the resume.

**Job Objective.** Place your job objective directly after your contact information. The job objective should reflect your employer research by specifying a job title or type of work. Highlighting the required skills can also be appropriate. For example:

> **Job Objective:** Waiter in an exclusive restaurant where my knowledge of international cuisine will be an added service to customers.

Tailor your objective as specifically as possible. The general objective above could be tailored to an advertisement for a waiter in a French restaurant:

> **Job Objective:** Waiter in a four-star French restaurant where my knowledge of the French language and cuisine will be an added service to customers.

**Capabilities Section.** Review the Career Actions you completed in Chapters 2 and 3 to extract qualifications and skills that best match your job target. List those in order of importance as they relate to your position objective.

Because this section is a focal point for employers, stress your qualifications and accomplishments. Include examples such as (a) numbers of years of experience in a specialized field or use of a specialized skill and (b) accomplishments achieved on the job and during volunteer work or other community or school activities.

If you don't have strong work experience related to your job objective, use the functional resume format and the capabilities summary to place strong emphasis on your accomplishments and skills in areas other than paid work experience.

## CHOOSE THE RIGHT WORDS

Use a thesaurus to find the best words to describe your capabilities and accomplishments.

**Keyword Section.** Always place your keyword section at the top of your resume (as illustrated in our examples). Some employers quickly review electronically submitted resumes in their e-mail programs. If they don't see what they're looking for in the first or second screen of information, they may not consider the resume further.

Your keyword section should be a concise list of nouns or short phrases describing your primary abilities that match the job target. Emphasize the following:

- **Hard skills** (Examples: financial analysis and project management)
- **Position titles** (Examples: accountant, sales representative)
- **Software skills** (Examples: *Excel*, *Quattro Pro*, and *Word*)
- **Appropriate, well-known abbreviations or acronyms** (Examples: *Unix*, *RN*, and *BA*)

Format this section as a concise paragraph listing of focused terms and phrases. The terms are best formatted by capitalizing the first word of each term and all proper nouns and by placing a period at the end of each term; this helps the computer identify where one term ends and the next begins. See Figure 9-15 on page 154 for an example.

In selecting keywords and acronyms, think *nouns.* The computerized resume-search typically seeks nouns. In searching for AutoCAD drafters, the computer looks for nouns such as *CAD, engineer, AA degree, certified drafter, Computer-Aided Drafting, AutoCAD Release 13/14, wiring diagrams,* and *physics.*

**REMEMBER:** Keyword choices are critical. A potential employer may never read your resume unless it first passes the computer search by getting several "hits." Getting a "hit" means the computer matches a word (keyword) in your resume to one it is seeking. Keywords alone, however, won't get you the interview or job. They will just get you through the first selection process.

**"Use the right word, not its second cousin."**
—Mark Twain

In the body of your resume, always provide proof of the qualifications you list in the keyword section. This proof should be in the form of experience, education, or skill summaries. Notice how this is done in the sample electronic resume illustrated in Figure 9-15 on page 154.

**Work Experience.** List your most recent job first, and end with the earliest job you held. For each job, list the dates of employment, the company's name, and a brief, results-oriented description of the job. In your description, give specific examples of accomplishments. For example, state how you increased sales, decreased costs, reduced errors, and improved speed of processing. Quantify where possible (by percentage, by a specific dollar figure, by a number of items produced or sold, etc.).

If you have held increasingly more responsible jobs with an employer, show this here. It demonstrates reliability and your ability to learn and achieve on the job. List only the new responsibilities and accomplishments for each promotion. Don't restate continuing job duties; these will be assumed by the reader. (See Figures 9-12a and 9-12b for an example.)

If you have little work experience, list part-time and summer work, school-sponsored internships, volunteer work, and community involvement. Emphasize all skills developed or accomplishments achieved in these experiences—even if they don't relate directly to your job target. For example, if you have just graduated and you worked throughout your schooling, one of your accomplishments might read:

> Earned 65 percent of school expenses by working part-time during school year, full-time in summers.

This demonstrates positive working ability and potential for learning. Employers consider these qualities real pluses, particularly in entry-level applicants.

**Other Experience.** Use this section to bring out other experience pertinent to your job objective. Include activities such as membership or leadership in professional or trade associations; honorary groups; and social, service, and school organizations. All these activities show that you are well rounded and able to work with others. List any offices held or awards earned.

Instead of the heading "Other Experience," consider options that may be more appropriate for you, such as "Awards and Honors," "Volunteer Work," "Community Service," "Certificates Earned," and "Professional Associations."

Figure • 9-4: Include summer jobs on your resume.

**Education.** List your education in reverse chronological order. List the names of technical schools, colleges, and universities you have attended, the years of attendance, and the degree(s) or certificates earned.

If you are (or will be) a recent graduate with limited work experience, highlight school activities and achievements in the education section. Support your job objective by listing your related major(s), minor(s), and courses. For example, the liberal arts student with courses in business will benefit from listing these courses when applying for a business job.

If you have several years of work experience pertinent to your job objective, emphasize your work experience and condense the education section of your resume.

Research your target employer to find out whether the GPA is a desirable or required listing on the resume. If your accumulated GPA is low but your GPA in your major or minor is high, list the latter only (GPA in accounting: 3.8). If your overall GPA is high and you graduated with honors, put it on your resume—it won't hurt!

**Military Service.** Include on your resume any military experience relevant to your job objective, emphasizing pertinent training, responsibilities, and accomplishments. Emphasize any rapid progressions, significant promotion(s), and special commendations. Usually, military service is listed in the experience section. If you have an exemplary record, however, you can put it under a separate heading for emphasis. Don't use military jargon; use civilian terms.

**Personal Data.** Omit personal data from your resume. Fair employment laws prohibit employers from requesting information about height, weight, age, gender, marital status, race, religion, and so on.

**References.** Research to find out whether your target employer prefers you to submit references with your resume. Employers expect applicants to have references, but employers differ regarding when they want to see an applicant's reference list.

Don't underestimate the importance of having strong references available, however. A reference is a person who can recommend you to prospective employers as a good worker or student or as a person with admirable personal qualities.

Now that you have reviewed the resume-writing guidelines, you are ready to develop your own resume. The Resume Outline form on page 167 will help you create an outline. Gather the following forms to help you with this activity:

- The documentation of your personal data, education and training, skills, etc. (**Career Actions 2-1, 2-2, 2-3, 2-4,** and **2-5**).
- Your Job Qualifications Profile (**Career Action 7-4**).

**Complete Career Action 9-2**

# CAREER ACTION 9-2

## Outline Your Resume

**DIRECTIONS:** Prepare the outline of your resume now. Use the assignment form provided on page 167 to outline your resume, or create your draft in a word processing program, using the form as a reference.

Once you've completed the form in **Career Action 9-2**, number each section of the outline, ranking it in order of its importance and relevance to your job objective. Present the material in your final resume in this order. For example, if your education is more important than your work experience, put education in a more prominent position.

**Tailor your resume to best support your objective.**

## Step Five: Finalize and Produce Your Resume

The next step in creating your resume is to use your outline as a reference in drafting your actual resume. Finally, evaluate and revise your information as necessary to create a job-winning resume.

**Produce Your Resume.** The general layout of your paper resume provides employers with their first impression of you. Give your resume a professional look:

- Omit the heading RESUME at the top of your document.
- Single-space the body of your resume, and double-space or triple-space between sections or items in the resume. (Remember: Your final resume should be only one page in length unless you have extensive work experience.)
- Use white or light-colored 8 1/2-by-11-inch paper.
- Frame your resume attractively with one-inch margins on all sides.
- Use white space effectively. Purposely incorporate areas of white space to draw attention to important parts of your resume, giving it an organized, uncrowded look.
- Capitalize the first letters of keywords or phrases, and place a period after each of these.
- Use headings in all capital letters, and indent text to emphasize resume parts. (Don't overdo this.)

## Tips for Preparing a Winning Career-Change Resume

Most of us will make more than one career change in our lifetimes. Below are tips for successfully revising your resume to fit a new career objective. See Chapter 20 for other important considerations in making a successful career change. A realistic new career target is one for which you have already developed relevant, related skills. To revise a resume to be used for a new career, follow the tips below:

1. Begin by making a list of all your work skills, knowledge, and experience.
2. Use a colored pen to place a check mark in front of each item on your list that matches or closely matches the needs of your new career target.
3. If necessary, change the wording of the items you checked to better fit your new career target. Use a thesaurus and your new career research to help identify appropriate terms. For example, in changing from a classroom teacher to an industry trainer, the terms *trainer*, *facilitator*, and *presenter* will be more appropriate than *teacher.*
4. Create new resume skill and experience headings by grouping related items from your updated skills list into categories. Create a heading to describe each category.
5. Now that you have appropriate content, you can begin drafting and refining your new career resume.

Compare the "Before" and "After" excerpts from the functional format resume shown below, and see Figures 9-13 on page 151 and 9-14 on page 152 for an example of a career-change resume in the combination format.

### Excerpts From "Before" Resume

**Job Objective:** Service manager in the automotive repair industry

**Auto Repair Customer Service**
Scheduled appointments; performed pre-inspections, achieved upgrade sales on 95 percent of accounts, quoted estimates, and wrote work orders; performed post-repair inspections; and explained statements to customers. Increased referrals from customers by 43 percent.

**Parts Management**
Managed ordering and stocking of mechanical and auto-body parts inventories; selected suppliers and negotiated vendor discounts that averaged 25-30 percent below wholesale; reconciled shipping invoices to billing statements; and approved payments.

**NOTE:** See Figure 9-13 (resume example on page 151).

### Excerpts From "After" Resume

**Job Objective:** Insurance adjuster in the automotive repair industry

**Claims Management**
Scheduled client appointments, determined mechanical and auto-body damages within 45 minutes, negotiated repairs with clients and insurance companies, prepared job documentation (pictures, work orders, billing), performed post-repair inspection, and explained statements.

**Cost Containment**
Obtained clients' agreement to use appropriate after-market and/or rebuilt parts on 98.7 percent of jobs; located replacement parts; negotiated price, delivery, and discounts, averaging 25-30 percent below wholesale; returned unused parts for credit; reconciled billing discrepancies; approved payments.

**NOTE:** See Figure 9-14 (resume example on page 152).

## MAKE IT PERFECT

Make sure your resume has no misspelled words, typing mistakes, or format errors. Any of these flaws could cause your resume to be rejected immediately.

**Make Your Resume Easy to Scan.** Since more and more companies are scanning hard copy resumes for storage and processing, you need to create a scannable resume by using formatting that is both attractive to the eye and easy to scan. A scannable resume must be stripped of certain word processing codes so scanners can read the text clearly and convert the resume into an ASCII text document. Employers can then store the ASCII document on computer or transfer it to other hiring departments.

Scanners may misinterpret improperly formatted characters. The following "Do's and Don'ts" explain how to format your resume so it will scan clearly and keep you in the running for an interview.

**DO:**

1. Use a clean overall format. Visual legibility is extremely important.
2. Use simple, clean fonts like Arial and Times Roman.
3. Use a font size of 10 to 14 points. The ideal font size is 12 points.
4. Use acceptable character enhancements and codes such as bolding, centering commands, solid bullets, and regular and indent tabs.
5. Print your resume on a high-quality printer in black ink, on one side of white or light-colored 8 1/2-inch x 11-inch paper. (You may have a printing firm reproduce your resume by using the photo-offset printing method. The cost is reasonable, and the print quality is acceptable for scanning. A standard copy machine does not produce a copy of high enough quality to ensure scannability.)

**DON'T:**

1. Don't use a highly formatted style such as a newsletter layout or columns. Scanner software assumes that the text reads conventionally from left-to-right in one column.
2. Don't use special justification (adjustable spacing between characters). Use the standard left-margin alignment so that each letter is clearly visible.
3. Don't use underlining, italics, shadows, white letters on a black background, or colored text. These all can blur or corrupt the scanned message.
4. Don't include graphic images and other graphics, such as vertical and horizontal lines and boxes. (You can use a horizontal line if you leave adequate white space above and below it so that the line doesn't touch any letters.)
5. Don't fold or staple the resume (creases and staple marks can cause scanning errors).

Examples of scannable paper resumes are shown in Figures 9-10, 9-11, and 9-14. This format may be perfectly acceptable for all the resumes you send out. If you think it is important to have a more dramatic format, however, send the simpler resume and take your more heavily formatted traditional resume to the interview.

**Complete Career Action 9-3**

# CAREER ACTION 9-3

## Draft Your Resume

**DIRECTIONS:** Review the resumes on pages 137-154. Use colored ink to mark sections of these models that are useful to you. Resumes typically should contain all the "Standard Resume Sections" listed below. The optional sections should be included when they support your main job objective.

**Standard Resume Sections:**

- Name and Contact Information
- Capabilities or Keyword Section
- Job Objective
- Education
- Work Experience
- Other Experience

**Optional Resume Sections:**

- Military Service
- References
- Personal Information

Prepare a written draft of your resume, using your resume outline as a reference. Be selective about the quality and quantity of information you include; make every word count. Emphasize your qualifications and measurable accomplishments.

Career Database Appropriate

**Revise the Content.** After you have drafted your resume, review it with careful attention to every detail. Use a colored pen to highlight areas that could be improved.

Once you have reviewed your draft, rewrite your resume, strengthening each area you marked. Eliminate unnecessary words; substitute stronger, clearer terms for weak ones. Your goal is to answer "yes" to all the Resume Review Questions at the right.

After reviewing your draft, check the professional guidelines presented earlier in this chapter, and complete **Career Action 9-4**.

Sample resumes (Figures 9-5 through 9-15) on pages 137-154 provide good models to help you prepare your own winning resume. Examine the content and format of each one and the summaries provided. Mark the examples that are most useful for your needs.

### RESUME REVIEW QUESTIONS

- Is it concise, free of unnecessary words and information?
- Does it include positive qualities and accomplishments using measurable terms and action verbs?
- Does it stress my job qualifications?
- Do my listed qualifications support my stated job objective?
- Is it logically organized, and is the information presented in order of importance and relevance to my job objective?
- Have I used keywords effectively?

**Complete Career Action 9-4 on page 156**

**KIMI R. OKASAKI**
148 Barrister Avenue • Tucson, Arizona 85726
(520) 555-9088 • E-mail: KOkasaki@provider.net

---

**OBJECTIVE**

Administrative Assistant for MegaMall Property Management Company

**EDUCATION**

Associate of Applied Science, 2000, Community College, Tucson, AZ
Major: Administrative Office Technology GPA 3.6

Related Courses and Skills

- Advanced Word Processing (MS Word, WordPerfect for Windows)
- Text input at 75 wpm
- Dictation transcription at 60 wpm
- Spreadsheet (Excel, Quattro Pro) and Database Management (Access, Paradox)
- Records Management
- Bookkeeping I and Computerized Bookkeeping (Peachtree)
- Ten-key at 250 spm
- Presentation Software (PowerPoint, Presentations)
- Office Management
- Internet Software (MS Explorer, Netscape Navigator)

**EXPERIENCE**

**Community Volunteer, Tucson, AZ** December 1993-Present

- Girl Scout Leader, Troop 566, 1998-Present
- National Diabetes Foundation Volunteer of the Year, 1999
- Secretary-Treasurer, Valley Elementary Parent-Teacher Organization, 1996-1998 Published printed and electronic newsletters, answered e-mail, and maintained correspondence; set up customized spreadsheet to track results of three fund-raisers that reduced reporting time by 50 percent; designed database for 500 student families; kept books for two years and satisfied yearly CPA audits.
- Cub Scout Den Mother, Troop 354, 1993-1996

**Katz Department Store, Tucson, AZ** March 1992-December 1993

- Sales Supervisor, Part-time: Supervised four sales clerks; trained new sales employees. Computed daily cash receipts; balanced two registers; attained highest part-time sales volume; and had fewest sales returned.

**Value Variety, Tucson, AZ** Summers 1990, 1991

- Sales Clerk, Floater: Provided complete customer service in sales and returns. Coordinated weekly inventory deliveries.

Figure • 9-5: Chronological resume sample

**KIMI R. OKASAKI**
148 Barrister Avenue • Tucson, Arizona 85726
(520) 555-9088 • E-mail: KOkasaki@provider.net

---

**OBJECTIVE** Administrative Assistant for MegaMall Property Management Company

**EDUCATION**

Associate of Applied Science, 2000, Community College, Tucson, AZ
Major: Administrative Office Technology GPA 3.6

**PROFESSIONAL SKILLS**

**Document Preparation**: Expert using MS Word, WordPerfect, PowerPoint, and Presentations. Enter text at 75 wpm and transcribe dictation at 60 wpm. Integrate tabular data and graphics into documents using Access, Paradox, Excel, and Quattro Pro. Write, format, and proofread printed and electronic business correspondence, reports, and newsletters. Research topics on the Internet (Netscape, MS Explorer).

- Published printed and electronic newsletters and maintained correspondence for Valley Elementary School Parent-Teacher Organization (VES-PTO) for two years.

**Spreadsheet Management**: Set up and maintain Excel and Quattro Pro spreadsheets.

- Designed spreadsheet to track results of three fund-raising activities for VES-PTO, which reduced reporting time by 50 percent.

**Database Management**: Configure, maintain, and generate reports with Access and Paradox.

- Designed and maintained an information database to enable VES-PTO to study parent participation of 500 student families.

**Bookkeeping**: Perform manual (ten-key by touch at 250 spm) or computerized (Peachtree) bookkeeping functions from journal entry to end-of-period reports.

- Maintained books for VES-PTO for two years and satisfied yearly CPA audits.
- Computed daily cash receipts and balanced two registers as part-time sales supervisor of a department store.

**Human Relations**: Successfully cooperate with store managers, representatives of delivery companies and community organizations, and the general public.

- Held positions of responsibility in four community organizations over the last eight years; chosen 1999 National Diabetes Foundation Volunteer of the Year.
- Worked in two department stores: promoted to supervisor; trained new sales clerks; coordinated weekly inventory deliveries; provided customer service in sales and returns; attained highest part-time sales volume and had fewest sales returned.

**EXPERIENCE**

| | |
|---|---|
| Community Volunteer, Tucson, AZ | December 1993-Present |
| Katz Department Store, Tucson, AZ | March 1992-December 1993 |
| Value Variety, Tucson, AZ | Summers 1990, 1991 |

Figure • 9-6: Functional resume sample

**KIMI R. OKASAKI**
148 Barrister Avenue • Tucson, Arizona 85726
(520) 555-9088 • E-mail: KOkasaki@provider.net

---

**OBJECTIVE** Administrative Assistant for MegaMall Property Management Company

**RELATED CAPABILITIES**

- Word processing in MS Word and WordPerfect for Windows
- Spreadsheet generation with Excel and Quattro Pro
- Database design and maintenance using Access and Paradox
- Text input at 75 wpm and dictation transcription at 60 wpm
- Printed and electronic business correspondence, reports, and newsletters written, formatted, and proofread
- Presentation preparation using PowerPoint or Presentation software
- Internet research and e-mail correspondence using Netscape or MS Explorer
- Bookkeeping using Peachtree and ten-key by touch at 250 spm
- Proven ability to work successfully with store managers, delivery companies, community organizations, and the general public

**EDUCATION**

Associate of Applied Science, 2000, Community College, Tucson, AZ
Major: Administrative Office Technology GPA 3.6

**EXPERIENCE**

**Community Volunteer, Tucson, AZ** December 1993-Present
- Girl Scout Leader, Troop 566, 1998-Present
- National Diabetes Foundation Volunteer of the Year, 1999
- Secretary-Treasurer, Valley Elementary Parent-Teacher Organization, 1996-1998
  Published printed and electronic newsletter and maintained correspondence; set up customized spreadsheet to track results of three fund-raisers that reduced reporting time by 50 percent; designed database for 500 student families; kept books for two years and satisfied yearly CPA audits.
- Cub Scout Den Mother, Troop 354, 1993-1996

**Katz Department Store, Tucson, AZ** March 1992-December 1993
- Sales Supervisor, Part-time: Supervised four sales clerks; trained new sales employees. Computed daily cash receipts; balanced two registers; attained highest part-time sales volume; and had fewest sales returned.

**Value Variety, Tucson, AZ** Summers 1990, 1991
- Sales Clerk, Floater: Provided complete customer service in sales and returns. Coordinated weekly inventory deliveries.

Figure • 9-7: Combination resume sample

**SONYA REED**
2332 Clovis Boulevard • Savannah, Georgia 31401
(912) 555-4549 • sreed@provider.net

**OBJECTIVE**

Hospital Medical Records Technician position requiring the ability to perform detailed tasks, to change priorities quickly, and to communicate well

**EDUCATION**

Associate of Science, 2000, Savannah College of Georgia
Major: Health Information Technology GPA 3.6
**Related Courses and Skills**
• Medical Terminology • Clinical Classification • Health Information Management
• Health Records Processing • Health Data • Introduction to Health Law and Ethics
• Disease Conditions • Word • Excel • Access • PowerPoint • MS Explorer

**CERTIFICATION**
Accredited Record Technician, 2000

**EXPERIENCE**

- **Community Hospital, Savannah, GA** January 2000-May 2000
Clinical Internship. Under the direction of the Medical Records Supervisor, assisted Records Technician to review and assign diagnosis codes and DRGs. Abstracted appropriate information and retrieved medical records. Assisted chiefly with Medicare/Medicaid coding for three months. Checked charts into and out of Records Department.

- **Family Practice Partnership, Savannah, GA** July 1998-December 1999
Evening Receptionist. Answered telephone, scheduled appointments, and kept waiting room neat. Checked patients in, obtained insurance and billing information, and pulled charts for nurses. Copied requested records for transport to other medical offices. Provided cheerful, efficient service to patients; awarded Superior Service Certificate in 1998 and 1999.

**ASSOCIATIONS**

Community Hospital Candy Stripers, 1998 to present
American Health Information Management Association, 1998 to present

Figure • 9-8: Hospital Medical Records Technician Objective

## Summary of Information Emphasized on Figure 9-8: Reed

1. **Objective**

Sonya uses an industry-standard job title to state her job objective concisely. To capture the attention of employers and to advertise her work characteristics, she includes job-related competencies that her targeted employers list in job postings.

2. **Education**

Sonya also puts her degree near the top of her resume to reinforce her job qualifications. She worked evenings during the two years she was in school and still earned a respectable GPA, so she includes this information on her resume. In addition, she lists classes from her major that are especially pertinent to employers and includes the computer programs she knows.

3. **Certification**

Since Sonya just graduated and has limited work experience, she places her national certification at the top of the resume to emphasize her qualifications and to show that she takes her profession seriously.

4. **Experience**

Sonya's internship through Savannah College of Georgia allowed her to learn and work at a local hospital. Because her internship lasted five months, provided hands-on experience, and is directly pertinent to her job objective, Sonya places it in the Experience section of her resume. Notice how Sonya describes her activities in specific industry terminology.

Although Sonya's job at the family practice clinic was at a medical facility, she did not have any responsibilities that are directly applicable to her current job objective. She puts her award for superior service at the end of her job description to demonstrate that her job performance is above average.

5. **Associations**

The two associations on Sonya's resume reinforce her interest in the medical field. She adds her volunteer work because she knows that her targeted employers value and promote community service.

**Maria Banta**
415 S. 23rd #43
Fresno, California 93701
(209) 555-7878

---

**OBJECTIVE**

Seeking a receptionist position for a flexible, reliable person who has a strong work ethic

**QUALIFICATIONS**

- Typing at 45 words per minute
- Windows, MS Word (Advanced), Outlook
- Ten-key at 245 strokes per minute
- Excel and Access data entry
- Formatting business correspondence
- Filing: alphabetic, numeric, geographic
- Operating high-speed, collating copy machine
- Multiline telephones

**EDUCATION**

State University, Fresno, CA
Office Occupations Class, Certificate, August 2000
GED Certificate, February 2000

McCaine Adult Education Center, Clovis, CA
MS Word: Levels I, II June 1999

**WORK EXPERIENCE**

**Fruitland West, Fresno, CA** **Summer 1999**

Cherry Sorter
Received a raise the second day for being one of the three fastest workers. Always arrived on time; promoted to Head Sorter.

**Trail Mushroom, Clovis, CA** **1994 to 1999**

Crew Leader
Promoted to Crew Leader in 1995. Calculated weekly time cards and posted daily attendance records for 16 to 20 people. Left when company closed.

Picker
Picked and sorted mushrooms 35 percent faster than the company average.

Figure • 9-9: Receptionist Objective

## Summary of Information Emphasized on Figure 9-9: Banta

**NOTE:** Figure 9-9 illustrates Maria's excellent job of translating personal attributes—strong work ethic and reliability—into measurable benefits for an employer.

1. **Objective** — Maria states a clear objective and stresses the strong personal attributes that enhance her job performance.

2. **Qualifications** — Maria positions her skills at the top of her resume to assure the prospective employer that she is qualified for the entry-level job stated in her objective. Notice how the typing and ten-key skills are measured in terms meaningful to an employer.

3. **Education** — The most current schooling is listed first. Maria's educational information explains where she learned the skills related to the job objective on her resume.

4. **Work Experience** — Since her work experience is limited and not directly transferable to the receptionist position she is seeking, Maria emphasizes on-the-job accomplishments that demonstrate her value to the employer:

   "Received a raise on the second day for being one of the three fastest workers. Always arrived on time; promoted to Head Sorter."

   "Promoted to Crew Leader in 1995. Calculated weekly time cards and posted daily attendance records for 16 to 20 people."

   "Picked and sorted mushrooms 35 percent faster than the company average."

## LOUELLA K. HINES

1247 Madison Road • Columbus, Ohio 43216 • (614) 555-5799 • LHines@mail.com

**OBJECTIVE** Computerized Accounting Systems Auditor I

**KEY SKILLS**

- Education in accounting practices and computer systems
- Programming competence in COBOL and RPG
- Practical experience in EDP accounting applications
- Good knowledge of MS Word, Excel, Access, DOS, and Windows
- Proven interpersonal skills in an auditing environment
- Experienced in AS/400, PC, IBM MVS, and Novell LAN operations

**EDUCATION**

**Bachelor of Business Administration, 2000** • Clermont State University, Columbus, OH
Major: Computer Information Systems • Minor: Internal Auditing

**Relevant Courses of Study:**

- Analysis, Design, and Auditing of Accounting Information Systems
- Internal Auditing • Information Systems Auditing • Accounting Applications
- Database Management • Advanced Corporate Finance • Cost Accounting

**Senior Internship:**
Under the supervision of the Managing Field Auditor of American Interstate Bank, performed internal audits on the safety deposit box operations of five local branches. Reviewed the audit findings with the branch managers. Compiled final report and presented it to the Chief Operating Officer.

**EXPERIENCE**

**Alexander & Swartz, Columbus, OH** 9/99 to Present
**Part-time Assistant Staff Auditor.** Assist in audits of cash, accounts receivable, and accounts payable for mid-sized firms that use AS/400s. Interface with clients, audit RPG programs, and write audit reports as member of the Business Services Assurance and Advisory team.

**Micronomics Company, Columbus, OH** 6/97-9/99
**Part-time Programmer's Assistant.** Designed, documented, coded, and tested COBOL program subroutines for order-entry system on Novell PC network. Achieved a 95 percent average program-accuracy rate on test runs. Also cataloged and filed new programs and program patches for the company's software library.

**Clermont State University, Columbus, OH** 9/95-6/97
**Part-time Computer Operator Aide.** Using MVS system, copied files for backup. Verified accuracy of reports and scheduled print sequences. Recommended schedule changes that improved efficiency of backup procedures by 28.5 percent.

**ASSOCIATIONS**

Information Technology Management Association, 1995 to present
Columbus Computer Club, 1994 to present

Figure • 9-10: Computerized Accounting Systems Auditor I Objective

## Summary of Information Emphasized on Figure 9-10: Hines

**NOTES:** Figures 9-10 and 9-11 illustrate how to tailor a resume for two diffent job objectives. Because this employer prefers it, Louella uses a one-page, scannable resume.

1. **Objective** — The title "Computerized Accounting Systems Auditor I" is clearly understood in the field.

2. **Key Skills** — Louella incorporates keywords in this section to highlight the education, specialized knowledge, and practical experience she possesses that relate directly to the Computerized Accounting Systems Auditor I job objective. She shows that she can be immediately productive.

3. **Education** — Because the job Louella wants requires expertise in two fields—computer systems and accounting systems—she emphasizes the courses that combine the skills from both areas. She addresses the requirements of her job objective by stressing the auditing experience she obtained through the class project. She also emphasizes proven interpersonal skills—critical to acquiring and retaining clients.

4. **Experience** — *Alexander & Swartz.* Louella provides proof of her interpersonal and on-the-job auditing skills in computerized accounting. She supports the most important qualifications needed for her job objective.

   *Micronomics Company.* By stating a measurable accomplishment, Louella shows that she gets results.
   *Clermont State University.* The addition of another concrete accomplishment strengthens her credibility as an achiever.

5. **Associations** — Membership in professional organizations related to the job objective demonstrates a commitment to remaining current with the trends in the field—something employers value highly.

**LOUELLA K. HINES**

1247 Madison Road • Columbus, Ohio 43216 • (614) 555-5799 • LHines@mail.com

**OBJECTIVE** Information Systems Analyst I position in a financial environment requiring system design, programming, investigation, and reporting skills

**KEY SKILLS**

- Education in computer systems and in accounting practices
- Proven interpersonal skills and team skills in a financial setting
- Programming competence in COBOL and RPG
- Practical experience in computerized order entry and EDP accounting applications
- Good knowledge of Excel, MS Word, Access, DOS, and Windows
- Experienced in AS/400, PC, IBM MVS, and Novell LAN operations

**EDUCATION**

**Bachelor of Business Administration, 2000** • Clermont State University, Columbus, OH
Major: Computer Information Systems • Minor: Internal Auditing

**Relevant Courses of Study:**

- System Analysis and Design • Systems Development • Quantitative Analysis
- Advanced Programming • Data Communications • Database Systems
- Information Systems Auditing • Advanced Corporate Finance • Statistical Techniques

**Senior Internship:**
Installed a five-PC Novell LAN, three printers, and associated software (MS Office and PowerPoint) for a small marketing services business. Assisted the consulting systems analyst in customizing proprietary statistical program for marketing research applications.

**EXPERIENCE**

**Alexander & Swartz, Columbus, OH** 9/99 to Present
**Part-time Assistant Staff Auditor:** Assist in audits of cash, accounts receivable, and accounts payable for mid-sized firms that use AS/400s. Interface with clients, audit RPG programs, and write audit reports as member of the Business Services Assurance and Advisory team.

**Micronomics Company, Columbus, OH** 6/97-9/99
**Part-time Programmer's Assistant:** Designed, documented, coded, and tested COBOL program subroutines for order-entry system on Novell PC network. Achieved a 95 percent-average program-accuracy rate on test runs. Also cataloged and filed new programs and program patches for the company's software library.

**Clermont State University, Columbus, OH** 9/95-6/97
**Part-time Computer Operator Aide:** Using MVS system, copied files for backup. Verified accuracy of reports and scheduled print sequences. Recommended schedule changes that improved efficiency of backup procedures by 28.5 percent.

**ASSOCIATIONS**

Information Technology Management Association, 1995 to present
Columbus Computer Club, 1994 to present

Figure • 9-11: Information Systems Analyst I Objective

## Summary of Information Emphasized on Figure 9-11: Hines

1. **Objective** — The title "Information Systems Analyst I" is clearly understood in Louella's field, specifies the level of expertise and authority she is qualified to handle, and clarifies her area of interest and expertise. She highlights pertinent skills, implying flexibility, thoroughness, and responsibility.

2. **Key Skills** — Since computer systems and accounting practices are primary skills required in financial work, Louella highlights these skills to meet the Information Systems Analyst I job objective. Accenting mainframe languages and hardware, microcomputer software, and experience in order entry and accounting applications stresses her flexibility. She emphasizes the names of hardware, operating systems, and program languages with which she is experienced to demonstrate immediate ability to use these skills.

3. **Education** — Louella highlights courses that best support this job objective. Practical experience gained in a directly related internship demonstrates her scope of knowledge and dependability. She omits her moderate GPA.

4. **Experience** — *Alexander & Swartz.* Louella uses action verbs and highlights her responsibilities and knowledge. She backs up her claim to have "proven interpersonal and team skills in a financial setting."

   *Micronomics Company.* Her claim to program design and coding skill is supported with a measurable achievement.

   *Clermont State University.* Louella reinforces her image for getting results by stressing another accomplishment (28.5 percent increase in efficiency).

5. **Associations** — Demonstrates continued professional growth.

**LAURENT CHACON**

1015 Cambridge Way • Houston, Texas 77001
(409) 555-2422 • Fax (409) 555-2423 • E-mail: LChacon@provider.com

**OBJECTIVE**

Marketing Product Line Manager for wireless data communications company

**KEYWORDS**

Market development. Team leader. Solution sales. RFP and RFQ responses. Presentations. PowerPoint. Project management. PERT charts. Gantt charts. MS Word. Excel. Access. Internet browsers. Local Area Network. LAN. Wide Area Network. WAN. Novell certification. Wireless technology. UNIX. C++. Bachelor of Science of Electrical Engineering. Master of Business Administration.

**QUALIFICATIONS**

- Managerial and technical education: BSEE, MBA
- Strong skills in marketing strategies development and implementation
- Knowledgeable and professional interaction with customers, sales force, engineers, and manufacturing personnel
- Team leader for product line introduction
- Proven project management skills
- Proficient with LANs (wired and wireless), WAN hardware and protocols, T1 Carrier networks, analog and digital telecommunications transmissions, UNIX, C++, and real-time embedded software

**PROFESSIONAL EXPERIENCE**

**NETLINK INC, Dallas, Texas** **1995-Present**

- Marketing Manager, Southwest Division 1998-Present

Manage marketing operations in Texas, Nevada, Arizona, and New Mexico. Supervise a sales and service force that has an average annual growth rate of 153 percent, and participate in executive-level strategic planning meetings. Direct the development and implementation of marketing plan for a banking application of LAN/WAN products;

Figure • 9-12a: Marketing Product Line Manager Objective

results so far include sales to 50 percent of the Southwest Division customer base. Led team whose 1999 sales strategies have doubled NETLINK's market share in the finance industry and expanded the customer base in hospitals by 125 percent.

- Sales and Service Manager, Southwest District 1995-1998

  Supervised account executives and increased district sales 300 percent in two years. Directed on-time, under-budget openings of offices in Houston and Dallas. Improved customer satisfaction 100 percent through systems-support teams that provide four-hour turnaround on service calls. Analyzed competitive forces in the Southwest and reported findings at quarterly planning meetings with upper management.

- Engineering Product Development Coordinator 1992-1995

  Member of company start-up team developing ultrafast, self-contained, secure, low-power wireless transmission technologies. Responsible for coordinating hardware and firmware integration. Supervised component testing, provided engineering support for component production, and assisted in real-time embedded software development. Acted as marketing interface during technical presentations to customers.

**University of South Texas, Houston, Texas**
**Small Business Development Center** **1990-1992**

- Intern: Technical Industries

  Guided by the Center Director, assisted small businesses specializing in technical products to establish vendor sources, design and implement testing procedures, solve production problems, and train workers in manufacturing techniques.

**EDUCATION**

- University of South Texas, Houston, Texas MBA, 1992
- Mid-State College, Austin, Texas, cum laude BSEE, 1990

**ASSOCIATIONS**

- National Association of Consulting Engineers, 1995-Present
- Information Technology Management Association, 1990-Present; President, 1999
- American Society for Quality Control, 1997-Present
- Member, Board of Directors, Texas Red Cross, 1993-Present

Figure • 9-12b: Marketing Product Line Manager Objective—page two

## Summary of Information
## Emphasized on Figure 9-12a and Figure 9-12b: Chacon

**NOTE:** Laurent's extensive experience justifies a two-page resume.

1. **Objective** — The focused objective reflects Laurent's ability to state goals clearly.

2. **Keywords** — Laurent uses industry-specific vocabulary that search programs will recognize. He places a period after each keyword phrase to show where one ends and the next begins.

3. **Qualifications** — The managerial and technical capabilities that make Laurent an effective and productive leader in this field are summarized here.

4. **Professional Experience** — NETLINK INC: *Marketing Manager*. Laurent emphasizes measurable achievements because this field is very results-oriented. Laurent proves competencies claimed in the Qualifications section

   *Sales and Services Manager.* Laurent documents leadership, marketing strategies, and customer service achievements. Referring to the management level of the business planning team emphasizes the responsible scope of his job as well as the respect he has earned.

   *Engineering Product Development Coordinator.* This position is vital to Laurent's success because it gives Laurent credibility with technically knowledgeable customers and with the engineering and manufacturing elements in any organization.

   University of South Texas, Small Business Development Center: *Intern.* This internship is valuable because it reassures employers that Laurent understands the structure and scope of the entire business process.

5. **Education** — Laurent has credible, impressive professional experience and does not need to emphasize specific courses taken. He places the educational background near the end of the resume because, at this point in his career, employers are more interested in accomplishments than in education.

6. **Associations** — Membership in related professional organizations demonstrates a commitment to remaining current with field trends—a quality respected by employers. Employees who contribute to the business community enhance the organizational image.

**DEANE G. CAREY**

126 Granada Avenue | St. Paul, Minnesota 55106 | 612-555-6469

---

**OBJECTIVE** Service Manager in Multi-line Dealership

**RELATED QUALIFICATIONS**

- Associate of Applied Science, Automotive Technology, 1990, Midwest Community College
- Proven supervisory, negotiation, and communication skills in retail repair services
- Excellent sales and customer service skills in dealership environment
- ASE-Certified Service Adviser, Auto Technician, and Auto Parts Specialist
- Safety-Kleen-Certified Hazardous Waste Compliance Trainer (1999)
- Reynolds and Reynolds Parts Database, ADP Shoplink/Photolink, Word, and Excel

**EXPERIENCE**

- **Fix-It-Right Auto Body** **1998-Present**

  **Damage Analyst**

  Estimated auto body repair costs and closed 25 percent more sales than the shop objective. Negotiated initial and supplemental estimates with insurance adjusters. Ordered parts and negotiated a 25 to 30 percent discount rate; scheduled auto body and mechanical repairs. Prepared job documentation: hard copy pictures or digital images, job costs, and invoices. Explained charges to customers and collected accounts receivable. Increased customer referrals by 43 percent. ASE and ICAR-Certified in Damage Analysis and Estimating (1999).

- **MegaLine Dealership** **1990-1998**

  **Service Adviser, Ford Line,** 1996-1998

  Scheduled client appointments, estimated repair costs, and wrote repair orders. Upgraded sales on 65 percent of routine maintenance orders and increased repeat-customer base 56 percent over two years. Coordinated workloads of five technicians. Reviewed repair orders and explained billings to clients. Attained a 98 or 99 percent Customer Service Index (CSI) all three years. ASE-Certified (1997) in Service Advising, Warranty and Policy Administration, and Warranty Claims Preparation.

  **Senior Parts Specialist,** 1993-1996

  Filled parts requests from shop technicians, and coordinated rush orders, returns, and manufacturers' warranties. Supervised three Parts Specialists who worked with retail customers on Saturdays. As Parts Specialist, provided front-counter service to walk-in retail customers; received and checked shipments, stocked parts, and boxed and shipped returns to suppliers. (ASE-Certified Parts Specialist, 1995)

  **Automotive Technician,** 1990-1993

  ASE-Certified in Engine Performance (1993), Engine Repair (1993), Electrical/Electronic Systems (1992), Heating and Air Conditioning (1992), and Brakes (1992). Averaged 136 percent of flat-rate and maintained a .05 percent come-back rate.

Figure • 9-13: Service Manager Objective

**DEANE G. CAREY**

126 Granada Avenue St. Paul, Minnesota 55106 612-555-6469

**OBJECTIVE** Insurance Adjuster in Automotive Collision Repair Industry

**RELATED QUALIFICATIONS**

- Licensed Insurance Adjuster, State of Minnesota, January 2000
- Associate of Applied Science, Automotive Technology, 1990, Midwest Community College
- Proven negotiation and customer service skills in automotive collision repair industry
- ASE-Certified in Damage Analysis and Estimating; ICAR-Certified in Collision Repair 2000
- ASE-Certified Service Adviser, Auto Technician, and Automobile Parts Specialist
- Competent with laptops and PCs with Windows
- Reynolds and Reynolds Parts Database, ADP Shoplink/Photolink, CCC, Word, and Excel

**EXPERIENCE**

- **Fix-It-Right Auto Body** **1998-Present**

  **Damage Analyst**

  Estimated auto body repair costs and closed 25 percent more sales than the shop objective. Negotiated initial and supplemental estimates with insurance adjusters. Ordered parts and negotiated a 25 to 30 percent discount rate; scheduled auto body and mechanical repairs. Prepared job documentation: hard copy pictures or digital images, job costs, and invoices. Explained charges to customers and collected accounts receivable. Increased referrals from customers by 43 percent.

- **MegaLine Dealership** **1990-1998**

  **Service Adviser, Ford Line,** 1996-1998

  Scheduled client appointments, estimated repair costs, and wrote repair orders. Upgraded sales on 65 percent of routine maintenance orders, and increased repeat-customer base 56 percent over two years. Coordinated workloads of five technicians. Reviewed repair orders and explained billings to clients. Attained a 98 or 99 percent Customer Service Index (CSI) all three years. ASE-Certified (1997) in Service Advising, Warranty and Policy Administration, and Warranty Claims Preparation.

  **Senior Parts Specialist,** 1993-1996

  Filled parts requests from shop technicians, and coordinated rush orders, returns, and manufacturers' warranties. Supervised three Parts Specialists who worked with retail customers on Saturdays. As Parts Specialist, provided front-counter service to walk-in retail customers; received and checked shipments, stocked parts, and boxed and shipped returns to suppliers. (ASE-Certified Parts Specialist, 1995)

  **Automotive Technician,** 1990-1993

  ASE-Certified in Engine Performance (1993), Engine Repair (1993), Electrical/Electronic Systems (1992), Heating and Air Conditioning (1992), and Brakes (1992). Averaged 136 percent of flat-rate and maintained a .05 percent come-back rate.

Figure • 9-14: Insurance Adjuster, Automotive Repair Specialist Objective

## Summary of Information Emphasized on Figure 9-13 and Figure 9-14: Carey

Deane Carey has spent ten years in the automotive repair industry and has now decided he wants to change careers. The variety and challenge of working as an insurance adjuster in the automobile collision repair industry appeals to him because it requires all his technical, computer, and customer service skills.

Figure 9-13 illustrates Deane's former resume; Figure 9-14 shows the resume he will use to apply for a position as an insurance adjuster. Compare the sections of the two resumes to see how he has tailored the presentation of his qualifications for his new job objective.

1. **Objective**

   Notice how Deane has changed the wording in his new resume (Figure 9-14) to reflect clearly his new objective.

2. **Related Qualifications**

   Deane uses this section to capture the interest of employers and to convince them that he has what it takes to do the job successfully.

   To persuade employers quickly that he has the technical expertise needed to succeed as an insurance adjuster, Deane inserts his state license before his degree at the beginning of his resume. He also adds the appropriate industry-respected certifications to reinforce his technical qualifications and to assure employers that he is uniquely capable of protecting them from fraudulent claims.

   Notice how Deane supports his new job objective by highlighting different competencies. In Figure 9-13 (Service Manager), he had noted his supervisory, negotiation, communication, sales, and customer service skills. These are the capabilities successful service managers use to increase profits and to build repeat business. In his new resume, however, Figure 9-14 (Insurance Adjuster), Deane emphasizes the negotiation and customer service skills that prepare him to save the insurance company money while keeping customers and vendors happy.

   Deane still ends the Related Qualifications section with a list of his computer skills, but he adds additional job-related items. Placing this information in the Qualifications section emphasizes that employers can save training time and costs by hiring Deane.

3. **Experience**

   In this section, Deane reinforces the claims made in the Related Qualifications section by showing specific responsibilities and accomplishments in directly related job skills. He details where, when, and how he used the competencies and skills he stated. By the end of the resume, employers remember that Deane is well-qualified, well-experienced, and has a track record of productive accomplishments. Deane gets an interview!

DANIEL RYAN
1205 Koch Lane * Seattle, WA 98115
(206) 555-1010 * dryan@provider.net

OBJECTIVE

Computer Network Support Technician for multi-location network

KEYWORDS

AAS Degree. Peer-to-peer. UNIX operating system. UNIX command line utilities. TCP/IP LAN. WAN. Network utilities. AIRNET. Menu utilities. System backups. ANSI C fundamentals. V Standards. BBS remote log-in to network servers. TCPON remote monitoring. MS Word. Access. Excel. MS Explorer. Windows NT. NOVELL. UUCP. Enthusiastic. Team player. Excellent interpersonal skills.

EDUCATION

Associate of Science, Computer Network Support Technology, 2000
Seattle Technology College, Seattle, WA
Related Courses and Skills
* Peer-to-Peer Networking Structures
* TCP/IP LAN Transport System * UNIX/ANSI C
* Remote Computing * Network System Administration
* Networking Technologies * Technical Report Writing
* Interpersonal Communications

Technician Internship at TechnoNet, Inc. January-May 2000
Assisted technicians installing and reconfiguring multi-location, wireless, AIRNET (Adaptive Interferometric Radio Network Enhancement Technology) long-range data networks.

EXPERIENCE

**Seattle Technology College September 1998-May 2000
Computer Lab Technician, Part-time: Assisted faculty and students with hardware and software-related problems on IBM-compatible personal computers. Assembled, installed, and added PCs to the network throughout campus. Answered 95 percent of trouble calls within 90 minutes.

**ComputerStop SuperStore May 1998-Present
Installation and Repair Technician, Part-time: Assembled computers, added hardware and software upgrades, provided in-store and on-site repairs to computers and peripherals. Named "Employee of the Month" four times in 18 months.

ASSOCIATIONS

Tech CORPS, Volunteer, 1998-present
PC Users' Club, 1995-present

Figure • 9-15: Computer Network Support Technician Objective (electronic resume)

## Summary of Information Emphasized on Figure 9-15: Ryan

Daniel wants a job in a medium- or large-sized firm that has an extensive network. Many of the firms he would like to work for recruit IT (Information Technology) employees through Internet posting sites, so Daniel prepares a cyber-friendly, electronic resume. He pays particular attention to formatting:

a. Uses no word processing codes
b. Uses only standard characters available on his keyboard
c. Uses Courier font in 12-point
d. Use a 6.5-inch line length
e. Saves the resume as an ASCII file for easy transmission

1. **Objective** — Daniel has researched the job market and knows the types of positions open to people with his skills. He writes a concise, targeted job objective. Employers reviewing resumes quickly can immediately identify what jobs match his qualifications.

2. **Keywords** — Because Daniel knows that cyber-resumes are often sorted and selected by resume-searching programs, he puts a "Keyword" section at the top of his resume. Notice how he separates the keywords and phrases with periods. He wants any resume-search program to mark his resume for further evaluation, so he uses this section to describe his skills with industry-specific terms that will increase the number of "hits" on his resume.

3. **Education** — In addition to his degree, Daniel shows courses he has taken. Because the course names are long, he separates them with asterisks and spaces. The course listings also use industry terminology and add other opportunities for search programs to pull his resume.

   Daniel puts his internship experience in the Education section. His exposure to a networking configuration different from the traditional wired configuration is very important because it expands his capabilities in employers' eyes.

4. **Experience** — Daniel's experience is complementary to his job objective. Notice how he uses measurable accomplishments that are meaningful to employers. He knows that employers want to hire people who meet deadlines and who produce quality results.

5. **Associations** — Tech CORPS is made up of individuals and businesses that donate and/or install computers, software, and networks in schools and other educational institutions. Daniel's community service relates directly to his job target, shows his commitment to his community, and helps him keep current in his field.

# CAREER ACTION 9-4

## Critique Two Resumes

**DIRECTIONS:** Assume you're evaluating candidates for an entry-level job as a staff accountant for a major accounting firm.

You are to compare and evaluate two top applicants–John Griffin and Ralph Greenwood. Their qualifications are almost identical. One has documented his qualifications much more convincingly, however, than the other.

Read their resumes (Figures 9-16 and 9-17 on pages 157-158). Determine which resume is more effective. Evaluate every word carefully to determine exactly why one resume is considerably better than the other. Be thorough, keeping in mind that your resume will be scrutinized in this way during your job search.

Identify the strengths and weaknesses of each resume. Why is one better than the other?

After completing **Career Action 9-4**, apply the same critical eye to finalizing your own resume. It must be perfect to pass the critical inspection of those who will be evaluating it and comparing it with resumes of your competition.

SUCCESS TIP

**Prepare and evaluate your resume draft, make corrections by applying effective writing techniques, and develop a final, perfect resume.**

**Complete Career Action 9-5**

# CAREER ACTION 9-5

## Complete Your Paper Resume

**DIRECTIONS:** Use a word processor to prepare your final paper resume. If you hire an expert to prepare your resume, be sure also to request an electronic file of your resume so you will have the file for future revisions or updates.

Proofread and edit the content until it's perfect.

**REMEMBER:** Your resume must be perfect! There is no room for error in keying, grammar, or punctuation. Get help from someone who has exceptional editing and grammar skills.

Career Database Appropriate

**JOHN R. GRIFFIN**

2440 Windom Way, Apt. 34 | Los Angeles, CA 90063 | (213) 555-4668

---

**OBJECTIVE**

Entry-level Staff Accountant

**KEY QUALIFICATIONS**

- Experienced in invoicing, accounts receivable and payable, general ledger, inventory control
- Self-starter, team player, goal-oriented, willing to travel
- Attention to detail, accuracy, and deadlines
- Strong communication, problem-solving, and customer service skills
- Proficient in Word, Excel, Access, Windows, Quickbooks Pro
- Worked with PC network in client-server environment

**EDUCATION**

**Bachelor of Business Administration, Accounting, 2000**
University of Los Angeles GPA 3.5

**Relevant courses of study:**

- Analysis and Design of Accounting Information Systems
- Information Systems Auditing • Managerial Accounting
- Cost Accounting • Tax Accounting • Financial Accounting
- Intermediate Accounting I, II, III • Commercial Law

**Senior Internship, Project Leader:**
Coordinated student team analyzing inventory system of a small trailer-manufacturing company. The recommended just-in-time ordering and improved parts control systems reduced yearly carrying costs by 55 percent.

**EXPERIENCE**

**O'Keefe and Associates, Los Angeles** **9/98 to Present**
**Part-time Bookkeeper:** Use Quickbooks Pro to invoice clients, post income and expenses, process accounts payable, reconcile general ledger accounts, and prepare monthly balance sheets and P&L statements. Update expense-tracking spreadsheets for each client. Reconcile monthly bank statement. Initiated shorter invoicing cycle and introduced discounts for prompt invoice payment; reduced A/R cycle to 35 days.

**Rand and Company, Los Angeles** **6/96 - 8/98**
**Part-time Retail Sales Clerk:** Sold 175 percent of quota. Awarded "1997 Outstanding Employee/Customer Relations" certificate.

**RELATED ACTIVITIES**

Vice President, Beta Alpha Psi Accounting, 2000
Member, Information Science Association, 1997-Present
Member, Debate Team, 1996-1997

Figure • 9-16: Staff Accountant, Audit Division, Public Accounting Firm Objective

Ralph Greenwood
6780 Greenbriar Street
Los Angeles, CA 90067

***Education:***

University of Los Angeles, Los Angeles, CA
B.B.A., Accounting, June 2000
Grade Point Average: 3.5

***Major Courses of Study:***

Commercial Law, Cost Accounting, Economics, Principles/Management, Auditing, Statistical Techniques, Programming Systems, Principles/Finance, Managerial Accounting, Systems Analysis & Design, and Intermediate Accounting I, II, III

***Experience:***

January to May 1998
Department of Accounting, University of Los Angeles: Senior Internship Coordinator of student team that analyzed inventory system of a small retail store. Recommendations to adopt just-in-time ordering and improved stock control saved company a significant amount of time and money.

1998-Present
Westworth and Company, Los Angeles. Part-time Bookkeeper. Responsibilities include: invoicing customers, posting income and expenses, handling accounts receivable and payable; preparing income statements and balance sheets, operating PC computer in client-server network with Microsoft software and Quickbooks Pro; reconciling bank statements; and updating client expense-tracking spreadsheets. Shortened time needed to invoice clients and to receive payments.

1996-1998
Tueller's Men's Shop, Los Angeles. Part-time sales. Duties included: making retail sales; maintaining merchandise displays; assisting with inventory; assisting with cashing out; and maintaining orderly stockroom.

June 1994-February 1996
Woodland General Nursery, Los Angeles. Stock maintenance staff. Duties included: unloading new merchandise; arranging merchandise in assigned locations; maintaining orderly and clean grounds; carrying and loading purchases for customers; dispensing with disposable containers and other waste. Assisting with watering, feeding, spraying, and general care of nursery items.

***Other Activities:***

*Beta Alpha Psi*—Accounting, officer; Member, *University of Los Angeles Student Center*—1998-1999; *University of Los Angeles Swim Team*, member, 1996-1997.
Hobbies: Swimming, reading, computers, piano, travel.

***Reference:***

*University of Los Angeles Career/Placement Center*, 1300 J Street, Los Angeles, CA 90063

Figure • 9-17: Staff Accountant, Audit Division, Public Accounting Firm Objective

**Evaluate Your Resume.** Once you have edited your resume, proceed to the most critical step: evaluation. Careful proofreading and evaluation of your resume is absolutely essential.

Recruit help from one or two objective members of your support system who have good writing and proofreading skills. Ask these people to review and critique your resume carefully. This assistance is vital to developing your successful resume.

## DISTRIBUTING YOUR RESUME

After developing your resume professionally, you'll want to distribute it effectively. Give your general resume to your job search network members. It will give them the basic information they need to help you find prospective employers.

### Customizing Your Resume

Tailor your resume for individual employers by using terminology and descriptions that address the needs stated in their notices and advertisements of job openings. Also customize your resume for employers who specifically request your resume. Follow the employer's instructions for the method of delivery: standard or overnight mail, facsimile or electronic transmission, or hand delivery.

### If You Are Asked to Send Your Resume via E-Mail

Some employers request that traditional or scannable resumes be sent as e-mail attachments so they can print and provide an attractive hard copy for appropriate hiring personnel. If you are requested to do this, ask what word processing software and operating system (Windows or Mac, for example) is preferred.

### DO NOT RELY ON YOUR RESUME ALONE TO GET INTERVIEWS!

It's a big mistake to send out several copies of your resume and then wait for the telephone to ring. Two to three days after sending your resume, follow up with a call to make sure your resume was received. Your call reminds the receiver about you and increases your name recognition.

Figure • 9-18: Don't expect your resume to do all the work. **Always call** an employer several days after you send in your resume. Remember, be positive and professional. Every contact counts!

Follow their requirements exactly to ensure that the receiver downloads your resume in a readable form. To ensure that employers can read your resume, state in your e-mail message the word processing software and operating system you have used.

## CONVERTING YOUR TRADITIONAL RESUME TO A CYBER-RESUME

Some employers request that candidates submit electronic or "cyber-resumes." Key differences distinguish cyber-resumes and paper resumes.

### ASCII Text Format

Cyber-resumes are relatively plain and unattractive because they must be ASCII (also called **.txt**, Text Only, or DOS text) documents stripped of all word processing codes to transmit correctly from an e-mail program or Internet Web site into an employer's resume tracking software.

### Keyword Emphasis

Although a keyword section may be optional in a more traditional resume, a keyword section must be included in a cyber-resume because cyber-resumes are electronically searched for keywords. The goal of the cyber-resume is to generate the largest possible number of keyword hits from the automated search software.

Therefore, you should add keywords and synonyms to your traditional resume. Keyword choices are critical. To help you identify the keywords for your job objective, review the information about keywords under the heading "Step Four: Fine-Tune Each Section of Your Resume." See pages 129-132.

**Use appropriate keywords in cyber-resumes.**

**Complete Career Action 9-6**

## CAREER ACTION 9-6

### Identify Appropriate Keywords

**DIRECTIONS:** Review your final paper resume carefully. Circle terms you could appropriately use in the keyword section of your cyber-resume. Then make a complete list of keywords (industry terms, acronyms, terms that describe job positions, experience, education skills, etc.) and synonyms you can use to strengthen a cyber-resume.

**Career Database Appropriate**

## SPECIAL TIPS FOR CYBER-RESUMES

**As you prepare your cyber-resume, keep these tips in mind:**

1. **Use standard section headings.** Use standard headings like those in a traditional paper resume; for example, Objectives, Keywords, Experience, Education, Qualifications, and Honors. (See the example in Figure 9-15 on page 154.)

2. **Include a keyword section.** In your keyword section, summarize your most relevant qualifications by using nouns tailored to the employer's needs.

3. **Use specific terms.** Use specific words, not vague descriptions.

4. **Use specialized terms.** Use industry-specific appropriate acronyms and buzzwords. Be sure to spell the acronyms correctly (search software will not generate positive hits on your resume if the terms aren't correct).

5. **Emphasize nouns.** Include noun forms of industry-specific terms and nouns that describe strong interpersonal skills, such as *team player* and *self-starter.* Search software frequently looks for noun forms.

6. **Practice transmitting.** Send your electronic cyber-resume and cover letter or e-mail introduction to a friend and to yourself to see how well the documents survive the cyberspace transfer before you actually send them to an employer.

7. **Back up your files.** Using a new filename, save your resume in ASCII format to a disk so that you have a backup you can use to customize your cyber-resume for specific employers.

8. **Preserve confidentiality.** When posting your resume to the Internet, it is important to retain your own confidentiality; include only your e-mail address, not your home address or telephone number.

9. **Keep up to date on electronic resume technology.** Technology changes quickly; keep your knowledge of scanning technology and cyber-resume preparation current by reviewing employer preferences, taking additional technical training, and checking out the Internet resources listed in this chapter.

**NOTE:** Contact the potential employer to find out if you should fax or mail a scannable resume as a backup to your cyber-resume. Find out who should receive this hard copy, and address your cover letter to that individual. Sending a backup resume creates an opportunity to sell your qualifications in a visually appealing format.

## Cyber-Resume Formatting and Transmission Guidelines

Get the edge on your competition by formatting your electronic cyber-resume correctly. Demonstrate superior knowledge and preparation by using correct formatting that eliminates the possibility of employers receiving documents with wildly erratic line lengths and unreadable garbage. Follow the instructions below to be sure your resume meets the employer's electronic expectations.

The instructions assume that your traditional paper resume was created with word processing software.

Figure • 9-19: You may be asked to submit your resume electronically. Read this section carefully to learn how to prepare and transmit an effective cyber-resume.

1. **Follow employer directions.** Obtain and read all employer instructions for creating and sending your electronic resume. If the instructions are incomplete or vague, send an e-mail message or call to request clarification.

2. **Open the file containing your traditional or scannable resume.** While in your word processor:

   a. Change the text to Courier 12-point font so you can see how your resume will look to the receiver. The default font for electronic transmission is Courier because e-mail programs can always translate Courier easily.

   b. Eliminate multiple columns.

   c. Change line lengths to 6.5 inches. If your line lengths are longer, the receiver may see uneven, confusing line lengths. Enter two hard returns between paragraphs.

   d. Using the search and replace function, search for all tabs and replace them with the appropriate number of spaces to achieve desired format clarity.

   e. Check the grammar and spelling of your resume content.

   f. Replace bullets with asterisks.

   g. **Eliminate special characters,** such as the copyright symbol, ampersands (&), and mathematical symbols.

   h. Use the "save as" command to give this document a **new name** and to save it as "text only with line breaks," or as a **.txt**, or an **ASCII.txt** file.

   i. Close the file, and exit the word processing program. (This step removes most remaining word processing codes.)

3. **Open the document in your standard text-editing program**, such as Windows Notepad **(not in your word processing program)**. Using this standard text-editing program creates the cleanest possible ASCII file—the key to a professional electronic image.

   a. Make sure your name is on the first line with no other text (otherwise, resume-search programs will be confused; they look only for a name on this line.)

   b. Start most lines at the left margin**.** Centered text (even if centered by using the space bar) does not always transmit cleanly.

   c. Enter headings in uppercase. **Do not use uppercase throughout the document**; uppercase is hard to read.

   d. If you list more than one telephone number, be sure to place each telephone number on a separate line and label each, such as "home phone," "work phone," or "message phone."

   e. Consider length. Because of the addition of keywords and the need to keep all text at the left margin and to use a line length of no more than 6.5 inches, your cyber-resume may become two or three pages long in your text editor program. Don't worry about keeping your e-mail resume to one page in this standard text-editing program; however, try to limit the document to two pages.

   f. Save your resume again as a **.txt** or **ASCII.txt** document. Leave the file open.

**Format cyber-resumes carefully to ensure clear transmission to and receipt by employers.**

4. **Select all (highlight) the text in this document, then copy and paste it into your e-mail message window.** Or paste the text into the resume field at employer or recruitment Web sites (such as Career-Mosaic, Career Path, and Monster.com).

5. While in your e-mail window, prepare your e-mail message to the receiver. Never send a resume without a short introduction or a cover letter.

6. In the subject line of the e-mail, include the job title and/or reference number of the position for which you are applying.

7. To insert a cover letter written in your word processor: First, create an electronic cover letter (see Chapter 10). Then, in your e-mail message window containing your cyber-resume, place your cursor above your cyber-resume and paste a copy of the electronic cover letter into your e-mail message. Or, you could key in a brief message at the beginning of your e-mail message that states you are submitting your resume. Be sure your message or cover letter is error-free.

8. Key a line of asterisks or equal signs between your cover letter or message and your resume. This marks where your cover message ends and your resume begins.

Review the sample cyber-resume (Figure 9-15 on page 154) to see how these resume guidelines are applied.

## Posting Cyber-Resumes Correctly

Follow the guidelines below for posting cyber-resumes to the Internet through the Web site of an employer or a recruitment company:

1. Follow the Web site instructions exactly.

2. If the Web site provides an open block for your resume, highlight and copy your cyber-resume and paste it into the block.

3. If the Web site provides a fill-in-the-blanks, online resume form, copy and paste appropriate sections of your cyber-resume into the form. You may need to key in new text, which must be proofread carefully before sending.

**Complete Career Action 9-7**

## CAREER ACTION 9-7

### Create and Post Your Cyber-Resume

**DIRECTIONS FOR PART 1:** Following the formatting guidelines presented, convert the resume you created in **Career Action 9-6** to a cyber-resume. Be sure to give it a different name so that you will still have the original file for your paper resume.

**DIRECTIONS FOR PART 2:** In *WebGuide*, select "Your Job Search." Go to Activity 3 "Prepare an Online Resume." Choose one or more resume-posting Web sites (Monster.com, Career Mosaic, ResumeCM, Creative Job Search) and review the instructions for creating an online, fill-in-the-blanks form for posting your cyber-resume into a Web site block. If possible, practice filling in a cyber-resume form or posting your cyber-resume. Print your findings, and bring examples to share with your class.

If you do not have *WebGuide*, access Monster.com, Career Mosaic, or another site of your choice and complete the actions noted above. Refer to "Internet Resources for Resume Information" on the next page for several suggested Web sites and addresses.

**Career Database Appropriate**

**SUCCESS TIP**

**Use the Internet to locate current resume preparation tips and as a means for delivering your cyber-resume.**

## SPECIAL RESUME REMINDERS

To ensure your resume gets the best possible results, follow these reminders:

**Be Honest.** An untrue statement could eliminate you from further consideration for a job. Employers pass such information on. Never volunteer negative information about yourself, however. If you were fired from a job, don't list this on your resume. Discuss this during an interview, if necessary.

**Omit any references to salary.** Salary should not be discussed until after you have had adequate opportunity to discuss your qualifications during the interview. Presenting salary expectations in your resume weakens your negotiating position. If employers require your salary expectation, use broad numbers; for example, "the mid-thirty thousands."

Figure • 9-20: Employers always scan keyword sections of resumes carefully—prepare yours well.

## INTERNET RESOURCES FOR RESUME INFORMATION

| WEB SITE NAME | INTERNET ADDRESS |
| --- | --- |
| America's Job Bank | http://www.ajb.dni.us |
| Career Mosaic | http://www.careermosaic.com |
| CareerPath | http://www.careerpath.com |
| eResumes & Resources | http://www.eresumes.com |
| Monster.com | http://www.monster.com |
| Archeus Resume Writing Resources | http://www.golden.net/~archeus/reswri.htm |
| Virtual Job Fair | http://www.virtualjobfair.com |
| JobStar | http://www.jobstar.org |

**NOTE:** Also review individual employer Web sites for their instructions regarding resume preparation and submission.

## CHECKLIST FOR PREPARING A WINNING RESUME

Check each of the following actions you are currently taking to increase your career success:

- ☐ Write a clear, appropriate job objective to focus your entire resume.
- ☐ Tailor your resume to support your objective effectively.
- ☐ Choose the most appropriate format for your resume to best support your objective.
- ☐ Use numbers and action verbs to describe accomplishments.
- ☐ Tailor your resume to meet the needs of the employer. Match your resume to the job description: Use specific terms and industry terminology.
- ☐ Prepare and evaluate your resume draft; make corrections by applying effective writing techniques; and develop a final, perfect resume.
- ☐ Use appropriate keywords in cyber-resumes.
- ☐ Format cyber-resumes carefully to ensure clear transmission to and receipt by the employer.
- ☐ Use the Internet to locate current resume preparation tips and to deliver your cyber-resume.

## CRITICAL THINKING QUESTIONS

1. When should an applicant use separate objectives or resumes?
2. In what order should you present your resume data to best support your own job objective?
3. Why is it effective to list a job objective followed immediately by a listing of related capabilities?
4. How is the cyber-resume transmitted to employers?

# CAREER ACTION 9-2

## Resume Outline

**Your Name:** ______________________________

**Your Address:** ______________________________

______________________________

**Your E-Mail Address:** ______________________________

**Telephone Number:** ______________________________

**Pager/Message Number:** ______________________________

**Fax Number:** ______________________________

**POSITION OBJECTIVE:** *(Refer to the sample job descriptions you were instructed to collect earlier.)*

______________________________

______________________________

______________________________

______________________________

**RELATED CAPABILITIES:** *(Use terms and keywords related to your target job to describe your capabilities and accomplishments.)*

______________________________

______________________________

______________________________

______________________________

______________________________

______________________________

______________________________

______________________________

CONTINUED ON NEXT PAGE

# CAREER ACTION 9-2

(CONTINUED)

**WORK EXPERIENCE:** *(Emphasize accomplishments stated in measurable terms, if possible. Start with the most recent job first, listing each job in reverse chronological order, ending with the earliest experience.)*

**Dates Employed: From** ____________________ **To** ____________________

**Company Name:** ______________________________________________

**City** ______________________________ **State** ________ **ZIP Code** ______________

**Job Title & Description:** ______________________________________

______________________________________________________________

______________________________________________________________

**Dates Employed: From** ____________________ **To** ____________________

**Company Name:** ______________________________________________

**City** ______________________________ **State** ________ **ZIP Code** ______________

**Job Title & Description:** ______________________________________

______________________________________________________________

______________________________________________________________

**Dates Employed: From** ____________________ **To** ____________________

**Company Name:** ______________________________________________

**City** ______________________________ **State** ________ **ZIP Code** ______________

**Job Title & Description:** ______________________________________

______________________________________________________________

______________________________________________________________



CONTINUED ON NEXT PAGE

# CAREER ACTION 9-2

(CONTINUED)

**EDUCATION:** *(List in reverse chronological order, most recent first, if you have attended more than one school. Do not list high school if you have higher-level schooling unless the high school is considered highly prestigious.)*

| Name of School | City, State | Degree(s)/Certificate(s) | Years Attended |
|---|---|---|---|
| | | | |
| | | | |
| | | | |

*(For students with little or no work experience, expand the educational section.)*

Major(s): ______________________________

Minor(s): ______________________________

GPA: ______________________________

Relevant Courses of Study: ______________________________

______________________________

**SCHOOL-RELATED ACTIVITIES:** *(Organizations, clubs, tutorial experience, honor groups, internships, leadership, etc.)*

______________________________

______________________________

______________________________

**OTHER RELATED ACTIVITIES/EXPERIENCE:** *(Internships, volunteer work, membership or leadership in professional or trade associations, community organizations, social organizations, service clubs, etc. List the name of the program or organization, a brief summary of your experience, accomplishments, activities, and the dates involved.)*

______________________________

______________________________

______________________________

CONTINUED ON NEXT PAGE

# CAREER ACTION 9-2

(CONTINUED)

**MILITARY SERVICE:** *(If applicable, list the branch of service, your highest rank, training received, areas of specialization, major duties, skills and knowledge developed, and location of service.)*

______________________________________________

______________________________________________

**INTERESTS:** *(List interests that are related to your job target and that demonstrate well-rounded abilities, including interaction with people, manual dexterity, intellectual pursuits, artistic ability, physical fitness, strength, continuing education, and personal/professional development.)*

______________________________________________

______________________________________________

**REFERENCES:** *(List your references here. Also have them prepared and available should a prospective employer request them.)*

**Name and Title:** ______________________________

**Company Name and Address:** ______________________________

______________________________________________

**Telephone:** ______________________________

**Name and Title:** ______________________________

**Company Name and Address:** ______________________________

______________________________________________

**Telephone:** ______________________________

**Name and Title:** ______________________________

**Company Name and Address:** ______________________________

______________________________________________

**Telephone:** ______________________________

CHAPTER 10

# Perfect the Application and Cover Letter

> "Through their resumes and cover letters, applicants should project the qualities of focus on total customer satisfaction, quality, and neatness, which are essential in the luxury hospitality industry. Employees are hired based on a selection process to ensure each person's philosophies are in line with those of The Ritz-Carlton."

*Anand Rao*
*Corporate Director of Organizational Development*
*The Ritz-Carlton Hotel Company, L.L.C.*

## *In this chapter you will:*

- Discuss and practice effectively completing an application for employment.

Use the Internet to search for additional cover letter strategies that may be useful to you.

- Write an effective cover letter that includes a request for an interview.

You will be screened into or out of an interview (and the job) on the basis of your job search paper package: resume, cover letter, and employment application. If you carefully completed the activities for Chapter 9, your resume should be top-notch. In this chapter, we present tips and activities for preparing winning employment applications and cover letters. Remember: The qualified job applicant who does only an average job of preparing these documents will be screened out; applicants with equal qualifications who prepare these documents well remain in the running for the job. Chapter 10 explains exactly how you can stay in the running by completing the application correctly, writing a results-oriented cover letter, and using the Internet to search for additional, useful tips in these areas.

# PREPARING THE EMPLOYMENT APPLICATION

In this section, you will learn how to complete an employment application correctly and professionally. This will help ensure that your application is not eliminated in the screening process so you can remain a viable job candidate.

## How Important Is It?

Many job applicants greatly underestimate the importance of the employment application. Employers use the application to obtain standard information from all applicants. Many job seekers think of the application as something to get through quickly so they can get on with the interview. Wrong! This idea can be fatal to your job search. Employers consider application forms, cover letters, and resumes carefully to select interviewees and to weed out people who don't look qualified on paper.

SUCCESS TIP

**Follow the instructions on the application exactly, and make your application perfect; it's a primary screening tool.**

## Application Forms Vary

Employers design their application forms to obtain the information they consider most pertinent to making hiring decisions—information that applicants might omit from cover letters or resumes. By obtaining the same information from all applicants, employers can more easily compare all of their backgrounds and qualifications. While the cover letter and resume expand on applicants' qualifications and either improve or lessen their chances of getting interviews, the application is one main tool for screening candidates.

Many employers computerize applicant information, scanning applications and filing the information electronically. Some have applicants fill out computerized applications. They retrieve applications on the basis of specified categories of information (job objective, educational background, specialized skills, work experience, etc.). Employers use these categories of information to compare applicants. If you omit important information, your application may be passed over. This brings us to one of the most important requirements in preparing an employment application: **Follow the instructions exactly!**

Both the length and complexity of application forms vary greatly. Some are relatively simple; others are lengthy. Often, technical jobs require comprehensive application information.

Some organizations use long, complex applications with questions requiring detailed information. These are designed to test applicants' *endurance* (a desirable employee trait). Additionally, some organizations include questions that require applicants to summarize their philosophies of the job or occupational field, thus testing the knowledge and personal values of the applicants.

As you prepare applications for employment, treat every question seriously and completely. Even if an application is long, maintain high quality in all your answers. Those who don't are the first to be eliminated in this screening process. If the application is extremely long, complete it at home, taking two or three days to work out the best possible answers.

## Get an Application Ahead of Time

Whenever possible, don't fill out the application in the employer's office. Why? Because you need to practice fitting your answers into the spaces provided on the form. (Often, space is limited, and you have to abbreviate information.) You also need time to word your answers well. Employers judge applications heavily on neatness, completeness, and accuracy, as well as on the quality of the answers. It usually takes more than one try to achieve the wording and effect you want.

Figure • 10-1: Visit a company you are interested in, and ask for a job application form. Take it home to study and complete.

## TIPS FOR COMPLETING A WINNING APPLICATION:

1. Read and follow the directions. Prepare each section slowly and carefully.
2. Make your application neat, with legible handwriting or correct data entry—no smudges or rumpled edges.
3. Use the correct lines or spaces for your answers.
4. Practice on a copy of the application, squeeze in as much positive information about yourself as possible, and abbreviate to fit information in the spaces provided.
5. Answer every question. Use N/A (not applicable) if the question does not pertain to you. This shows that you did not overlook the question or skip it purposely.
6. Use perfect spelling, grammar, and punctuation. Use specialized terminology correctly. (You never get a second chance to make a good first impression!)
7. Include a second telephone number of a person who is readily available and willing to take messages for you. You can't afford to miss calls from employers!
8. Make certain all information is accurate (dates, addresses, telephone and fax numbers, names—*everything*).
9. Be honest. Employers check the facts and immediately eliminate any candidate who has supplied false information.
10. Date and sign the application. Some organizations invalidate an application if it is not signed and dated!

**Copy the Application, and Use It as a Draft.** Get the application ahead of time, take it home or have the employer mail one to you, make a copy of the original, and use the copy as a working draft. If you can't get an application ahead of time, get one from a competitor or closely related organization and practice filling it out. Then, you can use it as a guide if you are required to fill one out in your target employer's office. Always get an application ahead of time to practice and perfect the information.

**Read the Directions First!** By reading through the entire application, from the first to the last question, you can see how requests for information may be interrelated, which helps you determine which questions require more or less detailed answers. You will also avoid duplicating information, ensure that you write information in the right places, and learn what other information you might need before completing the application.

As you read your practice copy, use a colored pen to mark all special directions so you don't overlook or misunderstand any of these while completing your application.

If you don't fully understand a portion of the application or if you do not know exactly what type of information the employer is seeking, call and ask. Following directions is important to employers, so be sure to demonstrate this quality when you apply for a job.

## Complete Each Section of the Application Carefully

Suggestions for effectively completing the major parts of a typical application are presented in this section.

**Personal Information.** As you fill out your application, read all instructions carefully. Look at the first part of the sample application shown in Figure 10-2, and notice the following:

- The last name is to be listed first, followed by the first name, and then the middle name or initial. Most applications are designed this way. Don't make a bad first impression (immediately demonstrating that you can't follow directions) by listing your name in the wrong order.

**ABC Company** — **Application for Employment**

**PERSONAL**

| NAME (Last) | (First) | (Middle) | Social Security Number | |
|---|---|---|---|---|
| Marzinelli | Evelyn | Sue | 606-00-0088 | |
| PERMANENT ADDRESS (Street) | (City) | (State) (ZIP) | How Long? | Telephone No. |
| 6518 Willow Way | Boise, ID | 83706 | 2 years | 208-555-1170 |
| List relatives now employed by ABC Company | | | | Message Phone |
| None | | | | 208-555-7677 |
| Have you previously... | ☐ applied to OR ☐ been employed by ABC Company? | Where and when? | N/A | |

Figure • 10-2: Personal Information Section.

- This application only asks for a permanent address. Some applications call first for a current address and then a permanent address. If your application calls for both, as a courtesy, you should repeat your current address under the permanent address section, rather than leave it blank or write "same as above."

- The applicant listed a second telephone number where messages can be received. (Good! If you are out pounding the pavement for a job, you can still get the call for an interview this way.)

- The applicant put N/A (not applicable) next to the request to list the names of any relatives employed by the organization, indicating no relatives work for that organization.

- Because the applicant had never applied to or been employed by the company, neither box was checked in the last portion of the personal segment of the application. Then, the applicant wrote N/A in the box labeled "Where and when?"

**NOTE:** As an alternative to using N/A for questions that do not apply, type or use a black ink ballpoint pen and a ruler to draw a line through the response area.

**Position Objective.** Figure 10-3 shows the position objective section of a job application form. Note the following tips for filling out this section:

## Your Application Can Screen You In or Out

Do a top-notch job of preparing your application. The application is a primary applicant-screening tool.

- Be sure to list a *definite position objective.* Employers are not impressed with applications that list "anything" as the position desired. (It hints of desperation or lack of confidence in your job qualifications and may also project a lack of focus or direction.)

- Since salary is such an influential factor in employment, we recommend using "negotiable" as the reply to the question of salary desired. Don't risk eliminating yourself before you have a chance to present your qualifications in the interview. Save discussion of salary until the employer has expressed a definite interest in you. (Besides, the employer could have more money in mind than you say you will require. Why lose such an advantage up front?)

**NOTE:** If the position has been advertised at a set and nonnegotiable salary, list that figure in the "Salary Desired" response area.

| POSITION | | |
|---|---|---|
| Position Desired<br>Sales Supervisor | | Salary Desired (per month)<br>Negotiable |
| Willing to relocate? ☑ Yes ☐ No | Do you want ☑ Full-time ☐ Part-time | Date Available for Work<br>Immediately |

Figure • 10-3: Position Information Section.

Your circumstances and preferences will determine answers to the remaining position questions.

**Education.** Your education will be covered in a section of the application blank such as that in Figure 10-4. Remember the following points when filling out this section:

- This sample lists one high school and one community college. If you have attended more than one high school, just list the most recent one and indicate the year you received your diploma. List your GPA if it is called for. If you have attended more than one college or other post-secondary school or institute, list the most recent one first and work back to the first one attended. If necessary, attach a separate, typed list of additional schools you have attended.

- If space is provided to list subjects of study, research, or other activities, list examples of your well-rounded capabilities and activities related to your job objective.

| EDUCATION | | | | |
|---|---|---|---|---|
| Schools | Name and Location of School | Degree, Certificate, or Diploma | Year Received | Major |
| High School | Idaho Falls High School<br>Idaho Falls, ID 83402 | Diploma | 1998 | ------ |
| College | Central Community College<br>Boise, ID 83704 | A. A. | 2000 | Marketing |
| Business, Technical, Other | -------------- | ------ | ---- | ------ |

Figure • 10-4: Education Information Section.

**Employment History.** The employment history (or work experience) section of our sample application is shown in Figure 10-5. The entries are explained below.

- If your application provides enough space, do as was advised for the resume: Use action verbs, and describe accomplishments in results-oriented terms.

- Even if you have been fired before, never list the reason for leaving as "fired." A better choice is "laid off." Because organizational downsizing is common, this terminology can get you into an interview.

**References.** Whenever possible, tie your references directly to your work experience. Most prospective employers value good references from former reputable employers because former employers know firsthand how you performed at work. Notice in Figure 10-6 how the first two references are tied to the employment history shown in Figure 10-5 on page 177.

**NOTE:** Some applications specify that your references be people other than former employers or supervisors. In this case, you should not list them! This is an example of why it is so important to read every word of the application carefully.

## EMPLOYMENT HISTORY

| Most Recent Employer | From (Mo./Yr.) / To (Mo./Yr.) | Supervisor | Salary |
|---|---|---|---|
| Kevington's Emporium | 12/8/98 – present | Pat Swenson | 7.00/hr. |

| | Describe Major Duties/Accomplishments |
|---|---|
| **Employer's Address:** 3315 Front Street, Boise ID 83705 | Train and supervise sales staff of six. |
| **Telephone:** (208) 555-7624 | Achieved highest sales award last three months. |
| **Your Job Title:** Assistant Sales Supervisor | Promoted to supervisor after only six months. |
| **Reason for Leaving:** still employed | |

| Employer | From (Mo./Yr.) / To (Mo./Yr.) | Supervisor | Salary |
|---|---|---|---|
| Crown Sportswear | 6/1/98 – 11/30/98 | Connie Pratt | 5.75/hr. |

| | Describe Major Duties/Accomplishments |
|---|---|
| **Employer's Address:** 1800 Orchard Street, Boise ID 83704 | Customer sales and preparation of all merchandise displays. |
| **Telephone:** (208) 555-8224 | In charge of closing three nights per week. |
| **Your Job Title:** Sales Clerk | |
| **Reason for Leaving:** took new job | |

| Employer | From (Mo./Yr.) / To (Mo./Yr.) | Supervisor | Salary |
|---|---|---|---|
| Value Market Variety | 12/1/96 – 5/5/98 | Trevia Levitt | 5.15/hr. |

| | Describe Major Duties/Accomplishments |
|---|---|
| **Employer's Address:** 460 Park Way, Idaho Falls, ID 83402 | Customer sales. |
| **Telephone:** (208) 555-5770 | Stocked inventory. |
| **Your Job Title:** Sales Clerk | Selected "Employee of the Month" twice in one year. |
| **Reason for Leaving:** moved to college location | |

Figure • 10-5: Employment History Section.

## REFERENCES

| Name | Address | Telephone | Occupation | Years Known |
|---|---|---|---|---|
| Pat Swenson (Kevington's Emporium) | 3315 Front Street Boise, ID 83705 | (208) 555-7624 | Sales Manager | 2 |
| Trevia Levitt | 460 Park Way Idaho Falls, ID 83402 | (208) 555-5770 | Supervisor | 4 |
| Dr. Robert Cornwell | Business Dept. Central Community College Boise, ID 83704 | (208) 555-2821 | Professor Marketing and Sales | 2 |

Figure • 10-6: References Section.

| By my signature below, I certify that all answers on this application are true and complete to the best of my knowledge. I understand if my answers are found to be untruthful, my application may be rejected or my employment terminated. | |
|---|---|
| Date<br>June 4, 2000 | Signature<br>Evelyn S. Marzinelli |

Figure • 10-7: Applicant Statement.

**Applicant Statement.** As shown in Figure 10-7, be sure to date and sign your application. (Be careful to list the correct year. It is a common error and could affect the time your application is retained in an active file.)

**REMEMBER:** Some employers do not consider the application valid unless it is signed.

**Request to Contact Your Current Employer.** If your application asks for permission to contact your current employer, answer *yes* only if your current employer is aware of your job search and approves; otherwise, protect your current job with a reply of *no.*

"The only place where success comes before work is in a dictionary."

—Vidal Sassoon

**If You Must Complete the Application on the Premises.** If you must complete the application on the employer's premises, take:

- Your completed sample application to be used as a guide.
- Two or three black ink pens.
- Your Social Security card, driver's license, proof of citizenship, certificates, union card, grade transcripts, or related items pertinent to your occupational field. (Use these to verify the accuracy of data you must record from them.)
- Your resume. You can use it as a reference for details.
- A pocket dictionary and a calculator.

**Check Your Work.** Once you have completed your application, always check it thoroughly for errors, neatness, completeness, and quality of answers. Be sure you can answer *yes* to each of the following questions:

**Application Checklist**

- ☑ Did you follow all directions?
- ☑ Did you handwrite in black ink or key information correctly? (Black ink copies best.) Or did you use a computerized application form and then print and check the final results carefully before submitting your application?
- ☑ Did you answer all questions?
- ☑ Is your application perfectly free from errors (typing, spelling, grammar, punctuation)?
- ☑ Did you use complete and accurate addresses in the references section?

- ☑ Is the content of every answer correct and well phrased?
- ☑ Does the application look attractive (neat and clean, no smudges or wrinkles; is printing or typing pleasing to the eye)?
- ☑ Did you sign and date your application?

## When to Submit Your Application

The best time to submit your employment application depends on (a) the status of job openings with your prospective employer(s), (b) whether or not they will give you applications, and (c) their preferences. Once again, your research on the industry and prospective employers is essential.

Resources for obtaining this information include current employees of the firm, the human resources department of the firm, knowledgeable experts in the field who can advise you, the area chamber of commerce, and your school career services staff.

Unless your research indicates that the employer does not want candidates to submit unsolicited applications, obtain an application and submit it along with your resume and cover letter. This demonstrates more initiative than applicants who don't bother to do this. Note, however, that some employers consider unsolicited submission of an application to be too "pushy." Do your research.

Figure • 10-8: Remember, the job application is yet another screening device you need to pass on your way to getting an interview and a job.

**Complete Career Action 10-1**

# CAREER ACTION 10-1

## Complete Your Own Actual Application or a Sample Application

**DIRECTIONS:** Using the guidelines presented in this chapter, complete your own application for employment. If at all possible, obtain and use an actual application from an employer in your job target industry—even one from your actual target employer. Using one from your job target industry provides the best preparation and practice. Complete the application for practice and for use as a model when you fill out your actual applications for employment.

## JUMP-STARTING YOUR COVER LETTER

Your cover letter introduces you to prospective employers. It must be well written, designed to get the reader's attention and interest, and able to convince the reader to interview you and consider you for employment. Review the section on using good writing style and organization in Chapter 9; these techniques also apply to writing a good cover letter.

Most employers expect a cover letter because it demonstrates the type of professionalism and initiative they want in an employee. Sending or taking your resume to employers without a cover letter could cost you further employer consideration.

Always tailor the content of your letter to fit each employer. In addition, vary the content somewhat, depending on which of the following three situations is applicable:

1. **Responding to an advertised opening for a specific job.** Figure 10-10 on page 186 is an example of a cover letter responding to an advertised opening.

2. **Contacting someone whom a member of your job search network has suggested (a networking cover letter).** See the example in Figure 10-11 on page 187.

3. **Writing to a potential employer who has not advertised a position opening.** See the example in Figure 10-12 on page 188.

The following guidelines explain how you can develop a strong, persuasive cover letter.

## EMPHASIZE WHAT YOU CAN DO FOR THE EMPLOYER

Your cover letter should stress how you can meet the employer's needs. It should be like a business proposal showcasing the value you can offer, not just a petition for an interview.

### Tailoring Your Letter

Applicants whose cover letters are not tailored to meet the employer's needs are often eliminated. Tailor every cover letter; refer to your employer and industry research. This is easy to do using word processing.

**Demonstrate Your Knowledge of the Organization/Industry.** Make your cover letter personal yet professional. Use your company research to personalize your letter. Mention your interest in a new or popular product of the organization; expansion of the firm; recent organizational accomplishments; reputation for reliability, quality, product, or customer service; humanitarian efforts; a special achievement of the person you're writing to, or the organization in general (a promotion, award, current activity, or project).

**Do Not Overdo It.** Don't use words that are too emotional or too gushy for a business setting: "I *love* to design computer graphics to enhance specialized publications" or "I believe the ABC Company has a *wonderful* employee training program." (Say instead, "I know the ABC Company has an excellent employee training program.")

**Emphasize How You Can Meet Employer Needs.** Reflect the employer's needs outlined in the job opening announcements or advertisements. If your current job target deals only with accounting, a vague listing of accounting qualifications and computer specialization will not be as effective as a reference to strong accounting abilities (with the computer specialization referenced as a backup).

Also, if you are considering more than one position, such as an accounting technician or computer specialist, highlight the appropriate skills, experience, and education for each job you target.

SUCCESS TIP

**Tailor your cover letter to the employer, and make it perfect. Applicants who do a good job stay in the running!**

## Addressing Your Letter

Some organizations don't accept unsolicited applications, resumes, or cover letters. Often, applicants who address communications to the human resources department get a form letter stating that no applications are currently being accepted.

**Find Out Who Hires.** To boost your chances, address your letter to the person who has hiring authority for the position (particularly the one who would be your boss—the department head, manager, or person who would supervise your work).

How do you get the right person's name? If you don't yet know who to address your cover letter to, consider one of these methods:

1. Call your target employer, and say you are doing career research and want to address a letter of inquiry to the person who specializes in your career area. Get the person's full name and title; verify the spelling and mailing address. When you call, always introduce yourself, get the name of the person you talk with, and thank that person by name for her or his help. Always say you are a student or are doing research. This person could possibly help you later, and using names establishes a courteous, friendly tone.
2. Go to the human resources office (if your target employer has one); ask whether it has an employee organizational chart you could use as part of your career planning class or personal research. Someone in the office may consider reviewing it with you to explain the organizational responsibilities of the department heads. This could help you target the department head you should address your cover letter to.

If this method seems inappropriate for your job search, ask members of your job search network to help you devise a workable approach. Use your creative ability, dare to be different, but always be courteous and businesslike. These traits also separate the employed from the unemployed!

SUCCESS TIP

**Contacting the targeted department head personally can get you in the door sooner.**

**The Human Resources Department or the Specific Department Head?** If you send your cover letter and resume only to the human resources department, the person who heads the department you are interested in might never see it. If you send your letter directly to the person you would work for, your chances of getting an interview will be greatly increased; but the human resources department could resent your circumventing them.

How do you handle this situation? If the employer is accepting applications, send one letter and resume to the human resources department and one to your targeted job department head. You can indicate in your letters that you have sent similar communications to each of these people. The worst that can happen is both letters will wind up in the human resources department. If the employer is not officially accepting applications, send your cover letter and resume to the department head only. If it is persuasive enough, you could still get an interview!

## NEVER ADDRESS YOUR LETTER "TO WHOM IT MAY CONCERN"

Unless responding to a blind advertisement, this impersonal approach never impresses the person who reads the letter (if anyone bothers to, since it is not addressed to anyone).

### FINE POINTS FOR PREPARING JOB SEARCH LETTERS

Use a word processor to prepare your letter, and print it using a quality printer and high-quality bond paper, 8 1/2-by-11 inches. Use the same paper for both your resume and cover letter.

- Use an acceptable business letter format. (See the samples in this chapter and in Appendix A.)
- Be certain the final letter is perfect—free from errors (no typographical, spelling, grammatical, or punctuation errors).
- Make sure the paper is wrinkle and smudge free.
- Incorporate specialized terminology for your industry where appropriate.
- Sign each letter.

## PREPARING YOUR LETTER

Keep the following pointers in mind as you develop your letter:

1. Use effective writing techniques, and project a likable, energetic, and skilled image (see Chapter 9).
2. Address your letter to the appropriate person in the organization, using the correct full name, title, and spelling (no abbreviations except for Mr., Dr., Ms., etc.).
3. Emphasize what you can do for the organization, not what you want from it.
4. Don't use overblown or empty words to describe your abilities. For example, avoid the terms *effectively* and *efficiently*; use specific, measurable terms instead (my program *increased* reported customer satisfaction by *35 percent*).
5. Use a friendly tone; avoid one that is overbearing or too familiar, emotional, desperate, humorous, or self-important.
6. Project confidence in your qualifications and interest and enthusiasm for the job.

7. If the job will likely require you to relocate, state your willingness to move. (If you aren't willing to move, don't apply.)

8. Do not try to convince the employer that you are a "wonder person" capable of unrealistic performance. This smacks of overkill and is a turn off to employers. Do make an effort to convey your skills as a team player.

9. Relate your qualifications to the needs and interests of the prospective employer.

10. Remember to sign each cover letter.

# DEVELOPING WINNING COVER LETTER CONTENT

Help the employer by keeping your cover letter brief (four or five paragraphs—no longer than one page). Be sure your cover letter does not just duplicate exactly the data in your resume. (What busy employer wants to read the same thing twice?) Also make sure that what you say in both your resume and cover letter does not contain contradictions.

Figure • 10-9: If you write a convincing cover letter, the employer will be eager to talk with you when you make your follow-up telephone call.

## What to Include in Your Cover Letter

The following items should be included in the letter:

1. If you had any previous communication with the person you're writing to, refer to it to help him or her remember you.

2. If you have a contact who knows the person you are writing to, mention your contact's name in your letter.

3. Explain how you learned of and why you are interested in the employer, and state the type of position you are seeking.

4. Include at least one sentence that shows your knowledge of the company. This demonstrates initiative and interest.

5. Emphasize your qualifications for the job (one or two results-oriented descriptions of accomplishments and capabilities that show how you can benefit the employer and handle the job).

6. State that your resume is enclosed.

7. Include a request for an *interview* (not a bid for a job!) even if no openings are available now.

8. Include a courteous closing sentence.

### The Opening

Begin by introducing yourself and stating your purpose. Explain how you know of the employer and why you are interested in this particular organization; state the type of job you are seeking.

If you are responding to an announced job opening, refer to the advertisement or announcement, the date of the notice, and where you found it (newspaper, Internet job posting, professional journal, employment agency, or the company human resources department). Some employers list several job openings at one time; help your reader (and yourself) by identifying the one you are referencing.

If you know someone who would be influential and recognized by the reader, get permission, and use that person's name as a reference in your letter.

The following example is a networking cover letter sent by Kimi Okasaki, who is seeking an administrative support position. Kimi mentions the name of a person well known to the addressee.

> ***"Miguel Sandoval from the Health Services Bureau recommended I talk with you about the possibility that you may need an administrative support person with experience in educational and community activities. Your new five-year educational and community plan is soundly developed, and I believe my five years of experience as a volunteer in the Valley Parent-Teacher Organization (VPTO) and the Diabetes Foundation would be useful in helping you achieve success in the plan."***

## Your Sales Pitch

This section focuses on your qualifications for the job. Make this paragraph a results-oriented summary of your assets, specifically highlighting one or two accomplishments that demonstrate your suitability for the job. Do not duplicate information exactly from your resume in your cover letter.

> ***"Through my volunteer work, I learned about the disease prevention techniques your department teaches to day-care workers. The potential to combine helping families, defeating disease, and doing work I enjoy is irresistible. I have recently completed an Associate of Applied Business degree, majoring in Business and Office Education, with an overall GPA of 3.5. As Secretary-Treasurer of the VPTO, I used Excel and Word to generate and merge letters and address labels for 500 student families."***

## The Closing

In the closing, make a bid for an interview (not a job!). Research shows that an active close (in which you say you will call to request an interview) leads to more interviews. A passive close (in which you request the reader to call you), however, can lead to higher-quality interviews. A third approach, which is used below, combines the strengths of both styles.

> ***"Enclosed for your review is my resume. I would appreciate meeting with you and discussing the possibility of our working together. I will call you on Thursday to request an interview, or you may reach me at 555-9088. I would welcome the opportunity to contribute to the community outreach efforts of the Department of Disease Prevention.***
>
> ***Sincerely,***
> ***Kimi Okasaki***

**SUCCESS TIP**

**In your cover letter, state the position you are applying for, highlight your related capabilities, and request an interview.**

**Complete Career Action 10-2**

# CAREER ACTION 10-2

## Use the Internet to Research Cover Letter Strategies

**NOTE:** Since the content of Web sites is subject to change without notice, the links listed below may not match the current content of the sites referenced in this assignment.

**DIRECTIONS:** Visit the sites indicated below to locate and summarize at least four strategies for writing a successful cover letter. Look for new ideas that may be useful to you. Write a summary of your findings, or print copies of the data. If you find new information or information that varies from that in your textbook, research further and discuss the topic(s) in the classroom, with your career services staff, and with interview specialists.

***WebGuide* Activity:** At the *WebGuide* Main Menu, select "Your Job Search." Complete activity #4, "Write your cover letter," by visiting the site listed and summarizing key strategies for writing successful cover letters.

**Internet Activity:** Access the following Web sites, and summarize key strategies for writing successful cover letters.

**Monster.com** http://www.monster.com/
(Look under "*resumes*" and "*letters*")

**CareerLab** http://www.careerlab.com/
(Look under Cover Letter Library — **excellent resource** on the topic.)

**CAREERMagazine.com** http://www.careermag.com/

**College Grad Job Hunter** http://www.collegegrad.com/
(Look under Resumes and Cover Letters)

148 Barrister Avenue
Tucson, AZ 85726
April 20, 20--

Ms. Kris George
Office Manager
MegaMall Property Management Company
P.O. Box 555
Tucson, AZ 85726

Dear Ms. George:

Please accept my application for the administrative assistant position advertised in last Sunday's edition of the *Arizona Bugle*. As a Scout Leader involved in a promotional project last fall, I appreciated MegaMall's offer to let us hold our event at no charge in the center of the mall. I would welcome the chance to work in such a civic-minded organization.

I am an energetic, detail-oriented person who has strong administrative and computer skills, retail and community service experience, and the ability to work well with people from all walks of life. In addition, I have held positions of responsibility in four community organizations over the last eight years and was chosen 1999 National Diabetes Foundation Volunteer of the Year.

As you can see from my resume, I thrive in a busy atmosphere that involves many different tasks, the opportunity to work with people, the satisfaction of meeting deadlines, and the chance to excel. I would appreciate an interview to discuss the possibility of my joining your staff. I will call you next week to request an appointment, or you may call me at your convenience at (520) 555-9088.

Sincerely,

Kimi Okasaki

Kimi Okasaki

Enclosure

Figure • 10-10: **Cover letter responding to an advertised job opening**

2440 Windom Way, Apt. 34
Los Angeles, CA 90063
June 29, 20--

Ms. Stephanie Nolan
Manager, Auditing Staff
Nolan Henry O'Leary Public Accountants
1410 Granada Avenue 7th Floor
San Francisco, CA 94115

Dear Ms. Nolan:

Meagan White at Sharon and Associates indicated that you are interested in hiring an accounting graduate who has some experience in the field. My degree and special interest is in Accounting/Information Systems. Please consider me for a place on your well-respected auditing team.

For the last two years, I have been working part-time as the full-charge bookkeeper for a small industrial consulting firm in Los Angeles. My practical experience includes opening, posting, and closing the books; completing federal and state corporate tax returns; and creating templates using Excel. In addition, I assisted an outside consultant in upgrading the software of the customized accounting system. Once the upgrade was installed, it was also my responsibility to work with the consultant to identify and resolve discrepancies between the two systems.

During my senior year at the University of Los Angeles, I had the chance to lead an internship research team. We studied the operations of a local accounting firm, accompanied its auditors to several client sites, and assisted in the audit of a small retail store. These experiences cemented my interest in auditing as a career field.

I am confident in my ability to make a positive contribution to Nolan Henry O'Leary Public Accountants and am enclosing a copy of my resume for your review. I will call you next week to request an appointment, or you may reach me at (213) 555-4668. Thank you for considering my request. I am looking forward to meeting you.

Respectfully,

John Griffin

John Griffin

Enclosure

c: Meagan White, Sharon and Associates

Figure • 10-11: **Networking cover letter**

846 Cameron Way
Phoenix, AZ 85012
December 10, 20--

Mr. Gary Whaley
District Sales Manager
Computeriferals Company
Rallings City, NY 10099

Dear Mr. Whaley:

Computeriferals has earned my respect. I have used and repaired peripherals from most of the leading manufacturers in my studies as a Business Systems/Computer Repair major and in my job as a sales representative at ComputerChoice. I know that you build quality products, and I want to sell quality products—Computeriferals.

Over the last two years at ComputerChoice, I initiated the outside sales of PCs and laptops to small businesses and, working part-time, increased overall sales 50 percent. Because of my background in computer equipment repair, I was also successful in negotiating a service contract with a customer who has five offices within the greater Phoenix area. Although I have enjoyed working in the local market, the wider scope of Computeriferals presents an appealing challenge.

Even if you have no current openings, I would appreciate meeting with you to discuss your requirements for sales representatives. My resume is enclosed for your convenience. I will call next week to request an appointment, or you may reach me at (602) 555-9873.

Respectfully,

Christopher Lipsmeyer

Christopher Lipsmeyer

Enclosure

Figure • 10-12: **Cover letter inquiring about an unadvertised position**

# CAREER ACTION 10-3

## Cover Letter Outline and Draft

**PART 1: OUTLINE**

**DIRECTIONS:** Use the Cover Letter Outline form on page 195 to organize and outline your basic cover letter (keeping in mind that it should be tailored to fit each employer's needs). Don't try to write a perfect letter at this point; just work at getting the essence of your message on paper. You will refine it afterward.

Review the sample cover letters provided in Figures 10-10, 10-11, and 10-12 on pages 186, 187, and 188.

**PART 2: DRAFT YOUR LETTER**

**NOTE:** No worksheet is provided for this part. Use your own paper to complete it.

**DIRECTIONS:** Using your cover letter outline and related job target research information, compose your cover letter draft. Make it concise, tailored to the employer's needs, and courteous. Most important, demonstrate how you can benefit the employer.

**Career Database Appropriate**

## Review and Edit Your Letter

Review and edit your cover letter draft by using the colored pen system recommended for the development of your resume. Be choosy (downright nitpicking!) about the words you use—every word counts!

## Get an Outside Critic

Ask a member of your network who has strong communications skills and who also knows your background to critique your letter carefully. Most of us find it very difficult to critique our own resumes and cover letters well because we overlook important aspects (like punctuation, omission of details, etc.) while concentrating on the wording. Your critic may think of additional items you should include that you have overlooked. Sources for outside reviewers and critics include the following:

- **A hiring expert you know**—someone who can tell you how your cover letter compares with the ones she or he reviews and how you can improve yours.
- **A professional friend or acquaintance** who knows you and your work well enough to help clarify confusing statements or to spot where you have omitted or neglected to emphasize important information or qualifications.
- **A professional who does not know you well** to serve as a final test for your cover letter, reading to learn about you from the letter. Choose a good writer who will give honest criticism, not someone who will automatically say the letter is fine. You need solid suggestions for improvement.

Complete Career Action 10-4

# CAREER ACTION 10-4

## Prepare Your Final Cover Letter

**DIRECTIONS:** Now polish your cover letter draft, emphasizing your qualifications and making the content clear and concise. Use a thesaurus to find just the right shades of meaning. As you prepare your final cover letter, remember that the same four words used to describe a good resume apply to your cover letter:

**IT MUST BE PERFECT!**

After your cover letter is completed, review it with thorough attention to detail; even *one error* can eliminate you in the employer's paper screening.

When you think your letter is perfect, ask an outside critic to review it one more time slowly and carefully, looking for even the smallest error. This is critical to the success of your cover letter. Print the final letter on top-quality paper.

Career Database Appropriate

Figure • 10-13: Ask a member of your network who has strong communication skills to critique your cover letter carefully.

## PREPARING A COVER LETTER FOR THE INTERNET

The emergence of the electronic job market has created the need for the electronic or *cyber-resume* discussed in Chapter 9. In addition, many employers require electronic cover letters to be transmitted through e-mail or to be posted on their Internet home pages.

Follow the guidelines below to prepare and transmit an electronic cover letter:

1. Turn to Chapter 9 of this textbook, and review the instructions under the section heading "Cyber-Resume Formatting and Transmission Guidelines" on page 162. Use the same general formatting instructions in steps 1 and 2 of that section:

   a. Retrieve your final cover letter created in your word processing program.

   b. Remove all special word processing coding, and use a 6.5-inch line length.

   c. Use the "Save As" command to give this document a new name and to save it as *text only with line breaks*, or as a **.txt**, or an **ASCII text** file.

2. Close the file and exit the word processing program.

3. Open the ASCII cover letter in your standard text-editing program, such as Windows Notepad or SimpleText for Macintosh.

   a. Clean up the formatting to create clean line lengths and to eliminate any errors.

   b. Save this file under another name.

4. Transmit your cover letter to the employer by either:

   a. Copying and pasting it or retrieving it into your e-mail program and sending it to the employer as an e-mail message.

   b. Pasting it into the cover letter block in the job application section of the employer's Web site.

**Format electronic cover letters to transmit correctly: Follow employer instructions, save as ASCII or .txt, and clean up in text editor.**

## PREPARING YOUR CAREER PORTFOLIO

Begin assembling your Career Portfolio by identifying your skills and experiences that relate directly to your career target. Consider carefully what you have done or accomplished that best demonstrates those qualifications. For example, to demonstrate a strong background in accounting, include in your portfolio your transcripts listing appropriate coursework; a diskette containing samples of budgets developed and accounts receivable or payable reports prepared; a letter of recommendation from an employer for bookkeeping or accounting work performed; etc.

For a traditional portfolio, you can use a three-ringed binder that holds 8 1/2-by-11-inch pages. File and categorize all your portfolio documents in file folders or by tabbed sections in the binder. Use sheet protectors, diskette protectors, and other appropriate accessories to protect and professionally display your portfolio items. Larger portfolios (17 × 22 inches) are appropriate for art designers, journalists, advertising specialists, and technical writers to store and categorize oversized documents and credentials.

In preparation for you interviews, you can create a customized Interview Marketing Kit composed of items you select from your Career Portfolio that pertain to a specific job interview. During the interview, you can extract items that best demonstrate your qualifications for that job, giving you an edge over other job candidates who don't prepare portfolios. Reference to your portfolio items during the interview depends on your job target. If an employer requests a portfolio of your work prior to the interview, the interview will likely include significant portfolio focus.

## BENEFITS OF ASSEMBLING PORTFOLIO ITEMS

- Provides tangible proof of abilities, experiences, and accomplishments that demonstrate past performance and are indicative of future success.
- Demonstrates a process of critical thinking, analyzing, planning, and preparation.
- Helps manage and organize career-related job search information into a usable format.
- Illustrates initiative and creativity.
- Boosts the interviewee's confidence and sense of preparation.

You can also transmit portfolio items via the Internet, videotape, or computer disk. Using electronic media provides unlimited access to companies worldwide.

Technology, however, cannot substitute for the value of personal contact and dialogue gained in a traditional interview.

**Complete Career Action 10-5**

## TAPPING INTO YOUR NETWORK FOR JOB LEADS

Employers base their hiring decisions largely on trust. They are most likely to hire people they know or who are referred by people they know. This is why we continue to emphasize that your job search network is the number one source of solid job leads.

## CAREER ACTION 10-5

### Online Portfolio Research

**NOTE:** Since the content of Web sites is subject to change without notice, be aware that the links listed below may not match the current content of the Web sites referenced in this assignment.

1. If you are using *WebGuide: Your Online Career Search*, go to "Your Job Search" and then "Build your portfolio." Complete activity #5.
2. Or access the two Web sites below, and review the career portfolio information. Then compile a list of items to include in your portfolio.

**University of Colorado at Denver:** http://www.cudenver.edu/public/career/search.html

**Ball State University:** http://www.bsu.edu/careers/portfoli.html

## Networking Process

Once you complete your job search paper package, contact your network to expand your employment options. Because your network members are statistically the strongest job lead source, they can form the bridge to your perfect job. Follow the networking guidelines below for best results. They are listed in order of preference for maximum results:

1. **Make an appointment to meet in person.** Make appointments with the most viable of your networking members. Appointments get the best results. In each meeting, briefly review your job objective and ask for recommendations. Give each a copy of your cover letter and resume and ask for feedback on the content and quality. Be organized and respect each person's time.
2. **Make a telephone call.** If you can't get an appointment, make a telephone call. Briefly review your job objective and ask for recommendations. Ask whether you can send a copy of your cover letter and resume to get their feedback.
3. **Send a networking letter.** If you can't get a meeting or reach the person by telephone, send a networking letter (see instructions below.)

## Networking Letter

A networking letter tells your network about your job search goals and requests specific help with the process. This letter contains a basic informational core, as well as personalized comments tailored to the recipient. The employment success rate from these letters is high.

Tailor your networking letter by considering the individual strengths of your network members. Ask a good writer for advice in improving your resume; ask for help in identifying specific employers or for direct job leads. You can also request meetings with some network members to brainstorm strategies.

## NETWORKING LETTER FEATURES

- Friendly tone
- Enthusiastic content
- Concise message
- Professional format and no errors
- Confident, upbeat style
- Clear expression of job target
- Clear request for specific help
- Reference to resume, which is attached

# DISTRIBUTING YOUR COMPLETE JOB SEARCH PAPER PACKAGE

Once you have completed your resume and cover letter and know how to complete an employment application, you're ready to submit a solid job search paper package (application, resume, and cover letter).

How you distribute your job search documents is also important. Consider the following tips regarding distribution:

1. **Regular Mail.** If you mail your documents, put them into a large envelope so you don't have to fold them. If the employer faxes or scans your letter after receiving it, folds in the paper can cause errors in the process.
2. **E-Mail or Fax.** Some employers specify that they want you to e-mail or fax the documents; do what they say! Follow the e-mail instructions provided in Chapter 9.

## FOLLOWING UP WITH A TELEPHONE CALL

Applicants who follow up with a telephone call to employers after sending cover letters and resumes are dramatically more successful. Two important reasons for this are (a) employers see follow up as an indication of initiative and confidence, and (b) busy employers may actually intend to call an applicant but get sidetracked. Applicants who call save the employer time and often speed a hiring decision.

Call about three or four days after the employer receives your letter, and say something like this: "This is Dona Orr calling from Raleigh. I sent you a letter and resume regarding the system support programming job and wanted to make sure you received it." This simple telephone call is often a deciding factor in getting an interview; always increase your odds with this call.

SUCCESS TIP

**After sending your job search paper package, follow up with a telephone call to increase your chance of securing an interview.**

## CHECKLIST FOR APPLICATIONS AND COVER LETTERS

Check each of the following actions you are taking to increase your career success:

- ☐ Make the applications perfect.
- ☐ Tailor cover letters to employers; make them perfect.
- ☐ State the positions you are applying for, list related abilities, and request an interview.
- ☐ Format electronic cover letters correctly.
- ☐ Follow cover letters with telephone calls.

## CRITICAL THINKING QUESTIONS

1. What are possible consequences of not filling out an employment application completely and according to the instructions?
2. Should you mention a salary figure in the application? Explain.
3. Think of a probable employer you would like to interview with. Explain exactly how you plan to find out who to address your cover letter to. Write the name, title, and address of the person in your answer.

# CAREER ACTION 10-3

## Cover Letter Outline and Draft

**Part I: Cover Letter Outline**

**Your Mailing Address:** ______________________________

______________________________

______________________________

**Telephone Number:** ______________________________

**Date:** ______________________________

**Name & Title of Addressee:** ______________________________

______________________________

______________________________

**Salutation:** **Dear:** ______________________________

**Paragraph One, Opening:** (Include name of referral if you have one; state your position objective.) ______________________________

______________________________

______________________________

______________________________

______________________________

______________________________

______________________________

______________________________

______________________________

# CAREER ACTION 10-3

(CONTINUED)

**Paragraph Two, Your Sales Pitch:**

(Tailor it to the opening.)

**Paragraph Three, Closing:**

(State that your resume is enclosed, and request an interview.)

**Complimentary Close:**

Sincerely,

Type Your Name Here

PART 4 • YOUR INTERVIEW

# Interview Like a Pro

> "It's okay to be nervous. Nervousness gets your adrenaline going, which can actually help you in an interview. As a headhunter, I am constantly interviewing candidates for all kinds of positions. My advice is to really listen in an interview. If you don't understand a question, ask the interviewer for clarification."
>
> *Beth Hare, President*
> *Criterion Search Group*

***In this chapter you will:***

- Prepare interview responses to demonstrate enthusiasm and interest in the position and in the organization.
- Identify nonverbal behaviors to enhance your interview performance.
- Prepare a "60-Second Interview Commercial."
- Identify the core elements of successful interviewing and ways to succeed in your interview.
- Summarize the fine points for interview success that are applicable to your job search and career planning.
- WWW Use the Internet to locate and summarize interview strategies.

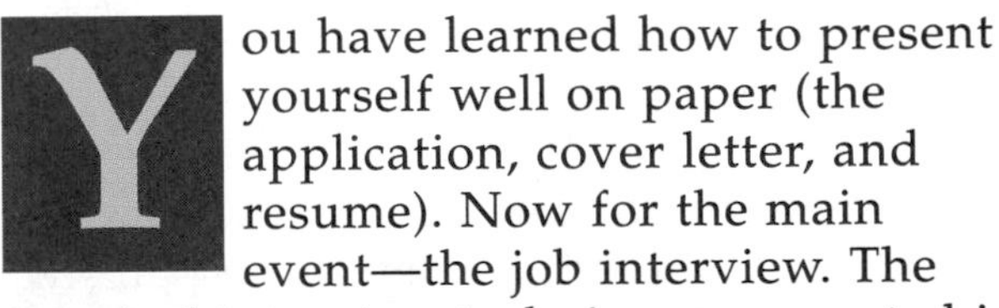

You have learned how to present yourself well on paper (the application, cover letter, and resume). Now for the main event—the job interview. The practical interview techniques presented in this chapter work. These techniques are based on broad, ongoing research with professional interviewers. These hiring specialists represent diverse employment fields and organizations throughout the United States. Our research also includes thorough review and testing of successful job-seeking program techniques.

## THE CORE OF SUCCESSFUL INTERVIEWING

You will be screened into an interview because you appear qualified on paper. The employer uses the interview to learn whether you have the personal qualities to fit in the organization and to further confirm your work performance qualifications.

## MAKE THE FIRST 30 SECONDS COUNT!

When first meeting, people often form opinions about others within 30 seconds or less. You can learn to use these power-packed seconds to your advantage! This first 30 seconds can make or break an interview. Read on to learn how to make it work for you!

We have researched extensively what techniques and behaviors applicants can develop to communicate best that they are professional and competent. Projecting these qualities gives job applicants a decided edge over their competition.

In this research, the key question we asked is "What influences interviewers to perceive applicants positively during interviews?" We found that the *image*, *appearance*, and *attitudes* applicants project during interviews are as influential as their skills in getting ahead.

In fact, in the time it takes applicants to walk across the room, say "hello," and sit down, interviewers say they form *strong opinions*. These opinions are primarily based on the four areas listed in "Impact on Interview" above.

### IMPACT ON INTERVIEW

| Areas: | Impact on Interview: |
|---|---|
| 1. Attitude | 40 percent |
| 2. Image and Appearance | 25 percent |
| 3. Communication (verbal/nonverbal) | 25 percent |
| 4. Job Qualifications | 10 percent |

### Applicants Are Screened on Paper First

You are selected to interview on the basis of your resume, cover letter, and application. Employers request these beforehand so they can review your education, work experience, and qualifications and compare them with those of other applicants. Employers don't have time during the interview to evaluate this information in detail.

### The Interview Focuses on You as a Person

One main purpose of the interview is for the employer to get to know the applicant as a person. Your *image and appearance* are the first things the interviewer will evaluate—and first impressions can influence the entire interview. Your *attitude* (the essence of your personality), however, is the biggest factor of your success in the interview. Job qualifications also count during the interview, and it's your responsibility to summarize them well.

## Your Attitude—The Number One Factor

Attitude is the number one factor that influences an employer to hire. Below are some ways you can exhibit a good attitude.

1. **Project an air of confidence and pride.** Act as though you want and deserve the job, not as though you are desperate.

2. **Demonstrate enthusiasm.** The applicant's level of enthusiasm often influences employers as much as any other interviewing factor. The applicant who demonstrates little enthusiasm for the job will never be selected for the position.

3. **Demonstrate knowledge of and interest in the employer.** "I really want this job" is not convincing enough. Explain *why* you want the position and how the position fits your career plans. You can cite opportunities that may be unique with this firm or emphasize your skills and education that are highly relevant.

4. **Perform at your best every moment.** There is no such thing as "time out" during the interview. While in the waiting room, treat the secretary or receptionist courteously; learn and use his or her name—the interviewer often requests this person's opinion of applicants.

5. **Concentrate on being likable.** Research proves that you *must be liked* by the interviewer if you are to be hired. The interviewer is interested in hiring someone who is pleasant, someone others will like spending time working with daily. Make efforts in the following areas:

   - Make certain your appearance is appropriate.
   - Be friendly, courteous, and enthusiastic.
   - Speak positively.
   - Use positive body language.

6. **Remember: The interview is a two-way street.** Project genuine interest in determining if you and the employer can mutually benefit from your employment.

**Project enthusiasm and a positive attitude in interviews. Often, a less experienced applicant with greater enthusiasm for the job is hired over competitors who are more qualified.**

Complete Career Action 11-1

# CAREER ACTION 11-1

## Project Enthusiasm, Positive Attitude, and Interest

**DIRECTIONS:** Prepare a list of statements you can use in your interview that demonstrate sincere enthusiasm and interest in the job, company, and other relevant aspects of your target employer. Back up your statements by referring to your research.

## Image and Appearance: The Cover on Your Book

Have you ever looked at a display of CDs or books and been drawn to one that had an appealing cover? The same concept applies in your interview. Remember: By the time you have walked into the room and sat down, the interviewer will have decided whether or not you will be considered for the position. Your image and appearance, combined with the attitude you project, will determine this first impression. Never underestimate the importance of your image and appearance; they count 25 percent as a positive or negative hiring factor.

### PACKAGE YOURSELF PROFESSIONALLY

Cosmetic firms are well aware of the impact of the package; some spend six times as much for the package as for the product inside! Products packaged attractively far outsell those that are not.

Whenever possible, visit your target employer before the interview to observe the working atmosphere, conditions, and dress code. Use this information to determine how to dress for your interview. *A word of caution:* Even if the employer permits casual dress on the job, you should demonstrate initiative and enhance your professional image by dressing more formally for your important business meeting—the interview. This also projects respect for the employer, which increases your likability.

**Conservative Dress Is Right.** When applying for an office or professional position, most interviewers expect you to wear businesslike clothes.



For men and women, a conservative suit of quality fabric is generally appropriate. For women, a conservative, tailored dress or coordinated skirt and blouse are also appropriate, especially when worn with a matching jacket. In most cases, women who wear slacks to an interview lower their chance of being selected.

**Appear Clean and Pressed.** Make sure your clothes are clean and pressed, in good repair, comfortable, and well fitted. (Shoes that pinch and clothes that are too tight restrict comfortable movement.) Visit top-notch clothing stores, and get help from experienced salespeople in selecting a coordinated interview outfit. You don't have to buy your outfit in an expensive store; you can usually duplicate it closely in a less expensive shop.

**Wear the Best Color.** Color is the most dynamic tool for dressing to enhance appearance. Learn which colors best complement your skin, eyes, and hair coloring. A good test is to note when you get repeated compliments on a color you wear. Good books are available on the subject of dressing for business success and on personal color analysis.

Traditionally, blue and gray are reliable color choices for interview suits, jackets, slacks, and skirts. Strengthen your image by using your best colors in your accessories—scarves, ties, shirts, blouses, and so on.

**Research Dress Expectations.** A business suit is not appropriate for every interview. Base your clothing choice on employer and career field research. Would a sport coat and dress slacks be more appropriate for your employer target, or would less formal slacks and a neat shirt and tie be better? Would a skirt and blouse be more in line with the employer target? Never dress too casually. T-shirts, jeans, tennis shoes, or other casual or faddish items cost applicants the job.

**Lose the Nose Ring and Baseball Cap.** In most cases, if you try to make a bold statement against business world conformity, you can kiss the job good-bye. For example, a male who wears an earring, a woman who wears several dangling earrings, or people who wear base- ball caps or nose rings to the interview might as well stay home.

Review the pictures of job applicants in Figures 11-1 and 11-2 below. Which outfit do you think is more likely to help the applicant get a job in a professional business or office setting? Why?

**Impeccable Grooming Is a Must.** You must be immaculately groomed. Be a model of cleanliness, and always use a deodorant. "Never let 'em see you sweat!"

**Look Alert!** Being well-rested projects a healthy, alert image; get plenty of sleep the night before. Taking good care of yourself with a healthful diet, exercise, and adequate rest is an important lifetime investment in your successful career.

**Project professionalism. Dress and groom yourself neatly and appropriately.**

Figure • 11-1: Even though it may be appropriate for a casual business office, this casual attire is inappropriate when applying for a professional business or office position.

Figure • 11-2: A conservative suit is appropriate dress when applying for a professional or office position.

## Verbal Communication

Start your verbal communication off right—use the interviewer's name in your greeting. This conveys respect, which aids your likability. (In some cases, you will be interviewed by more than one person at a time. See Chapter 13, "Be Prepared for Any Interview Style.") Find out, memorize, and use the names of everyone who will be interviewing you.

**State Your Name and the Position You're Seeking.** When you enter the interviewer's office, begin with a friendly greeting and state the position you're interviewing for: "Hello, Ms. Adams, I'm Ann Richards. I'm here to interview for the accounting position." If someone else has already introduced you to the interviewer, simply say, "Good morning, Ms. Adams." Identifying the position is important because interviewers often interview for many different positions.

**"Remember that a person's name is, to that person, the sweetest sound in any language."**

—Dale Carnegie

**Concentrate on Projecting a Pleasant Voice Tone.** It isn't always *what* you say that creates a positive or negative reflection of your attitude, but *how* you say it. Using a pleasant voice tone (friendly, courteous, and energetic) also enhances your likability.

**Tape Yourself for Practice.** Ask a friend to give you a practice interview to evaluate your voice tone. Have your friend ask you some of the sample questions from Chapter 14. Tape your questions and answers and listen to them; then decide where you could improve. If your voice is high pitched, work on lowering it; if you speak too softly, increase the volume; and so on. Above all, speak in a warm tone that has energy.

**Use Positive Words and Phrases.** One of the most important interview goals is to keep the content completely positive so that the interviewer's final impression is "Yes, this is the person for the job!" Use a positive vocabulary and eliminate all negative terms.

**Emphasize Your Strengths—Even When Discussing an Error.** Emphasize your strengths and abilities that are relevant to the job. Although you don't need to bring up a past shortcoming, do not try to cover up one if it emerges during the interview. Face it head-on, and explain what you learned from the experience. Turn a negative into a positive by demonstrating that you learn from mistakes.

If the interviewer asks you about the circumstances, explain briefly; don't make excuses or blame others. Remember: The interviewer is human, too, and probably has made a few mistakes—at least one! You create a better impression by being honest, candid, and sincere.

Never lie during the interview, and be prepared to state why you left previous employment if you are asked. Never speak unfavorably about your previous boss or firm. Interviewers often believe that you would do the same if you left their companies. Maintain your business and professional integrity throughout the interview.

**Sound Good.** Grammatical errors can cost applicants the job. Use correct grammar, word choice, and a businesslike vocabulary, not an informal, "chatty" one. Avoid slang. When under stress, people often use their "pet" phrases (such as "you know") too often. This is highly annoying and projects immaturity and insecurity. Ask a friend or family member to help you identify any speech weaknesses you have, and make a list of them. Practice eliminating these habits.

**Avoid Credibility Robbers.** Avoid using words and phrases that rob credibility and make you sound indecisive, or lacking in credibility. Eliminate the following credibility robbers from your vocabulary.

- **Just or only.** Used as follows, "I *just* worked as a waiter" or "I *only* worked there part-time" implies lack of pride in your work or that you don't consider it meaningful. Any work is meaningful; it demonstrates initiative.
- **I guess.** This sounds uncertain—definitely *not* the image you want to project!
- **Little.** As in "This is a *little* report/project I wrote/developed." Don't belittle your accomplishments!
- **Probably.** This suggests doubt unnecessarily: "The technique I developed would *probably* be useful in your department." This sounds more convincing: "I believe that the technique I developed would be useful in your department."

**NOTE:** This is a small sample of words and phrases that can diminish your image, but it is designed to illustrate the concept. Ask members of your support system to help you identify other verbal credibility robbers and to remind you when you use them.

**Additional Tips.** Following are additional tips for effective communication.

- **Keep the interview businesslike.** Do not discuss personal, domestic, or financial problems.
- **Try to demonstrate a sense of humor.** Nearly every employer looks for job applicants with a sense of humor. It's an important factor in working well with other people, and it's a sign of intelligence. Use humor only when appropriate, however, and don't tell jokes—they're not suitable for the interview. One of the safest forms of humor is to make yourself the subject.

Figure • 11-3: Practice answering interview questions with a member of your support network. Think about what you say and how you say it.

- **Don't ramble.** Be concise, yet not curt, with your replies. Rambling is frequently a nervous response. Answer questions with required information, adding anything you think is relevant or especially important; then stop talking or ask a question.
- **Focus on your goal.** Keep coming back to the main purpose in the interview: determining how you and the employer can mutually benefit. If the conversation strays too far from this subject, bring it back in that direction. Get feedback from the interviewer so that you know clearly how you are coming across. Stop and ask: "Do you think my skills in that area would be helpful to you?" If the answer is *yes,* you know you're on the right track. If the answer is *no* or unclear, clarify how you are qualified for the job.

## Nonverbal Communication (Body Language)

We are all experts at sending and receiving nonverbal messages. Nonverbal communication, or *body language,* is powerful. A severe frown can melt the warmest smile; a yawn during a speech speaks for itself. What emotions or qualities do you associate with these behaviors: (a) hands on hips and glaring face, (b) extreme fidgeting, (c) lack of eye contact, (d) slouched posture, (e) uplifted posture, (f) pleasant, relaxed smile, (g) limp handshake?

During your interview, your body language is a major factor. If you speak persuasively during your interview but your body language conveys arrogance, lack of enthusiasm, excessive nervousness, or other negative messages, the interviewer typically will be more influenced by your negative body language than by what you say.

Three sources of communication affect the listener or receiver: verbal communication, voice qualities, and nonverbal communication. The impact of each of these sources is illustrated in Figure 11-4. Because nonverbal communication is so influential, focus energy on sending positive nonverbal messages to maximize your interview effectiveness.

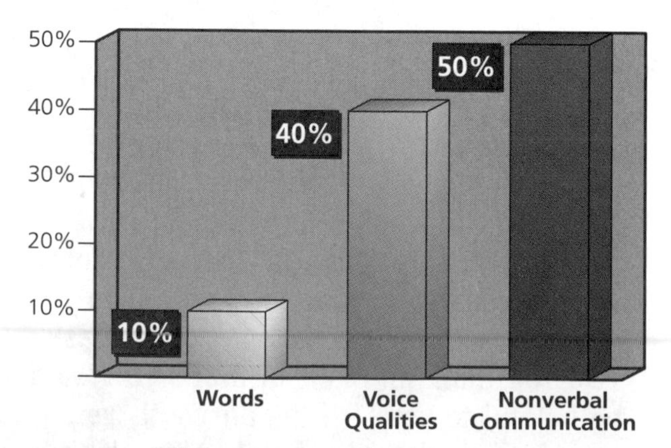


Figure • 11-4: Three Sources of Communication: The impact of each.

**NOTE:** Even though the words you use have the least impact in communication, the content must be appropriate for the situation (this is where your research pays off). You must also speak correctly (to project professionalism and competence).

**Use Positive Body Language to Your Advantage.** Follow the easy body language pointers below. They will speak well for you during your job search and will help you achieve important goals throughout your career. Also pay attention to the body language of others.

1. **Relax.** (Easy for us to say...) If you're tense, your body language will project the tension.

   a. Most important, *be well rested* for the interview so that you will be alert.

   b. Complete your research on the industry, organization, and interviewer *ahead of time.* Stop preparing the night before the interview; then relax and let your preparation pay off the next day.

   c. On the day of the interview, do some exercise that increases your heart rate, such as stretches and running. Exercise is one of nature's best techniques for relaxing your body and your mind.

   d. Change your position in your seat occasionally; this relaxes body tension and breaks the rigid feeling that nervousness can cause.

   e. Don't hurry movements, and breathe deeply to aid relaxation.

   f. Smile—it's a great tension breaker (for you and the interviewer)!

   g. Visualize your success in detail. Project enthusiasm and likability; concentrate on your capabilities.

## BODY LANGUAGE PACKS A WALLOP!

Body language has the greatest impact of the three sources of communication; it carries more impact than the words you say. To succeed in interviews, keep your body language positive.

2. Give a firm **handshake**. Because touch is the keenest physical sense, your handshake will greatly bolster or detract from your credibility. The best handshake is firm and accompanied by confident eye contact and a pleasant smile.

3. **Make eye contact.** Making good eye contact is essential to achieving effective communication. It conveys that you really care about what the person has to say. It also conveys confidence, intelligence, competence, and honesty. This does not mean you should glue your eyes to the interviewer; it does mean you should look at the interviewer, especially when he or she is talking. Break the eye contact at natural points in the discussion. Avoid letting your eyes dart back and forth circling the room. If you are extremely uncomfortable looking directly into the eyes of the interviewer, look at the forehead; it gives the impression of looking into the eyes.

**NOTE:** In a group interview, make sure you give eye contact to each person periodically.

4. **Maintain good posture.** Good posture conveys that you are composed, respectable, alert, and strong. Sit, stand, and walk with your head up and your back straight. Slouching conveys that you are bored, disinterested, lazy, or unintelligent. Crossing your arms and legs can be interpreted as being closed or stubborn.

Figure • 11-5: For a successful interview, match your body language to your interviewer's.

5. **Project a pleasant facial expression.** Aim for a pleasant, uplifted facial expression. Avoid frowning, licking your lips, clenching your jaw, or any other nervous or downturned expression.

6. **Don't fidget.** Fidgeting is distracting and makes you look nervous, self-conscious, or unsure of getting the job.

7. **Mirror communication behaviors of the interviewer.** Some people have intense and highly energetic body language and voice qualities; others are much more relaxed in both. People are most comfortable communicating with others who have styles similar to their own. Subtly "mirror" or match your interviewer's style, speed and tone of your voice, but don't overdo it; *never* mirror negative behavior.

   Much has been written about this technique (called neurolinguistic programming)—more than can be included here. Give thought to reading more about this skill and developing the ability.

## ADDITIONAL BODY LANGUAGE DON'TS AND DO'S

### DON'T:

- Don't bring your hand to your face; it can be interpreted as insecurity.
- Don't nod your head too much or tilt it to one side. Both actions detract.
- Don't grimace or frown, and don't blink too frequently.

### DO:

- Do sit with your body slightly to the side, rather than directly facing the interviewer. This tends to promote an attitude of openness and a relaxed atmosphere.
- Do keep your hands apart to avoid fidgeting. Rest them on the arms of the chair, and keep them still. Don't be a "white knuckle" interviewee; keep your hands relaxed, not in tight fists.

**NOTE:** To practice developing positive body language, arrange your own videotaped practice interview. Review the tape.Watch carefully for body language that needs correction.

**Communicate That You Are Trustworthy.** During your interview, it is important to convey that you are trustworthy and, therefore, believable. Interviewers will *not* hire people they think are not trustworthy.

Conveying trust is almost entirely a nonverbal function. It requires convincing the listener's emotional brain center through positive nonverbal messages. The sense of trust is emotionally based, learned in infancy and early childhood, and remains permanently embedded in our brains. We learned to trust those who exhibited specific nonverbal behavior: those whose body language and facial expressions conveyed warmth, competence, caring, and self-assurance. This is exactly how, as adults, we first evaluate the trustworthiness of others.

How can you convey these trustworthy, believable qualities: *warmth, caring, competence, self-assurance?* You can do this through your nonverbal communication: (a) a firm, warm handshake; (b) a pleasant facial expression and direct eye contact; (c) erect posture (sitting and standing); (d) an energetic, pleasant voice tone; and (e) a tall, deliberate walk.

**Develop Assertive Body Language.** Concentrate on sending assertive messages and eliminating passive or aggressive nonverbal habits. These three styles are defined below:

1. **Assertive Body Language.** This body language is relaxed, open, and confident. It agrees with and supports your words and conveys competence, self-assurance, caring, and credibility.

2. **Passive Body Language.** This body language looks nonenergetic and diminishes credibility by conveying insecurity, weakness, anxiety, and a lack of self-assurance and competence.

3. **Aggressive Body Language.** This body language appears brash and overbearing and sends offensive messages that convey hostility, pushiness, intimidation, and a domineering attitude.

**Complete Career Action 11-2**

## CAREER ACTION 11-2

### Body Language Self-Inventory

**DIRECTIONS:** Turn to page 220, and complete the Body Language Self-Inventory. This assignment will help you identify passive or aggressive body language habits you can begin eliminating to increase your communications effectiveness.

**Watch Your Interviewer's Body Language.** Watch to see what the interviewer's body language is saying. The interviewer may lean forward, signaling you to expand on what you are saying. If the interviewer shuffles papers, looks around the room, or gives other nonverbal clues that you should finish speaking, heed the signal.

Keep listening and watching to determine whether what you are saying is clearly understood. Retreat from a subject if you observe that it is not being well received.

**SUCCESS TIP**

**To project trust and credibility quickly, use positive body language in the first 30 seconds and throughout the interview. Focus on pleasant facial expression, good posture and eye contact, and a strong handshake.**

## Listening: The Silent Power Play

Concentrate on listening to every word. Never interrupt the interviewer, even if you're certain you know what will be said; this is considered rude. If the interviewer asks a question you don't understand, politely ask the person to repeat it. If you don't understand the question fully, you won't be able to respond adequately. Listen to the interviewer carefully for important details regarding the job requirements, the organization, or the department so you can respond appropriately.

**Silence Is Sometimes Used as a Power Play.** The interviewer may ask a question, you provide the proper response, and then the interviewer doesn't respond. An experienced interviewer may use this technique to test your confidence and ability to handle stress or uncertainty.

If you experience this silence power play, never retract your statement—just wait calmly. You have no obligation to continue talking if you answered adequately. By doing this, you will pass the "test" and project a mature, confident image. Break a long silence by asking whether the interviewer needs more information or by asking a related question. Be prepared to handle silence.

**You Can Also Use Silence.** If asked a difficult question, giving an answer too quickly and without enough thought could work against you. You're entitled to think carefully about the question and prepare your response. The employer wouldn't want you to solve problems on the job without adequate thought and planning.

## Emphasizing Your Qualifications

In your interview, you must convince the employer that you are the best-qualified person for the job. If you don't, you won't be hired. To convince the employer, you need to focus on how your skills and experience can benefit the employer. The way you handle discussion of your qualifications will be a determining factor.

Getting hired can be compared to making a sale. In this case, the products are you and your capabilities. You complete the "sale" by effectively emphasizing how your capabilities can benefit the employer.

**Develop and Use a "60-Second Commercial."** To help make the sale, we recommend you develop a **"60-Second Commercial."** This "commercial" is a power-condensed summary of the benefits you can offer. As a starting point, think of the times you have provided benefits to an employer or volunteer organization.

Focus on the following benefits outlined in "Emphasize Employer Benefits in Your Commercial."

### EMPHASIZE EMPLOYER BENEFITS IN YOUR COMMERCIAL

Employers are persuaded to "buy" (hire) the one who can offer benefits in one or more of these areas:

- Increasing sales/profits/productivity
- Decreasing costs
- Saving time
- Solving problems
- Increasing convenience
- Enhancing image
- Improving relationships
- Increasing accuracy or efficiency

Can you give examples of times when you have provided any of these benefits to organizations?

**Give Examples of Measurable Accomplishments and Transferable Competencies.** The key is to provide evidence of your capabilities or "proof by example." For instance, if you are skilled at improving work efficiency, give specific examples of demonstrated ability. The use of numbers increases credibility:

NO: "I work efficiently.'

YES: "I developed an order processing system that reduced processing time by 20 percent."

Figure • 11-6: During your interview, be prepared to speak of your accomplishments. Use the 60-Second Commercial technique to sell yourself.

Since employers are looking for flexible employees, also emphasize your transferable skills, such as ability to (a) handle diverse responsibilities, (b) manage yourself (attendance, punctuality, and problem solving), and (c) work well with others.

Be sure your 60-Second Commercial represents you authentically. If it doesn't, it can lead to a mismatch between you and the company. A lack of honesty can eliminate you from the competition; don't sell what you can't deliver.

Take your 60-Second Commercial to the interview. If you have a brief memory lapse, you can save the day by skimming it quickly for the main points before your interview, but *never read from the commercial.*

**Keep Your Commercial Concise.** Assume that your target employer requires you to summarize your qualifications for the job in a 60-second videotape. Just as in a television commercial, your own interview commercial must be short and to the point.

**Tailor Your Commercial to Each Employer.** **Career Action 11-3**, on page 211, guides you through the development of a persuasive summary of your qualifications tailored for each employer.

**Make the sale: Deliver a polished "interview commercial" emphasizing the heart of your qualifications. Include measurable accomplishments whenever possible.**

Review the sample qualification commercials on the next page to see how they focus on employer benefits, emphasizing the applicant's results-oriented accomplishments and transferable competencies. Notice how they are phrased in the "proof by example" format and are concise phrases, rather than complete sentences. (In an actual interview, you would use complete sentences.)

**Complete Career Action 11-3 on page 211**

## 60-SECOND COMMERCIAL SAMPLE #1

- **Job Target** Sales representative with Axion Inc., a consumer product company
- **Experience Credentials** Two years in retail sales at Computer Logistics, Inc.
- **Education Credentials** BA in sales and marketing
- **Proof of Benefits Provided**
  - Increased school newspaper revenues 22 percent as advertising assistant
  - Voted "Most Helpful Clerk" by customers in Service Excellence contest at Ralston Pharmacy
  - Received performance ratings of "excellent" in accurate, quick sales for two years at Computer Logistics, Inc.
- **Related Job Skills/Preferences**
  - Highly skilled in record keeping, use of personal computers, business math
  - Enjoy travel, open to relocation
- **Transferable Competencies**
  - Maintain professional appearance and have good communication skills
  - Strong interpersonal relations skills

## 60-SECOND COMMERCIAL SAMPLE #2

- **Job Target** Graphics/text specialist position with Action Publishers
- **Experience Credentials** Worked 18 months as graphics/text processing assistant, Westville State College Print Center
- **Education Credentials** Associate of Applied Business Degree, Westville State College
- **Proof of Benefits Provided**
  - Developed priority scheduling method resulting in 99 percent on-time delivery
  - Developed three graphic-intensive brochures that were selected by school for national student recruitment campaign
- **Related Job Skills/Preferences**
  - Key 70 w.p.m.
  - Skilled in English usage
  - Proficient in Word, Excel, graphics design, and desktop publishing software
  - Operate personal computers, printers, networks, and other office equipment
  - Enjoy all aspects of document/graphic development
- **Transferable Competencies**

  Punctual, self-starter, resourceful in information management, skilled in computer technology, excellent language skills

# CAREER ACTION 11-3

## 60-Second Commercial

1. **Prepare a rough draft.** On separate paper, prepare a rough draft of your basic commercial.

2. **Use short phrases, not full sentences.** The goal is to say the most about your qualifications in the fewest possible words.

3. **Name your targeted job position and the employer.**

4. **Summarize education and training briefly.** Review your resume and **Career Action 2-1: Education and Training Inventory** as a reference.

5. **Focus on "Proof of Benefits Provided."** Describe relevant examples of your work performance and accomplishments and successful use of your job-specific skills. Whenever possible, use numbers or percentages to measure the success. Also, emphasize benefits you can provide for the employer.

6. **List your job skills and transferable competencies most relevant to the job target.** Review **Career Actions 3-1** and **3-2** on pages 48 and 51 for the lists of top job-specific and transferable skills.

7. **Tailor each commercial, and prepare a commercial card.** Use your commercial draft as a base, and tailor it for each target employer. Then transfer the information from the tailored commercial to a 60-Second Commercial card.

Career Database Appropriate

**Polish and Focus the Content.** The point is to prepare a brief, polished summary of your qualifications. It should contain the heart of your sales message, emphasizing how you can benefit the employer. Think of it as your interview billboard saying "Here's what I can do for you!" This helps the interviewer focus on the strengths you have to offer.

**Deliver Your 60-Second Commercial.** To target an opening for your "commercial," you can ask the interviewer to review the scope of the job responsibilities and the reason for the opening. Pay attention to the answer. If necessary, probe further to clarify what the employer really needs. Then discuss the benefits you can offer to meet those needs. Pick from your master "60-Second Commercial" items that best fit the needs expressed by the interviewer—that's good selling!

Be ready for any situation; practice delivering the full-length and a shorter version of your commercial (a 60-second and a 30-second version). Remember that the more often "buyers see or hear a sales message, the more likely they buy." Whenever possible, weave your commercial into the interview more than once—perhaps the longer version first, followed later by the shorter one. Twice is not too often, but use good judgement—don't overdo it.

If the person interviewing you isn't an experienced interviewer (which can happen), you *must* take the initiative to deliver your commercial. An untrained interviewer may never ask you to summarize your qualifications. Make certain this doesn't happen in *your* interview.

**Complete Career Action 11-4**

## HELP INTERVIEWERS REMEMBER YOUR STRENGTHS

Always deliver your interview commercial—even if you only get 30 seconds to do it!

## CAREER ACTION 11-4

### Summary of Core Areas of Successful Interviewing

**DIRECTIONS:** Write a summary discussing how you can apply in your own job search the interview strategies presented thus far in Chapter 11. Explain specifically how you can apply the techniques presented relating to each of the following:

1. Attitude
2 Image and Appearance
3. Verbal Communication
4. Nonverbal Communication
5. Listening
6. Job Qualifications

## USING YOUR PORTFOLIO ITEMS AND AN INTERVIEW MARKETING KIT

Preparing well for interviews definitely gives applicants a competitive edge. By doing so, you will project professionalism and organizational skills and increase your own sense of readiness.

### Select Portfolio Items

Before each interview, select the items most appropriate for the job target from your Career Portfolio (see Chapter 3, "Your Career Portfolio" and also see "Career Portfolio" and "Interview Marketing Kit" in "Appendix C: Career Management Tools"). Place the portfolio items you select in the Interview Marketing Kit described below.

### Prepare and Use an Interview Marketing Kit

To round out your interview preparation, assemble and take with you an "Interview Marketing Kit." Use a professional-looking binder or small attaché case to carry selected portfolio and other items. A regular briefcase is not recommended because interviewers could view it as "overkill." The items to include in your kit are listed on the following page.

## INTERVIEW MARKETING KIT CONTENTS

1. **Items from Career Portfolio for this interview:**
   - Job-related samples of your work, if applicable (this can be from your work and/or educational or training experience)
   - Required certificates, licenses, transcripts, or other related documents
   - Spare copies of your resume
   - Letters of recommendation
   - List of references appropriate for this job
2. **A copy of your 60-Second Commercial** summarizing your qualifications for the job (skills, education, experience)
3. **A notebook with a list of pertinent questions** you can ask during the interview (see Chapter 14)
4. **Professional preparation items**
   - Pens and pencils
   - An appointment calendar

Well in advance of your interview, prepare your 60-Second Commercial and the list of questions you want to ask. For guidelines in developing your questions, refer to the section in Chapter 14 entitled "Questions from You." Arrange the portfolio items in your Interview Marketing Kit to best show how your abilities relate to the employer's needs.

**"When your work speaks for itself, don't interrupt."**

—Mark Twain

### Practice Using Your Marketing Materials

To capture the interviewer's attention, refer first to an item representing one of your most outstanding accomplishments. Save another exceptional item to use toward the end of your interview to leave a favorable last impression.

Practice using your portfolio items so the actual delivery will be smooth. Have a friend give you a mock interview, and practice referring to your portfolio items at key points during the interview.

Suppose the interviewer asks, "How important do you think it is to keep up with changing technology?" At this point, you could say, "I think it is very important, and I have taken several classes to update my software skills. The most recent was a PowerPoint class. Would you be interested in seeing a few of the PowerPoint slides I made?" If you actually used the slides on a job, you could explain their application. By rehearsing, you will be able to work the portfolio into the interview naturally.

Figure • 11-7: Use your portfolio materials wisely in an interview situation.

SUCCESS TIP

**Be prepared and organized; take with you an Interview Marketing Kit containing items from your career portfolio and other items you may need in the interview.**

## Portfolio Cautions

Relying on only the portfolio items to persuade employers during interviews is a big mistake; it's like a speaker relying only on a set of slides. The focus of the interview is still on you. Your personal appearance and your nonverbal and verbal communication skills are essential. The portfolio items are a visual aid to add further dimensions in selling your qualifications.

## TWO INTERVIEWS A DAY ARE ENOUGH!

Performance levels typically drop after two interviews in one day. Don't jeopardize your chances; take a breather and gear up for the next day.

**REMEMBER:** Never misrepresent yourself in the portfolio items; the work must be your own. Be prepared to reproduce the work if requested to do so during pre-employment testing.

Part of your research must include learning whether or not your targeted employers are likely to be interested in reviewing a career portfolio during interviews. Some employers do not want, nor do they have time, to review portfolios during the interview.

Select your portfolio items to match specific employers and jobs. Do not use every item in your primary portfolio for every interview.

## Referring to Your Portfolio Items and Taking Notes

Before you refer to any portfolio items in your Interview Marketing Kit and before making notes, ask whether the interviewer has any objections. Pay attention to the answer, and do not refer to items or make notes if the interviewer prefers that you don't.

An exception is referring to your appointment calendar, if necessary. If you need to schedule a follow-up meeting or activity, having your appointment book handy projects organization. The time to confirm future appointments is immediately. Tomorrow could well be a lost opportunity; the interviewer is most likely to make a future commitment while you're still in the interview.

### "Murphy's Law" Survival Pack

With a little planning, you can avoid a sabotaging "Murphy's law" experience. Prepare a separate survival pack containing personal hygiene items (tooth-brush and paste, comb, even deodorant), a spare tie or nylons, and anything else you might need to look, smell, and be your best under any circumstances. Put your gear in a zippered pouch that fits neatly into your Interview Marketing Kit, or if you travel by car, store it in your car.

## INTERVIEW DISQUALIFIERS

The following is a list of important reminders. Avoid committing any of these blunders. Any one of these could lose you the job.

1. Don't sit down unless the interviewer invites you to; waiting is courteous.
2. Don't bring anyone else to the interview; it makes you look immature and insecure.
3. Don't smoke.
4. Don't put anything on or read anything on the interviewer's desk; it's considered an invasion of personal space.
5. Don't chew gum or have anything else in your mouth; this projects immaturity.
6. If you are invited to a business meal, don't order alcohol. When ordering, choose food that's easy to eat while carrying on a conversation.
7. Don't offer a limp handshake; it projects weakness. Meet a handshake firmly.

## WRAP UP THE INTERVIEW IN YOUR FAVOR

To wrap up the interview in your favor, always clarify what to expect next in the interview process and restate your qualifications.

### Clarify What to Expect Next

You must know what to expect next in this interview process. Before you leave the interview, always clarify the following:

1. What, if anything, should you do in the way of follow-up to the interview?
2. How long will you have to wait before the hiring decision is made? (If you are considering another job, this is especially important.)
3. How does the interviewer prefer that you follow up (by telephone, by letter, or in person)?

The following sample dialogue shows how to get this information:

YOU: When may I expect to hear whether or not I am selected for the position?
INTERVIEWER: We'll notify all applicants of our decision within two weeks.
YOU: Do you mind if I check back with you?
INTERVIEWER: I prefer that you don't until we notify you.

or

INTERVIEWER: No, I don't mind.
YOU: How would you prefer I do that? (by telephone, by mail, in person?)
INTERVIEWER: I prefer you to telephone my assistant.

You are clarifying *how* you will be notified of the hiring decision, *when* you will be notified, *whether* the interviewer objects to your checking back, and *how* the interviewer prefers that you check back. In every instance, you are helping yourself in the job campaign.

### The Clincher

As you near the close of your interview, make it a point to ask a question in a courteous tone, similar to this example:

> ***"Would you please summarize the qualifications you're looking for in filling this position?"***

Once the interviewer has answered, you can restate your skills, experience, and other assets that meet these needs. (Run your 60- or 30-Second Commercial one more time!) This important "clincher" technique gives you one last chance to make the sale—to market the products (you and your qualifications for the job). People remember best what they hear first and last in any communication.

Figure • 11-8: End the interview as positively as you started it. Be sure you and the interviewer agree on the next step.

## CLOSE THE INTERVIEW SKILLFULLY

Some applicants lose the race for the job by not clearing the final hurdle—*closing the interview skillfully.* Don't let down for a moment on your posture, attitude, and verbal and nonverbal communication skills. Follow the closing techniques below to close your interviews skillfully.

- Watch for signs from the interviewer that it's time to close the interview. Signs include asking whether you have any further questions, tidying up papers on the desk, pushing the chair back, or simply sitting back in the chair. Take the cue. Don't make the interviewer impatient by droning on at this point.

- If the person is not skilled at interviewing, you can help wrap up the interview smoothly by asking: "Is there anything else you need to discuss with me? I know you are busy, and I appreciate the time you have given me for this interview."

- Request a commitment from the interviewer to notify you when the applicant has been selected. Imply that this is not the only job you are considering: "By what date will you make your decision on this position? I'd appreciate knowing within the next two weeks so I can finalize my plans."

- Before you leave, make certain you clarify any follow-up activities the interviewer expects from you. If a second interview is arranged, write down the date, time, place, and name of the person who will be interviewing you. If you are to provide additional information, credentials, or references, make a note and verify it before you leave.

- If you're interested in the job, say so! Just as in effective sales, the person who *asks* is most likely to *get*. Interviewers are impressed with expression of interest; candidates who directly express it strengthen their position. Offer a simple statement such as, "I'd be pleased to be a part of this organization," or, "After talking with you, I'm convinced this is the job I want, and I believe my qualifications would be an asset to the XYZ Corporation. Please consider me seriously for this position."

**SUCCESS TIP**

**Close the interview skillfully. Pay close attention to the interviewer's signals for closure. If possible, run your "commercial" one more time to focus on your capabilities. Always find out how you should follow up and when a hiring decision will be made.**

- As you leave, remember to use the interviewer's name: "Thank you for providing me with this interview, Ms. Adams."

- Be conscious of your posture as you stand up, keeping your shoulders back and head up. A warm smile and firm handshake will confirm your friendly and positive attitude. Once you leave the interviewer's office, you are still interviewing! Thank the receptionist or secretary by name, and add a brief parting greeting.

Review Figure 11-9 to reinforce the areas that employers consider most important during the interview.

**Complete Career Action 11-5**

**Complete Career Action 11-6**

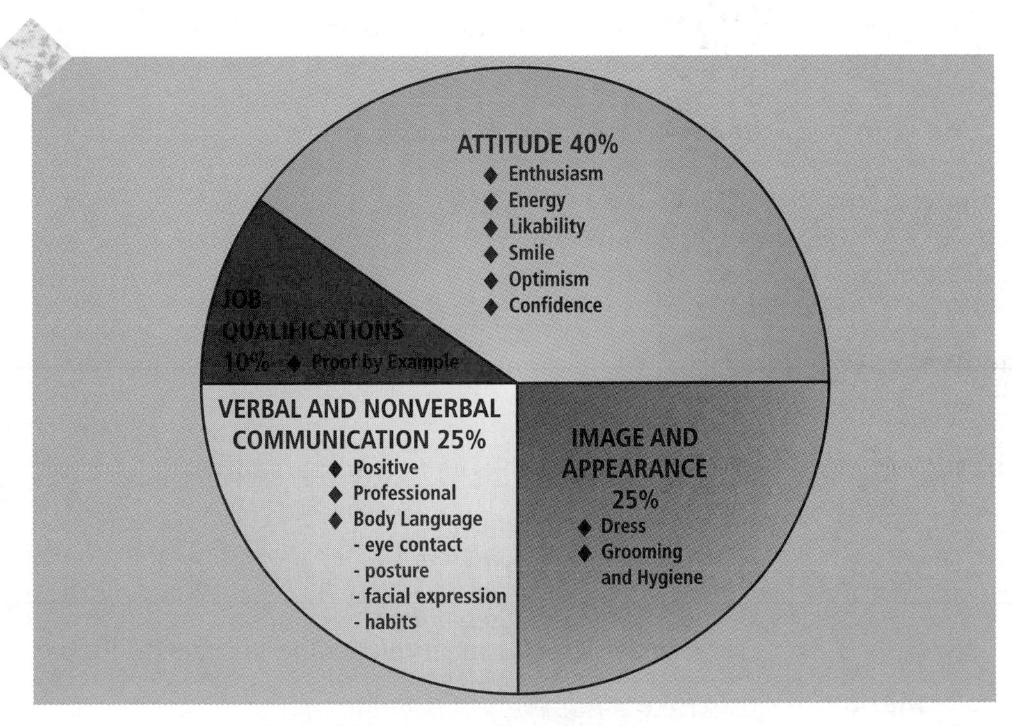


Figure • 11-9: How you are rated during the interview.

# CAREER ACTION 11-5

## Summary of Fine Points for Interview Success

**DIRECTIONS:** On separate paper, write a summary of how you plan to apply the information presented about each of the following aspects of interviewing.

1. **Your Interview Marketing Kit.** What will yours consist of?
2. **Your Murphy's Law Survival Pack.** What should be in yours?
3. **Interview Disqualifiers.** Which apply to you?
4. **How to Wrap Up the Interview in Your Favor.** Summarize how you plan to wrap up your interview favorably. Explain how you will find out what method of follow-up contact the interviewer prefers.
5. **Close the Interview Skillfully.** Summarize how you plan to end your interview.

# CAREER ACTION 11-6

## Use the Internet to Research Interview Strategies

**DIRECTIONS:** Visit the sites indicated below to locate and summarize at least four strategies for effective interviewing. Look for new ideas that may be useful to you. Write a summary of your findings. If you find new information, research further and discuss the topic(s) in the classroom, with your career services staff, and with interview specialists.

***WebGuide* Activity:** At the *WebGuide* Main Menu, select "Your Job Search." Complete activity #7, "Prepare for your interview." Visit the sites listed, and summarize key strategies for effective interviewing.

**Internet Activity:** Access the Web sites below; summarize strategies for effective interviewing.

| **Internet Web Sites:** | **NOTE:** Web site links and content are subject to change. |
|---|---|
| Monster.com | ***http://www.monster.com***<br>(Look under "*interviewing*" and "*portfolios*") |
| CAREERMagazine | ***http://www.careermag.com***<br>(Look under ***Articles*** for interviewing and portfolios) |
| Job Choices Online Magazine | ***http://www.jobweb.org/jconline***<br>(Look under "*interviewing*" and "*portfolios*") |

## CHECKLIST FOR INTERVIEWING LIKE A PRO

Check each of the following actions you are currently taking to increase your career success:

- ☐ Project enthusiasm and a positive attitude in interviews; they are big factors in hiring.
- ☐ Project professionalism; dress neatly and appropriately, and be clean and neat.
- ☐ Use positive verbal communication; use positive terms, and avoid grammatical errors, slang, and credibility-robbing terms.
- ☐ Use positive body language in the first 30 seconds and throughout the interview to project trust and credibility quickly.
- ☐ Make the sale: Deliver a polished interview commercial that emphasizes qualifications and includes measurable accomplishments whenever possible.
- ☐ Be prepared and organized; take to the interview an Interview Marketing Kit containing appropriate portfolio items.
- ☐ Close the interview skillfully. Pay close attention to the interviewer's signals for closure; run your commercial one more time to focus on capabilities; find out how to follow up and when a hiring decision will be made.

## CRITICAL THINKING QUESTIONS

1. What aspects of the applicant do interviewers focus on most?
2. How can the job applicant demonstrate positive attitudes during the interview?
3. What negative nonverbal habits are most important for you to eliminate to improve your interview abilities?
4. What is the most important information the applicant must convey to the interviewer?
5. What are the two most important items of information you should include in your 60-Second Commercial?

# CAREER ACTION 11-2

## Body Language Self-Inventory

### PART 1

**DIRECTIONS:** (a) Review the following nonverbal descriptions, and place a check mark next to each item that describes your body language habits. (b) Review your answers, and circle any that are aggressive or passive; make a list of those. (c) In Part 2, prepare a list of the habits you think are most important to change. (d) Then take action to correct these habits, and get others to remind you when you exhibit them.

#### POSTURE

| Behavior | Style | Behavior | Style |
|---|---|---|---|
| ☐ comfortably straight | Assertive | ☐ intimidating | Aggressive |
| ☐ relaxed, well balanced | Assertive | ☐ wooden, stiff | Passive |
| ☐ open, not cramped | Assertive | ☐ slumped shoulders | Passive |
| ☐ stiff, rigid | Aggressive | ☐ slumped back, spine | Passive |
| ☐ arms/legs crossed | Aggressive | | |

#### HANDSHAKE

| Behavior | Style | Behavior | Style |
|---|---|---|---|
| ☐ appropriately firm | Assertive | ☐ held too long | Aggressive |
| ☐ interlock thumb/first finger | Assertive | ☐ limp (weak, wimpy) | Passive |
| ☐ shake elbow through hand | Assertive | ☐ from wrist through hand | Passive |
| ☐ held appropriate time | Assertive | ☐ held too briefly | Passive |
| ☐ a "bone crushing" grip | Aggressive | ☐ grasping fingers only | Passive |

#### FACIAL EXPRESSION

| Behavior | Style | Behavior | Style |
|---|---|---|---|
| ☐ open, relaxed | Assertive | ☐ clenched jaw | Aggressive |
| ☐ frowning | Aggressive | ☐ wrinkling forehead | Passive |
| ☐ sullen, moody | Aggressive | ☐ biting or licking lips | Passive |
| ☐ tight lips, pursed mouth | Aggressive | ☐ constant smiling | Passive |



CONTINUED ON NEXT PAGE

# CAREER ACTION 11-2

(CONTINUED)

## EYE CONTACT

| Behavior | Style | Behavior | Style |
|---|---|---|---|
| ☐ relaxed, direct, comfortable | Assertive | ☐ looking down or away | Passive |
| ☐ staring off, bored expression | Aggressive | ☐ blinking rapidly | Passive |
| ☐ looking down nose | Aggressive | ☐ shifting focus, no eye contact | Passive |
| ☐ direct stare | Aggressive | | |

## VOICE QUALITIES

| Behavior | Style | Behavior | Style |
|---|---|---|---|
| ☐ clear | Assertive | ☐ too loud | Aggressive |
| ☐ controlled, but relaxed | Assertive | ☐ arrogant or sarcastic | Aggressive |
| ☐ warm, pleasant tone | Assertive | ☐ monotone | Passive |
| ☐ energized/suitable emphasis | Assertive | ☐ whiny | Passive |
| ☐ too rapid | Aggressive | ☐ too soft or too slow | Passive |
| ☐ too urgent | Aggressive | ☐ too nasal | Passive |

## GESTURES

| Behavior | Style | Behavior | Style |
|---|---|---|---|
| ☐ some positive head nodding | Assertive | ☐ hands on hips | Aggressive |
| ☐ some hand gestures | Assertive | ☐ clenched or pounding fists | Aggressive |
| ☐ composed, not erratic | Assertive | ☐ tilting head to one side | Passive |
| ☐ open hand (conveys trust) | Assertive | ☐ bringing hand to face | Passive |
| ☐ leaning toward speaker | Assertive | ☐ excessive head nodding | Passive |
| ☐ pointing finger | Aggressive | ☐ any form of fidgeting | Passive |

CONTINUED ON NEXT PAGE

# CAREER ACTION 11-2

(CONTINUED)

## DISTRACTING NONVERBAL HABITS

| | Behavior | Style | | Behavior | Style |
|---|---|---|---|---|---|
| ☐ | fiddling with any object | Passive | ☐ | scratching | Passive |
| ☐ | use of fillers (um, uh, etc.) | Passive | ☐ | stroking beard, mustache | Passive |
| ☐ | jangling keys, coins, etc. | Passive | ☐ | biting nails | Passive |
| ☐ | fiddling with hair | Passive | | | |

## OTHER HABITS (List any other similar habits you have.)

| | Behavior | Style | | Behavior | Style |
|---|---|---|---|---|---|
| ☐ | ____________ | ______ | ☐ | ____________ | ______ |
| ☐ | ____________ | ______ | ☐ | ____________ | ______ |
| ☐ | ____________ | ______ | ☐ | ____________ | ______ |

**Part 2**

**DIRECTIONS:** Review your self-assessment; then make a list of negative nonverbal habits you plan to change. List them in order of importance (most important change first).

## MY GOALS FOR IMPROVING NONVERBAL COMMUNICATION

1. ______________________________
2. ______________________________
3. ______________________________
4. ______________________________
5. ______________________________

CHAPTER 12

# Master the Art of Getting Interviews

"Present yourself with confidence when communicating with a potential employer. Your own confidence will help convince them that you are the best person for the job. A genuine sense of enthusiasm conveys the high energy and interest level that employers want. Enthusiasm also helps sustain you during the job-search process, encouraging you to follow up, maintain contact and keep a positive outlook—all things that, ultimately, will distinguish you from the crowd."

*Charlene Crusoe-Ingram*
*Vice President of Organization and People Development*
*Coca-Cola USA*

## *In this chapter you will:*

- Develop written scripts for interview bids to be made through personal visit or by telephone.
- Practice delivering your bid for an interview.

Use the Internet to research job search telephone strategies.

To land your target job, you first need to get an interview. Sound strategies for succeeding in this essential job search step are outlined in Chapter 12. Techniques for arranging interviews directly and indirectly are presented.

# DIRECT BIDS FOR INTERVIEWS

You can use four direct methods of contacting employers for an interview: personal visit, telephone, standard letter, or Internet communication. Once you identify a "hot" employer prospect, your goal is to get an interview. Statistically, the most productive methods are face-to-face or telephone contact. Don't write a letter when you can call, and don't call when you can make a personal visit. If you can't visit or call, a standard letter or Internet communication is appropriate. Review your 60-Second Commercial, resume, and cover letter that you prepared earlier. Tailor your bid for an interview by emphasizing your strengths and experience most relevant to the needs of each prospective employer.

## Tips for Verbal Effectiveness in Interview Bids

To increase your success rate in landing interviews, focus on being courteous, likeable, professional, persuasive, and resourceful. Follow the guidelines below to project likability and professionalism in face-to-face and telephone interview bids:

- Use a friendly tone and moderate pitch and speed.
- Use correct grammar.
- Speak distinctly and confidently.
- Eliminate slang and annoying filler expressions ("um," "uh," or "you know").
- Always be courteous.
- Emphasize your qualifications before requesting an interview.

Figure • 12-1: Personal contact—by phone or in person—is the best way to make contact for an interview.

**NOTE:** Respect the person's time; most businesspeople will have only a few minutes for your visit or call. If you sense this is not a good time, say something like, "I'd be glad to call/visit you at a more convenient time, if necessary." Never act irritable; remain composed and professional.

**SUCCESS TIP**

**When you ask for an interview, provide a reason for a *yes* answer by emphasizing your qualifications before requesting the interview!**

## The Focus of Your Interview Bid

The focus of an effective interview bid should be on how your abilities can benefit (even be essential to) the employer. Your employer research is vital and should include finding out who is in charge of the department that could benefit most from your abilities. This is the target person for your interview bid.

Review the 60-Second Commercial you developed in Chapter 11 (**Career Action 11-3**, on page 211). Use a brief modification of it as the base for your bid for an interview.

**SUCCESS TIP**

**When you make a bid for an interview in person, prepare as if you were going to an actual interview. First impressions influence the outcome.**

## Making a Bid through a Personal Visit

A direct bid for an interview through a personal visit is statistically the most successful method of getting interviews. It is difficult for people to ignore you when you are standing in front of them. Here are guidelines for making a successful bid for an interview in person:

1. **Dress for the part.** Dress and groom yourself as if for an actual interview—perfectly.
2. **Research the firm thoroughly beforehand.**
3. **Be prepared.** Take your Interview Marketing Kit (Chapter 11) with you, including your 60-Second Commercial and your resume.
4. **Pay special attention to the "gatekeeper"** (the person between you and the employer): the secretary, receptionist, supervisor, or human resources specialist. Actively and courteously seek that person's help (see "Breaking Secretarial Barriers" later in this chapter).
5. **Present the most concise, action-packed version of your 60-Second Commercial**, and then make a bid for an interview.
6. **Thank your contact by name** for his or her time and consideration.

**IMPORTANT!** If you don't get an interview, ask for referrals to another department or company that might need your abilities.

Study the bid on page 226 for an interview made during a personal visit to an employer. The applicant highlights qualifications, demonstrates knowledge of the employer and the industry, and expresses interest in the job—just the right approach!

**Complete Career Action 12-1**

# CAREER ACTION 12-1

## Develop Your Personal Bid for an Interview

**DIRECTIONS:** Read the sample script in Figure 12-2 on page 226; then write or key a script that would be appropriate to use in making a bid in person for an interview.

## SCRIPT OF A BID FOR AN INTERVIEW MADE IN PERSON

**OBJECTIVE:** Administrative Support Position in a Medical Center

◆ **The Opening:**

"Hello, Mr. Selland, my name is Jaleesa Williams. My instructor, Gerald Johnston, recommends your Information Services Department at Saint Francis Hospital for its well-organized systems design. I just completed my degree in information processing with emphasis in medical transcription and terminology."

◆ **60-Second Commercial Excerpt:**

"I worked 18 months as an information processing specialist at Lewis State College while finishing school. I'm proficient in Word, Excel, Access, PowerPoint, and Outlook software. I operate personal computers, networks, and general office equipment. I also type at 70 words per minute and am skilled in English usage."

◆ **The Bid for an Interview:**

"I've developed some time-saving methods for processing and managing merge documents that are appropriate for your department. Would you possibly have time for me to review them with you today, or would one day next week be convenient?"

◆ **Close the Sale:**

"Next Tuesday at 10 A.M.? I appreciate your willingness to meet with me so soon, Mr. Selland. I'll look forward to meeting with you then. Thank you and good-bye."

Figure • 12-2: Script of a bid for an interview made in person

**Prepare your script and practice asking for an interview before you make a real request.**

### Requesting an Interview by Telephone

The telephone can be your powerful ally. It demands immediate attention from the person who answers it and reduces the time you need for initial inquiries. Use the telephone to survey employers and to determine whether they're viable targets for employment. Follow up with personal visits to the most likely prospects.

### Tips for Using the Telephone Persuasively

Good telephone communication skills will affect the success of your entire working career. You can develop these skills just as you develop any other skill. To prepare and make persuasive job search telephone calls, (a) follow the methods outlined on page 227 in "Guidelines for Organizing and Making Telephone Calls," and (b) review the "Script of Telephone Bid for an Interview" in Figure 12-3 on page 228.

## Guidelines for Organizing and Making Telephone Calls

1. **Determine the purpose of your call first.** Is it to get the name of the employer? Is it to request information? Is it to request an interview?

2. **Learn all you can about the organization before calling.** Get the name of the person you need to contact before you call to request an interview. You may need to make a preliminary call to get this.

3. **Write out your script completely.** Beforehand, summarize the key points you need to cover in your call. Pattern your script after the samples in this chapter, and refer to your 60-Second Commercial. List all the information you need to obtain from your contact. The script or outline is essential! It helps you organize your message, sound intelligent and well prepared, and provides a good reference in case you forget items.

4. **Smile when you speak on the telephone.** The muscles used to smile actually relax the vocal cords and create a pleasant voice tone. Try it—it works!

5. **What do you say when someone answers the telephone?**

   a. Identify yourself first: "Hello, this is Brenda Bernstein." (Secretaries who screen calls are immediately suspicious of callers who don't give their names or don't state why they are calling; so be straightforward, and eliminate suspicions instantly.)

   b. Identify your purpose for calling: Deliver your bid for an interview, or use a practiced indirect strategy for getting through to the employer.

   c. Get the name of the person who answers: Ask, "Could I please have your name in case I need to talk with you again?" (Write it down! Using this person's name can make him or her far more receptive to helping you.)

   d. Clarify the details: Clarify any follow-up activities you are to complete (pick up an application, supply additional information or references, keep an appointment, etc.). Always verify the time and place for any meetings; get the correct spelling and pronunciation of the names of people you will meet with.

   e. Thank the person by name.

**NOTE:** If you need practice before actually calling for an interview, use "Indirect Strategy Sample A," presented later in this chapter. You could ask all the questions in this sample by telephone or request a meeting to discuss them. Study the telephone script of an interview bid in Figure 12-3, and notice how qualifications, knowledge of the employer and the industry, and interest in the employer are incorporated.

**Complete Career Action 12-2 on page 228**

## SCRIPT OF A BID FOR AN INTERVIEW MADE BY TELEPHONE

**OBJECTIVE:** Sales Representatve Position

◆ **The Opening:**
"Hello, Ms. Hope. This is Stephen Rogowski. I'm just completing research comparing the product quality and service records of computer network manufacturers. I'm impressed with the results XYZ Company has achieved, and I'm interested in learning about your sales representative position."

◆ **60-Second Commercial Excerpt:**
"I'm completing my degree at Lewis State College in sales and marketing and have two years of successful retail sales experience. I also worked as the advertising assistant for our school paper and increased sales by 18 percent this year."

◆ **The Bid for an Interview:**
"Would it be possible to arrange a meeting with you to discuss your sales goals and how I might contribute to them?"

◆ **Close the Sale:**
"Thank you, Ms. Hope. I look forward to meeting with you next Tuesday, the 18th, at 2:30. Good-bye."

**NOTE:** Ask for referrals if you don't get an interview. For example:
"I appreciate your time, Ms. Hope. Could you suggest anyone who might have a position in my field in another department or in another organization?"

Figure • 12-3: Script of a bid for an interview made by telephone

# CAREER ACTION 12-2

## Develop and Practice Bids for an Interview

**PART 1 DIRECTIONS:** Write or key a script that would be appropriate to use in making a telephone bid for an interview with your prospective job target(s).

**PART 2 DIRECTIONS:** Once again, you can turn to your support system for assistance. Do some role playing, and practice following the guidelines below: Deliver your telephone or personal visit bid for an interview to your support system helper.

1. Tape your delivery, play it back, critique it, and improve it where necessary.
2. Request your helper to ask you questions that require more detail about your qualifications.
3. Practice responding when your helper makes excuses for not scheduling an interview.
4. Practice presenting your qualifications persuasively.
5. Practice turning objections into acceptance.
6. Persevere.

### Requesting an Interview by Letter

If you are relying on your cover letter and resume to attract interviews and you have prepared these documents well, you are ready to make your interview bid. First, find out which method is appropriate for your target employer: sending your request by regular mail, fax, or e-mail. Second, review the instructions in Chapter 10 for preparing and distributing your cover letter.

If you don't receive responses from your cover letter and resume within two to three weeks, reinforce the bid through a telephone call or personal visit.

**"The people who get on in the world are the people who get up and look for circumstances they want, and if they can't find them, make them."**

—George Bernard Shaw

### Responding to a Job Posted on the Internet

If you find a job posted on the Internet through a general job-posting site or a specific employer's Web site, follow the instructions provided exactly. Often, employers want you to e-mail or fax your resume and a cover letter to them. They may use a special code to identify a specific job opening; be sure to include it in your cover letter. They may also have an online resume form you fill out or a block into which you can paste your resume or letter. All of these options become your technical "bid for an interview."

## INDIRECT STRATEGIES FOR LANDING INTERVIEWS

To reach an employer, bypass a secretary, or find the hidden job market, you may need to use an indirect strategy that will lead to a request for an interview. Indirect requests for interviews are especially important during times of high job competition.

### Getting Through to the Employer

When job competition is high, many employers are flooded with applicants. They may issue a temporary no-hire policy, which makes personal contact difficult because employees are instructed to notify applicants that no interviews are being scheduled.

This is the time to use initiative and persistence. Develop a persuasive reason to contact the person with hiring authority in your target organization.

An indirect strategy can create opportunities to meet people in your job target organization who can arrange an interview for you. Although you should not make a direct bid for a job during a meeting arranged indirectly, you can discuss your experience and abilities. You may actually convince your contact you would be an asset to the organization—exactly your intention! Also ask if the employer might need your skills in the future or if your contact could suggest another organization or department that could use someone with your qualifications.

The indirect strategies shown in Figure 12-4 on page 230 provide a natural lead to discussing your qualifications. Consider using any that seem appropriate for your job search, or ask members of your support system to help you develop another strategy.

### Breaking Secretarial Barriers

The "gatekeeper" (the secretary, receptionist, or human resources staff) who must screen all job applicants can help, hinder, or destroy your chance for a job with the organization. This person's influence on your job campaign could be considerable, so you

## INDIRECT STRATEGIES FOR GETTING AN INTERVIEW

### ◆ Indirect Strategy Sample A

Ask to arrange a brief meeting with the employer to discuss professional associations and publications in your field. Once you meet, ask whether he or she could recommend a professional association that would keep you informed of industry developments, technology, and trends. Also ask for the name of good professional publications or Internet resources that deal specifically with your field. Also ask whether your contact could refer you to anyone else for further advice on this topic.

### ◆ Indirect Strategy Sample B

*For limited work experience related to your job target*

Call to ask for assistance with your career planning and educational preparation: "Hello, Mr. Cuevo, this is Celia Lee. I'm completing an assignment for my career planning course and would appreciate your assistance with some of the research. I'm seeking opinions from people who are recognized and experienced in the field of (your field), which is why I'm calling you. My skills lie in the area(s) of ________________. Could you help me identify positions within (your career field) for which these skills would be most useful? I'd also appreciate your recommendations regarding additional course work and preparation I might need."

### ◆ Indirect Strategy Sample C

*For limited work experience related to your job target*

Sample C is similar to Sample B but has a minor variation: "My major is ________, and my career objective is ___________________. I would appreciate your helping me identify elective course work or a minor (another minor) that would strengthen my educational preparation and support my career goal."

### ◆ Indirect Strategy Sample D

*Request help in the development of your resume*

"Hello, Ms. Pappas. This is Mildred Hayward. You've been highly recommended to me by Dr. Ivarsen of the Data Processing Department of Nevada College. I'm developing a professional resume and would very much appreciate your critiquing it."

### ◆ Indirect Strategy Sample E

*Follow-up call to Sample B or or C*

Four to six months later, follow up Sample B or C. Call back to say: "Hello, Mr. Cuevo. This is Celia Lee. You gave me some excellent advice six months ago. Would you consider evaluating my preparation now?" Ask to arrange a meeting, and then approach it as you would an interview—totally prepared! Remember: This person advised you earlier. If you followed the advice, he or she could consider hiring you for demonstrating initiative and intelligence. (After all, it was his or her idea, so it must be a good one!)

Figure • 12-4: Summary of indirect strategies for getting an interview

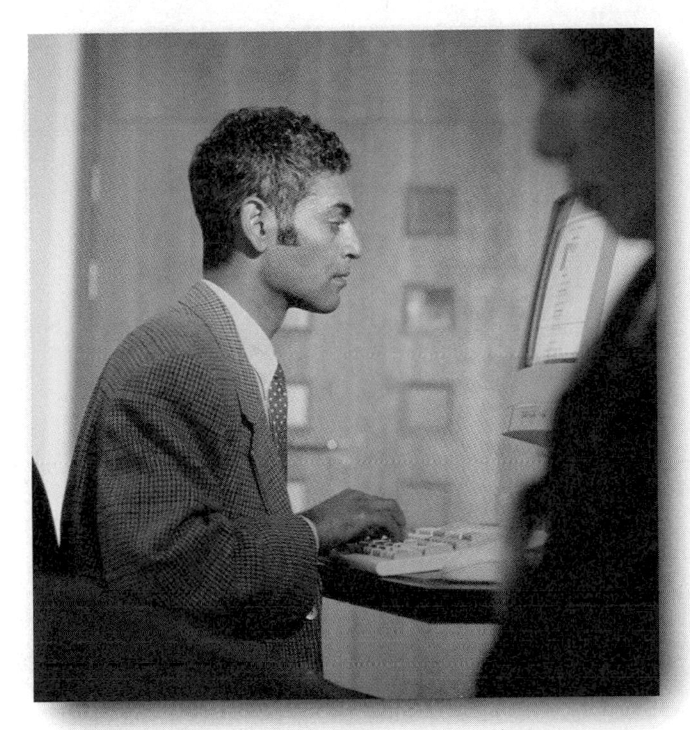

Figure • 12-5: The "gatekeeper" can be a barrier or a resource in your pursuit of an interview.

need to use good diplomacy skills. The following recommendations will help establish a good relationship.

- Express respect for the organization, perhaps referring to its reputation for professionalism, reliability, or leadership. A gatekeeper who is happily employed with the organization will likely agree with your comments and may help you.

- Make as much effort to get the gatekeeper on your side as you do to get the employer to hire you. Be personable, courteous, and enthusiastic.

- As in the interview itself, notice the gatekeeper's surroundings. An interested comment from you about a family portrait, a wall decoration, or a desk item can relax the atmosphere. If the gatekeeper seems receptive, you can discuss your job search; you may get useful assistance!

- Ask for the gatekeeper's help in arranging an interview with the employer, indicating your awareness of busy schedules; ask the gatekeeper to suggest the best time to contact the employer. Ask if you could speak with someone else who could tell you more about your areas of interest.

SUCCESS TIP

**Always treat "gatekeepers" (secretaries and receptionists) courteously and professionally. They are often the keys to connecting with the hiring authority.**

## Uncovering the Hidden Job Market

You could uncover the hidden job market mentioned in Chapter 6. These jobs are not advertised. In fact, employers may be unaware they have positions you could fill. It's up to you to make an employer aware of your potential and possibly create a job in the process.

**Research and Prepare.** To uncover the hidden job market, you need to research carefully and learn as much as possible about the employer's products or services, structure, and so on. Then you need to analyze how your qualifications can be useful, even essential, to the employer. Prepare a dynamic 60-Second Commercial emphasizing how you could benefit the employer, and get someone skilled in writing to help you polish it. The key is to identify how you could provide a useful service or how you could save or make money for the organization.

Find out who is in charge of the department that could use your assets—your hidden job market target. Practice and polish your hidden job market sales pitch.

A member of your support system could help you by playing the role of your contact and critiquing your presentation.

SUCCESS TIP

**Tap into the hidden job market. Resourceful applicants create jobs by researching employer needs well and by showing how their abilities meet the needs exactly.**

**Encourage the Need for Your Capabilities.** Armed with thorough employer research and a 60-Second Commercial that illustrates how you can benefit the firm, you could uncover a job the employer hasn't even considered.

Think big! The hidden job market is limited only by your imagination. You have everything to gain by tapping into this market in your bids for an interview.

## Going through the Human Resources Department

If your target employer has a strict policy requiring all applicants to be processed through the human resources department, you may have follow the procedures. Usually, your first step will be to submit an application, a resume, and a cover letter.

If the organization is interviewing, the first interview will likely be a screening interview given in person by a member of the human resources staff. Note, however, that some screening interviews are conducted by telephone to save time and money. One purpose will be to verify the information in your cover letter, application, and resume. Also during this screening interview, you will be judged on your self-confidence, composure, intelligence, and personality. Projecting energy, enthusiasm, and confidence are essential during screening interviews.

Figure • 12-6: If you have a screening interview with human resources staff, project poise and enthusiasm.

> **"If you only knock long enough and loud enough at the gate, you are sure to wake up somebody!"**
>
> —Henry Wadsworth Longfellow

If you perform well during a screening interview and if your qualifications appear to be adequate, you may be scheduled for a departmental interview. If the employer doesn't have openings in your area, find out how to keep your file active and how you can remain informed of the hiring status for the position.

## Employment Agencies/Contractors

If you are planning to use employment agencies or contractors in your job search, your interviews for jobs will be arranged by them. Read each agency's agreement thoroughly to be certain you are satisfied with the method of interviewing. Clarify the procedure carefully before agreeing to it. Review the information presented on employment agencies and contractors in Chapter 6.

## Develop a Plan When Your Targeted Job Is Not Open

If your preferred employer is not scheduling interviews because the company has absolutely no openings, reevaluate your goal.

If your ultimate goal is still to work for this organization and you think it is worth waiting for, develop an effective waiting plan. The following guidelines may help:

1. **Take another job during the waiting period.** This work experience can improve your value. During your interim job, you can polish your current skills, develop new ones, and establish a reputation as a valuable employee.

2. **Follow up.** Call your target employer after you have had some time in your interim job and when you think employment opportunities have improved. Ask whether the employer would consider reevaluating your qualifications in light of your new experience, or ask for additional suggestions to improve your employability.

3. **Check back periodically.** Call the human resources department of your target employer to remain informed of the hiring status and to reaffirm your interest. This helps keep you first in line for openings.

### TAKE ACTION

Make those calls; send letters; check the Internet. Successful achievement never starts with *if*, *but*, or *later*.

If you consider more than one organization to be a prime employer, don't let one discouragement slow you down. Review the techniques presented in this chapter, and rally your efforts toward your next target. Preparation, practice, action, and perseverance pay off!

**Complete Career Action 12-3**

## CAREER ACTION 12-3

### Use the Internet to Find Strategies for Getting Job Interviews

**DIRECTIONS:** Conduct an Internet search to find additional tips for getting job interviews. You may want to look for special tips on using the telephone effectively in the job search. Look for new ideas that may be specifically useful to you. Write a summary of your findings, or print copies of the data.

Use the following Internet resources or others of your choice to conduct this search:

**Internet Web Sites:**

| | |
|---|---|
| CAREERMagazine | http://www.careermag.com |
| Monster.com | http://www.monster.com |
| CareerLab | http://www.careerlab.com |

## CHECKLIST FOR MASTERING THE ART OF GETTING INTERVIEWS

Check each of the following actions you are currently taking to increase your career success:

- ☐ When you ask for an interview, provide a reason for a *yes* answer by emphasizing your qualifications before requesting the interview.
- ☐ When you make a bid for an interview in person, prepare as if you were going to an actual interview. First impressions influence the outcome.
- ☐ Prepare your script and practice asking for an interview before you make a real request.
- ☐ Always treat gatekeepers (secretaries and receptionists) courteously and professionally. They are often the key to connecting with the hiring authority.
- ☐ Tap into the hidden job market. Resourceful applicants create jobs by researching employer needs well and by showing exactly how their abilities meet the needs.

## CRITICAL THINKING QUESTIONS

1. Explain which method of making a bid for an interview you think will be most effective in your own job search and why.
2. What are some advantages to making bids for interviews by telephone, rather than by letter?
3. Get creative. Think of an employer you could realistically target for a hidden job market position. Describe the needs of this employer on the basis of your research. Then describe special skills and knowledge you have that could represent a "hidden job" you could perform to meet the employer needs.

CHAPTER 13

# Be Prepared for Any Interview Style

> We give a one-on-one interview the first time we interview an applicant. If we bring them back for a second interview, we have two people interview them. Usually, we can get more in-depth in the second interview because the applicant is less nervous. If we are seriously considering hiring the person, we will send them to a staff member that is equal to their level to ask any questions and ensure a good match.
>
> *Ron Taylor, CPA*
> *Partner*
> *Robinson, Maynard & Associates*

## *In this chapter you will:*

- Conduct direct employer research to learn about styles of interviews used in your field.
- Use the Internet to search for additional useful information on interview styles.
- Prepare a summary of the information from this chapter and from your research that is most pertinent to your job search.

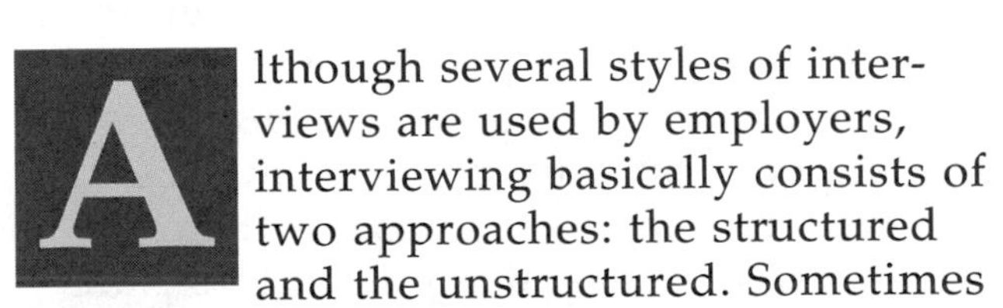

Although several styles of interviews are used by employers, interviewing basically consists of two approaches: the structured and the unstructured. Sometimes styles are combined within one interview. At other times, the interview usually falls into one of the two approaches. Once you have a job interview scheduled, you will greatly improve your chance of success if you find out what style of interview it will be. Usually, the human resources department or receptionist will explain the general interview style and process to you.

## THE INTERVIEW CONNECTION

In all interviews, try to give the interviewer a picture of your personal attributes as well as of your experience, skills, and other job qualifications. Make your verbal and nonverbal messages positive, incorporating posture, facial expressions, voice qualities, and so on that convey competence, friendliness, energy, and enthusiasm. This helps to make the interviewer feel comfortable and to create an open tone, which improves the chance for a successful interview. This helps both you and the interviewer relax and improves the natural flow of conversation. When under less tension, you can better communicate the information necessary for a good interview.

## THE STRUCTURED INTERVIEW

The structured interview is often used by professional interviewers who work in the human resources department or who are part of a corporate team, panel, or other trained interviewing group. The interviewer often uses a planned pattern of questioning, sometimes recording your responses and making notes on a checklist or interview rating form. Many use the same list of questions for each job applicant to ensure fairness in interviewing. The approach is formal and focuses on obtaining factual information. Sometimes a highly structured approach doesn't give the interviewer adequate information about the applicant's personality and attitudes.

**Be friendly, courteous, and positive to establish rapport with interviewers and to help relax the tone of overly structured interviews.**

### The Behavioral Interview

In the *behavioral interview*, the interviewer uses questions aimed at getting the applicant to provide specific examples of how he or she has successfully used the required job skills. If you have completed the activities in Chapter 12, you are ready to handle this style of interview. Your 60-Second Commercial contains the "proof by example" descriptions of your capabilities most relevant to the job target. This is exactly what interviewers are looking for in a behavioral interview.

Figure • 13-1: In a behavioral interview, the interviewer might ask you to role play a situation, such as counseling an unhappy employee.

Topics frequently included in a behavioral interview involve the following skill areas: (a) organizing and planning, (b) communications, (c) problem solving and decision making, (d) team building, (e) creativity, (f) flexibility, (g) motivating self and others, (h) coping with conflict, time constraints, stress, and so on, and (i) job-specific knowledge and technical skills.

The following are typical examples of behavioral interview inquiries:

1. Give me an example of how you have managed conflict well.

2. Give me an example of your ability to be a team player, motivate yourself and others, cope with time constraints, etc.

3. Describe your leadership experience. Give examples that show your leadership style.

4. Describe exactly how you have used this software, equipment, or tool in the past.

**In behavioral interviews, provide the "proof by example" descriptions of your capabilities; include relevant parts of your 60-Second Commercial.**

## The Human Resources Department (Screening) Interview

Large organizations often require applicants to be interviewed first through the human resources department. The *screening interview* is used to identify qualified applicants for the next level of interview and to screen out those who don't have the basic qualifications. Your objectives in this interview are to make your qualifications clear and to try to find out exactly who makes the final hiring decision.

If the interviewer does not give you this information during the interview, politely ask who will make the final hiring decision. If you are qualified for the job, this will accomplish two things: (a) The interviewer will feel more obligated to arrange an interview for you with the hiring authority, and (b) you can attempt to arrange the interview if the human resources department doesn't.

Although it is best to work through regular organizational channels, if your attempts are unsuccessful, try to arrange the interview yourself. Some employers are impressed with an applicant who doesn't give up; other employers may be annoyed that protocol was not honored. If the human resources department will not help you, setting up your own interview is worth a try—and you just might get the job! Always take this approach with care; never be abrasive or "pushy."

The interviewer may use a rating sheet to evaluate each applicant. Review Figure 13-2, a typical interview rating form, and notice the categories of evaluation.

Remember that the goal of your screening interview is to be scheduled for the next required interview. If the screening interviewer does not tell you, ask what to expect next, who is responsible for making the final hiring decision, and when this decision will be made.

As a rule, you should expect to have no fewer than two interviews with an employer before a hiring decision is made. Some organizations give three or four interviews before selecting an applicant. A hiring decision is rarely made during the first interview. If you are scheduled for a follow-up interview, you are definitely in the running, so review and polish your interviewing skills. Keep your chin up, your smile broad, and go for the win!

## INTERVIEW EVALUATION

**APPLICANT:** ____________________ **DATE:** ____________________

**POSITION:** ________________________________________

| | POOR | FAIR | GOOD | VERY GOOD | EXCELLENT |
|---|---|---|---|---|---|
| Resume, Application, Cover Letter | | | | | |
| Attitude/Interest/Enthusiasm | | | | | |
| Communication Skills | | | | | |
| Knowledge of Job/Company | | | | | |
| Education/Training | | | | | |
| Related Experience | | | | | |
| Team Interactive Skills | | | | | |
| Leadership Ability | | | | | |
| Coping Ability (stress, conflict, time demands, etc.) | | | | | |
| Motivation/Goals | | | | | |
| Judgment, Decision Making, Maturity | | | | | |
| Organizational/Planning Skills | | | | | |
| Demonstrated Performance/ Achievements | | | | | |
| Appearance (appropriate dress, grooming) | | | | | |

**COMMENTS:** ________________________________________

**Conclusion:** Considering the observations made above and the applicant's qualifications, do you think this person should be considered for the position?

**YES NO RESERVATIONS:** ______________________________

**INTERVIEWER'S SIGNATURE:** ______________________________

Figure • 13-2: **Typical interview rating form**

## The Campus Interview

Some organizations give *campus interviews* for graduating students in such fields as engineering, electronics, business management, data processing, accounting, retail sales, and marketing. These are prearranged screening interviews, and the techniques vary, depending on the organization. They are usually structured interviews, but several styles are used, such as the stress interview, the "tell me about yourself" interview, or a panel interview. Each style is explained in detail later in this chapter.

Campus interviews are generally scheduled through the school's career services office. The schedule is closely observed, and the interviewer is forced to evaluate each candidate quickly. (The average interview time is twenty to thirty minutes.) In this type of interview, keep your remarks as concise and to the point as possible. Most interviewers are professionally trained and know how to guide applicants through the fact-finding process. Let the interviewer take the lead, and respond as concisely as you can without omitting pertinent information about your qualifications.

**In screening interviews on campus or given by an employer's human resources department, always find out what the next step in the hiring process will be and who makes the final hiring decision.**

**"The spirit, the will to win, and the will to excel are the things that endure."**

—Vince Lombardi

Figure • 13-3: Don't miss out on any job interview opportunities. Check your school's bulletin board to see what organizations will be interviewing on campus.

## The Board or Panel Interview

In a *board or panel interview*, you talk with more than one person. Focus on the person questioning you at the time, but don't ignore the others. Being relaxed and projecting a self-assured attitude are important. Review the techniques dealing with attitude and relaxation in Chapter 11.

Before the interview, get and memorize the names of every member of the panel. Then, during the interview, draw a diagram of the interviewers as they are seated, and label the seats with their names (see Figure 13-4 on page 240). At the close of the interview, thank each one by name and shake hands with each as you leave.

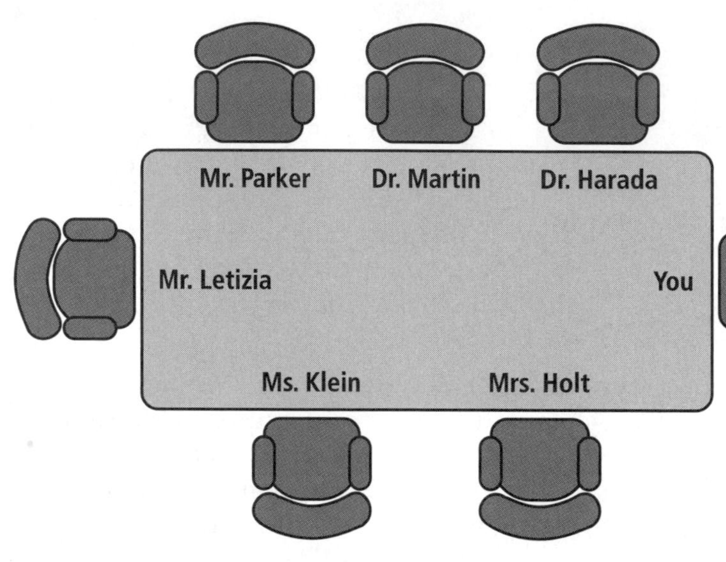


Figure • 13-4: Seating diagram for a panel interview

## The Team Interview

The *team interview* may be given by a group of three to five employees. Usually, these people have been trained in interviewing techniques. They meet prior to the interview to determine the subject areas each team member will cover with the applicant. A few common questions may be asked by all the team members to give the applicant more than one chance for adequate expression.

> **"Things turn out best for people who make the best of the way things turn out."**
>
> —John Wooden

In this style, the applicant meets individually with each member of the team; the team and the applicant do not meet together at one time. After the interviewing is completed, the team members meet to evaluate the applicant's performance and to identify the best candidate. This method gives applicants a chance to meet with several personality types, increasing their chances of establishing rapport with one or more interviewers.

Before a team interview, learn the names of the members and, if possible, learn something about their areas of expertise. Use this information to help enhance your performance. Also give consistent answers to the individual members.

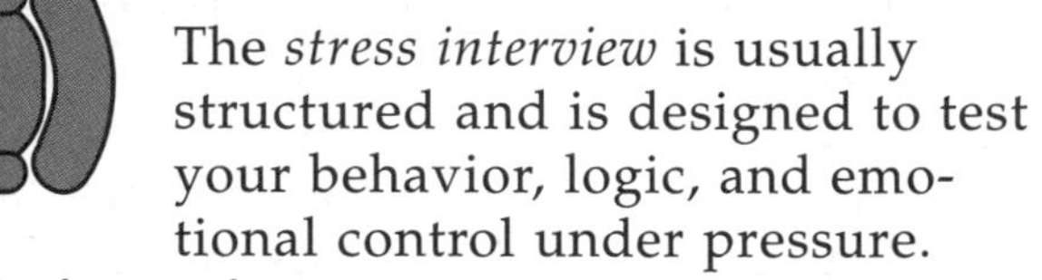

## The Stress Interview

The *stress interview* is usually structured and is designed to test your behavior, logic, and emotional control under pressure. This form of interview is not used routinely. Stress makes it more difficult to assess job qualifications and personal attributes because applicants often become guarded in response to the stress. Stress questions are often reserved for jobs that involve regular pressure. Some stress questions, however, are routinely asked in other types of interviews—even informal ones. Every job occasionally has a crisis situation.

A skillful interviewer may use some stress techniques in combination with an unstructured interview approach to get a well-rounded picture of your personality. The following are some techniques used in stress interviewing:

- Remaining silent following your remark
- Questioning you rapidly
- Placing you on the defensive with irritating questions or remarks
- Criticizing your responses or remarks

An interviewer may use a stress technique unintentionally. If you encounter one, do not react. Take a deep, calm breath, demonstrate control, and be courteous. This type of behavior earns perfect marks in the stress test! (Refer to Chapter 14 for specific examples of stress questions and suggested responses.)

## The "Tell Me about Yourself" Interview

In the *"tell me about yourself" interview*, the interviewer takes a few minutes to build rapport and then says, "Tell me about yourself." Be prepared to handle this style effectively. Once the interviewer asks this question, he or she makes only enough comments to encourage the applicant to keep answering. The purpose is to see whether applicants focus on their qualifications for the job and how the employer would benefit by hiring them. Do not ramble on about your life history—a sure way to disqualify yourself on the spot. Ask questions such as, "What exactly do you want to know about—my work experience, educational experience, skills, or extracurricular and community activities?"

Your objective in this case is to highlight your capabilities (personal attributes, accomplishments, skills, pertinent training, work experience, etc.). After you think you have covered these, ask, "Would you like me to clarify or expand any area for you?" This helps you focus on the information the interviewer wants.

**If the interviewer says, "Tell me about yourself," focus completely on your qualifications for the job. Don't talk about your life history.**

## The Corporate Ladder Interview

Large organizations sometimes schedule *corporate ladder (or multilevel) interviews*. The first rung of the ladder is the human resources department interview, which screens for applicants qualified to progress to the next step. The next interview is usually with a divisional manager or department head and is more detailed and specific regarding your relevant qualifications, skills, and experience.

From this step, you might have one or two more interviews, perhaps with a department manager, followed by the immediate section supervisor for the position. Each step will be progressively more specific in evaluating your suitability for the job. If you are asked the same question by more than one person, try to elaborate creatively while maintaining consistency. The key is to keep your enthusiasm high. This is an endurance test, so keep fueling yourself with positive thinking and expectations. And lean on your support system!

SUCCESS TIP

**To ace multilevel interviews in which you are interviewed by several people, keep your answers consistent and maintain energy and enthusiasm.**

## The Telephone Interview

The *telephone interview* is a cost-effective screening device. If you expect to be interviewed by telephone, prepare by getting a member of your network to role-play the interviewer. Practice delivering your 60-Second Commercial and giving responses to typical interview questions. The following tips will help you succeed in a telephone interview:

1. Post your resume and 60-Second Commercial where you can refer to them easily, and eliminate all distractions.

2. Focus on why you are interested in working for the prospective employer (on the basis of your research and understanding of the employer's products or services, current developments, philosophies, etc.).

3. Be courteous and friendly; let the caller lead the conversation, but add questions of your own.

4. Stand up, smile, and speak directly into the mouthpiece while you're talking; this gives your voice more energy and a pleasant tone.

5. If you need time to think about a question, avoid using repetitive phrases to buy time, and simply say, "Let me think about that."

6. Use the "Clincher" technique described in Chapter 11: Ask what skills, knowledge, and qualities the employer is looking for in filling the position. As the interviewer answers, jot down the qualities you have that match; then describe them to emphasize how you meet their needs.

7. As you wrap up the interview, ask what the next steps will be.

8. Follow up. Call back one or two days later, thank the interviewer for his or her time, and restate your interest in the position. If necessary, leave this message by voice mail or send an e-mail or fax message.

## The Computer-Assisted Interview

Some companies use *computer-assisted interviews* to screen applicants. The applicant is taken to a computer workstation and given instructions on how to take the interview. The interview typically consists of 50 to 100 computerized multiple-choice and true/false questions that are scored automatically. Some computer-assisted interviews include essay questions that are reviewed by recruitment specialists or managers. Answer the questions in the same way you would for a face-to-face interview. Emphasize your related skills thoroughly, but don't exaggerate your abilities. Be as concise as possible, avoiding overly long responses or a negative focus on any topic. Be consistent in your answers; some programs search for contradictions. Also avoid pausing too long to respond; some systems flag abnormally long pauses because it takes longer to think of a lie than to tell the truth.

Benefits of computer-assisted interviews include ease and cost effectiveness of data collection, consistent gathering of information from all applicants to keep the playing field level, and avoidance of personal bias from the interviewer. The primary drawback is that computers are not able to assess personal qualities such as attitude and enthusiasm. These can be observed in follow-up interviews, however.

## The Internet Computer-Assisted Interview

The *Internet computer-assisted interview* is a version of the computer-assisted interview. The Internet interview is useful for long-distance applicant screenings because it saves travel time and other expenses.

In an Internet interview, the employer will contact you and give you a password. Through the Internet, you log on to their in-house computer by using the password and complete an interview that is essentially the same as the computer-assisted interview.

**In computer-assisted interviews, be consistent in your answers and avoid long pauses for responses.**

## The Task-Oriented Interview

In the *task-oriented interview*, applicants are asked to demonstrate their skills by performing specific tasks. This style gives employers a chance to assess skills and knowledge in a realistic, rather than theoretical, way. It also gives applicants a chance to showcase their abilities and to assess their interest in the type of work they would be doing. Always research to find out whether your target employer uses this style of interviewing, and if so, try to find out the types of skills you could be expected to demonstrate. Then practice beforehand.

Figure • 13-5: Some companies ask applicants to demonstrate job-specific and/or transferable skills. Find out if this technique is common to your field or targeted employer.

## The Internet Video Interview

The *Internet video interview* involves using two-way video to conduct a "face-to-face" interview over the Web by having cameras attached to computers at two separate locations. Currently, this method is not widely used because it requires using highly compatible equipment at both ends. As video conferencing becomes more common on computers, this style will probably be used more frequently.

To succeed in this style of interview, follow the techniques outlined in Chapter 11 for standard face-to-face interviews. *Tips:* Dress appropriately, project energy, establish good eye contact with the camera, use positive body language, maintain good posture, and avoid fidgeting.

**Complete Career Action 13-1**

# CAREER ACTION 13-1

## Research Interview Styles

**Part 1: Personal Contact Research**

**DIRECTIONS:** Contact at least two organizations in your field similar to your actual job target, and arrange a brief meeting to research interview styles. Make certain they understand that this is not a bid for an interview. In making your appointment and following through with this outside assignment, follow the guidelines for conducting a successful outside assignment given in Chapter 7.

**The Research Meeting Steps:**

1. During your meetings, ask your contacts to explain the style of interviewing they use to evaluate applicants for positions similar to the one you will be targeting.

CONTINUED ON NEXT PAGE

# CAREER ACTION 13-1

(CONTINUED)

2. Ask what criteria (skills, experience, education, attitudes, personal qualities, etc.) they use to evaluate applicants.

3. Ask for specific examples of positive and negative actions and comments of applicants.

4. Take notes of information you find useful.

5. As always, act professionally and thank the people who help you. Follow up with a thank-you note.

**Part 2: Internet Research**

**NOTE:** Since the content of Web sites is subject to change without notice, be aware that the links referenced below may not match the current content of the Web sites referenced in this assignment.

**DIRECTIONS:** Use the Internet to search for information on interview styles that could be useful to you.

***WebGuide* Activities:** Access "Your Job Search" from the Main Menu. Go to Activity #7. Access each of the sites listed, and summarize information that describes different types of interviews, or print your findings.

**Internet Activities**

Use your favorite search engine, one of those listed below, or other employment-focused Web sites to search for information on different styles of interviews. Search for the interview style(s) you expect to be most prevalent in your field (telephone interview, behavioral interview, campus interview, etc.). Summarize key points you find useful, or print relevant articles.

**Internet Search Engines:**

| | |
|---|---|
| Alta Vista | http://www.altavista.com |
| Excite | http://www.excite.com |
| Infoseek | http://www.infoseek.com/careers |
| Lycos | http://www.lycos.com |
| Yahoo | http://www.yahoo.com/business/employment |

## THE UNSTRUCTURED INTERVIEW

The unstructured approach to interviews is generally taken by people who are not professionally trained in interviewing. It tends to be more informal and conversational in tone. The unstructured approach is often used in small businesses and given by the owners or managers of the firms. In this case, interviewing job applicants is one of many responsibilities of the interviewer; it is not the primary job assignment, as in the case of a human resources specialist in a large organization.

**SUCCESS TIP**

**In unstructured interviews, the most important point is to be sure you present your qualifications thoroughly. If an untrained or unstructured interviewer doesn't focus on extracting this essential information, make sure you bring it out!**

Unstructured interviewing is often more successful at bringing out the personal qualities of the applicant (attitudes, feelings, goals, and human relations skills) than the structured interviewing. The questions are usually broad and allow interviewees to express their personalities.

Untrained interviewers, however, may be less skilled in discussing job qualifications; the conversation may get bogged down in unimportant details. In this case, you need to be the "professional interviewee." You can aid the interviewer by asking questions to learn about the full scope of the job and by communicating all your skills, experience, and attributes that apply to it.

## THE BAD INTERVIEW

Some interviews are not good; in fact, some are grim. After learning the details of the job, you might be convinced that you don't want it. The interviewer may be inept at interviewing, making it difficult for you to perform well. Do not stop trying, however. Do your best to be the professional interviewee. You can always learn something beneficial, and it provides you a chance to polish your interviewing skills. Don't let down; it could cost you a future reference or a good job lead from the interviewer. If you have a bad interview, chalk it up to experience.

## THE UNSUCCESSFUL INTERVIEW

As a general rule, a job applicant must have several interviews before a good job is offered. Getting a top-notch job is a full-time job and often requires several interviews and some rejections. Harness the energy of negative feelings from rejections; turn them into a positive force. Fueling your determination will help you land the job you want most.

Again, remember that you can learn from in-terviews. If you aren't offered the job, ask the interviewer to suggest ways you could improve your interviewing skills or whether you appear to be lacking in any area of skill, training, or experience. This information is the starting point for succeeding in your next interview.

**Complete Career Action 13-2 on page 246**

# CAREER ACTION 13-2

## Summarize Interview Styles Pertinent to Your Field

**DIRECTIONS:** Review all the information in this chapter and your findings from the personal contact and Internet research (**Career Action 13-1**, on pages 243 and 244). On a separate sheet of paper, prepare a report describing the styles of interviews you expect to be most prevalent in your field. Also describe techniques you have learned that would help you succeed in these interview styles.

### CHECKLIST TO PREPARE FOR ANY INTERVIEW STYLE

Check each of the following actions you are currently taking to increase your career success:

- ☐ **Overly structured interviews:** Be friendly and positive to establish rapport and a relaxed tone.
- ☐ **Behavioral interview:** Provide proof by example of your capabilities.
- ☐ **Screening interview:** Find out what the next step will be/who makes the hiring decision.
- ☐ **Board, panel, team interview:** Learn and use the names of all interviewers.
- ☐ **Stress interview:** Keep your cool and dont react!
- ☐ **Tell me about yourself interview:** Focus completely on your job qualifications.
- ☐ **Multilevel or Corporate ladder interview:** Keep answers consistent and maintain energy.
- ☐ **Telephone interview:** Post your resume/commercial close by; stand up, smile, and eliminate distractions.
- ☐ **Computer-assisted interview:** Give consistent answers; avoid long pauses.
- ☐ **Unstructured interview:** Present qualifications thoroughly.

## CRITICAL THINKING QUESTIONS

1. How can job seekers benefit by learning what style of interview is typically given by their target employers?
2. What benefits can you gain by trying to relax the atmosphere of a highly structured interview?
3. Which style(s) of interviewing do you expect to be most prevalent in your job search? What techniques can you use to maximize your performance in the style(s)?

CHAPTER 14

# Navigate Interview Questions and Answers

"All of the agents in our company work on straight commission. If the very first question an agent asks in an interview is, 'What is the commission?' I know that the agent is only out for himself or herself. I want agents working for me who will put the clients' interests first."

*Ross Riley, President*
*Agency Development Corporation*

*In this chapter you will:*

Use the Internet to search for useful additional information on interview questions and answers.

- Write out appropriate answers for frequently asked interview questions, and write suitable questions to ask during your interview.

The core of your interview is the question-and-answer period, and it should include questions and answers from both the interviewer and you. To ace your interview, generally let the interviewer take the lead; interviewers usually consider applicants' efforts to control to be rude. You, too, however, should ask questions—for two reasons: (a) to verify that this is the employer you want to work for and (b) to demonstrate initiative and preparation. Chapter 14 presents a comprehensive overview of common interview questions, tips for answering these effectively, and samples of meaningful questions to ask.

## FOCUS ON YOUR JOB QUALIFICATIONS

Persuasively discussing your strengths and how they can benefit the employer requires some preparation. Consider the positive capabilities and personal qualities your coworkers, supervisors, teachers, and others have recognized and noted about you. Review your 60-Second Commercial and your resume, and write out examples of your positive performance related to the job target requirements.

What examples demonstrate your organizational skills and orderly mind? Have you developed better methods of performing tasks or working with people? How have you motivated people successfully? Can you cite examples of effective problem solving? Are you creative? Can you give examples of handling detail work well? Are you always dependable and cooperative? What activities have you been involved in that demonstrate each of these? Are you flexible, able to work independently without regular supervision, and able to work effectively in a team? Choose these types of examples to showcase what you can do for the employer. Focus on your qualifications in the question-and-answer period of your interview.

**Focus on "Proof by Example." Respond persuasively to questions about your abilities; give measurable examples of successfully applying them in work, school, and other activities.**

## PREPARE FOR INTERVIEWER QUESTIONS

Questions asked by interviewers generally fall into four categories: general information questions, behavioral questions, character questions, and stress questions. Following are lists of the most commonly posed interview questions. Study the questions and suggested answers; in **Career Action 14-2**, you will write your responses to these questions. Writing and rehearsing this script will help you answer questions successfully during your interview.

### General Information Questions

General information questions are designed to obtain factual information about you. These questions usually cover your skills, education, work experience, and so on.

1. **Why do you want this job?** (Be prepared for this one; every employer wants to know the answer.)

   **Suggested Answer:** "My skills and experience are directly related to this position, and my interest lies especially in this field." Then relate examples of your experience, education, or training that are pertinent to the job you are seeking; base this on your employer and job research. Emphasize your interest in developing your career in this area. *Don't* ever say you want the job because of the pay and benefits. If you are impressed with and knowledgeable about the reputation of the firm, say so; and add that you would be pleased to be a part of the organization. Don't overdo it, however; overt flattery is usually a turnoff to interviewers.

2. **What type of work do you most enjoy?**

   **Suggested Answer:** Play your research card; name the types of tasks that would be involved in the job. By doing this, you demonstrate your research and how you are qualified for the position.

3. **What are your strongest skills?**

   **Suggested Answer:** Review your abilities and accomplishments and your 60-Second Commercial. Use these to develop your answer to this question. Again, try to relate your skills to those required in the position for which you are applying.

4. **What are your long-range career goals, and how do you plan to achieve them?**

   **Suggested Answer:** Although this is usually an information-oriented question, it can be a stress question if you trap yourself by appearing overly aggressive, too ambitious, or lacking in ambition. Employers look for loyalty in return for their training investment and are not interested in hiring someone who plans to stay in an entry-level job just until something better comes along. Emphasize your strengths, state that your goal is to make a strong contribution in your job, and state that you look forward to developing the experience necessary for career growth.

   Employers are impressed with people who show initiative; they often perform better than those who have no plans for self-improvement. Mention plans to continue your education and expand your knowledge to become a more valuable employee.

5. **Are you a team player?**

   **Suggested Answer:** Teamwork is highly valued in today's workplaces, so a positive answer is typically a plus. Give examples of your successful team roles (as a leader, as a member, and as a partner) at school, on the job, and in clubs or other activities.

Figure • 14-1: Review your self-assessment from Chapter 2. Use school and sports activities and accomplishments in other jobs when responding to questions about teamwork, character, and personal strengths.

6. **Do you have a geographical preference? Are you willing to relocate?**

   **Suggested Answer:** If the job requires relocation, this question is important. If you have no objection to relocating, make this perfectly clear. If you do have objections, this could be a stress question. Be honest in your answer. If you don't like being mobile, say so; otherwise, you will undoubtedly be unhappy in the job.

7. **Under what management style do you work most efficiently?**

   **Suggested Answer:** "I am flexible and can be productive under any style. The management style I enjoy working with the most is ____________." (This shows you to be flexible and casts no negative connotations. It also answers the primary question.)

**Prepare and rehearse responses to typical interview questions. The result can determine your interview and career success.**

## Behavioral Interview Questions

The behavioral job interview is used widely today and is based on the premise that past performance is the best way to predict future behavior. Behavioral questions probe specific past performance and behaviors through questions such as: "Describe one of the most challenging assignments you've had, and explain how you handled it." This may be followed by several more in depth probes aimed at getting further details, such as, "Explain what problems you encountered." "How did you overcome them?" Some behavioral questions probe for negative experiences; in responding to these, focus on what you learned from the experience or what actions you took to improve.

To prepare for these interviews, recall scenarios of your experiences that illustrate how you have performed or behaved on the job. Write out examples that demonstrate good performance, and also be ready to describe how you have handled difficult situations. Students with little work experience should focus on class projects and group situations that illustrate your task performance and interpersonal behavior.

A good model for your answers is based on four elements: (1) describe the situation, (2) explain the actions you took, (3) describe the outcomes, and (4) summarize what you learned from the experience.

**Example:** Describe an accomplishment that demonstrates your initiative.

**Answer:** "While working part-time as a Computer Lab Technician for Seattle Technology College, our department had been receiving several complaints about service response time. I set a personal goal of answering all trouble-shooting calls within 90 minutes. I recorded the exact response time for each call and maintained the 90-minute response goal for one full semester. I was awarded the Customer Service Certificate for this performance."

Whenever possible, give positive examples that demonstrate measurable achievements. Or when describing a less positive experience, emphasize what actions you took to correct weaknesses or poor performance. By giving specific examples, you establish credibility and believability that can translate into a job offer. Some additional examples of behavioral interview questions are listed below:

1. Tell me specifically about a time you worked under great stress.

2. Describe an experience when you dealt with an angry customer or co-worker.

3. Give me an example that would demonstrate your ability to adapt to change.

## Character Questions

Character questions are used to learn about personal attributes, such as integrity, personality, attitudes, and motivation.

1. **How would you describe yourself?**

   **Suggested Answer:** Emphasize your strongest personal attributes, and focus on those relevant to your target job. Review your capabilities and accomplishments. Appropriate responses include:

"I'm punctual and dependable; I haven't been late for work or missed one day in the last two years at my current job." "I get along well with others; in fact, I've been chosen by my co-workers to represent them in our company's monthly staff meetings." Give specific examples of your strengths. Don't just say, "I'm a hard worker," or, "I'm dependable"; give concrete examples. Other leads include, "I learn quickly," "I like solving problems, for example...," "I like contributing to a team," and, "I like managing people."

2. **What rewards do you look for in your career?**

   **Suggested Answer:** Don't stress monetary rewards. Emphasize your desire to improve your skills, to make a valuable contribution to the field, and to become better educated. These show initiative, interest, and professionalism. You may mention you expect an income that matches your performance.

3. **Of what accomplishment are you most proud, particularly as it relates to your field?**

   **Suggested Answer:** Relate an accomplishment that demonstrates special effort and initiative—perhaps one that surpassed normal requirements. For example, at your last job you recognized the need for improving communications within the organization. You designed a questionnaire that was completed by representatives of every department. Management initiated the changes suggested, and communications improved in the areas identified.

   **Another example:** You purchased a computer with earnings from your part-time job and then used the equipment to start your own business preparing term papers, resumes, and other items for students and instructors from your school and community. The earnings paid for 80 percent of your school costs.

4. **Do you work well under pressure?**

   **Suggested Answer:** Be honest in your answer. If you prefer to work at a well-defined job in an organized, calm atmosphere, rather than one that involves constant decision-making under pressure, say so. Otherwise, you may wind up in a job that is a constant source of tension. If you like the challenge of pressure, either in decision making or in dealing with people, make this clear.

   Keep in mind that a large company may have more than one working environment. For instance, an administrative support job in the customer relations department would likely involve more interactive pressure with the public than a support job in the data processing department.

## Stress or Problem Questions

Stress questions are asked to determine how you perform under pressure (controlled and composed or nervous and unsettled). They are also used to find out whether you are good at making decisions, solving problems, and thinking under stress.

Some questions may be aimed at clarifying issues the interviewer perceives as a possible problem, such as being over-qualified or under-qualified, having physical limitations, and lacking dependability (if your resume shows many different jobs).

**Preparing Answers to Stress Questions.** Prepare to answer any possible problem questions that are based on your resume or personal circumstances. Look at stress questions as an opportunity (with preparation) to demonstrate that the issue is not a problem as it relates to your ability to do the job. **Career Action 14-2** will help you prepare by writing out responses to possible stress questions. The next step is to rehearse them: either tape-record yourself giving the question(s) and prepared response(s) or ask a member of your support network to help you role-play the practice. Revise the responses on the basis of feedback.

Figure • 14-2: Answer difficult questions honestly and directly. Address the employer's needs and concerns.

**Remaining Cool under Stress.** Always keep your cool; remain focused, take three to five calming deep breaths, and tell yourself "I can do this." If you get a question you are totally unprepared for, don't just blunder on; use the *"That's a good question, let me think about that for a minute"* technique. This can buy you the time to respond well. You want to demonstrate that you can handle stress professionally; you don't just react, you think it through and remain composed.

1. **Why do you think you are the best candidate for this job?**

   **Suggested Answer:** Prepare for this one—it might also be phrased "Why should I hire you?" Ask the interviewer to highlight the important objectives and challenges of the job. Then explain how you could handle them. Focus on how you can benefit the employer, giving examples of increasing productivity, saving money, increasing sales, and so on. Summarize accomplishments, skills, and experience that are pertinent to the job, followed by, "How does that seem to fit your requirements?" This now shifts the focus from you to the interviewer, helping reduce stress for you. The key, in this case, is to get the interviewer involved in developing your answer. This buys you time to develop an appropriate answer. (Be careful about appearing evasive or overcontrolling.)

2. **Why do you want to leave your current job?**

   **Suggested Answer:** This question is often posed to determine whether you have a problem with your current job. Accentuate the positive—you are seeking a new challenge, you have mastered your present job and are seeking advancement, you prefer not having to commute so far, and so on. If you do have a problem with your current job, avoid discussing it. If you think you must discuss it, state it briefly and unemotionally. Get back to the positive by explaining that you think this organization would provide a good opportunity for career growth.

3. **Why have you held so many jobs?**

   **Suggested Answer:** Naturally, employers are impressed by a work history that implies stability and dependability. Often, people have valid reasons for holding numerous jobs. Some jobs are seasonal (agriculture, landscaping, and recreation); some jobs involve frequent relocation (engineering, construction); and some jobs are profoundly affected by the general economy. You may have held a variety of summer jobs while completing your education. Capitalize on this; it shows initiative and provides you with broad working experience.

You may also have accompanied your spouse, who was required to relocate frequently. If you just hopped around frequently, mention that previously you wanted to obtain a broad base of experience and that now your goal is to apply this experience to long-term employment and development of a career.

4. **What is your weakest point?**

   **Suggested Answer:** "My weakest point is accounting (unless you are applying for an accounting position!), so I'm completing a beginning course at the college. It's going well, and I plan to take the advanced course next semester." The point is to acknowledge any weak point and to explain your plan for improving in this area. Never volunteer a weakness you think is a major requirement for getting the job. Explain how you have or plan to overcome the weakness (through practice, education, planning, etc.).

5. **Have you ever been fired from a job?**

   **Suggested Answer:** If you have been fired, use terms such as *laid off* or *terminated;* they sound less negative. Be honest about the reason for your termination. Briefly explain the situation, and mention that you have learned from the experience. End your response on a positive note.

   If you have been laid off for a legitimate reason, such as downsizing, loss of company business, or a lagging economy, remember that this is *not* being fired from a job. Therefore, there is no need for you to mention this in answer to number 5. If quitting a job was your own decision, remember to use more positive language, such as, "I left," or, "I decided to leave."

6. **Does your current employer know you are planning to leave?**

   **Suggested Answer:** If your current employer is aware of this fact, say so. If not, and especially if you depend on your current income, make this clear. Say you would prefer that your current employer not be informed of your job search until a firm job offer is made and that you would give at least two weeks' notice before leaving. (This demonstrates good ethics and a sense of responsibility—both pluses for you!)

Remember that some questions are not purposely posed to be stressful, but they may be stressful to you. For instance, if the interviewer asks, "Does your employer know that you are planning to leave?" and the answer is "yes" because your spouse is being transferred, the question will not be stressful to you. If, however, the reason for leaving is that you can no longer tolerate working for your current employer, the question will probably be stressful.

**SUCCESS TIP**

**Prepare and practice for stress questions. Keep your cool, breathe deeply, use positive self-talk, and take time to think. Demonstrate stress skills—thinking it through and remaining composed.**

**NOTE:** Interviewers may ask you about the use of drugs or advise you that drug screening is required before applicants are approved for hire. For more information regarding drug screening, see Chapter 15.

### Illegal Questions

Federal law and many state laws have classified some interview questions as inappropriate. Technically, few questions are illegal. What may be illegal is how the information is used—and the main illegal reason is discrimination in hiring on the basis of gender, age, race, national origin, or religion.

Be aware that outright discrimination is fairly uncommon today. Often, questions that might appear to be illegal are asked innocently by untrained interviewers not familiar with the laws, and the questions are not intended to be discriminatory.

If you complain about a question being illegal or unfair and refuse to answer, you probably won't be offered the job. You certainly have the right to refuse, but you must weigh the situation: Is it worth jeopardizing the job over this question, or does the interviewer appear so offensive that you don't want to work for the organization? You decide and act accordingly.

The most effective approach is to answer the question in a polite, honest manner. Provide proof by example of your ability to meet the employer's expectations, as in the following example:

**Interviewer:** Do you have children?

**Applicant:** Yes, and appropriate child care is a top priority for me, so I'm thorough in arranging dependable daily and alternative care. It pays off; I've never had to miss a day of work or school for child care purposes (emphasizing planning and management).

## SHOW 'EM YOU CAN TAKE THE HEAT!

Anticipate the stress or illegal questions; prepare and practice appropriate responses. This gives you the edge in demonstrating your ability to handle stressful situations calmly and skillfully—just the behavior employers want.

## PLAN NOW: YOUR QUESTIONS COUNT!

Making the interview an effective two-way communication is important; prepare to ask pertinent questions. Outline questions that will help you learn more about the employer and the position as well as questions that show initiative and preparation. Don't ask questions about salary until the employer makes a job offer.

### Good Questions to Ask

Asking appropriate questions demonstrates interest, confidence, and intelligence. Study the following sample questions carefully; then write out your own questions as part of **Career Action 14-2**.

1. **Do you have a training program for this position; if so, would you describe it?** This demonstrates interest in the job and a desire to perform it well.

2. **Will you describe the duties and tasks in a typical workday for this position?** The answer will help you better understand the scope and emphasis of the job. It may be just what you want, or you may learn that it is not the type of work you are seeking. The information will be important to you in considering a job offer.

3. **May I have a copy of the written job description?** Getting a job description can help you tie your qualifications to those required for the job.

4. **Could good job performance in this job lead to career growth opportunities with the company?** This will help you determine whether this is a dead-end job or whether the company encourages employee career growth.

5. **Will the responsibilities of this position expand with time and experience on the job?** The answer could also give you insight into whether this is a dead-end, no-growth job.

6. **Could you tell me about the people I would be working with? To whom would I report, and who would be my peers and subordinates?** The answer can help you evaluate how you might fit in this position.

7. **Do you require any more information about my qualifications or experience?** This gives you an opportunity to clear up any misunderstanding or lack of information. It also gives you another chance to run your 60-Second Commercial, reemphasizing just how well you are qualified.

**Prepare and ask appropriate questions; this demonstrates interest, confidence, and intelligence.**

## Turnoff Questions to Avoid

Following are some questions most disliked by employers. *Do not ask these;* they make the applicant sound pushy and uninformed, and they diminish likability.

1. **What does this company do?** You should have done your research well enough to know exactly what the company does. This question will make you appear uninformed and unqualified. Employers are *not* looking for employees who know nothing about their business!

2. **Do you have any openings?** This makes it easy for the employer to respond with a flat "no." Improve your chances by asking, "May I submit an application?"

3. **How much sick leave and vacation time will I get?** Do not ask this during a first interview. Although employee benefits are important, asking specifically about vacations or sick-leave projects a negative attitude. Prior to making a final decision about a job offer, however, you should obtain this information. Employers appreciate the importance of major benefits to prospective employees.

4. **Are you hiring?** This question is too direct. It pressures the interviewer. Making the interviewer feel uncomfortable makes you less likable and, therefore, lessens your chances for employment. Express interest in the job, and do your research first to determine whether the company is hiring.

5. **Will I have an office?** This suggests too much emphasis on where you will work, rather than interest in the work.

## SPREAD OUT YOUR QUESTIONS, AND DON'T OVERDO IT

Prepare to ask three to five well-chosen and appropriate questions. Don't ask all your questions at the end of the interview. Interject them naturally at appropriate intervals throughout the meeting. Keep your questions positive; avoid asking any that could elicit negative reactions from the interviewer.

6. **What time do I have to be at work in the morning? or How long do you give for lunch?** This does not project an enthusiastic interest in the work!

**Complete Career Action 14-1**

**Avoid questions that make you unlikable; these include questions that are too direct, that your research should have answered, or that are pushy.**

# CAREER ACTION 14-1

## Use the Internet to Search for Interview Question-and-Answer Tips

**DIRECTIONS:** Use the Internet to search for additional tips on interview questions and answers that could be useful. Summarize key points or print relevant articles.

***WebGuide* Activities:** Access "Your Job Search" from the Main Menu. Go to Activity #7, and click on *Career Development Center Internet Checklist*. Under the heading "Contents," click on "During the Interview." Then scroll to and click on "Best Interview Questions Asked during Job Interviews."

**Internet Activities:** Check these Web sites as well as Internet search engines for tips on interview questions and answers. If you want to know more about handling illegal questions, include this topic in your Internet search.

**Internet Web Sites**

America's Employers ***http://www.americasemployers.com***
(Click on ***Job Search Essentials***, ***Prepare for Interviews***, then click on ***FAIQs***. (FAIQs stands for Frequently Asked Interview Questions.)

Career Strategies, Inc. Online! ***http://www.careerstrategiesinc.com***
(Click on ***Applicant Services***, then ***Career Resource Center***, ***Interview Tips***, and ***Commonly Asked Interview Questions***.)

Job Options ***http://www.joboptions.com***
(Click on ***Career Tools***, then on ***Interviewing***; select appropriate articles.)

## APPLY Q-AND-A SAVVY STRATEGIES

Employers rate the following as top-notch strategies for interview question-and-answer performance.

- **Be enthusiastic.** Enthusiasm is a top quality that employers look for when hiring.
- **Pause to think before you reply.** If you are uncomfortable with a question, go back to the familiar; stress your assets. Use the "thinking pause" to buy time to answer well. One of the following phrases can be used:

*"Could we return to this question? I'd like to think about it for a moment."*

*"That's a good question." or "Let me see..." (This works if you need only a little extra time.)*

- **Be candid and honest.** Be realistic in expressing your preferences and dislikes. You won't be happy in a job that doesn't fit.
- **Do not use canned responses.** Tailor your answers to fit your goals, objectives, and personality, as well as the goals and needs of the employer.
- **Be concise.** Keep to the point, but avoid being curt or too brief in your responses.
- **Answer in complete sentences, and speak correctly.** Answer in complete sentences; avoid using slang, incorrect grammar, or repetitive terms, and always speak clearly.

Figure • 14-3: The right strategy can be the key to a successful interview.

- **Be positive.** Positive thinking promotes positive behavior and speech, a positive image, positive responses, and a positive atmosphere. It also projects enthusiasm, self-confidence, and initiative.
- **Fill in gaps.** If you sense that the interviewer thinks you have an area of weakness, communicate how you plan to eliminate the weakness or round out your qualifications—perhaps by completing research or course work in the area.

Complete Career Action 14-2 on page 258

# CAREER ACTION 14-2

## Question-and-Answer Planning Sheet

**DIRECTIONS:** Use the Question-and-Answer Planning Sheet on page 259 to write answers to typical questions you anticipate, and write sample questions you can ask during your interviews. Use the suggestions presented in this chapter, the Career Actions for Chapter 3, and your 60-Second Commercial as references in writing answers on the planning sheet. Tailor your answers to your targeted job. Emphasize your qualifications for the job at every opportunity, and use positive, action-oriented words.

**Career Database Appropriate**

## CHECKLIST FOR INTERVIEW QUESTIONS AND ANSWERS

Check each of the following actions you are currently taking to increase your career success:

- ☐ Focus on proof by example. Respond persuasively to questions about your abilities; give examples of applying them in work, school, and other activities.
- ☐ Prepare and rehearse responses to typical interview questions.
- ☐ Prepare and practice for stress questions. Keep your cool, breathe deeply, use positive self-talk, and take time to think. Demonstrate stress skills—thinking it through and remaining composed.
- ☐ Prepare and ask appropriate questions; this demonstrates interest, confidence, and intelligence.
- ☐ Avoid questions that make you unlikable; these include questions that are too direct, that your research should have answered, or that are overly pushy.

## CRITICAL THINKING QUESTIONS

1. What should be your main objectives during the question-and-answer portion of the interview?
2. Why is it important for the applicant to pose some questions during the interview?
3. What specific types of questions do you need the most preparation for to be ready for your interviews? List two examples, and include the answers you plan to give.

# CAREER ACTION 14-2

## Question-and-Answer Planning Sheet

### GENERAL INFORMATION QUESTIONS

1. Why do you want this job?

2. What type of work do you enjoy doing most?

3. What are your strongest skills?

4. What are your long-range career goals, and how do you plan to achieve them?

5. Are you a team player? Give examples.

6. Do you have a geographical preference? Are you willing to relocate?

7. Under what management style do you work most efficiently?

CONTINUED ON NEXT PAGE

# CAREER ACTION 14-2

(CONTINUED)

## CHARACTER QUESTIONS

1. Describe an accomplishment that demonstrates your intiative.

_______________________________________________

_______________________________________________

2. Describe an experience where you dealt with an angry customer or co-worker.

_______________________________________________

_______________________________________________

3. Give an example that demonstrates your ability to adapt to change.

_______________________________________________

_______________________________________________

4. How would you describe yourself?

_______________________________________________

_______________________________________________

5. What rewards do you look for in your career?

_______________________________________________

_______________________________________________

6. Of what accomplishment are you most proud, particularly as it relates to your field?

_______________________________________________

_______________________________________________

7. Do you work well under pressure?

_______________________________________________

_______________________________________________



CONTINUED ON NEXT PAGE

# CAREER ACTION 14-2

(CONTINUED)

## STRESS QUESTIONS

1. Why do you think you are the best candidate for this job? (or) Why should I hire you?

_______________________________________________

_______________________________________________

2. Why do you want to leave your current job?

_______________________________________________

_______________________________________________

3. Why have you held so many jobs?

_______________________________________________

_______________________________________________

4. What is your weakest point?

_______________________________________________

_______________________________________________

5. Have you ever been fired from a job?

_______________________________________________

_______________________________________________

6. Does your current employer know you are planning to leave?

_______________________________________________

_______________________________________________



CONTINUED ON NEXT PAGE

# CAREER ACTION 14-2

(CONTINUED)

## QUESTIONS AND TOPICS TO AVOID

1. Why should you avoid asking, "What does this company do?"

______________________________

______________________________

2. How can you improve on this question: "Do you have any openings?"

______________________________

______________________________

3. Should you ask specifically about sick leave and vacation time? Why or why not?

______________________________

______________________________

4. Why shouldn't you ask, "Are you hiring?"

______________________________

______________________________

5. List below any other questions that interviewers dislike from applicants (based on your outside research or reading).

______________________________

______________________________

## Q-AND-A SAVVY STRATEGIES

**DIRECTIONS:** Review the "Apply Q-and-A Savvy Strategies" in this chapter. List those strategies that are most applicable to your job search. Add any others you may have identified through your Internet research.

## YOUR QUESTIONS

**DIRECTIONS:** Review the questions in the section "Plan Now: Your Questions Count!" Then, on separate paper, write out the questions you want to ask during your interviews. Put the questions in your own words, and get help from a member of your support system. Add questions that are pertinent to your job search, goals, and objectives.

CHAPTER 15

# Ace Employment Tests and Negotiations

> **"Our computerized preemployment tests help determine the marketability of each applicant. If the applicant does well on the assessment tests, we are more likely to place him or her in a position that requires more skills and pays better."**
>
> *Jennifer Evans*
> *Branch Manager*
> *Kelly Services*

*In this chapter you will:*

Use the Internet to research current salary information for your field.

- Identify and summarize employment testing procedures used and compensation packages offered in your field for the type of job you are seeking.
- Summarize guidelines for negotiating the compensation package.
- Summarize how to deal effectively with job offers.

Chapter 15 presents strategies for performing successfully in preemployment tests and drug screening, negotiating a fair compensation package, and evaluating and accepting job offers.

# ACE EMPLOYMENT TESTS

Doing your homework is a sure way to improve educational test scores, and it's also important to succeed in employment tests. As part of your pre-interview research, find out whether the organization requires preemployment testing. If a test is involved, find out whether it's a written, oral, combination, or computerized test. Does it test technical knowledge, skills, manual dexterity, personality, special abilities, or other job-related capabilities? Try to find out what will be tested and how it will be tested.

Well in advance of asking for an interview, contact the employer to learn about the preemployment testing procedures. Speak with the human resources staff or the office manager, and ask the person to describe any testing procedures used.

## The Personality Test

The personality test is the one exception to the "do your homework" rule. Because this type of test is usually designed to determine whether your personal and behavioral preferences are suitable for the work involved, advance study doesn't apply. Answer all questions honestly. If your personality doesn't match the job, you won't be happy in it.

## The Skills Test

If you will be taking a skills test, start today to review, practice, and improve. No matter how good your skills are, they can be improved with practice, which increases your employability. A word of caution, however: Quit preparing one or two days before your test. Cramming until the last minute increases anxiety and usually results in lower performance. Another benefit of polishing your skills is that you will begin your new job with greater confidence and ease.

Figure • 15-1: Employer testing requirements vary. You could be asked to take some simple skills tests or more detailed technical testing.

## The Technical Test

If you will be required to take an oral or written test for a professional position, try to get some samples of the technical questions that are asked. Resources for learning about the types of questions are the employer's human resources department, other employees in the company, people who have taken the test, and people who have taken similar tests in your field. Libraries and bookstores also have sample tests.

If you can find sample questions or even general topics that will be covered in the technical test, write out answers to the possible questions. The important thing in technical tests is to *be as complete as possible* in your answers. The purpose of the test is to find out how much you know about the subject.

## The Computerized Preemployment Test

The computerized preemployment test is useful for large applicant screenings because it saves time and other expenses. The test may be very general in content, or it could be a skills or personality test.

Typically, applicants take these tests at the employer's site. You receive instructions on how to use the computerized test program and then are given a specified amount of time to complete it. The results are usually scored electronically and generated in a report. These results are then analyzed by human resources personnel. The best advice for performing well on these tests is to do your best and not try to outwit the test. Also, avoid using absolutes like *never* and *always*. These words can signal an extreme personality or lying. If it is a skills test, pre-practice can help improve your score.

**SUCCESS TIP**

**Research to learn what types of tests are given by your target employer. To sharpen your performance for skills tests, practice ahead; for technical tests, study concepts. Don't try to prepare for personality tests; answer honestly to ensure a good match between you and the job.**

## Taking Employment Tests

Employment testing may be an important factor in an employer's hiring decision. Follow these guidelines to perform at your best:

1. Eat properly before the test, and be well rested. A sluggish body and brain diminish test performance.
2. Do some physical exercise before your test to improve your circulation and your ability to relax and concentrate.
3. Arrive ten to fifteen minutes early to avoid being rushed or tense.
4. Most firms provide more than enough time to complete tests, so don't rush into poor performance. Always ask, however, exactly how much time is allowed for the test.
5. Before beginning the test, read it carefully to clarify the instructions and to determine how many points are assigned to each question. If you run short of time, first answer the questions carrying the largest number of points. If the points aren't indicated on the test, ask the person monitoring it how the questions are weighted.
6. Ask whether points will be deducted for any questions you don't answer. If so, be sure to answer every question. If not, don't spend a lot of time on questions you can't answer easily. (Save those until last!)
7. Always clarify any directions or questions you don't understand before you start the test.
8. Many tests are objective—often multiple choice. In true-false questions, extreme statements are often false (for example, choices that contain the words *all*, *never*, or *always*). Statements that are moderate are often true.
9. Double-check to make certain you haven't missed any questions. Remember: Your first response is usually the correct one. Don't change answers unless you are sure you made a careless mistake.
10. On general math tests, usually expect some simple addition, subtraction, multiplication, division, fraction, percentage, and decimal problems. Many math tests also include several word problems.
11. Advanced math tests will be geared to your field (engineering and statistical analysis, for instance). Consult others who have taken similar tests to determine what you should review. Your educational and working experience are the primary preparation for this type of test.

12. Oral tests or boards are generally given for advanced college degrees and senior management/supervisory positions. These test the technical knowledge of the applicant. Ask a colleague and/or an instructor in your field to meet with you and to review important technical aspects of your field with you. Review and study major principles beforehand, and use the meeting to summarize these elements.

## PREPARE FOR DRUG SCREENING

Drug screening as a preemployment requirement for large and small organizations is becoming the norm. Be prepared for the possibility that you will be asked to take a drug test before being hired. Employers can refuse to hire you if you refuse to take the test.

Take drug screening seriously. Applicants who test positively for drug use or who admit to use of illegal drugs may be screened out of the job immediately. Never give flippant answers to questions about drug use; they could be interpreted negatively.

Policies for drug screening vary considerably from one employer to another. As part of your employer research, find out what the drug screening procedures and requirements are. Make certain the testing incorporates fair and accurate procedures. Your school career services counselor should have current information about this topic. Be sure you obtain all information available.

**NOTE:** To protect yourself, before you are tested, report to the employer any prescription or over-the-counter drugs you are taking. Some can result in a false positive test.

Figure • 15-2: Drug testing is required by many companies. To protect yourself before you are tested, ask your doctor or pharmacist for a list of any prescription or over the counter drugs you are taking. Some can result in a false positive test.

SUCCESS TIP

**Take drug screening seriously. Find out what the employer's drug screening procedures are, and to avoid a false-positive result, report any over-the-counter drugs you are taking.**

## NEGOTIATE FOR TOP SALARY AND BENEFITS

The topic of compensation (salary and benefits) is inevitable if you are being seriously considered for the job. To put yourself in the strongest bargaining position, try to postpone discussion of salary until you receive a job offer. If you bring up the topic of salary too soon, the interviewer's focus could shift too far away from your qualifications, costing you the job. As with any sale, first concentrate on what the "buyer" will gain (your qualifications) before focusing on the price (your compensation).

**SUCCESS TIP**

**Postpone discussion of salary until you receive a job offer. This is your strongest bargaining strategy because the employer will already be convinced that you are the person for the job.**

## The Compensation Package

Salary is not the only important factor in assessing the value of a job; benefits and potential for earnings growth are also important considerations. Base your salary requirements on your worth (the benefits you can offer the employer). Consider carefully what benefits are most important to you: health or life insurance, investment or retirement programs, flextime, and so on. Research to know the going rate. Increase your chances of being offered the best compensation by including these topics in your employer and industry research. Talk with leaders in your field, with people holding positions similar to your target job, and with area placement specialists.

## Salary

Some employers provide printed job descriptions that include a fixed salary listing or offer salary information on their Internet Web sites. Other job notices include a salary range, or the salary may be open. Often, you can find out what the range or approximate salary is for the position from the employer's human resources department. In some cases, however, employers don't give out this information. They may give you only the bottom of the range; rarely will they give you the top of the range. Having a general idea of the range is better than having no idea. Your career services office can help you research both salary and benefits packages through its local contacts and publications such as ***Job Choices,*** published by the National Association of Colleges and Employers.

If the salary is fixed, as may occur in some union or government jobs, you must decide whether it is acceptable. If the salary is negotiable, however, always try for a salary that is at the top of the range. (You can agree to accept a salary lower than the top level, but if you offer to take the lowest end of the range first, that's probably what you will get.) Study the salary negotiation tactics on page 268 (related to negotiable salaries), and prepare to bargain your way up the pay scale.

**Complete Career Action 15-1 on page 269**

**"The man who simply drifts into success in any field of human activity is almost as rare as the ship that drifts aimlessly into a safe harbor."**

—John Milton Gregory

## "ANYONE CAN NEGOTIATE THEIR SALARY—THIS MEANS YOU!"

Jack Chapman, author of *Negotiating Your Salary: How to Make $1,000 a Minute*, describes his TOP salary negotiating tip:

"OK"

Bam! Those two letters just cost you plenty!

Can you tell how much they cost you? Choose one: Those two letters...

A. Canceled your reservations for a $5,000 two-week dream trip to an exotic location.

B. Burned the blueprints for the $10,000 addition to your house.

C. Yanked your kid out of college because you were $25K short.

How could those two letters be so powerful? Easy—"OK" is what most people say in response to a salary offer. They mean "I'll accept what you've just offered, thank you." Depending on where your salary is to begin with, you could lose A, B, or C. But you could also keep it, and more besides, if you learn even one small negotiating technique: Change the "OK" to a "Hmmm," and watch what happens.

A simple "Hmmm" instead of "OK" can change a $25,000 salary into $28,000 and finance your new computer system. And $45,000 can be pushed to $50,000, affording you that much-needed two-week vacation.

Don't worry that the employer will change his or her mind about hiring you just because you ask for more. If you've interviewed well (and you must have done that or you wouldn't be getting an offer!), you're the front-runner already. Choosing the second best or going through the whole recruiting-interviewing-hiring process again will cost a company much more than $1,000 to $5,000 anyway in the long run. Odds are, you'll get that little extra, and the employer will still consider it a good bargain to avoid that hassle.

And what's the worst that happens if you don't? Your new boss will know that you believe you're worth more and treat you better.

No matter what your level, there's easy money to be made by changing "OK" to "Hmmm."

# CAREER ACTION 15-1

## Use the Internet to Research Current Salary Information

**NOTE:** Since the content of Web sites is subject to change without notice, be aware that the links listed below may not match the current content of the Web sites referenced in this assignment.

**Part 1**

**DIRECTIONS:** Access one of the first two Web sites listed below. Using "The Salary Calculator" on either site, compute the cost of living differences between two cities you would consider working in for this exercise. Print the results.

1. Access **WSJ Careers** ***http://www.careers.wsj.com***
   (Click on ***Salaries and Profiles***; then click on ***The Salary Calculator***.)

2. Access **HomeFair** ***http://www.homefair.com***
   (Under "Tools & Calculators," click on ***The Salary Calculator***.)

**Part 2**

**DIRECTIONS:** Access the following Web site, and then complete the steps outlined below the Web name and address.

Access **America's Job Bank** ***http://www.ajb.dni.us***
(Click on ***Job Market Info***; then click on ***Wages and Trends***. Select a Job Family; then click on ***search***. Select one occupation, and select one state; then click on ***search***. Print or summarize in writing the Occupation Report. Identify the wage ranges listed for the occupation.)

# SALARY AND BENEFITS NEGOTIATION TACTICS

1. **Do not accept the job offer without discussing the salary and benefits.** You can bring it up by asking, "What salary range do you have in mind for the position?" Then ask about the benefits.

2. **Whenever possible, let the interviewer bring up the topic of compensation (salary and benefits).**

3. **Aim for a salary that equals the peak of your qualifications.** The higher you start, the higher the offer is likely to be. Always state your requirement in a range (upper twenties, mid-thirties), making it broad enough to negotiate. Don't specify a low end. If you suggest one, the employer will likely select it.

4. **If the interviewer asks what salary you want, a good response is, "What figure or range is the company planning to pay?"** This gives you a starting point for negotiation. If it's higher than you expected, you help yourself by not stating a lower figure first. If it's lower, you now have a place to begin negotiations.

5. **When the interviewer presses you for your salary requirement, a good reply is,** "The national average for a person with my experience, education, and training is $_____. Considering the cost-of-living factors here, I would expect a salary in the upper _____." (State your range, and be sure to research the facts first!)

6. **If the interviewer brings up the subject of salary too early in the interview** (before you have adequately covered your qualifications), delay discussion of the topic, saying something like, "Actually, the position itself is more important to me than the salary. Could we first discuss the position a little more?"

7. **While discussing salary, always return to your assets.** Review all you have to offer the company.

8. **Once you state your salary range, do not back down,** particularly if you think it is equal to your qualifications. The employer will respect confidence about the quality and worth of your work. Base your range on careful research.

**"Reach high, for stars lie hidden in your soul. Dream deep, for every dream precedes the goal."**

—Anonymous

9. **Do not discuss any other sources of income, and do not moan about your expenses.** Keep focused on this negotiation.

10. **Always discuss the fringe benefits** (insurance coverage, pension plans, paid vacations, etc.) along with the topic of salary.

11. **Ask what criteria are used to determine compensation increases and the frequency of salary reviews.** If benefits and salary increases are good, they can offset a somewhat lower starting salary.

12. **If the salary offer is made in a letter and the salary is too low, arrange an appointment to discuss it right away.** Bargaining power is far better in person than by letter or telephone.

13. **If the salary isn't acceptable, state the salary you would accept,** and close by reaffirming your interest in the company and the job. If the interviewer says, "I'll have to think about your requirements," wait one week; then call back. You may receive a higher or compromise offer. If the interviewer gives you a flat "no," express regret that you were unable to work out a compromise, and restate your interest in the position and the organization. Send a follow-up thank-you letter within two days; it could swing the decision in your favor. In any case, you will complete the negotiations professionally and leave a positive impression.

**Complete Career Action 15-2**

# CAREER ACTION 15-2

## Employment Test/Salary and Benefits Planning Sheet

**DIRECTIONS:** This outside assignment will help you succeed in employment tests and negotiate effectively for both fair salary and benefits. As the base of your outside research in this assignment, use Parts 1 and 2 of the "Employment Test/Salary and Benefits Planning Sheet," provided on page 275. Then complete Part 3 of the form, "Summary of Strategies for Negotiating Compensation."

# EVALUATE AND NEGOTIATE JOB OFFERS

Before deciding on a job offer, it's important to be sure it meets your career planning needs and goals. The following guidelines will help you assess job offers wisely.

## How to Evaluate a Job Offer

Because the decision to accept or reject the job offer affects your lifetime career plans, consider this important decision carefully. Include the following factors in your evaluation of a job offer:

Figure • 15-3: Think carefully about the job offer in terms of your financial needs and career goals. You may want to discuss the offer with a member of your network.

- **The job itself:** Is the scope acceptable? Is the work interesting to you? Will you work in teams or alone?
- **The organization and personnel:** Do you feel comfortable with the organizational structure and the people you have met?
- **The salary and benefits:** Is the salary commensurate with your abilities and comparable with the competition? Does potential exist for increases?
- **Career development opportunities:** Will you have adequate opportunities for professional growth (through training, continuing education, and experience)?
- **The values and philosophies of management:** Are they compatible with your own?
- **Expense considerations:** What expenses will be required for relocation, housing, cost of living, and so on?
- **How the job meets your goals:** Consider carefully how this job fits into your long-range career goals.

Job offers are made by telephone, by letter, or in person. If the offer is made by letter, you have time to think it over carefully and less emotionally than if the offer is made by telephone or in person. You might want to discuss the job offer conditions with a member of your support system, a family member, a career planning specialist, or all of these. Respond to the offer quickly so that you don't jeopardize it in any way.

If the offer is made by telephone or in the interviewer's office, request time to think it over. Occasionally, interviewers will offer to increase the salary or benefits on the spot if that appears to be your main concern regarding the job offer. This is particularly true if they are *convinced* you are the right person for the job and they don't want to interview any other applicants. If this should happen, more power to you! Even if this doesn't happen, it is still in your best interest to take at least one day to consider the advantages and disadvantages of the job offer. (Make certain that waiting one day won't be an imposition. This courtesy also helps avoid returning the next day to accept the offer and finding someone else has the job!) Be sure you understand all conditions and elements of the job before you decide.

If you have absolutely no doubts or objections concerning the job offer, accept the offer on the spot with enthusiasm. This will reinforce the employer's confidence in your interest in the job.

SUCCESS TIP

**Consider all aspects of the job offer (the job and company, compensation, growth opportunities, and expense considerations). Before accepting, negotiate to improve areas of concern and to provide the best career opportunity for yourself.**

## Accept the Offer Professionally

If you accept the job offer orally, follow up immediately in writing, summarizing the conditions of the offer, stating the position title, starting date, salary, and other pertinent items. (Your employer may do the same, but this helps ensure mutual agreement regarding all conditions of the offer.)

Notify any other organizations you have interviewed with that you have accepted a job. This is important because you may deal with these people in your new job, or you may want to contact them in the future regarding employment.

Contact everyone who served as a reference and everyone who helped with your job search; tell these people of your new job and thank them for their help. People you thank are more likely to assist in the future if you seek a new position or advancement in your career.

Figure • 15-4: When accepting a job offer, let the employer know how pleased you are.

## Reject the Offer Professionally

If you decide this is not the job for you, notify the employer by telephone first if possible. Then also politely decline the offer in a letter, thank the employer for the job offer, and wish the employer future success.

## Economics May Influence Your Decision

Your final decision may be influenced by economics—the need to earn a living. If the offer meets most of your requirements but is not a perfectly logical career step, your decision still could be to accept the job. If so, take the job with a determination to excel. This is an opportunity for you to establish a reputation for dependability, creativity, excellent job performance, initiative, and the ability to work well with others—all while taking home a regular salary. Accept the challenge, and view it as preparation for the next step in your career development.

**Complete Career Action 15-3**

# CAREER ACTION 15-3

## Planning for Dealing with Job Offers

**DIRECTIONS:** On a separate sheet of paper, answer the following questions.

1. List every factor you should weigh in considering a job offer. Be thorough in your answer. You might want to discuss it with a member of your support network, a placement counselor, or both. Include those factors that are specific to your personal job search, as well as those general factors discussed in this chapter.
2. Explain how you can best respond to a job offer made in person
   a. if you *think* you want the job.
   b. if you are *certain* you want the job.
   c. if you *do not* want the job.
3. How can you best respond to a job offer made by telephone?
4. List the follow-up steps you should take in accepting a job offer.
5. How should you professionally reject a job offer?
6. If economic conditions require you to accept a job that is not exactly what you are aiming for, how can you best approach this new job? What are the benefits of doing this?

## CHECKLIST TO ACE EMPLOYMENT TESTS AND NEGOTIATIONS

Check each of the following actions you are taking to increase your interview and follow-up success:

- ☐ Research to learn what types of tests are given by your target employer. To sharpen performance in skills tests, practice ahead; for technical tests, study concepts.
- ☐ Take drug screening seriously. Find out what drug screen procedures are used, and to avoid a false-positive result, report any over-the-counter drugs you are taking.
- ☐ Postpone discussion of salary until you receive a job offer.
- ☐ Consider all aspects of the job offer: the job and company, compensation, growth opportunities, and so on. Before accepting, negotiate to improve areas of concern.

## CRITICAL THINKING QUESTIONS

1. Review "Ace Employment Tests" in this chapter. Summarize those pointers that apply to your job search campaign.
2. Is it more advantageous for the applicant to bring up the subject of salary first? Why?
3. What is an appropriate response for you to make when an interviewer asks what salary you are looking for?
4. Base your answers to these questions on your salary information research: (a) What is the entry-level salary for the job you are seeking? (b) What salary range do you plan to seek in your job search? On what do you base this?

# CAREER ACTION 15-2

## Employment Test/Salary and Benefits Planning Sheet

**DIRECTIONS:** Contact two employers in your field to learn about their employment testing, salary ranges, and benefits offered for the type of job you are seeking. Answer the following questions.

**Part 1: Employment Test Questions**

1. Do you require prospective employees to take employment tests?

______________________________

______________________________

2. What kinds of tests are given (personality, skills, technical, computerized, other)?

______________________________

______________________________

3. Would you please describe the test (written, oral, skills, computerized, other).

______________________________

______________________________

4. What types of questions are in the test (multiple-choice, true-false, fill-in-the-blank, essay, other)?

______________________________

______________________________

5. Would you please explain how the test applies to the job itself?

______________________________

______________________________

6. Could a person study for the test(s)? If so, could you recommend specific methods of study and resources?

______________________________

______________________________

7. Do you require prospective employees to take drug tests? If so, what is the procedure?

______________________________

______________________________

CONTINUED ON NEXT PAGE

# CAREER ACTION 15-2

(CONTINUED)

**Part 2: Negotiating Salary and Benefits**

**DIRECTIONS:** Obtain and write out answers to the following questions.

1. Does this position have a fixed salary or a salary range?

___

2. If the salary is fixed, could you tell me the amount?

___

3. If the salary is in a range, could you tell me the range?

___

4. Is the salary negotiable?

___

___

5. What criteria are used for determining the salary for this position?

___

___

6. Are salary raises offered for excellent job performance? If so, what criteria are used?

___

___

7. What is in the typical complete compensation package (benefits)?

___

___

**Part 3: Summary of Strategies for Negotiating Compensation**

**DIRECTIONS:** Review the "Salary and Benefits Negotiation Tactics" on page 269. Use a separate sheet of paper to summarize in your own words the tactics you plan to use in negotiating the compensation package (salary and benefits). Add any tips you have found in your Internet or other research.

CHAPTER 16

# Practice for Your Successful Interview

> **"I ask applicants various situational questions, such as 'What would you do when ...' The way they answer these questions tells me whether or not they have experience in early childhood development. I look for people whose philosophy on teaching is in line with our philosophy. In addition, if an applicant is friendly and has good posture, it shows me that she or he is comfortable and confident."**
>
> *Jerinel Maynard*
> *Administrator*
> *Columbia Heights Preschool*

*In this chapter you will:*

- Review the techniques for successful interviewing, and arrange a practice interview with a member of your support network.
- Arrange a dress rehearsal interview with an employer in your field.
- Evaluate both your practice and dress rehearsal interviews.

Chapter 16 provides vital interview rehearsal activities, including interview practice with a member of your support network, followed by a dress rehearsal interview with an employer in your field. These activities will sharpen your interviewing skills and boost your competitive edge. The payoff could be just the job you are looking for!

# REVIEW INTERVIEW TECHNIQUES

To prepare for your practice interviews, review all of Chapter 11, "Interview Like a Pro." Prepare and perform in your practice interview as if it were the real thing. A summary of the key points for effective interviewing follows.

## Preparing for the Interview

To ensure the best results from your practice interviews, prepare first:

1. **Take the time to look your best.** Eat well and be rested, immaculately groomed, and appropriately dressed. Appearance has a major impact on interviewers—make it positive.

2. **Strengthen your performance with positive behaviors.** See Chapter 1 (positive self-talk and expectations, visualization, etc.).

3. **Review the Career Actions in Chapters 2, 3, 9, and 11.** Focus on your capabilities, accomplishments, 60-Second Commercial, resume, and specific qualifications for your job target.

4. **Assemble your Interview Marketing Kit** (see Chapter 11), and take it with you.

5. **Allow travel time;** arrive a few minutes early.

To improve actual interview performance and confidence, first schedule and participate seriously in practice interviews.

Figure • 16-1: If possible, arrange for one or two people to observe and critique your practice interview.

## During the Interview

Follow the summary of successful interview techniques below to polish your performance:

1. **Remember there is no "time out" from the moment you enter the building until you leave.** Maintain good posture, project energy and enthusiasm, think good thoughts. **Smile!** Be courteous to the secretary or receptionist; use his or her name.

2. **Use the interviewer's name** in your greeting. Identify yourself and the position you are applying for.

3. **Be likable and relax.** Be courteous, friendly, and show interest in the position.

4. **Remember that the impact of body language and voice tone is a major factor in interviewing.** Keep it positive and friendly.

## INTERVIEW PRACTICE IS A MAJOR COMPETITIVE EDGE

Users of *Your Career: How To Make It Happen* emphasize that the practice interviews improve their actual interview performance by as much as 100 percent! They say this valuable practice enhances their preparation, increases their self-confidence, improves the image of competence they want to project, and reduces their anxiety about the process—all of which improves their performance in actual interviews!

5. **Stress your qualifications** and your interest in benefiting the company and advancing yourself.
6. **Ask a few appropriate questions.**
7. **Be prepared to negotiate skillfully for salary.**
8. **Remain calm if asked a stress question.** Allow yourself time to plan an effective answer.
9. **Close the interview skillfully.** Use the "clincher" (ask the interviewer to summarize the most important qualifications for the job; then stress your related abilities).

## SCHEDULE A PRACTICE INTERVIEW

Schedule a practice interview for yourself with a member of your support network (a friend, family member, or acquaintance), preferably someone experienced in interviewing who knows you personally. Ask one or two others to observe this practice interview, and get their recommendations for improving your performance.

Dress and groom yourself as you would for an actual interview, and practice all the interviewing techniques presented in Chapter 11.

**REMEMBER:** Any job offer should be spontaneous from the employer. Asking directly for a job contradicts your request for help in *practicing* your interviewing skills. If your contact makes an offer or provides leads or suggestions, however, follow up immediately if you are interested.

**IMPORTANT NOTE:** If at all possible, arrange to have your practice interview videotaped. This will be the most valuable feedback on your performance you can get—firsthand review.

**Complete Career Action 16-1 on page 280**

## FOLLOW GUIDELINES FOR PRACTICE INTERVIEWS

The following interview guidelines will help you carry out your practice interview successfully.

- **Prepare and take your Interview Marketing Kit** (directions in Chapter 11). Practice showcasing relevant items from your portfolio at appropriate points in your practice interviews.

# CAREER ACTION 16-1

## Arrange Your Own Practice Interview

**DIRECTIONS:** Schedule your practice interview with your support network members (one interviewer and one or two observers). Use the sample questions in Chapter 14 as a guide for your practice session. You can make a copy of them for the "interviewer" and include any stress questions or others you want to rehearse. Encourage the interviewer to expand on the questions if possible, tailoring them to your job target to give you relevant interview practice.

**REMEMBER:** If possible, arrange to have your practice interview videotaped.

- **Dress as you would for an actual interview;** you will be rated on your appearance.
- **Provide your interviewer with copies of your cover letter, resume, and employment application.**
- **Review the Interview Critique Form** (on page 286) to become familiar with the areas to be evaluated. Note this form is designed to get an overview of your interview skills.
- **Give the interviewer and observers copies of the Interview Critique Form.**
- **Send a thank-you letter to everyone who helps you.**

SUCCESS TIP

**Ask your "interviewers" to evaluate your practice and dress rehearsals by using the Interview Critique Form.**

## HAVE INTERVIEWERS FILL OUT CRITIQUE FORM

Make copies of the Interview Critique Form at the end of this chapter; give copies to the interviewer and observers. After the practice interview, ask them to use the form to evaluate your performance, to identify your strengths and weaknesses, and give suggestions for improvement. Identify and correct areas of weakness now—before your actual interview.

Figure • 16-2: The final touch: Arrange a "dress rehearsal" interview with an employer in your field.

## SCHEDULE A DRESS REHEARSAL

Several people have actually received job offers from those who gave them practice interviews. Others have obtained leads that developed into ideal jobs. This is why this practice is so important.

Prepare now to participate in a dress rehearsal with an employer in your field. This is your chance to rehearse and get feedback that will strengthen your actual interviews. Follow the guidelines below to schedule and participate in this important rehearsal:

1. **Make an appointment for your interview dress rehearsal.** Explain that this is a course assignment and that you would appreciate the employer's help in completing it. Say that you would like the interview to be as realistic as possible.

2. **Ask whether it would be possible to get an employment application form.** If so, pick it up, complete it carefully, and take it with you (along with your resume and cover letter) to the dress rehearsal.

3. **Verify the address and other details about the meeting, and thank your contact** for agreeing to help you with the assignment.

4. **Take your Interview Marketing Kit, and use it appropriately.**

Complete Career Action 16-2

## CAREER ACTION 16-2

### Participate in a Dress Rehearsal, and Evaluate Your Performance

**DIRECTIONS:** Contact an employer in your career field, and ask for help with a course assignment. Ask the employer to give you a practice interview and to complete a copy of the Interview Critique Form.

1. Dress appropriately.

2. Take a copy of the Interview Critique Form (provided on page 286) with you, and ask the interviewer to evaluate your performance by completing it during or after the interview.

3. After your rehearsal interview, evaluate your own performance; complete a copy of the Interview Follow-up and Evaluation Form (provided on page 283).

4. Within two days of your dress rehearsal, send a follow-up thank-you letter to the employer.

SUCCESS TIP

Summarize thoroughly what you learn from practice and rehearsal interviews, and send thank-you letters to those who help you.

**"The thing always happens that you really believe in; and the belief in the thing makes it happen."**

—Frank Lloyd Wright

## CHECKLIST FOR PRACTICING TO SUCCEED IN YOUR INTERVIEW

Check each of the following actions you are currently taking to increase your career success:

- ☐ To improve actual interview performance and confidence, first schedule and participate seriously in practice interviews.
- ☐ Ask your "interviewers" to evaluate your practice and dress rehearsals by using the Interview Critique Form.
- ☐ Summarize thoroughly what you learn from practice and rehearsal interviews; send thank-you letters to those who help you.

## CRITICAL THINKING QUESTIONS

1. Outline key points you want to remember from your responses to Career Action 11-4, Summary of Core Areas of Successful Interviewing. Also improve your 60-Second Commercial if necessary.

2. List the most important points you recorded in Career Action 14-2, Question-and-Answer Planning Sheet.

3. Review the salary negotiation information in Chapter 15 and your research findings from Career Action 15-2, Employment Test/Salary and Benefits Planning Sheet. Then answer the following questions:
   (a) What is the general salary range for the position you will be seeking?
   (b) To what should you equate your salary requirements?
   (c) Should you state your salary in a range or in a specific amount, and why?

# CAREER ACTION 16-2

## Interview Follow-Up and Evaluation Form

**NOTE:** Duplicate this form for follow up after every interview.

**DIRECTIONS:** Record a summary of the interview as soon as possible to avoid forgetting important details. Supply the general information about the employer and the interviewer(s). Answer the questions as completely as possible.

Name of Organization: ______________________________

Date of Interview: ______________________________

Name(s) and Titles(s) of Interviewer(s):

______________________________

______________________________

Address: ______________________________

Telephone: ______________________ Fax: ______________________

E-Mail Address: ______________________________

### Summary Activities and Questions

1. On a separate sheet of paper, write every question you can remember being asked during the interview. Take your time and be thorough. Do this before answering any of the following questions.

2. On the basis of the knowledge you gained in your interview and research, which of your qualifications would be the greatest assets in this job? Which of these qualifications do you think should be reinforced with the prospective employer in your follow up?

   ______________________________

   ______________________________

3. List any questions you think you answered inadequately. Then write out the best possible answer to these. Use additional paper if necessary.

   ______________________________

   ______________________________

## CAREER ACTION 16-2

(CONTINUED)

4. Did you forget to provide any important information that demonstrates your qualifications for the job? Explain in detail.

_______________________________________________

_______________________________________________

5. What questions did you intend to ask but either forgot or didn't have a chance to ask? Write these out now.

_______________________________________________

_______________________________________________

6. How do you think you could have presented yourself more effectively (appearance, body language, verbal communication, enthusiasm, describing qualifications, etc.)?

_______________________________________________

_______________________________________________

7. In what area(s) do you think you performed best in your interview? Why?

_______________________________________________

_______________________________________________

8. In what area(s) do you think your performance was weakest? What steps could you take to improve in these areas?

_______________________________________________

_______________________________________________

9. Describe any information you learned about the interviewer that might be helpful in establishing greater rapport in the future (philosophy, current working projects or objectives, personal interests or hobbies, mutual interests, goals, etc.).

_______________________________________________

_______________________________________________

# CAREER ACTION 16-2

(CONTINUED)

10. Should any point of confusion be clarified for the employer? Explain.

11. Are you scheduled for another interview with the organization? Record the date, time, place, and name(s) of the interviewer(s).

12. Record any other activities you either offered to follow up on or were specifically asked to follow up on by the interviewer (for example, provide references, transcripts, certificates, or examples of work).

13. What is the interviewer's preference for your follow up (by telephone, letter, in person)? Ask this question toward the end of your interview!

14. By what date did the interviewer indicate the hiring decision would be made?

# CAREER ACTION 16-2

## Interview Critique Form

Name of Interviewee: ______________________ Date: ______________________

Position Applied For: ____________________________________________

**DIRECTIONS:** Circle the appropriate rating of the interviewee (Excellent, Very Good, Good, or Needs Improvement) after each item listed below.

1. **Documentation** (Application for employment; resume; cover letter)
   Excellent Very Good Good Needs Improvement

2. **Attitude** (Interested in position; self-confident; likable; pleasant tone of voice; smiling)
   Excellent Very Good Good Needs Improvement

3. **Appearance** (Generally neat and tidy; appropriately dressed; alert; good hygiene)
   Excellent Very Good Good Needs Improvement

4. **Job Qualifications** (Education, skills, and experience suitable for position; good personal attributes; human relations capability, dependable, punctual, industrious)
   Excellent Very Good Good Needs Improvement

5. **Verbal Communication** (Speaks clearly with positive tone; uses good English; avoids slang or repetative words; emphasizes assets; courteous; uses name of the interviewer)
   Excellent Very Good Good Needs Improvement

6. **Nonverbal Communication** (Good body language and good eye contant; does not fidget)
   Excellent Very Good Good Needs Improvement

7. **Listening** (Does not interrupt, or respond too quickly; asks to have a question repeated if necessary; takes time to think through important questions; calmly endures silence)
   Excellent Very Good Good Needs Improvement

8. **Enthusiasm** (Demonstrates interest/energy through verbal and nonverbal communication)
   Excellent Very Good Good Needs Improvement

**COMMENTS:** Summarize any other observations you made during the interview. (Note favorable behavior, and provide suggestions for improvement where necessary.)

CHAPTER 17

# Interview and Follow Up

> **If you have not received feedback from a company that you interviewed with, don't hesitate to call. Persistence is often the key to furthering your career. Although I do not expect a follow-up call or letter after an interview, I am always pleased and favorably impressed when I do get one; it makes the candidate stand out from the rest.**

*Linda Stryker*
*Human Resources Manager*
*Square D/Groupe Schneider*
*www.squared.com*

## *In this chapter you will:*

- Review the summary of successful interview techniques.

Use the Internet to search for additional information on interview follow up that could be useful to you.

- Prepare an outline for a follow-up telephone call that could be used after interviews.
- Compose a simple follow-up thank-you letter to be used in addition to the follow-up telephone call.
- Prepare an outline of a formal follow-up letter that could be used after interviews instead of a telephone call.

Previous Career Actions (completing employer research, practicing to interview, and applying the eight success strategies outlined in Chapter 1) have prepared you to succeed in your actual interviews. Chapter 17 highlights important points for succeeding in your actual interview and outlines interview follow-up actions that can tip the hiring decision in your favor.

## INTERVIEW GAME STRATEGIES

To prepare for your successful interview, review the strategies covered earlier. Begin by reviewing all of Chapter 11, "Interview Like a Pro." Pay particular attention to **Career Action 11-3**, your 60-Second Commercial; **Career Actions 11-4** and **11-5**; and summaries of interview techniques. Also review **Career Action 14-2**, Question-and-Answer Planning Sheet, and your research on salary negotiations and the suggestions presented in Chapter 15.

**"Opportunity does not knock, it presents itself when you beat down the door."**

—Kyle Chandler

To connect most positively throughout your interview, focus on four areas: (1) Be likeable, (2) emphasize qualifications, (3) show enthusiasm and interest, and (4) use positive body language and voice qualities.

## THE INTERVIEW FOCUSES ON YOU AS A PERSON

If you are asked to interview, the employer is interested in *you!* Concentrate on being likable; remember that body language is just as important as the words you say.

## GOOD FOLLOW-UP MOVES

Interview follow up can increase your chances of getting the job by 30 percent or more because many applicants don't bother to do it! *Follow up* means taking action to evaluate your performance in interviews, to remind prospective employers of your qualifications for and interest in the job, and to encourage a speedy hiring decision (to hire you, of course). Good follow up reinforces your qualifications and helps you stand out favorably from the competition.

The key in follow up is *action.* The first step is to write an evaluation of your interview performance; the second step is to send a follow-up message to the interviewer by telephone or letter or through a personal visit.

### Evaluate Your Interview Immediately

Within one hour of every interview (or at the earliest possible time), summarize and evaluate your interview performance in writing. Do this for interviews that were great and for those that were poor. This is the best way to learn from the experience and to plan your successful follow-up strategies.

### Plan Your Follow-Up Strategies

After each interview, complete an Interview Follow Up and Evaluation Form (**Career Action 16-2**). Circle in red any notes that require follow up (information you need to clarify or reinforce with the employer, questions you want answered, areas of weak performance and ways to improve, and specific actions you need to take).

Determine which method of follow up is most appropriate. If, during your interview, you remembered to ask the interviewer how he or she wanted you to follow up, the decision has been made for you. If you forgot to ask this question, send a follow-up letter, rather than make a telephone call. If the interviewer approves of follow-up telephone calls, go ahead; a telephone call is more personal and lively and gives you quicker feedback. But also follow up with a letter; it provides a permanent reminder of you!

**Outline Your Follow-Up Message.** Whether your follow up is by telephone, letter, or both, first outline the message and include these topics:

1. List any questions you need to ask.

2. Summarize pertinent information you omitted or covered inadequately in your interview.

3. State specifically how the organization could benefit by hiring you (a brief rerun of or an excerpt from your 60-Second Commercial).

**NOTE:** Make your follow-up message brief and well polished. Choose your words carefully; include only the most important questions or information.

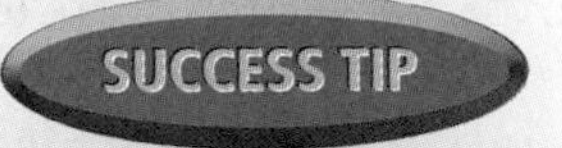


**Prepare a written script you can use for an interview follow-up telephone call.**

**Time Your Call.** Make your follow-up call within two days of your interview, while your name and the interview are fresh in the interviewer's mind. Mondays and Fridays are the worst days to contact employers because they are such hectic business days. Just before lunch or closing are also bad times. Below are some guidelines for the follow-up telephone call.

**Send a Brief Thank-You Letter, Too.** Even if you make your initial follow up by telephone, also send a brief thank-you letter

## SAMPLE FOLLOW-UP TELEPHONE CALL

- **Begin with a greeting and self-introduction.** "Hello, Ms. Hardaway. This is Terrell Hooks calling."
- **Demonstrate courtesy.** "Do you have a moment?"
- **Identify the position you interviewed for and the date of your interview.** "I want to thank you for meeting with me yesterday to discuss the Data Processing Systems Analyst I position."
- **Provide any important information you omitted.** "After reviewing our meeting, I realized I hadn't mentioned some pertinent information regarding my (education, work experience, qualifications, other)."
- **Reemphasize your qualifications.** If necessary, give a short, targeted version of your 60-Second Commercial, emphasizing exactly how your qualifications can benefit the employer.
- **If necessary, ask questions to clarify any points not covered adequately.** These may include a clearer description of the job responsibilities or clarification of salary, benefits, or other terms of employment.
- **Thank your interviewer, express your interest, and encourage a speedy hiring decision.** "Thank you again for the interview. I look forward to learning of your hiring decision soon. I believe we could benefit each other, and I'd be pleased to be a part of Ohio Central Power Company."

within 48 hours of your interview. If you made an effective telephone call, do not restate your qualifications in this letter. Just thank the interviewer, with no strings attached!

The thank-you letter brings your name favorably before the interviewer one more time, reinforcing your name recognition (a great advertising strategy). It also provides a positive written record of you in the employer's files. Review the brief thank-you letter (Figure 17-2) to be sent after a follow-up telephone call.

**Send a More Complete Follow-Up Letter when No Call is Made or to Add Information.** If the interviewer prefers follow-up in writing or if you think your interview performance was weak in any area and follow-up is vital to getting hired, send a more complete follow-up letter. This letter should include the following:

1. Reference to your interview and the position you are seeking
2. Clarification of any pertinent information omitted during your interview
3. A *brief* version of your 60-Second Commercial
4. A thank-you for the interviewer's time
5. A statement of enthusiasm for the job
6. Encouragement of a speedy hiring decision

Review Figure 17-3 on page 292 to see how these items are presented in the sample letter.

**NOTE:** The follow-up letter provides a permanent written record of your qualifications and professional courtesy. The employer can review it any time—a good way to keep your "commercial" running!

Figure • 17-1: A follow-up telephone call or letter tells a busy employer you are interested in the job, which could make the difference between being called back or disqualified. Follow up no matter how awkward it may feel!

SUCCESS TIP

**Draft a brief follow-up letter you can send after making a follow-up telephone call.**

SUCCESS TIP

**Draft a longer follow-up letter to add information or to use when no call is made.**

**Complete Career Action 17-1 on page 293**

2440 Windom Way, Apt. 34
Los Angeles, CA 90063
July 2, 20—

Ms. Stephanie Nolan
Manager, Auditing Staff
Nolan Henry O'Leary Public Accountants
1410 Granada Avenue, 7th Floor
San Francisco, CA 94115

Dear Ms. Nolan:

Thank you for the opportunity to interview for the position of Staff Auditor I with you and your team. Your invitation to join the first hour of the weekly staff meeting made me feel especially welcome—and sent me to the library to brush up on the finer points of the state's tax credit program for employers who train welfare recipients!

I would enjoy being part of your team and look forward to your hiring decision. Please call me anytime this week at (213) 555-4668.

Sincerely

John Griffin

John Griffin

Figure • 17-2: Sample of a brief thank-you letter

3493 Hydrant Heights
Denver, CO 80202
August 23, 20—

Mr. Frederick J. Gray Wolf
Jupiter Copiers, Inc.
3500 Main Street
West Palm Beach, FL 33408

Dear Mr. Gray Wolf:

The enthusiasm you shared this afternoon for the customer-centered philosophy behind the new Jupiter Print Center is contagious! I know from experience how satisfying it is to break new ground and to achieve results that exceed all expectations. The Jupiter management system sounds unique, innovative, and challenging.

During our meeting we talked about ways I could contribute to your marketing plan, but we didn't have time to discuss store operations. While I managed the parts and service operations of Start Business Systems, our team achieved and maintained a production efficiency rate that consistently placed us in the top five percent of the 160 shops nationwide. Sales of maintenance contracts increased every year I was in charge, and we had the lowest return rate for products of all the centers.

Thank you for talking with me about the new opportunities with Jupiter. Jupiter Copiers, Inc., will be a great success in West Palm Beach, and I would like to contribute to that success. As we agreed, I will call you next Thursday, but you can reach me before that at (303) 555-4886.

Sincerely,

Elena P. Valdez

Elena P. Valdez

Figure • 17-3: Sample of a more complete follow-up letter

# CAREER ACTION 17-1

## Search the Internet for Interview Follow-Up Tips

**NOTE:** Since the content of Web sites is subject to change without notice, be aware that the links listed below may not match the current content of the Web sites referenced in this assignment.

**DIRECTIONS:** Search the Internet for additional tips on interview follow up that could be useful to you. Summarize key points you find useful, or print relevant articles.

***WebGuide* Activities:** Access ***Your Job Search*** from the Main Menu. Go to Activity #7, and click on ***Career Development Center Interview Checklist***, then click on ***After the Interview***, and then ***Thank-You Letters***.

**Internet Activities:** Check the following Web sites for more tips on interview follow-up activities:

**Internet Web Sites:**

Monster Campus ***http://campus.monster.com***
(Click on ***Resumes & Letters***, and then on ***Sample Thank-you Letters***.)

CareerLab ***http://www.careerlab.com***
(Click on ***200 Cover Letters*** or ***200 Letters for Job Hunters***. These are excellent models. Then scroll to ***Say Thank You***, and browse through the many samples provided.)

National Business Employment Weekly ***http://www.nbew.com***
(Click on ***The Best From Our Pages***, then on ***Resumes, Networking, and Interviewing***. Check for new tips on interviewing. Note that articles change; browse for useful new ideas, and share with the class.)

**Internet Search Engines:**

| | |
|---|---|
| Alta Vista | ***http://www.altavista.com*** |
| Excite | ***http://www.excite.com*** |
| Infoseek | ***http://www.infoseek.com/careers*** |
| Lycos | ***http://www.lycos.com*** |
| Yahoo | ***http://www.yahoo.com/business/employment/*** |

**Connect With Your Support Network Again.** If a member of your support network is influential with your prospective employer, contact her or him to ask for additional support. A friendly follow-up call from this person to the employer could tip the scales in your favor.

An alternative to the follow-up call by a network member is a letter of recommendation sent to the employer from one or more people who can confirm your qualifications. Some employers routinely request letters of recommendation from former employers, managers, or supervisors of applicants. Arranging to have such letters sent on your own demonstrates initiative—another plus for you!

> **"Carry the image of victory in your heart."**
> —Fran Tarkenton

Figure • 17-4: It's appropriate to ask influential members of your network to "put in a good word" for you. Be sure to let them know you appreciate their help.

## WAITING GAME STRATEGIES

Waiting to hear about a hiring decision is frustrating. Your best strategy is action!

### Evaluate Your Performance; Identify Follow-Up Activities

After you complete your follow-up telephone call and letter, review your notes on the Interview Follow Up and Evaluation Form (**Career Action 16-2**). Concentrate on the positive aspects of your evaluation to keep your self-image positive. Check to be certain you have completed all follow-up activities you underlined in red.

**Complete Career Action 17-2**

**SUCCESS TIP**

**After each interview, evaluate your performance and identify ways to improve; list all necessary follow-up activities and complete them.**

# CAREER ACTION 17-2

## Follow-Up Telephone Call and Letters

### Part 1: Follow-Up Telephone Call

**DIRECTIONS:** Prepare a draft of a telephone call you can use to follow up an interview. Practice making the call to your helper in a role-playing situation. Answer the questions below to outline your telephone call.

1. Write an appropriate telephone greeting for the person who interviewed you. Follow it by a statement of your name and the position you were interviewed for.
2. Summarize any pertinent information you omitted during your interview.
3. Include any important questions you forgot to ask during the interview.
4. Present a short, casual version of your 60-Second Commercial one more time.
5. Express your interest in the job and your appreciation for the interview.

### Part 2: Brief Follow-Up Thank-You Letter

**DIRECTIONS:** Write a brief follow-up thank-you letter to use after you have made your follow-up telephone call.

### Part 3: Complete Follow-Up Thank-You Letter

**DIRECTIONS:** Draft a letter you could use as a follow up to your interview instead of a call. Answer the questions below to outline your letter.

1. Write an appropriate greeting and a reminder of the position you interviewed for.
2. Include any pertinent information you omitted from your interview.
3. Summarize your job qualifications briefly with the short version of your 60-Second Commercial.
4. Express your interest in the job and your appreciation for the interview.

## Call Back If You Don't Hear about the Decision

Check the last question on the Interview Follow Up and Evaluation Form: By what date did the interviewer indicate he or she would make the hiring decision? Call if you don't receive notice of the hiring decision by the date the interviewer gave. The following technique doesn't pressure interviewers:

> ***"Hello, Ms. Hardaway. This is Terrell Hooks calling. You indicated during our meeting that you expected to have a hiring decision by July 30. I might have missed your call if you tried to get in touch with me."***

This technique helps you with the waiting game by giving you current information about the hiring status. This demonstration of interest and initiative could also persuade the employer to hire you—it happens!

### CHECKLIST FOR SUCCESSFUL INTERVIEWING AND FOLLOW UP

Check each of the following actions you are taking to increase your interview and follow-up success:

- ☐ Review interview success strategies: Chapter 11, 60-Second Commercial, and Career Action 14-2, Question-and-Answer Planning Sheet.
- ☐ Prepare a written script for an interview follow-up telephone call. If necessary, include questions you forgot to ask in the interview or add information omitted.
- ☐ Draft a brief follow-up letter to send after making a follow-up telephone call.
- ☐ Draft a longer follow-up letter to add important information or to use when no call is made.
- ☐ After each interview, complete an Interview Follow Up and Evaluation Form. Take steps to improve areas of weak performance. Complete all follow-up activities necessary.

## CRITICAL THINKING QUESTIONS

1. Describe what makes good interview follow up.
2. Summarize the important topics applicants should include in their follow-up communication (telephone call or letter).
3. Summarize any follow up required after your dress rehearsal practice interview (Career Action 16-2).

CHAPTER 18

# So What If You Don't Get the Job?

"When things do not go the way you want them to go, it's time to ask yourself: What didn't work in the interview? What questions were you struggling with? What do you need to change? Ask people for honest feedback. Sometimes we need to check that the impressions we gave to others were what we intended."

*Roxanne Pellegrino*
*Educational Services Manager*
*Philadelphia Job Corps*

## *In this chapter you will:*

- Determine how to deal effectively with rejection in your job search.
- Evaluate your job search performance, and identify methods of improving it.

Getting a good job often requires more than one interview; it may take several tries before you land the job you want. Getting a rejection notice is not a great ego booster, but it's not a reason to stop your job search campaign. Think of it as a learning experience, and continue with your job search activities. Chapter 18 highlights practical strategies for reenergizing your motivation, reversing a rejection notice, and trying new angles to land a top job.

## COUNTER REJECTION WITH SUCCESS STRATEGIES

To counter natural feelings of rejection, the best defense is taking immediate positive action:

1. Maintain a positive attitude.
2. Evaluate your performance and your self-marketing package.
3. Connect with your network for support and rework your contacts.
4. Plan your next job search steps, and follow through.

**NOTE:** Taking a short breather helps you renew energy and enthusiasm. Allow yourself one day to do something you enjoy, to relax following rejection, but no longer. And *don't* use rejection as an excuse for giving up. Simply regroup—rework your action plans!

### Apply the Eight Success Strategies

Reread Chapter 1, focusing on the success strategies that project competence and strengthen esteem. Review your self-analysis forms from Chapters 2 and 3 (your talents, skills, qualifications, special accomplishments, and personal attributes). Also review your 60-Second Commercial. Remind yourself of your skills and positive accomplishments.

**SUCCESS TIP**

**After a job rejection, use positive thinking, actions, visualization, goal setting, and self-talk to recharge your motivation, fine-tune your job search campaign, and improve your performance.**

Figure • 18-1: Don't let a job rejection get you down. Use the secrets of athletes and other champions. Analyze your performance, visualize succeeding in getting a job offer, and move on.

## SUCCESS IS BUILT ON PERSEVERANCE

Winners in all fields agree: Perseverance is a major factor in their success. When they meet an obstacle, they find a way around it. Setbacks are not failures; you only fail when you quit trying.

### Practice Visualization and Positive Thinking Regularly

**Visualize** yourself performing successfully in your next interview and on your new job. Also make a conscious effort to think and **act positively** and to **use positive self-talk** and affirmation statements. Remember that these actions trigger positive physiological responses that will improve your performance.

# "NO" ISN'T ALWAYS THE FINAL ANSWER

Many job applicants have turned a first rejection into a job offer through effective follow up. Sometimes interviewers get an inaccurate first impression of an applicant. You can revise that impression through follow up; consider the following techniques:

1. **Call and clarify.** Place a timely call to provide missing information, correct misinformation, clarify qualifications, or restate interest. This can turn rejection into employment.

2. **Call and request a short follow-up meeting.** Explain that you have additional information, portfolio examples, or some other item you think the interviewer should consider before making a hiring decision. Ask for just ten to fifteen minutes to make your case. Do your homework, and prepare your telephone script before you call. Make the call organized and concise. This could be your employment ticket.

SUCCESS TIP

**Ask the interviewer to evaluate your performance. You need to base your rejection response on facts, not on assumptions; the information can help you identify areas that need improvement.**

## Get an Evaluation of Your Interview Performance

After receiving a rejection notice, if you're not sure where you fell short, call your interviewer and try to get an honest evaluation. If you are aware of the perceived shortcoming, though, prepare a strong written clarification to reference while making your rejection follow-up call. Here is a way of asking your interviewer for an evaluation:

> ***"Hello, Ms. Nguyen. This is Aaron Goldman. I received your letter stating I had not been selected for the job, and I appreciate the prompt notification. Could you tell me which areas of my preparation and qualifications need to be strengthened, and could you suggest methods of improving in these areas?"***

The interviewer may try to evade your question. Some employers are reluctant to offer specific opinions and are justifiably cautious about disgruntled applicants suing for unfair hiring policies. Even if you don't get concrete help, express your thanks.

**Prepare and Respond.** If the interviewer is willing to evaluate your performance and make suggestions for improvement, take notes. If you are prepared, briefly clarify your qualifications or clear up any misunderstanding right then. Use a friendly tone, and never react defensively. Remember: You asked for the opinion.

If you need more time to respond, wait and write out an effective response after your call. Then write, call, or visit in person to present your new information. A letter can become a permanent part of your application file and can be reviewed more than once, perhaps by someone else in the company who decides you have the required qualities.

**Set Up Another Meeting.** If the interviewer seems receptive, explain that you didn't convey your qualifications as completely as you had planned, and suggest that you meet once more to review them. Handled well, this approach demonstrates confidence, competence, and assertiveness.

## RESPOND TO CRITICAL EVALUATION:

- Be enthusiastic and pleasant.
- Think and speak positively.
- Visualize and focus on your accomplishments and qualifications. (Don't dwell on negatives.)
- Listen carefully and be open to suggestions.
- Add positive information about yourself.
- Do not debate negative impressions.

**Ask for Referrals.** If you reach a point where no further action would get you this job, always ask for other referrals.

> ***"Thank you again for your time, Ms. Nguyen. I have one more question. Could you recommend another department or company I could contact to discuss employment possibilities?"***

### Offer Additional Positive Information

Make your call or send your letter to add additional positive information and/or clarify your qualifications. The purposes should be (a) to provide added positive information, (b) to confirm your enthusiasm and interest in the job, and (c) to convince the interviewer that you are qualified for the job. Prepare your telephone script or letter, and review it with a member of your support network before going further.



## A TRUE CASE: REVERSING REJECTION

The following case illustrates how well-planned follow up can reverse a job rejection. Steve was graduating in engineering from a private university. He applied to several companies, but his first choice was Silar Corporation.

His resume, cover letter, and application for employment got him an interview. He thought the interview was successful because he felt comfortable with the interviewer and solidly demonstrated how his qualifications fit the needs at Silar. He was encouraged by the positive feedback from the interviewer.

Steve was shocked when he received a cordial letter of rejection a week later. The letter emphasized that his 3.2 grade point average didn't meet that of the competition. Many applicants would have accepted the rejection as final proof that this particular job wasn't within their reach. Not so with Steve.

He discussed the subject with his professors and other members of his support network and decided a follow-up telephone call would be appropriate. Steve had not made it clear during his interview that he had worked full-time while earning his university degree. In addition, Steve's performance was low in the first year while he

**SUCCESS TIP**

**Prepare and deliver a response to a rejection notice. Provide additional information or portfolio samples. This follow up can reverse the rejection.**

Figure • 18-2: When you get a job rejection, don't give up. Take it as a personal challenge to see if you can turn the situation around.

clarified his degree objective and learned to develop good study habits—typical of many students. Because his grades were excellent in the last three years, he thought that an appeal to Silar based on demonstrated improvement and achievement was in order.

"If opportunity doesn't knock, build a door."

—Milton Berle

## Steve's Success

Steve called the department manager he interviewed with at Silar Corporation. Steve noted that he had received the rejection letter but added that additional circumstances might be considered. He explained that he worked full-time during his four years in college and that he hadn't clearly identified his degree and career objectives until the latter part of his first year. After the first year, with clear goals in mind, his academic performance was excellent, including a 3.8 average in his engineering major.

Three days later, Steve received a call from the department manager offering him a job! The manager explained that Steve's initiative and belief in his qualifications convinced him and his colleagues that Steve had the qualities they were seeking.

SUCCESS TIP

**Always ask for referrals to another department or another company. Such leads often open new employment possibilities!**

## Your Success

Steve's technique, or a variation of it, has been used by thousands of applicants, and the results have been remarkably successful. You may have a perfectly valid reason for clarifying your qualifications. It takes courage and determination, but the possible reward for your effort is the successful conclusion of your job search. If you receive a rejection notice, you have nothing to lose and everything to gain by trying this tactic.

Word your rejection response carefully. Ask for help from a member of your support network who has the strongest communication skills. Work with this person to develop your rejection response by using the guidelines on the next page.

# PREPARING AND RESPONDING TO A REJECTION NOTICE

**Prepare Your Response:**

- Describe in writing the shortcomings that the interviewer perceives and that resulted in your rejection.
- Summarize any misunderstandings you think contributed to your rejection.
- Summarize important information you omitted during the application or interview process.
- Draft your rejection response, clarifying any misunderstandings, adding information you omitted, and expanding on your qualifications.
- Make your response positive, active, and pleasant. Don't dwell on negatives.
- Review and practice the content with a member of your network.

**NOTE:** Making this extra effort provides further proof of your initiative and interest in the job. This can be the factor that causes the interviewer to choose you.

**"We can do anything we want if we stick to it long enough."**

—Helen Keller

SUCCESS TIP

**Don't be afraid to reapply. You could be first on the backup list; employers save time and money hiring candidates from this list. So keep checking back to keep your name recognition high.**

## ANOTHER POSITION IN ANOTHER DEPARTMENT

If your rejection response doesn't land you this job, ask whether another position would be more suitable for you. Emphasize your enthusiasm for working for this employer, and ask whether you are more qualified to fill another position. This strategy encourages the interviewer to give you more consideration and can land you a "hidden job." If another position isn't available, ask for a referral to another employer. Employers are impressed by applicants who demonstrate initiative and confidence. If you project confidence and competence, you greatly increase your chances of convincing others of your potential.

## DON'T BE AFRAID TO REAPPLY

If you don't get a job with your preferred employer now, don't give up. Even if you take another job for a while, opportunities can develop later. If an opening comes up in the future, it's an advantage to be known by the employer because a known applicant saves valuable time in recruiting a new employee. Besides, you never know how close to being accepted you were. You might be at the top of the list the next time an opening occurs; keeping your name in front of the employer can put you first in line for the next position opening. Consider the following true story:

Janet applied to a large, well-known corporation for a job as an administrative secretary in the human resources department. The department manager interviewed her. She *knew* she did well in the interview, but she didn't get the job because someone was promoted from within (another common practice).

A month later, the manufacturing department manager found her file and interview rating sheet in the human resources department. He noted that the manager had decided not to hire Janet, despite excellent qualifications, because her personality was "too strong for the human resources department." The manufacturing department manager decided immediately that someone who was "too strong for the human resources department" was exactly what they needed in the manufacturing area. Result: The manufacturing department manager interviewed her and hired her at a higher salary than she would have been offered for the first position. Five years later, she was promoted to a supervisory position with a salary 125 percent above her starting salary.

## FOLLOW UP ON YOUR JOB SEARCH PERFORMANCE EVALUATION

To strengthen your job campaign, focus in two areas: (a) thinking and acting positively and (b) planning and taking specific actions. **Career Action 18-1** will help you outline practical actions to strengthen your search effectiveness.

**Complete Career Action 18-1**

## CAREER ACTION 18-1

### Action Plans: Job Search Campaign Improvement

**DIRECTIONS:** Complete the Action Plans: Job Search Campaign Improvement form on page 305. To summarize and evaluate your overall job search performance, answer the assignment questions thoroughly. Complete the follow-up actions required to improve your job search techniques.

**"To keep a lamp burning, we have to keep putting oil in it."**

—Mother Teresa

## CHECKLIST FOR RECHARGING YOUR JOB SEARCH CAMPAIGN

Check each of the following actions you are taking to increase your career success:

- ☐ Use positive thinking, actions, visualization, goal setting, and self-talk to recharge motivation and to improve the job search campaign.
- ☐ Ask the interviewer to evaluate your performance so you can base your response on facts and identify areas that need improvement.
- ☐ Prepare and deliver a response to a rejection notice. Provide additional information or portfolio samples, clarify qualifications or misunderstanding, and so on, as needed.
- ☐ Ask for referrals to another department or another company.
- ☐ Reapply at a later date. Call back periodically to check the hiring status.

## CRITICAL THINKING QUESTIONS

1. After a rejection, how should you approach your continuation of the job search?
2. Should you abandon your efforts to obtain a job with a prospective employer if, following your interview, you are notified that you were not selected for the position? Why?
3. What can you gain from seeking an evaluation of your interview performance from an interviewer who rejected you?
4. If all your efforts fail to result in a job offer, what last request should you make of the interviewer?

# CAREER ACTION 18-1

## Action Plans: Job Search Campaign Improvement

**DIRECTIONS:** Review your complete job search campaign thoroughly. Answer each of the following questions in detail. Include specific action plans you will take to improve where necessary. Check off each item as you complete the actions.

1. After reviewing my self-analysis activities in the Career Actions from Chapters 2 and 3, have I overlooked anything important that supports my job target? (List any items here, and summarize needed research or improvement.)

 ______________________________________________

 ______________________________________________

2. Have I checked with my support network to find out whether they have any new job leads? (List them here, and follow up immediately.)

 ______________________________________________

 ______________________________________________

3. Could my resume be improved or tailored to a new job target? How could it be improved? Who could do a good job of helping me with it?

 ______________________________________________

 ______________________________________________

4. Should I make additional telephone calls/personal visits or write additional letters to prospective employers? (List detailed actions on a separate sheet of paper, and then begin following up today. Don't put them off.)

 ______________________________________________

 ______________________________________________

5. Could my cover letters be improved? How could they be strengthened?

 ______________________________________________

 ______________________________________________

# CAREER ACTION 18-1

(CONTINUED)

6. Have I followed up on every interview—with telephone calls, letters, and personal visits? Have I followed up on the cover letters and resumes I mailed, on all job leads? (List any follow up needed in these areas.)

______________________________________________

______________________________________________

7. Have I done thorough research on my current job leads—enough to talk intelligently and persuasively about myself and the organization in an interview? (List here all research that must be completed.)

______________________________________________

______________________________________________

8. Have I tried every possible job source? (Refer to the list of suggested job sources in Chapter 6. List below any you could use now.)

______________________________________________

______________________________________________

9. Should I reapply with any employers? When?

______________________________________________

______________________________________________

10. Review Chapter 17; make sure you did a thorough job of interview follow up. Make note of any follow-up activity you omitted that might have improved your chance of being selected.

______________________________________________

______________________________________________

11. Have I scheduled my job search on my daily and weekly calendars? Do it now!

______________________________________________

______________________________________________

CHAPTER 19

# You're Hired! Succeed in Your New Position

> Never be afraid to ask questions. When you are new in your position, people don't expect you to know everything, and they anticipate that you will need some instruction. Be open to learning about everything you possibly can, even if it doesn't directly relate to your role or position. By soaking in as much knowledge as you can, you open opportunities for the future.

*Whitney Kilburn*
*Analyst*
*Andersen Consulting*

## *In this chapter you will:*

- Review guidelines for adjusting successfully and achieving peak efficiency in a new job.
- Evaluate your previous or current performance in a job, volunteer work, or other responsible activity.

Search the Internet for job and career success tips.

- Research your industry for tips on job success, promotion, and making a job change.

Chapter 19 presents guidelines for adjusting to your new job. These include techniques for developing successful interpersonal skills, achieving top work efficiency, quickly mastering new responsibilities, and learning how to prepare for a successful job performance evaluation. The importance of taking responsibility for achieving a high quality and quantity of work and for being adaptable to change is also emphasized. Once you master your job and are performing at your peak, you will likely be interested in working toward career development and advancement opportunities. This chapter also provides clear guidelines for earning a promotion and achieving career growth.

## ADJUST TO YOUR NEW JOB

All workers who start new jobs have one challenge in common: adjusting to the job. Adjustment includes learning to perform specific job functions, learning how the job relates to the business as a whole, learning to work with others (superiors, team members or co-workers, or customers), and understanding the formal and informal chain of organizational command. Mastering all these elements takes time and effort on your part and training assistance from your employer.

> "A man can succeed at almost anything for which he has unlimited enthusiasm."
> —Charles M. Schwab

Don't expect to achieve top efficiency overnight—it doesn't happen. Experiencing some anxiety in trying to learn so much new information and many new procedures is normal. Maintaining enthusiasm, eagerness to learn, and a positive attitude will help you adjust successfully.

Figure • 19-1: Expect to take some time to get comfortable in a new job and work environment. Don't let the learning curve get you down. Listen; stay positive; look, speak, and act professionally.

Starting a new job is an important personal and professional step that shapes your lifetime career. Successful careers are developed through planning and determination to succeed. You will achieve peak success through persistence and accumulation of skills, knowledge, and experience.

Your employer will want you to succeed; co-workers will help you get off to a good start. The following techniques will help you adjust to the organization and your job and to achieve a successful lifetime career.

### Attitude: The Most Important Success Factor

Employers hire and promote employees who have good attitudes and demonstrate enthusiasm and a positive attitude. Employees who demonstrate a defensive, negative, or disinterested attitude are not promoted and may eventually be terminated. Two employees with equal job skills but vastly different attitudes often develop widely different career paths. The one with a strong, positive attitude progresses steadily; the one with a negative attitude stagnates.

Approach new tasks, colleagues, and superiors with the attitude that you will do your best and that you expect the best from them, while being patient with their constraints. People most often live up to the expectations others have of them.

### Project a Positive, Professional, and Competent Image

People assume that the image you project is an example of the quality of work you do. Your image projects from three sources: your inner confidence, your outward appearance, and your verbal and non-verbal

## A POSITIVE, PROFESSIONAL IMAGE BOOSTS SUCCESS

Successful people think of themselves, see themselves, groom themselves, and talk about themselves as winners.

communication. Review the information on self-esteem, appearance, and communication skills in Chapters 1 and 11. Polish and apply these skills daily.

If you project an unsure attitude through your speech, appearance, and actions, you will be perceived as a tentative, unsure worker, even if your work is excellent. Purposely think, speak, dress, and act positively. This projects career-building confidence and competence.

Always projecting a positive, professional, and competent image gives you a competitive edge. For example, if you make an error, your professional image influences people to be more accepting of the error as a part of learning, rather than as a result of incompetence. Successful people act positively, practicing the eight success strategies until these become automatic habits.

### Develop and Practice Good Interpersonal Skills: Be a Team Player

Job success depends largely on the ability to work well with others. Studies repeatedly verify that job failure is most frequently based on poor interpersonal (behavior and attitude) skills, *not* on lack of skill.

**Be a Team Player.** Get along well with and assist others, show interest in their work, and work efficiently alone or with others. Team players are promoted first.

**Be Tactful.** The world's most successful people have these abilities in common: They are tactful, diplomatic, courteous, and helpful in dealing with other people.

**Treat People the Way You Want to Be Treated.** Help others accomplish their assignments, compliment them on work well done, criticize tactfully only when necessary, and listen to what they have to say. This behavior encourages others to treat you the same way.

When you need help with a project or are in line for a promotion, your reputation for working well with others will more likely be rewarded. Treat *all people* (your employer, peers, the custodian) with respect.

**SUCCESS TIP**

**Focus on three goals to help you adjust successfully to a new job: keep a positive attitude; project a professional, competent image; and be a good team player.**

## GET OFF TO A SUCCESSFUL START

When you're hired, your employer expects you to have the basic knowledge and skills to do the job. You acquired these through your education and prior work experience. The challenge now is to apply them to the best of your ability in performing your job.

Be a good learner and expand your abilities. You will be expected to become a productive employee within a reasonable training period. You can improve the quality and speed of your learning and performance by applying the following job mastery techniques.

## Job Orientation

Your employer is responsible for informing you of your job duties and for providing an orientation to the work procedures. You should also be told about work hours, parking requirements, and related information.

Your employer should explain when and how your performance will be evaluated. To help you focus your efforts and to achieve the best possible performance evaluation, find out immediately *just how and when your job performance will be evaluated.* If any of this orientation or job evaluation information is overlooked, request an explanation of it.

## Be Aware and Alert at All Times

Observe carefully the way work flows through your office or department, and be a good listener. This will help you adjust more quickly. By listening, you can detect subtle attitudes and unstated policies that influence business operations. Others also appreciate good listening skills and not needing to clarify information repeatedly.

## Learn about the Development of Your Area

Knowing the history of the employees and development of departmental procedures and policies can help you understand the logic behind, and the need for, your job responsibilities. This will help you perform your work to meet the employer's goals.

## Maintain a Question-and-Answer Notebook

As you learn each aspect of your job, use a notebook to record all your questions and the instructions you receive. Ask your supervisor what times are best for discussing your questions. This way, you can avoid annoying your supervisor with poorly timed interruptions. Maintaining your notebook is important for several reasons:

- You will improve your efficiency by following up regularly on areas of confusion or areas that haven't been explained.
- You won't have to repeat the same questions.
- Your supervisor will appreciate your courtesy and efficiency.

Remembering every detail required to master a new set of job tasks is impossible. A notebook provides a quick review and a reminder of tasks and procedures.

## Work Efficiently; Manage Time

Arrive at work exactly on time or a little early every day. Being on time gives you an edge of preparedness and an unhurried mind-set that improves work performance. Being late or rushed often causes pressure for you and your work team, interfering with efficient job performance.

**Determine Priorities.** Ask your co-workers and supervisor which tasks are most vital to the successful operation of your department. Determine which tasks are most important, and prioritize your work. Spending time on a menial task that can wait until a rush project is completed is inefficient.

### CONSTANTLY PRIORITIZE YOUR WORK

Do your most important daily tasks first. This avoids overlooking vital tasks during rush work periods.

**Use Time-Management Tools: Calendars, Job-Tracking Forms.** Keep your work calendar current, coordinate it with your work team, and check it daily to avoid overlooking deadlines, meetings, and other responsibilities. Keep a reminder notebook of tasks to be completed. Prepare a daily "To Do" list, and record the tasks in order of importance (record items from your notebook on the form). You can create computerized "To Do" or "Project Tracking" forms and then print copies as needed as a quick reference. Each day, do your best to complete as many things on your list as possible; always concentrate on the top priorities first.

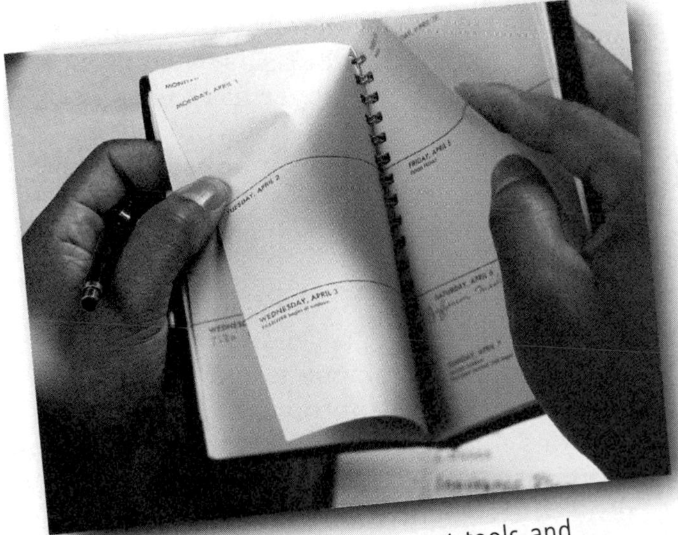

Figure • 19-2: Use time management tools and personal organization systems to keep track of your work and meetings.

**Develop Good Time-Management Habits.** Group tasks that are alike, and complete them in one block of time. For example, schedule one time to file or prepare documents and another to place all telephone calls. This helps you stay focused on one type of task and increases your productivity over a scattered approach.

**Keep Your Work Area Well Organized.** If your work area is disorganized, you can't locate resources efficiently; this decreases productivity and increases frustration.

## Be Dependable, Punctual, and Industrious

Be professional, hardworking, and accurate in performing your job. This sets a positive example for your coworkers; employers value and look for these qualities in retaining and promoting people.

**Maintain an Excellent Attendance Record.** Absenteeism causes work inefficiency, disruption of work flow, and lower productivity; places stress on workers who have to cover for the absent employee; and causes resentment and frustration. If you must be absent because of severe illness, serious emergency, or an unavoidable problem, let your employer know at the earliest possible moment.

Chronic absenteeism is not tolerated by employers and is an eventual ticket out the door. *Abuse* is the key word. Patterns of questionable excuses raise big questions in the employer's mind.

**Be Punctual.** Report to work promptly every day and after breaks or mealtimes. Also, be on time for meetings. Being late is not well accepted by others who always make an effort to be punctual. Always be on time! Being on time also means finishing projects or assignments when they are due.

**Demonstrate Initiative.** Personal initiative is a major promotional factor. After you've finished your assigned duties, *don't sit and wait for more work to be assigned.* Find an appropriate task to perform on your own, or ask how you can assist. Think creatively about better ways to do your job. Then research and plan how to implement your ideas. If a co-worker is overloaded, offer to help.

## Focus on People as Well as on Job Duties

The way you relate to the people in your work will influence your career success as much as the quality of your job performance—no matter how skilled or educated you are. Make time for your co-workers, supervisors, employer, clients, or customers.

**Be Courteous, Understanding, and Helpful.** Spend time with co-workers during breaks and mealtimes. Don't let yourself become a loner; it won't enhance career success.

**Be Aware of Organizational Politics.** Every office or organizational group has formal and informal politics, which are modified by changes in personnel. Learn who is respected (or even feared) in your place of employment. These people usually influence office politics greatly and are usually powerful within the organization. Learn to deal successfully with them.

**"The only certain means of success is to render more and better service than is expected of you, no matter what your task may be."**

—Og Mandino

Note, however, that *first impressions are not always accurate.* Take time to observe and learn the office politics; don't affiliate with any group until you're satisfied the group is reputable and in harmony with your philosophy and that of the employer.

## Manage Yourself

Learn to deal with difficult people, control your emotions, manage stress and conflict, and maintain a good health and fitness program. Good books and classes are available on all of these subjects if you need additional information. Also, manage your family and transportation; anticipate and prevent problems.

### BUILD A NETWORK

Build a network of people willing to help you understand how to work most efficiently and effectively in the organization.

## Learn to Accept Criticism Professionally

Because you are human, you will make an occasional mistake. Gasp! The challenge is to accept criticism maturely. When you work for someone else, you agree to perform according to that person's standards. By paying your salary, your employer has the right to criticize your performance or behavior if it doesn't meet established standards.

If the criticism is deserved, don't deny fault. Accept it graciously, and start making improvements. If appropriate, request suggestions for improving from the person who criticizes you. Learn from mistakes. If you think the criticism was not based on fact, tactfully present the evidence that supports your opinion.

If your employer or supervisor continually criticizes you unfairly, particularly in front of others, request a private meeting to discuss the reason. If the criticism continues even though you have made the recommended improvements, seriously consider seeking a position in another department or looking for another employer.

## Be a Supportive Employee

Employers value supportive employees. When you accept employment and a salary, the employer expects your support. Make an effort to speak well of the firm and its personnel to colleagues and to people outside the company. Employees who speak negatively about the employer, personnel, product, or service harm the employer's reputation. Employees who do this are often dismissed. If you are ultimately unhappy in the job and can see no way of improving your satisfaction there, move on.

## Demonstrate Maturity

Be responsible for your actions; always perform at your best level, and expect the same from others you supervise. Be aware of your strengths and weaknesses. Capitalize on your strengths, and make efforts to improve areas of weakness. Be self-reliant and self-disciplined. Maintain stable emotions in the office, leaving personal problems at home.

Figure • 19-3: Respond professionally to all formal and informal performance reviews. Listen to criticisms as an opportunity to improve.

## Prepare for Your Job Performance Evaluation

Learn how and when you will be evaluated on your job performance so you will know where to focus your efforts to achieve a good evaluation. At the same time, you will reduce chances that you will overlook an area considered important by your employer. You need to know, too, how heavily the employer weights each area of performance so you can concentrate on those that are most important. If you don't receive this information, ask your supervisor to explain the process.

If your employer uses an informal method of job evaluation, you should still ask what is considered good job performance and what criteria are used in determining promotions or raises. This will provide guidelines for your successful performance.

Many employers schedule annual, biannual, or quarterly meetings to review their employees' job performances in writing, orally, or both. Usually, the purpose of these evaluations is to identify strengths and weaknesses of each employee and to establish short-term and long-term goals of the employer and employee. A sample job performance rating form, representative of those used by many organizations today, is used as the worksheet for **Career Action 19-1**.

**SUCCESS TIP**

**To succeed in your job, manage yourself professionally. Work efficiently, be dependable, focus on people, and prepare for your performance evaluation.**

**Complete Career Action 19-1**

# CAREER ACTION 19-1

## Job Performance Evaluation

**DIRECTIONS:** Complete the Job Performance Evaluation form on page 319. If you have not held a paid job, evaluate yourself on volunteer work, internship work, or another significant activity in which you were responsible for carrying out assigned tasks, organizing and directing others, or both.

## SUCCEED IN TODAY'S CHANGING WORKPLACE

As emphasized in Chapter 4, today's technology and increasing workplace competition are escalating the pace of work and changing the way it is performed. Employers need employees who are flexible in adapting to change and who are able to work independently in making decisions and solving problems. Competition requires increased efficiency and production.

### Total Quality Management

Throughout the world, organizations recognize that to compete successfully, they must have well-developed quality control programs. Most have developed **Total Quality Management (TQM)** systems for this purpose. Increased competition is forcing us to speed up the development, production, and delivery of improved goods and services.

TQM requires each worker to take responsibility for achieving maximum productivity while continuously looking for ways to improve quality. Work teams are also emphasized as natural sources of ideas for improving processes. Many organizations place complete responsibility on employee work teams to supervise themselves—setting their goals, monitoring quality and quantity of work, evaluating job performance, and disciplining when necessary.

## MEET YOUR EMPLOYER'S NEEDS FOR TQM

To meet your employer's expectations and achieve peak career success:

1. Produce top-quality work.
2. Produce the highest possible quantity of work.
3. Be alert for problems and take action to prevent or solve them.
4. Contribute efficiently and effectively as a team member.

### Manage Change and Be Flexible

In addition to quality performance, focus on developing and improving your abilities to be flexible and to adapt to change.

**Be Flexible.** Expect differences (some major) between the way your employer conducts business and the methods you learned in school or on another job. Schools often teach theories, whereas work supervisors interpret and apply theories and techniques (often developing their own!) to accomplish specific work goals and tasks. Changing technology rapidly makes some textbook theories obsolete. Personalities also influence work methods: An outgoing person will use methods different from those used by a shy person.

A process may seem inefficient to you but may serve a valuable organizational purpose that is not immediately apparent to you. Presenting a know-it-all image to your supervisor or others is a sure way to alienate yourself, perhaps permanently. If you think a technique could be improved, request a meeting with your supervisor to clarify the reasons for the technique. Using thoughtful questions is a good technique to open the discussion.

There is a right time, place, and method for presenting your ideas or suggestions. Learn by observing how others present theirs. If the clarification by your supervisor still doesn't convince you that this is the most effective technique, explain the theory or technique you have learned or devised, offering it as a suggestion for consideration. Never try to bulldoze your idea through.

**Adapt to Change.** Rapid technological, global economic, and other changes require continual changes in work processes, tools, and equipment. You must be flexible in evaluating the need for or adapting to changes in procedures, equipment use, and so on. Office automation continually affects the way business is conducted and the way work is performed. Keep an open, flexible attitude toward change. Don't make yourself obsolete by stubborn resistance; you may miss an open door to a career development opportunity. Continually keep your skills and knowledge current through education and training.

**Complete Career Action 19-2**

# CAREER ACTION 19-2

## Use the Internet to Search for Current Job and Career Success Tips

**DIRECTIONS:** Search for articles on career success tips related to areas presented in Chapter 19 (succeeding in a new job, succeeding in today's changing workplace, or pursing a new career goal). Use any of the sites below or others you identify. **Write a summary of at least two articles for this assignment.**

1. **CAREERMagazine** ***http://www.careermag.com***

   (Check out the current columns on the home page, and click on ***Articles*** to browse through current articles and archives.)

2. **Careers, Not Just Jobs** ***http://www.careers.wsj.com***

   (Click on ***Succeeding at Work***; review articles on making the most of your career.)

3. **National Business Employment Weekly** ***http://www.nbew.com***

   (Browse through the articles and features on the home page, and choose any of interest to you.)

## PURSUE A NEW CAREER GOAL

Once you believe that (a) you have mastered your job responsibilities, (b) you have overcome any areas of weakness in your performance or skills, and (c) your employer is satisfied with your performance and understanding of the job, you may want to work toward a new career goal—a lateral move or a promotion, for example.

### Be Willing to Take on New or Additional Responsibilities

Find out exactly what new responsibilities would be included in any new position you seek. Once you decide on the goal, pursue it with an expectation of success, and be willing to accept, learn, and carry out all the duties. Make extra efforts to get any training you need to perform at the levels required.

> "Perpetual optimism is a force multiplier."
>
> —Colin Powell

### How to Earn a Promotion

Keep in mind that you don't *get* a promotion, you *earn* one! When you know you are adequately prepared for a promotion, take steps to demonstrate your qualifications for it. The following guidelines will help you achieve this goal:

- **Maintain and update your career portfolio.** Continually add to the career portfolio you have created through the exercises in this text. This is your collection of documents and other items providing evidence and examples of work accomplishments, certifications, skills, qualifications, and more. Throughout your career, add records of all work-related achievements, including samples of exemplary work, letters of recognition for a job well done, and other documents supporting your good job performance and related activities. Document all accomplishments that will help demonstrate your qualifications for a promotion.

**SUCCESS TIP**

**To succeed in the changing workplace, be a high-quality, top producer; be a problem solver; learn to adapt to and manage change; and be flexible.**

- **Seek a mentor.** A mentor is someone inside or outside your organization who can advise and coach you—someone respected and knowledgeable in your field. Seek advice from a mentor who is experienced in the areas you need to improve; don't limit yourself to seeking advice from just one mentor. Look for people who are sensitive to your concerns and those who help you learn new skills or take the time to explain the dynamics of your organization. Always keep your relationship businesslike. A true mentor will develop an interest in you, make you aware of useful resources, and arrange opportunities for you to meet key people and be involved in professional growth activities. Work hard to live up to his or her expectations for your professional performance.

- **Be professional.** Think, act, speak, and dress professionally. If you want the promotion, act as if you already fit the part.

- **Expand your knowledge and skills and keep up to date.** Keep current in your job and industry knowledge (current trends, technology, and improved methods of job performance). Correct any deficiencies immediately through reading, involvement in professional associations, training, and education. Submit written reports of what you learn to your supervisor or employer.

- **Do high-quality work.** Always do the best possible job and achieve the highest possible quantity and quality of work.

- **Increase your organizational awareness.** Learn all phases of the organization, its goals, and how each job is designed to meet the overall goals.

- **Increase your visibility.** Get involved in organizational committees at work. Find projects in which you can succeed. Show extra initiative, do more than is required, and demonstrate leadership.

- **Seek the promotion.** Once you have accomplished most of the items on this list, let your supervisor know you are interested in progressing and learning more. Demonstrate your ability to handle additional responsibility.

**Complete Career Action 19-3**

Figure • 19-4: To earn a promotion, increase your visibility by getting involved in cross-team projects and organization-wide planning committees.

# CAREER ACTION 19-3

## Research Your Industry for Tips on Job Success, Promotion, and Making a Job Change

**DIRECTIONS:** Complete the questionnaire provided for **Career Action 19-3** on page 322 (or design a questionnaire yourself). Survey knowledgeable people in your field, and record their answers.

## MAINTAIN YOUR NETWORK AND DATABASE

Once you're employed, send a thank-you note to each member of your network who helped you or expressed interest in your job search. Tell them about your new position, and keep your contacts for the next time you're ready to pursue a career goal.

Keep your database current; don't abandon it. You have done a great deal of work in completing the exercises in *Your Career: How to Make It Happen*. Remember that this information will be useful throughout your entire career. Save your work (this book, the written assignments, and your computer files); you'll be glad you did!

SUCCESS TIP

**To achieve new career goals, take on new challenges, broaden your skills and knowledge, seek a mentor, keep your career portfolio current, network, and increase your visibility.**

## CHECKLIST FOR SUCCEEDING ON THE JOB

Check each of the following actions you are currently taking to increase your career success:

- ☐ Focus on three goals to help adjust successfully to a new job: keep a positive attitude; project a professional, competent image; and be a good team player.
- ☐ Work efficiently, be dependable, focus on people, and prepare for evaluation.
- ☐ Be a high-quality, top producer; be a problem solver; learn to adapt to and manage change; and be flexible.
- ☐ Take on new challenges, broaden skills and knowledge; seek a mentor; keep your portfolio current; network; and increase your visibility.
- ☐ Keep your career-building network active. Maintain your career information database to use in future career development activities.

## CRITICAL THINKING QUESTIONS

1. On what is job failure most frequently based?
2. How can you most effectively learn your new job?
3. Why is it important for you to know how you will be evaluated on your job performance?
4. Why is it essential to adapt to change, and how can you demonstrate adaptability?
5. Once you have mastered your new job, explain the actions you would take to increase your professional development and to make yourself promotable: (a) List additional training or course work you could take to increase your knowledge and skills, (b) identify growth-oriented new responsibilities you would be interested in pursuing, and (c) list any other actions you could take to prepare for a promotion and increase your visibility.

# CAREER ACTION 19-1

## Job Performance Evaluation

**DIRECTIONS:** Rate your job performance in your current or past work experience, in volunteer or internship work, or in another significant activity in which you carried out tasks. In the space next to each Performance or Behavioral Category, place the rating code you think most appropriately represents your performance (O = outstanding, V = very good, G = good, A = acceptable, U = unacceptable). On the line below each item, give one or two examples of the performance. Then circle the topic headings you rated acceptable or below; make these your targets for improvement.

| Rating Code | Performance or Behavioral Category |
|---|---|
| ____________ | **ABILITY TO ACQUIRE AND USE INFORMATION AND FOLLOW INSTRUCTIONS** (Uses initiative in acquiring, interpreting, and following instructions and using references.)<br>List specific examples: ______________________________<br>______________________________ |
| ____________ | **INTERPERSONAL SKILLS** (Is tactful and understanding when dealing with people.)<br>List specific examples: ______________________________<br>______________________________ |
| ____________ | **BASIC SKILLS** (Is proficient in reading, writing, mathematics, listening, verbal and non-verbal communications.)<br>List specific examples: ______________________________<br>______________________________ |
| ____________ | **JOB SKILLS** (Demonstrates command of required knowledge and skills.)<br>List specific examples: ______________________________<br>______________________________ |
| ____________ | **THINKING SKILLS** (Generates new ideas, makes decisions, solves problems, and reasons logically.)<br>List specific examples: ______________________________<br>______________________________ |

CONTINUED ON NEXT PAGE

# CAREER ACTION 19-1

(CONTINUED)

_______ **ABILITY TO COOPERATE WITH OTHERS** (Works well with team members and under supervision, exercises leadership, works well with people of diverse backgrounds.)

List specific examples: ______________________________

______________________________

_______ **QUANTITY OF WORK** (Does required amount of work.)

List specific examples: ______________________________

______________________________

_______ **QUALITY OF WORK** (Does neat, accurate, efficient work.)

List specific examples: ______________________________

______________________________

_______ **PRACTICES GOOD WORK HABITS** (Maintains good attendance and punctuality, is dependable, follows safety/work procedures.)

List specific examples: ______________________________

______________________________

_______ **ATTITUDE** (Demonstrates enthusiastic interest and motivation.)

List specific examples: ______________________________

______________________________

_______ **TECHNOLOGY** (Works well with technology—tools, computers, procedures.)

List specific examples: ______________________________

______________________________

_______ **PERSONAL QUALITIES** (Demonstrates responsibility, initiative, self-confidence, integrity, and honesty. Practices good self-management, sets and maintains goals, exhibits self-motivation, is cooperative.)

List specific examples: ______________________________

______________________________



CONTINUED ON NEXT PAGE

# CAREER ACTION 19-1

(CONTINUED)



**Overall Evaluation of Performance and Behavior**

**Directions:** Review the rating codes (Outstanding, Very good, Acceptable, or Unacceptable) you placed in each category of your job performance evaluation on the previous pages. Then place a check mark below next to the rating you recorded most frequently.

____ Outstanding
____ Very good
____ Good
____ Acceptable
____ Unacceptable

**Employee's Short-Term Goals:** (List your short-term job or career goals here.)

______________________________________________________________________

**Employee's Long-Term Goals:** (List your long-term job or career goals here.)

______________________________________________________________________

**Suggestions for Improving Performance or Behavior:** (List steps you can take to improve your work performance or behavior.)

______________________________________________________________________

**General Comments Regarding Employee's Job Performance:** (Add any other appropriate comments to describe the quality of your work performance.)

______________________________________________________________________

**Signature of Supervisor:** (This is where your job supervisor would sign your performance evaluation.)

______________________________________________________________________

**Signature of Employee:** (This is where you would sign the peformance evaluation.)

______________________________________________________________________

**Date:** ______________________________________________________

# CAREER ACTION 19-3

## Research Your Industry for Tips on Job Success, Promotion, and Making a Job Change

**DIRECTIONS:** Arrange meetings with knowledgeable people in your field to learn the following: (a) how the job performance of employees is evaluated, (b) what techniques help ensure success on the job, (c) how employees can earn a promotion, and (d) what methods are recommended in making a job change. Use the following questionnaire, adding pertinent questions relevant to your field, or you design your own questionnaire.

1. What advice would you give a new employee (in a position similar to the one you are seeking) to help him or her adjust quickly to the job, company, and people the employee would interact with?

   ______________________________________________

   ______________________________________________

2. What advice would you give this person to help ensure the highest degree of job success?

   ______________________________________________

   ______________________________________________

3. What criteria do you use to evaluate the performance of such an employee? Do you have a job performance evaluation form I could review?

   ______________________________________________

   ______________________________________________

4. How can such an employee earn a promotion here?

   ______________________________________________

   ______________________________________________

5. If an employee must leave your company, what steps do you prefer the employee to take? How much notice do you expect? Do you prefer that the employee help train the replacement? Do you expect a letter of resignation?

   ______________________________________________

   ______________________________________________

CHAPTER 20

# Make Successful Job and Career Changes

**"In all of my job and career changes, I have looked at my decisions as investments. What is the cost, and what is the return? With each decision, I always consider the risks. I never plan to fail, but I try to be realistic and plan for the good and the bad."**

*Mark Richardson*
*Chief Executive Officer*
*Mid States Steel Company*

*In this chapter you will:*

- Focus on lifelong learning.
- Learn the difference between a job and a career; identify issues to consider when changing jobs or careers.
- Learn how to resign professionally.
- Identify factors to consider in relocating.

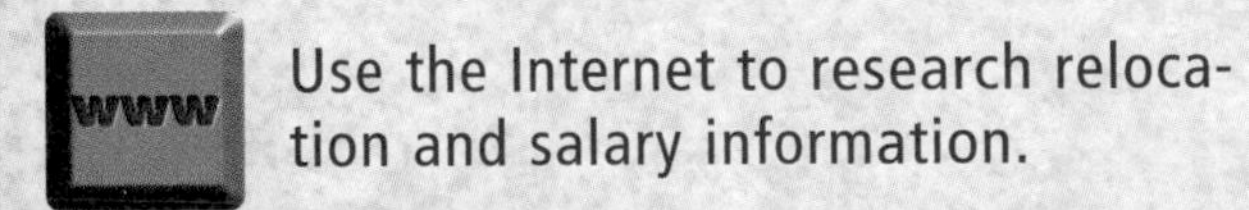


Use the Internet to research relocation and salary information.

- Recognize how to survive being laid off or fired.

This chapter defines the difference between a job and a career and presents strategies for determining whether you will want to consider changing your job or your career. People rarely spend their entire lives working in the same positions for the same employers at the same locations. In this chapter, you will discover the importance of lifelong learning and how to decide whether you should consider relocation, change of job, or change of career. Methods are also presented for effectively coping with relocation. In addition, you will receive advice on what to do if you are laid off or fired from your position.

## BE A LIFELONG LEARNER

Rapidly changing technology and a global economy are driving us into a fast-changing world. Not only are you likely to change jobs and even careers, but jobs and careers are changing dramatically and require those who wish to have successful careers to update quickly and continuously and add new skills. This means you need to develop and sustain the habit of continuing your education throughout your working life to avoid being left behind. You may do this through workshops, training programs, college courses, or other educational delivery systems. To ensure your employability in the future, you must make sure you always have the skills required to meet the demands of the changing workforce.

For example, auto mechanics who previously knew how to work on fuel carburetors had to learn the technology of fuel injection systems in order to continue to work in their career field.

Figure • 20-1: You can be a lifelong learner by keeping up with the latest technology in your field, learning another language, and taking on new challenges.

To remain a viable employee in the 21st Century, you must make lifelong learning a part of your career management plans.

**Keep yourself on the cutting edge of the workforce by continuing your education; lifelong learning is the ticket to continued employment in a rapidly changing world.**

## KNOW THE DIFFERENCE BETWEEN A JOB AND A CAREER

A **job** involves performing a designated set of responsibilities and duties for a specific employer. A **career** encompasses a family of jobs. Your career is your life's work. Thus, *high school history teacher for Washington High School* is a job, and *teaching* is the career. Similarly, *sportswear clerk for After Five Stores* is a job, and *retail sales* is the career.

Many people do not consider the difference between a job and a career; as a result, they spend a great deal of time and money changing careers when they only need to change jobs. In other cases, people change jobs repeatedly and continue to be dissatisfied because they are not in the right careers.

Most people will change jobs at least eight times during their working lives. With changes in technology and in their values and interests, it is also common for people to change careers at least once during their lifetimes. If you realize that your current employment situation is no longer satisfying, first consider whether the dissatisfaction is with your career or with your specific job.

# CAREER ACTION 20-1

## Career Changes

**PART 1 DIRECTIONS:** Identify a career (other than the example just given) for which new training has become necessary to remain employable; describe the career process change, and identify the type of education or training needed to meet the changing need.

**PART 2 DIRECTIONS:** Think about the career you are planning to pursue, and list at least two likely changes that will require further education or training.

If you are unhappy with your boss yet love your work, you may need to change jobs; but it doesn't mean you need to change careers. If you don't like the basic kind of work you are doing, though, you may need to consider changing careers.

**SUCCESS TIP**

**Before you change your job or career, analyze whether your discontent is from your specific job or from your career choice. Don't change your career just because you don't like your boss, and don't keep changing jobs when you really aren't well suited for your career.**

## UNDERSTAND WHEN YOU SHOULD CHANGE JOBS

You may want to consider a job change if (a) your current employer cannot offer you advancement, (b) a poor economy requires layoffs, (c) you wish to move to a new location, (d) your department is dissolved, (e) your philosophy conflicts with that of your current employer, or (f) you simply want a new challenge.

### Never Quit a Job before You Have a New One

If possible, begin and complete your job change while still employed. Because being employed is current proof that you do a job satisfactorily, you are considered much more employable when you are currently employed. As the mountain-climbing instructor says to students, "Never let loose of your support before you have hold of another one."

### Don't Rush into a Job Change without Adequate Planning

Give any change of jobs serious thought and planning. You will regret a hasty decision to take a new job if it turns out to be worse than your current one. The job may look good on the outside, but without proper research, you may find yourself in a situation that is as bad or worse than your current one. Evaluate your current job by asking yourself: Is there room for advancement to a higher position with my current employer? If the answer is *no* and you will not be happy staying in the same position, you have strong grounds for considering a new employer. If the answer is *yes*, there may be advantages to staying with your current employer.

## What Are the Advantages of Staying with Your Current Employer?

Seeking advancement or growth with your current employer can offer many advantages, including the following:

- Staying is less risky because you are already established and need not repeat the process of adjusting to new surroundings and people.
- Your reputation for job stability is improved by staying, rather than moving frequently from one employer to another.
- You will not lose accumulated benefits, such as vacation time, retirement, profit sharing, and insurance.

## What Can You Gain by Changing Employers?

Changing employers can also offer many advantages, including the following:

- You will increase job interest by becoming involved in new challenges, surroundings, and people.
- A job change may result in quicker advancement than you could achieve through seeking promotion within the same organization.
- You will gain knowledge, broaden your experience, and increase your support network, expanding your career growth opportunities.
- You will start with a clean slate as you develop your reputation for good job performance.

**SUCCESS TIP**

**Change to a new job after careful consideration of the advantages and disadvantages of staying in your current one. Avoid quitting your current position until you have obtained a new one.**

"An investment in knowledge pays the best interest."

—Benjamin Franklin

# KNOW WHEN YOU SHOULD CHANGE CAREERS

If, after thorough consideration, you decide that you aren't happy in your work and that a change to another job within the same field would not bring satisfaction, you may want to consider seriously a career change. Ask yourself the following questions:

- **Have I changed positions several times only to find that I am still unhappy?** Repeated changes of employment that don't improve job satisfaction may indicate a career problem, not a job problem.
- **Are my problems the result of personality or philosophical conflicts with my supervisor or fellow employees?** If so, it's more likely that you need a new employer instead of a new career. The exception occurs when the type of people usually found in your career field, regardless of the organization, don't fit your personality or philosophy.

- **Am I unhappy with the work environment?** If you don't like to work constantly at a desk, decide whether this is common to your career field or only to your job. Would you prefer outdoor work? You might want to look at other careers if your career doesn't provide the opportunity for this kind of work. Is the environmental problem common to the career or only to some jobs within the career field?

- **Am I constrained in expressing my values?** Again, is this a function of your job or your career?

- **Is this position interesting?** What are your interests? Are you blocked from meeting them in your career or just in your current job?

- **Am I frustrated that I'm not using my skills and abilities?** Is this a job-related or a career-related problem?

Even if you determine that your unhappiness is related to your career rather than to your current job, you still have to weigh the pros and cons of making a career change. Rarely can you just jump into another career without sacrifices. You must evaluate the advantages and disadvantages and whether you are gaining more than you are losing.

## Reassess

First, determine what alternative careers fit your interests and abilities. Study the options to decide which you would prefer. Apply the principles presented in Chapters 2 and 3. Then, after you have selected an alternative career, you need to discover what additional education or training you need, how long it takes to prepare for this field, and what it will cost. Also determine whether the education or training is available nearby and whether you can get the skills while continuing your current job or if you will have to return to school.

## Be Realistic

What are the job opportunities in the new field? Are those jobs in a desirable location, and will the pay meet your requirements? Be aware that when you change careers, you often have to start over at the entry-level salary.

Figure • 20-2: Never let loose of your support until you have hold of another.

**SUCCESS TIP**

**Change to a new career if you determine that your unhappiness is related to your career, not just to your specific current job, and that an alternative career is realistically available and will meet your needs.**

## Determine Your Risk Tolerance

What kind of risk taker are you? Are you willing to give up the security of your current position and career and take a chance? On the one hand, you may lose any seniority you have, you may lose benefits, and the change may reduce your retirement funds. On the other hand, do you expect to be significantly more satisfied in this new career? Does your research confirm that you have a good chance of achieving equal or greater financial stability as well?

In the final analysis, you will need to decide whether the probable advantages sufficiently outweigh the disadvantages and whether you are willing to assume any risk involved. You must also be prepared to discuss this risk taking persuasively with prospective employers who may question whether you will be happy with such changes. It will be important for you to convey to employers that you have considered this change carefully and that you believe the advantages outweigh the disadvantages. Each of us has a personal level of risk taking. You will need to determine yours.

**Complete Career Action 20-2**

## CAREER ACTION 20-2

### Career and Job Planning Application

**DIRECTIONS:** Consider your career development.

1. On separate paper, list the name of your current targeted career; then list three jobs you might hold within that career field.

2. List two issues you would need to evaluate if you were considering a career change, and list two issues you would need to evaluate if you were considering a job change.

# RESIGN PROFESSIONALLY

Resigning professionally is good career insurance. Make every effort to leave your current employer with good feelings; never leave in anger or hostility, no matter how dissatisfied you may be. Throughout the rest of your career, references from your past employers will be requested each time you seek a new job. For this important reason, *always* leave any job gracefully, pleasantly, and professionally.

Follow these guidelines to ensure that your resignation results in feelings of goodwill and willingness by your employer to provide a good reference for you.

1. Find out how your current employer typically reacts when learning that someone is looking for a new position. Does your employer become upset and fire that person or try to make it difficult for her or him to find new employment? Does your employer respond positively by offering to support the person in finding new employment? Or, even better, does your employer try to provide positive inducements, such as pay raises or promotions, to keep the person within the organization?

Figure • 20-3: Always resign professionally. Keep your reasons for leaving positive. Thank your boss for the development opportunities you've had. She or he can become part of your career network.

2. If your current employer responds positively to people leaving, it is advantageous to discuss your plans immediately. The employer may provide you with references, helpful suggestions, or even a better opportunity where you are.

3. If your current employer resents losing employees and even fires those seeking other opportunities, do not give notice that you are planning to leave until you have another firm offer. Remember: You are more employable if you are currently employed, and you don't want to jeopardize your current position.

**Always resign professionally: Your future may depend on it!**

4. Do your current job to the best of your ability through your last day on the job. You are most likely to be remembered by how well you performed at the end of your employment. This can greatly influence the quality of future references from this employer.

5. Update your career work portfolio before you leave. If appropriate, request letters of recommendation from supervisors. Assemble samples of your work that are pertinent and exemplary.

6. Plan for an orderly and efficient transition of your responsibilities to the person taking your place. If asked to help train your replacement, be as thorough as possible, taking care to explain your duties clearly and completely.

7. Give your employer at least two weeks written notice before you leave your current job. You should submit a formal letter of resignation. An appropriate sample is shown in Figure 20-4.

**Complete Career Action 20-3**

## CAREER ACTION 20-3

### Write a Letter of Resignation

**DIRECTIONS:** Review Figure 20-4 on page 330, and practice by preparing a letter of resignation for a position you currently hold or have held.

March 9, 20--

Mr. George Baker
Henson-Standlin Company
1414 Cromwell Avenue
Memphis, TN 38115

Dear Mr. Baker:

This letter is to serve as notice that I will be leaving the Henson-Standlin Company on March 31. I have taken a position as service manager with Gantry and Sons in Salem, Oregon.

I have truly enjoyed working for Henson-Standlin and view my employment here as a valuable experience and opportunity for professional development. Thank you for your guidance and assistance during the past three years; I sincerely appreciate it.

Best wishes to you for continued success.

Sincerely,

*Kelli Sullivan*

Kelli Sullivan

Figure • 20-4: **Sample letter of resignation**

# UNDERSTAND WHEN YOU SHOULD CONSIDER RELOCATING

Sometimes deciding to relocate is easy. You may have no commitments keeping you in your current location, or you might just prefer to be elsewhere. On the other hand, the reasons you cannot relocate may be compelling; deciding can be difficult. You may find yourself weighing several important factors to decide whether relocation is in your best interest. The most important issues are personal or family considerations and the impact on your career goals.

## Consider the Impact on Loved Ones

The impact of relocation on your loved ones generally is the most difficult part of this decision. Your spouse may have an excellent career position that would be lost if you relocated. You may have aging parents who require that you remain nearby. You have to weigh the advantages against any possible negative impact on your spouse, children, or other significant people in your life.

Good communication among those most affected is important. If you are married and your spouse works, together you will need to discuss openly the advantages and disadvantages to each other's careers. If you have children, you will also want to consider how they feel about moving and what the quality of the schools is in the new community.

## Consider Your Values and Interests

Another important factor is reviewing your values and interests to determine whether they are being met in your current location. For example, if you are living in Florida but love to snow ski and have an opportunity to live in Denver, clearly you can list one advantage of moving to Colorado.

## Consider the Costs Involved

The other main personal consideration is economic. What will relocation cost? Don't look just at the cost of a moving van. Expenses include utility connections and other start-up costs required to move into new living quarters. If offered a job in another location, what portion, if any, of these costs will your employer provide? Also research the differences in living costs.

The cost of housing, transportation, utilities, food, taxes (state, local, sales, etc.), insurance, and other portions of your budget may vary greatly from place to place. Get copies of the local newspaper from communities you are considering. Review grocery advertisements, classified listings for houses and apartments, and other indications of costs. Use your support network to identify individuals who may be familiar with this location.

The following Web sites can also help you in making important relocation decisions:

**JobStar** ***http://jobstar.org/*** links to some general and specialized surveys—click on ***Salary Info***.

**Homefair** ***http://www.homefair.com/calc/salcalc.html*** provides a cost-of-living calculator and links to comparisons of crime rates and other considerations as well as links to help with calculating moving costs.

**Rent Net** ***http://www.rent.net/aptguide.html*** provides information on rental costs in various locations and tips for evaluating specific rental properties.

## Consider the Impact on Your Career Goals

Another important area of concern is the impact on your career goals. Will this move provide the opportunity to gain valuable experience and advancement not currently available? How will the move look on your resume if, later on, you look for another new position? Is education or training available at the new location (not available where you are now) that would provide added benefits? Will you be exposed to new people who can help your growth and development? Review your career plans. Will relocating better help you realize those goals?

Your decision will vary, depending on your personal goals, needs, and circumstances. Base your relocation decisions on thoughtful and careful consideration.

**Consider the impact on your loved ones, your values and interests, costs involved, and the impact on your career goals in making relocation decisions.**

# USE RELOCATION TO GROW, NOT TO START OVER

Assume you have decided to relocate. What can you do to make this move as smooth and positive an experience as possible? How do you ensure that you will continue to move forward in your career?

Moving companies often provide free pamphlets describing the steps you need to consider, including handy checklists. Check the Internet and your library for information on moving. Some important career-related issues are discussed below to help you get off to a good start in your new location.

Figure • 20-5: Many companies pay some relocation expenses and/or provide support services. Find out what help is available to you.

## Research Pays Off

Learn as much as you can about your new community before you move. If you belong to professional associations, find out whether they have chapters in the new community, and arrange to transfer your memberships. If your association has a Web site, it will frequently have links to local chapters. This helps you get professionally involved immediately and expand your support network to your new location. Subscribe to a newspaper to become familiar with your new area. Most communities have Web sites providing a gold mine of information on the area in which they are located.

**Complete Career Action 20-4**

# CAREER ACTION 20-4

## Use the Internet to Research Other Work Locations

**NOTE:** Since the content of Web sites is subject to change without notice, be aware that the links listed below may not match the current content of the Web sites referenced in this assignment.

**DIRECTIONS:** Check the Web sites listed below to learn more about a community to which you might consider moving. Prepare a short report summarizing your answers to the following questions:

1. How does the climate/weather compare with the climate/weather where you live now?
2. What kinds of recreation and cultural opportunities are highlighted?
3. Is information on educational opportunities provided?
4. What cost-of-living information is provided?
5. What medical facilities are available?

**USA City Link** — http://www.usacitylink.com

**Virtual Relocation** — http://www.virtualrelocation.com

**Make your relocation smooth and positive by researching the new community prior to your move, and build a new support network immediately on your arrival.**

### Build a Support Network Branch

When you arrive in the community, work at establishing a broad support group. Get involved in the community. Volunteer to work in a charity or an organization that fits your interests. This is an excellent way to become involved in the community and to build your support network. You may also have the opportunity to learn new skills or enhance old ones through volunteer work. Make this effort early to speed the process of meeting new people, making new friends, and developing a healthy social network.

## KNOW WHAT TO DO IF YOU LOSE YOUR JOB

For many reasons, you might find yourself unemployed. Rapidly changing technology, economic downturns, and corporate mergers are a few of the reasons you might be laid off. Many people face this sometime during their working years. Sometimes employees are fired. Firing may occur as the result of a personality conflict, office politics, lack of skills, poor attitude, absenteeism, or other unpleasant circumstances. You may never have the experience of being fired, but it does happen. Regardless of the fairness involved, the results are the same—unemployment and the need to find a new job.

## Coping with a Layoff or Downsizing

In the case of permanent layoffs or downsizing, some notice is usually given. *Before* the actual layoff is the time to reapply the job-seeking skills presented in earlier chapters of this book. Acting quickly is important because being employed is one factor that makes getting hired easier.

Keep this book and the related assignment materials you have prepared. They provide a solid foundation that will make your next job search easier and more efficient. Updating and revising the efforts you have made here will help you through the process of finding any new job—after a layoff or by your choice. Immediately reactivate and rebuild your support and network groups. Review the materials on support and network groups in Chapter 5. Begin rebuilding a strong network by contacting people with whom you are close. Ask each of them to provide you with the names of two more people you can contact to expand your network. Pay special attention to what you learned in Chapter 1 to help you maintain your positive outlook.

**"When one door closes, another door opens; but we so often look so long and so regretfully upon the closed door, that we do not see the ones which open for us."**

—Alexander Graham Bell

## Surviving Being Fired

There is life after being fired! Should this misfortune be your fate, take heart that literally hundreds of thousands of people who lost their jobs sometime in their past are now happily and successfully employed. If you receive the proverbial pink slip, these are some immediate do's and don'ts:

- **Do** try to have a calm and non-threatening conversation with your supervisor to clarify the reason for your termination if you don't already know. Ask your supervisor for advice and support. Find out whether the organization offers out-placement assistance. By responding professionally, you can limit or eliminate a negative reference. You may even receive a positive reference and assistance in finding another position.
- **Do** analyze objectively what you may have learned from this experience. What did you gain from the work experience? What can you improve or avoid in future situations to make you a good employee for someone else?
- **Do** give yourself a day or two to reflect on what happened and to put it into perspective. Begin to think about a positive future. Review Chapter 1, and give your self-concept a much-needed boost.
- **Do** reestablish and rebuild your support system. You will need it now more than ever. Repeat the process you used to get your last position.
- **Do** reestablish and rebuild your network. Start contacting people and asking them to refer you to several others to get a strong network established again.
- **Do** review this text and all the information you developed to complete the exercises. Update your resume, and begin the job-hunting process anew. Carefully consider whether you need a new job or an actual career change.

- **Do** use the term laid off rather than fired in your responses when you have a job interview; laid off has less negative impact than fired. Discuss the situation briefly and in as positive a manner as you possibly can. Avoid negative statements about your former employer. Instead, emphasize positive things you have learned from this experience that will make you a valuable employee.

- **Don't** make things worse by verbally (or physically) attacking your supervisor or anyone else before leaving. Prospective employers are likely to contact your previous employer for references. Do not add to your problems now!

- **Don't** begin applying for jobs the same day you get the bad news. You won't be in the right frame of mind to make good decisions or to present a confident and positive image to another employer.

## FOCUS ON FUTURE OPPORTUNITIES

Literally hundreds of thousands of happily and successfully employed people have been fired sometime previously. You, too, can successfully survive termination if you focus on using it as an experience that will lead to a new opportunity.

- **Don't** focus on how unfairly you were treated and begin to identify all the injustices your former employer committed against you and other employees.

- Most important, remember that many people have been fired and have gone on to enjoy successful careers. This is the beginning of new opportunities, not the end of the world.

**Complete Career Action 20-5**

# CAREER ACTION 20-5

## Review Your Success Action Plan

In Chapter 1, **Career Action 1-5** on page 16, you accessed South-Western Educational Publishing's Web site and completed a Success Action Plan in which you identified a goal that was most important to you at the time. In addition, you were to identify success strategies described in Chapter 1 that you could use to accomplish the goal you identified.

**DIRECTIONS:** Now review your Success Action Plan, and note what progress you have made on this plan since you first wrote it. If you applied the strategies you outlined on the form, you should have made some good progress. Keep in mind the importance of using these strategies throughout your career to reach your fullest possible potential!

## CONCLUSION

The average American makes a minimum of seven job changes in a lifetime. (Some career changes are included in this number.) All the work you have done in this book to assess and document your experience, education, interest, goals and objectives, capabilities, and so on will be useful to you in the future. Keep this book, and use it throughout your successful career.

### CHECKLIST FOR MAKING A SUCCESSFUL JOB AND CAREER CHANGE

Check each of the following actions you are currently taking to increase your career success:

- ☐ Keep yourself on the cutting edge of the workforce by continuing your education.
- ☐ Before changing jobs or careers, determine whether your discontent is job-based or career-based.
- ☐ Consider the pros and cons of staying in your current job before making a change. Avoid quitting until you've secured another job.
- ☐ Change to a new career if it's realistically available and meets your needs.
- ☐ Always resign professionally: Your future may depend on it!
- ☐ In relocating, consider the impact on your loved ones, values and interests, costs involved, and impact on your career goals.
- ☐ In relocating, research the new community before moving, and build a new support network immediately on arriving.

## CRITICAL THINKING QUESTIONS

1. Why has lifelong learning become crucial?
2. List at least two benefits you could gain by changing employers when seeking a job change.
3. What actions should you take to resign professionally?

APPENDIX

# Sample Business Letters and E-Mail Formats

To project professionalism in your job search and career development written communications, always use appropriate business formats. Listed below are guidelines for formatting a business letter and an e-mail message. Illustrations of these document formats follow the guidelines.

**Business Letter Format (See model on page 338):** Use the following guidelines to format your business letters correctly:

1. Prepare standard business letters on 8 1/2-by-11-inch letterhead stationery. If you don't have your own letterhead stationery (not expected for an individual) use a high quality bond stationery.

2. Use the block style letter format illustrated on the following page. General guidelines for the placement of the letter parts are indicated on the illustration. A few specific tips are emphasized below.

3. The placement of the return address and date varies depending on the length of the letter.

   For an average length letter, begin the return address at the left margin and at approximately the two-inch top margin point; if the letter is long, place this section higher on the page to achieve a more balanced placement. Place the date directly under the return address and at the left margin.

4. Key a double space (two hard returns) between the salutation and the body of the letter, between each paragraph, and between the last line of the body of the letter and the complimentary close.

5. Key four hard returns between the complimentary close and the name of the sender.

**E-mail Message Format (See model on page 338):** Follow the guidelines below to format an e-mail message correctly:

1. **Format:** Use a heading similar to that of a standard business memo. Always include the *"To, From, Date, Subject"* information to communicate clearly and quickly. Most e-mail programs contain a form at the top of the message screen to fill in this information.

2. **Case:** Use the standard mix of upper and lower case letters—using all caps is like **SHOUTING ON THE NETWORK!** Entire messages in all capital letters are also extremely hard to read.

3. **Brief but complete:** Keep e-mail messages short and to one subject, but be sure to include all information necessary for the recipient to take appropriate action and to reach you.

4. **Professional:** As with hard-copy documents, your professional reputation is reflected in e-mail:

   a. Plan and organize the message.

   b. Prepare a draft, proofread and revise it.

   c. Be courteous.

   d. Use correct spelling and grammar.

# BUSINESS LETTER FORMAT

1008 North Lindsey Avenue
Boise, ID 83706
January 25, 20––

**(Begin writer's address at left margin at approximately the 2-inch top margin point. Starting line varies based on letter length.)**
**(Date)**

**(4 line spaces, 3 blank lines)**

Mr. Tom Scott
1235 Lake Hazel
Boise, ID 83709

**(Letter address at left margin)**

**(Always 2 line spaces, 1 blank line)**

Dear Mr. Scott: **(Salutation)**

**(Always 2 line spaces, 1 blank line)**

**** ***** **** * **** ** **** *** ** *** ** **** *** **** ***** *** ****** **(Body of letter.)**
**** * ***. ********* ****** * ******* ***** *** ***** *** * ****** *** **** *
***** ** *** ** **** ********* **** ** ***********.

**(All lines start at left margin.)** **(Always 2 line spaces, 1 blank line)**

**** **** **** **** *** * *** **** ** **** ** *** ********* ***. * **** ** **** *****
***** **** *** * *****.

**(Always 2 line spaces, 1 blank line)**

****** ***** **** ** * ***** *** **** **** *** **** *** ***** *** *** * ****** *** ** *
******. **** ** * ********* *** ******** ******** ** *** ********. ** **** *** ***
**************** **** **** ******* *** **** *********.

**(Always 2 line spaces, 1 blank line)**

Sincerely yours, **(Complimentary close at left margin)**

**(4 returns)**

**(Sender's written signature here)**

Mike Ashley **(Keyed name of sender at left margin)**

# E-MAIL MESSAGE FORMAT

**(E-Mail heading usually a form fill-in.)**

**Date:** September 8, 20--
**From:** Jack Mills
**To:** Lee Yordy, MacroTech Corporation
**Subject:** Confirmation of Meeting, September 12, 20-- **(Always include a subject!)**

This message is a confirmation of *** * ****** ******* **** ***** ** ******* *** *****
* ** ******* ****** ******** ** ******** **** ****** **** ****** ****. *** ****** ****
*** ******** *** ***** ***** ** ***** ****** **** ****. **(Body of message)**

** **** ******* **** ** ***** ****** *** ***** **** **** **** **** **** *** ** ** ***
*** **** ** ******* **** ** ***** ****** ***.

* **** *** **** **** *** * *** ***** *** ******** *** **** *** ** **** ***** **** * ****
*** *************.

**Contact Information:**
Jack Mills
E-mail address: mills@enterprise.com
Fax number: 707-555-3466
Telephone: 707-555-8220
Mailing address: 8200 Whitney Avenue, Vacaville, CA 95688

APPENDIX B

# Internet Resources

For Internet link updates, go to the *Your Career: How to Make It Happen* Web site at http://www.swep.com under post-secondary career development. If any of the Web addresses below don't launch, try deleting "www." from the address—some sites are dropping this designation.

## Career and Job Search Information Sites

These sites offer job search and career information on many important topics including interviews, resumes, cover letters, salary negotiation and salary ranges, relocation, and much more.

**Archeus Online:** *http://www.golden.net/~archeus/intres.htm*
(Provides comprehensive coverage of and links to interview techniques information.)

**Bolles Parachute Net Guide:** *http://www.tenspeedpress.com/parachute/front.htm*
(Excellent source of links to information regarding careers, employer research, and job search techniques.)

**The Riley Guide:** *http://dbm.com/jobguide*
(Offers many good links and information on job listings, resume posting, employer profiles, current articles.)

**JOB-HUNT.ORG:** *http://www.job-hunt.org*
(A huge master list of useful national links to job search and career development information.)

**JobWeb:** *http://www.jobweb.org*
(Sponsored by National Association of Colleges and Employers. Provides useful information on career management/job search and links directly to employers, a career fair database, and other job search sites.)

**Bureau of Labor Statistics:** *http://stats.bls.gov*
(Note: URL does not use standard "www." U.S. Bureau of Labor site containing national employment statistics, career planning information, Occupational Outlook Handbook, and more.)

**America's Career InfoNet:** *http://www.acinet.org*
(A comprehensive source of occupational and economic information for making informed career decisions.)

**BigYellow:** *http://www1.bigyellow.com*
(An online mega-telephone directory to locate phone numbers and addresses of all U.S. businesses.)

**CareerLab:** *http://www.careerlab.com*
(An excellent site with links to career management success information. Provides 200 cover, thank-you, and follow-up letter samples.)

**Careers, Not Just Jobs:** http://www.careers.wsj.com
(Offers job postings and extensive job search and career management information. Sponsored by the Wall Street Journal.)

**CareerPost:** http://www.washingtonpost.com/wp-adv/classifieds/careerpost
(Provides excellent job search and career development information and links to job postings.)

**Career Resource Center:** http://www.careers.org/index.html
(A comprehensive index of career-related links. Includes job postings and career advice.)

**Companies Online:** http://www.companiesonline.com
(Links to many corporate home pages.)

**Cyber Nation:** http://www.cybernation.com
(Features motivational articles and information by leading success authors and coaches.)

**Dun and Bradstreet's Million Dollar Directory:** http://dbisna.com/mdd/milldllr.htm

**eResumes & Resources:** http://www.eresumes.com
(A comprehensive guide to electronic and scannable resume preparation and more.)

**Federal Jobs Digest:** http://www.jobsfed.com
(A recruitment site with federal job listings, federal resume advice, and more.)

**High Technology Careers Magazine:** http://www.hightechcareers.com
(Provides hundreds of articles on career management—applicable to any occupation—and on high technology.)

**Homefair.com:** http://www.homefair.com
(An excellent site featuring extensive links and information on career and lifestyle management.)

**International Standards Organization:** http://www.iso.ch
(ISO Web site providing complete information about this global standards certification organization.)

**Job Choices Online:** http://www.jobweb.org/jconline
(An electronic magazine that presents career information and job-search advice to college students and recent graduates. Sponsored by the National Association of Colleges and Employers, NACE.)

**JobStar:** http://www.jobstar.org
(Provides national job search, career planning, and comprehensive salary information. Also lists California job openings and links for job information.)

**National Business Employment Weekly:** http://www.nbew.com
(A national publication offering current job-search and career-guidance articles and information.)

**Occupational Outlook Handbook:** http://stats.bls.gov/ocohome.htm
(A valuable tool for researching information about specific occupations.)

**Quintessential Career & Job-Hunting Resources Guide:** http://www.stetson.edu/~rhansen/intvres.html
(Excellent links to comprehensive job search and career management information.)

**Monster Campus:** *http://www.campus.monster.com*
(Offers comprehensive guidelines to help college students choose careers and find jobs. Topics covered include cover letters, resumes, interviewing, securing internships, networking, and finding a job online.)

**Team Management Systems:** *http://www.tms.com.au*
(Excellent source of research and information regarding team management and organizational development.)

**USA CityLink:** *http://www.usacitylink.com*
(Offers helpful information on most U.S. cities to use in making relocation decisions.)

**USA Jobs:** *http://www.usajobs.opm.gov*
(Official U.S. Government site for job/employment information provided by the U.S. Office of Personnel Management.)

**Wall Street Research Net:** *http://www.wsrn.com*
(A good resource for company research. Look under "Journal Search.")

## Recruitment Sites

These sites recruit employees and accept resumes for posted jobs; many provide career management information as well as links to employers' home pages or other employment-related Web sites.

**NOTE:** We recommend that students generally avoid using Internet sites that charge a fee for posting a resume because so many reputable sites do not charge.

**Monster.com:** *http://www.monster.com*
(A huge site providing job listings, job search and employer information, resume posting, and more.)

**CareerPath:** *http://www.careerpath.com*
(A major recruitment site with a large database of job listings, online resume posting, and career/job search information.)

**JobOptions:** *http://www.joboptions.com*
(Offers online recruitment; resume/job postings; job search, employer, and career management information.)

**CareerMosaic:** *http://www.careermosaic.com*
(A major online recruitment site. Offers information on several job search and career management topics.)

**America's Job Bank:** *http://www.ajb.dni.us*
(A joint effort of hundreds of offices of the State Employment Service. Also offers good salary information.)

**America's Employers:** *http://www.americasemployers.com*
(An online recruiting service offering many job-search resources. Developed by Career Relocation Corporation of America.)

**Beaucoup:** *http://www.beaucoup.com*
(An excellent collection of job recruitment and large corporate employer links.)

**CAREERMagazine:** *http://www.careermag.com*
(A good job posting recruitment and career information site.)

**Career Shop:** *http://www.careershop.com*
(Features job postings and job search/career development information and links.)

**CareerWeb:** *http://www.cweb.com*
(A resume posting site also offering career management information.)

**JobFactory Online:** *http://www.jobfactory.com*
(A large database of job openings in the U.S. including job application processes and comprehensive links to other employment-related Web sites.)

**NationJob Network:** *http://www.nationjob.com*
(A recruitment network and source of employer research.)

## Search Engines to Locate Employer Web Sites and Career Topics

To learn how to use search engines efficiently, access the following site and review the instructions provided.

**Web Search Strategies:** *http://home.sprintmail.com/~debflanagan/main.html*

These sites are good sources of information about any topic.

**AltaVista:** *http://www.altavista.com*
**DogPile:** *http://www.dogpile.com*
**Excite:** *http://www.excite.com*
**HotBot:** *http://www.hotbot.com*
**Infoseek:** *http://www.infoseek.com/careers*
**Lycos:** *http://www.lycos.com*
**SnapCom:** *http://www.snap.com*
**Yahoo! Employment:** *http://www.yahoo.com/business/employment*

## Financial Information-Centered Web Sites

These sites are good sources of financial information about prospective employers. (Only privately owned companies are listed on these sites.)

**American Stock Exchange:** *http://www.amex.com*
**New York Stock Exchange:** *http://www.nyse.com*
**NASDAQ:** *http://www.nasdaq.com*
**Wall Street Research Net:** *http://www.wsrn.com*

APPENDIX

C

# Career Management and Marketing Tools

Three important career management and marketing tools are recommended to help you reach your full career potential. These tools are discussed in various chapters throughout this text; they are further summarized below as a convenient reference:

## CAREER MANAGEMENT TOOL 1: LIFETIME CAREER DATABASE

A database is a collection of related information. In using this textbook, you will collect data you can use throughout your life to help achieve each new job and career goal. This data will consist of information you record in your *Career Actions* as well as drafts of job search documents you create. Altogether, this data will form your Lifetime Career Database.

### Compiling Your Lifetime Career Database

1. **Organize your data.** Set up a system for collecting, organizing, and updating your career information. You will need much of this data each time you seek a new job, advancement, or career.

   Your system may be as simple as files and index cards, or you can use computer software. For example, you might keep a computer database of job lead contacts and records of your education, training, and work experience. You can also store paragraphs in word processing files to use in creating resumes or cover letters. The important point is to collect the information in a format and location that is easy to retrieve and update throughout your career.

2. **Create a Lifetime Career Database File.** We recommend using a ring binder. Place 20 binder divider tabs, labeled Chapter 1 through Chapter 20, in the binder.

3. **File Completed Career Actions.** Place all of your completed Career Action forms or other written assignments behind the corresponding chapter tab in your Lifetime Career Database File. If you wish, use additional tabs with specific topic labels, such as "network list," "references," "resume," etc.

4. **Use computer files.** Whenever possible, use a computer to store information you will refer to repeatedly, update, or revise throughout your career (such as documentation of education/training, work experience; names and addresses of references and networking contacts; your resume, cover letters, and so on). Save your computer-generated files on a computer diskette, CD, or other media for easy updating or revision throughout your career.

   a. If you choose to use a computer to enter part or all of your answers to career action assignments, place a printout of your answers in your Career Action File.

   b. You can name your computer files by the career action number, for example: CA1-1, for Career Action 1-1; CA2-2, for Career Action 2-2. Or you may prefer to use specific topic filenames, such as "network," "references," "resume," etc.

**IMPORTANT:** Look for this notation at the bottom of selected Career Actions:

Career Database Appropriate

This indicates that some or all the information you record for this Career Action would be appropriate to enter using a computer program and to store on electronic media (diskette, CD, etc.).

# CAREER MANAGEMENT TOOL 2: CAREER PORTFOLIO

The career portfolio is an organized master collection of items demonstrating job-specific skills and work qualifications. You can select specific items for each interview from this master portfolio that best demonstrate how you meet individual employer's needs. Some examples of appropriate portfolio items include your resume; an official copy of your transcript(s); exemplary samples of your work, such as business writing, graphic art work, and printed samples from software presentations; evidence of sophisticated computer usage, such as desktop publishing and Web site creation; awards and commendations; work performance evaluations; and letters of reference.

Portfolio samples can be from paid or volunteer work, internships, cooperative education, clubs, community activities, and more. A comprehensive list of appropriate items and ideas for building your portfolio is presented below under the heading "Sample Portfolio Items."

**NOTE:** You will likely want to file original documents, such as school transcripts, in your Lifetime Career Database (described on the preceding page) and also place a copy in your Career Portfolio. This way you will retain a clean master and also have a copy for demonstration during interviews.

## Assembling and Using Your Portfolio

Begin by identifying your skills and experiences that relate directly to your job target. Then consider carefully what you have done or accomplished that best demonstrates those qualifications. For example, if you are seeking an accounting job, include your transcripts listing appropriate coursework; a diskette containing samples of budgets developed or accounts receivable or payable reports prepared; a letter of recommendation from an employer for bookkeeping or accounting work performed; and so on.

For a traditional portfolio, use a professional-looking three-ringed binder that holds 8 1/2-by-11 inch pages. File and categorize all your portfolio documents in file folders or by tabbed sections in the binder. Use sheet protectors, diskette protectors, and other appropriate accessories to professionally display and to protect your portfolio items. Larger portfolios (17-by-22 inches) are appropriate for art designers, journalists, advertising specialists, and technical writers to store and categorize oversized documents and credentials.

## Sample Portfolio Items

Portfolio components may include paper documents, diskettes and CD-ROMs, video or audiotapes, pictures, photographs, or other items that can be used to demonstrate your qualifications.

To aid in assembling your portfolio, review the following list of ideas for appropriate components. However, don't limit yourself to these—use your imagination, and strive for a close match with your target job.

## To Demonstrate Work Experience, Work Performance, and Credentials

- **Resume:** Include error-free copies of your resume printed on quality paper. This should be the first item in your portfolio.

**NOTE:** Include in your portfolio a computer disk copy of your scannable paper resume and your electronic "cyber-resume" for employers who prefer the disk format. Place the disk in a disk jacket.

- **Employer or Internship Performance Reviews:** Providing all comments are favorable, include copies of these reviews.
- **Licenses:** For professions requiring a license to work in the field.
- **List of References:** A listing of the names, addresses, phone numbers, and their association pertaining to you. Past employers, direct supervisors, and teachers are all good references.
- **Letters of Recommendation/Commendation:** These letters speak for themselves.

  **NOTE:** Some companies do not permit such letters to be written on company letterhead out of concern for legal liability, should an incorrect statement be written that could result in legal problems. Collecting letters of recommendation when possible is still a good idea.

## Education and Training

- **Diploma/Degree:** Place a copy of your diploma(s) or degree(s) in your portfolio; (place originals in your Lifetime Career Database).
- **Transcripts:** If your academic performance was good, keep copies of your transcripts in your portfolio to demonstrate this strength.
- **Certificates:** Professional certification (CPA, CPS, CET, PE, teaching certificates, etc.) is evidence of life-long learning. Certificates of completion for continuing education, specialized training, workshops, seminars, etc., are important because they, too, demonstrate career development.
- **Awards:** Perfect attendance on the job and in school; academic accomplishments; employee of the month, quarter or year are just a few examples of awards. Awards are proof of outstanding accomplishments and are of interest to employers.

## Samples of Work, Use of Technology and Information

- **Design Work:** Computer or manual drawings in the field of drafting can prove technical ability in mechanical, architectural, structural, or electrical designs. Computer-aided drafting design (CAD) work done in 2-D and 3-D is most impressive and highly sought today. Interior design work as it pertains to decorators may also be presented by drawings, photographs, and videotapes.
- **Art Work:** Also file samples of sketches, drawings, and paintings; photographs or video footage; or computer-generated items in your career portfolio.
- **Writing Samples:** The ability to communicate is important to employers. Authors, editors, and reporters should showcase their best works. Include samples of technical writing, business plans, institutional improvement plans, proposals, mission statements, or reports you have composed.
- **Software Generated Documents:** If you are preparing to graduate and lack related job experience, generate your best examples of electronic spreadsheets, database documents, newsletters, or presentation documents using presentation and graphics software. If you have on-the-job experience, include copies of your actual work.
- **Publicity/Press Coverage:** Articles highlighting your work; volunteer, community, or professional activities; or other special accomplishments. Sources: school, corporate, or professional publications such as newspapers, journals, magazines, etc.

## Other

- **Forms of Identification:** Once hired, many employers request at least two forms of identification to process your application. Place front and back photocopies of a valid driver's license, social security card, or photo ID in your portfolio for easy retrieval.

# CAREER MANAGEMENT TOOL 3: INTERVIEW MARKETING KIT

The Interview Marketing Kit is a professional-looking binder or case containing items selected from your Career Portfolio for each interview. During interviews, you can extract appropriate portfolio items from your Kit that demonstrate your qualifications. This tangible evidence of abilities often gives candidates a winning edge in competing for a job. Always choose items that match the needs of the specific target employer. After your interview, you can refile the items in your master Career Portfolio. In other words, your Interview Marketing Kit should be tailored and assembled using Career Portfolio items selected specifically for each interview.

The kit should also contain what we call a "Murphy's Law Survival Pack." These are supplies that can bail you out of a situation that could diminish your confidence and performance. They include rescue items such as a comb, toothbrush, breath freshener, a spare tie, or a spare pair of nylons.

## Selecting Portfolio Items to Place in Interview Marketing Kit

Before each interview, pull items from your Career Portfolio that best pertain to the specific job target and meet the employer's needs. Do not use every item in your primary portfolio for every interview. Place the items you select in your Interview Marketing Kit. Always arrange the portfolio items logically in your Interview Marketing Kit to best demonstrate how your abilities relate specifically to the employer's needs. Examples of appropriate items for your Interview Marketing Kit are listed below:

1. Items from your Career Portfolio that best support the needs of the organization you are interviewing with:
   - Job-related samples of your work, if applicable (from your work, educational, or training experience)
   - Required certificates, licenses, transcripts, or other related documents
   - Spare copies of your resume
   - Letters of recommendation
   - List of references appropriate for this job
2. Your 60-Second Commercial summarizing your qualifications for the job (see Chapter 11)
3. A list of pertinent questions you can ask during the interview (see Chapter 14)

**NOTE:** Review items 2 and 3 just before your interview—don't read from them during the interview.

## Using Portfolio Items During Your Interview

Always ask if the interviewer would like to see samples from your portfolio before displaying any of it. Even if the interviewer prefers not to review them, having portfolio items conveys that you are professional and organized. During the interview, you may still have an opportunity to offer a portfolio sample if the topic suggests it. Employers typically ask questions about your resume. At this point, you can use your portfolio items to support your responses. Never misrepresent yourself in the portfolio items—the work must be your own. Be prepared to reproduce the work if requested to do so during preemployment testing.

To capture the interviewer's attention, refer to one of your most outstanding accomplishments first. Provide evidence of the accomplishment with an appropriate portfolio item. Save another exceptional item for the end of your presentation or interview to leave a memorable final impression.

Have a friend conduct a mock interview with you, and practice referring to your portfolio items at key points during the questioning process. This will prepare you to make a smooth delivery during your actual interviews.

APPENDIX

# Reference Reading

## CAREER PLANNING AND JOB SEARCH


Bolles, Richard N. *The New Quick Job-Hunting Map.* Revised Edition. Berkeley, CA: Ten Speed Press, 1990.

Bolles, Richard N. *What Color Is Your Parachute?* Berkeley, CA: Ten Speed Press, 1999.

Chapman, Jack. *Negotiating Your Salary: How to Make $1000 a Minute.* Berkeley, CA: Ten Speed Press, 1996.

Criscito, Pat. *Resumes in Cyberspace.* Hauppauge, NY: Barron's Educational Series, Inc., 1997.

Crowther, Karmen, N. T. *Researching Your Way to a Good Job*. New York: John Wiley and Sons, 1993.

Crystal, John C., and Richard N. Bolles, *Where Do I Go From Here With My Life*? Berkeley, CA: Ten Speed Press, 1988.

Decker, Bert. *You've Got to Be Believed to Be Heard.* New York: St. Martin's Press, 1992. (Audio tapes are now available.)

Figler, Howard. *The Complete Job Search Handbook: All the Skills You Need to Get Any Job and Have a Good Time Doing It.* New York: Henry Holt & Co., 1988.

Jackson, Tom. *Guerrilla Tactics in the Job Market*. New York: Bantam Books, 1993.

Jackson, Tom. *Not Just Another Job.* New York: Times Books, 1992.

Jackson, Tom. *The New Perfect Resume.* New York: Doubleday, 1996.

Judy, Richard and Carol D'Amico. *Workforce 2020: Work and Workers in the 21st Century.* Indianapolis, IN: Hudson Institute, 1997.

*Job Choices.* Bethelem, PA: National Association of Colleges and Employers 2000. (Annual publication.)

Karl, Shannon and Karl, Arthur. *How to Get Your Dream Job Using the Web*. Albany, NY: Coriolis Group Books, 1997.

Kelly, Robert E. *How to Be a Star at work: Nine Breakthrough Strategies You Need to Succeed.* New York: Random House, 1998.

Kennedy, Joyce Lain and Thomas J. Morrow. *Electronic Resume Revolution*. New York: John Wiley and Sons, Inc. 1995.

Kennedy, Joyce Lain. *Hook Up, Get Hired! The Internet Job Search Revolution.* New York: John Wiley and Sons, Inc., 1995.

Lathrop, Richard. *Who's Hiring Who.* Berkeley, CA: Ten Speed Press, 1989.

Medley, H. Anthony. *Sweaty Palms—The Neglected Art of Being Interviewed*. Berkeley, CA: Ten Speed Press, 1992.

Michelozzi, Betty N. *Coming Alive From Nine to Five: The Career Search Handbook*. Mountain View, CA: Mayfield Publishing Company, 1996.

Molloy, John T. *The New Dress for Success.* New York: Warner Books, 1988.

Molloy, John T. *The New Woman's Dress for Success Book.* New York: Warner Books, 1996.

Naisbitt, J. & Aburdene, P. *Megatrends 2000.* New York: Smithmark Publishing, 1994.

Parker, Yana. *Damn Good Resume Guide, Third Edition.* Berkeley, CA: Ten Speed Press, 1996.

Podesta, Sandra and Paxton, Andrea. *201 Killer Cover Letters.* New York: McGraw-Hill, 1996.

Riley, Margaret, Roehm, Frances, and Oserman, Steve. *The Guide to Internet Job Searching.* Licolnwood, IL: VGM Career Horizons, 1999

Snodgrass, Jon. *Follow Your Career Star: A Career Quest Based on Inner Values.* South Pasadena, CA: 1996.

Washington, Tom. *The Hunt, Complete Guide to Effective Job Finding*. Bellevue, WA: Mount Vernon Press, 1992.

Yate, Martin. *Cover Letters That Knock 'Em Dead*. Holbrook, MA: Adams, Inc., 1998.

Yate, Martin. *Knock 'Em Dead: The Ultimate Job Seeker's Handbook*. Holbrook, MA: Adams, Inc., 1999.

## POSITIVE MENTAL ATTITUDE AND ASSERTIVENESS

Alberti, Robert E. and Michael L. Emmons. *Your Perfect Right*. San Luis Obispo, CA: Impact Publishers, 1995.

Axelrod, Alan and Jim Holtje. *201 Ways to Say No—Gracefully and Effectively*. New York: McGraw-Hill, 1997.

Baer, Jean. *How to Be an Assertive (Not Aggressive) Woman in Life, in Love, & on the Job: The Total Guide to Self-Assertiveness*. New York: NAL Ford-Dutton, 1991. (Audio tapes available 1991.)

Briles, Judith. *The Confidence Factor*. New York: Mastermedia, 1990.

Burnell, Ivan. *The Power of Positive Doing—12 Srategies for Taking Control of Your Life*. Center Ossipee, NH: IPO Publishing, 1999.

Carnegie, Dale. *How to Win Friends and Influence People*. New York: Simon & Schuster, 1982.

Covey, Stephen R. *The 7 Habits of Highly Effective People: Powerful Lessons in Personal Change*. New York: Simon & Schuster, 1990.

Davidson, Jeff. *The Complete Idiot's Guide to Assertiveness*. Old Tapan, NJ: MacMillan Publishing Company, 1997.

Gray, John. *How to Get What You Want and Want What You Get*. New York: Harper Collins, 1999.

Frankl, Viktor. *Man's Search for Meaning*. Boston, MA: Beacon Press, 1992. (Audio tapes available 1997.)

Hill, Napoleon. *Think and Grow Rich*. New York: Fawcett Book Group, 1996.

Jakubowske, Patricia and Arthur J. Lange. *The Assertive Option*. Champaign, IL: Research Press Company, 1978.

Moawad, Bob. *Increasing Human Effectiveness*. Tacoma, WA: ULIEDGE SYSTEMS, 1981. (Audiocassette program.)

Peale, Norman Vincent. *The Power of Positive Thinking*. New York: Prentice-Hall, 1996.

Peters, Thomas and Robert Waterman. *In Search of Excellence*. New York: Warner Books, 1993.

In Search of Excellence; *Lessons From America's Best-Run Companies*. Thorndike, ME: GK Hall & Co., 1997.

Peale, Norman Vincent. *Positive Principles Today*. New York: Fawcett Books, 1996.

Phelps, Stanlee and Nancy Austin. *The Assertive Woman—New Edition for a New Mellennium*. San Luis Obispo, CA : Impact Publishers, 1997.

Robbins, Anthony. *Unlimited Power: The New Science of Personal Achievement*. New York: Simon and Schuster, 1996.

Siegel, Bernie. *Prescription for Living*. New York: Harper Collins, 1998.

Swartz, David. *The Magic of Thinking Big*. New York: Simon & Schuster, 1987.

Tracy, Brian. *Maximum Achievement: Strategies that Unlock Your Hidden Power to Achieve*. New York: Simon & Schuster, 1995.

Tracy, Brian. *Thinking Big: The Keys to Personal Power and Maximum Performance*. Simon and Schuster, 1997. (Audiocassette.)

Waitley, Denis. *The Double Win*. New York: Berkley Publishing Group, 1986.

Waitley, Denis. *The New Dynamics of Winning*. New York: William Morrow Publishing, 1993.

Waitley, Denis. *The Psychology of Winning*. New York: Simon and Schuster, 1995. (Audiocassette.)

Ziglar, Zig. *See You At the Top*. El Toro, CA: Pelican Publishing Co., 1984.

# Index

## S



## T



## U



## V



## W